LEVERAGING AN EMPIRE

LEVERAGING AN EMPIRE

Settler Colonialism and the Legalities of Citizenship in the Pacific Northwest

JACKI HEDLUND TYLER

University of Nebraska Press
Lincoln

Library of Congress Cataloging-in-Publication Data
Names: Tyler, Jacki Hedlund, author.
Title: Leveraging an empire: settler colonialism and the legalities of citizenship in the Pacific Northwest / Jacki Hedlund Tyler, University of Nebraska Press.
Description: Lincoln: University of Nebraska Press, [2021] | Includes bibliographical references and index.
Identifiers: LCCN 2020041743
ISBN 9781496219046 (hardback)
ISBN 9781496227645 (epub)
ISBN 9781496227652 (mobi)
ISBN 9781496227669 (pdf)
Subjects: LCSH: Citizenship—Oregon Territory—History. | Citizenship—Northwest, Pacific—History.
Classification: LCC KF4700 .T95 2021 |
DDC 342.73/0830979509034—dc23
LC record available at
https://lccn.loc.gov/2020041743

Set in Monotype Bulmer by Mikala R. Kolander.

To Dr. David Stratton,
whose encouragement started
me on this journey

Contents

Illustrations

Tables

Preface

Daffodils

As in many places throughout the world, a variety of daffodils grow in the Pacific Northwest. Daffodils have found a home on multiple continents through merchants and travelers, primarily from southern Europe and northern Africa, since the sixteenth century. As the daffodil plant is difficult to cultivate from seed, the human exchange of daffodil bulbs explains its impressive immigration.[1] Rather than easily spreading through North America as a seed, therefore, the daffodil was carried west by people. The timeline of settler colonialism into the American West runs parallel to the cultivation of daffodils in the region.

Daffodils became popularized and associated with English gardens by the early nineteenth century, and their presence continued to move south and west with U.S. immigrants. Settlers to the American West, especially women, brought with them elements of their eastern homes to re-create those landscapes on foreign lands.[2] Yet, daffodils did not just accompany settler colonialism in the Pacific Northwest; the process through which daffodils have continued to grow in this region is somewhat reflective of the progression of colonial outposts themselves.

Gardeners have been encouraged to plant daffodil bulbs in clusters for them to successfully take root and to appear naturally occurring in a new setting, which creates "the impression of age . . . as if they had been formed by the multiplication over a period of years of one or two bulbs."[3] The illusion of permanence and attempts to claim authority over the land were also necessary for the continued influence of settler colonialism in the Pacific Northwest. The daffodil was not native to this region, but with each successful bulb more daffodils came until their presence appeared consistent and organic. The United States may not have viewed itself as a foreign colonizer with settler colonies in the mid-nineteenth century, but neither did the daffodil.

Acknowledgments

This project has been twelve years of research, writing, and revisions in the making. The road to this point, however, has spanned my lifetime, which is why I am indebted to all the family (especially my mom and sisters), friends, and teachers who have supported me in ways I cannot fully or appropriately express. Even if you are not aware of your influence, I hope to someday thank you in person, because this book would not have been possible without your assistance.

I have had the honor of working with some amazing historians and mentors over the years. Although the main premise for this book did not begin until my PhD program, History faculty members at Arizona State University—including Brooks Simpson—helped me discover my interest in political and legal history. At Washington State University I benefited from the knowledge and support of several History faculty members, including Jennifer Thigpen, Matthew Sutton, Robert McCoy, and Heather Streets-Salter (now at Northwestern University). To my PhD adviser, Peter Boag, only now as I begin to advise graduate students myself can I fully understand how much time and effort you have given to help me succeed. Your continued guidance and instruction are greatly appreciated. Furthermore, I am thankful for Washington State University's support of my research through the Pettyjohn Graduate Research Fellowship, Edward M. and Margery H. Bennett History Graduate Fellowship, and the College of Arts and Sciences Graduate Achievement Award.

I am also grateful to a number of wonderful libraries and archives throughout the Pacific Northwest that have helped me uncover critical materials for my research. In particular, I was fortunate enough to spend many months at the Oregon Historical Society Research Library, supported, in part, by their Donald J. Sterling Graduate Fellowship in Pacific Northwest History. Additional advice and feedback from Eliza Canty-Jones, editor of *Oregon Historical Quarterly*, is deeply appreciated. And thank-you to the wonderful family members (Dana Honn, Janet and Steve Sims) for giving me a home base during my research trips to Portland and Seattle. A big thank you to the Manuscripts, Archives, and Special Collections unit at Washington State University Library, in particular, Trevor Bond and Cheryl Gunselman. My research and knowledge of archives was exponentially supported by your assistance as well as through both the Jewett Archives Graduate Fellowship and the Robert W. Bucklin Archives Fellowship.

I am thankful for current support by Eastern Washington University and its funding for faculty development and research, as well as advice and encouragement from my colleagues in the History Department. A special thanks to my colleague Larry Cebula for serving as a reader late in the revision process. I promise to pay it forward in the future. On the topic of readers, again, a thank-you to my dissertation committee members and much appreciation to two readers whom I have the privilege to call my friends: Chelsea Mead-Borrell and my sister Jennifer Hedlund. Another reader, but also someone who helped me survive both graduate school and the publication process, is Mandy Link. I am eternally grateful for your help and thankful for your friendship.

To those at the University of Nebraska Press, in particular Bridget Barry, thank you for your time and dedication to making my dream of publishing a book a reality. I also want to thank the peer-review readers who took time to assist in this process, especially Coll Thrush, whose insight and recommendations were of great help and very appreciated.

Finally, to Keith Tyler, my best friend and husband. I am so grateful for your unwavering support and for you.

Introduction

A Colonial Outpost

> The people of Oregon being of different nations, and in a land over which no power exercised exclusive sovereignty . . . found it absolutely necessary to establish some rules, by the observance of which they could live together in peace and harmony.
>
> —"For the Spectator," *Oregon Spectator*, May 14, 1846

> The circumstances under which that government was called into existence, in the absence of all protection by Congress, the absolute necessity which then existed for the people to organize, protect, and legislate for themselves, cannot now be denied.
>
> —John P. Gaines, "Letter to the President," *Western Star*, December 12, 1850

William W. Bristow, a delegate to the Oregon Constitutional Convention, was born in 1826 at "about 3 o'clock in the morning in old Kentucky."[1] This was a claim he could not prove with original documentation when Oregon applied for statehood in the 1850s. Bristow lacked a birth certificate; moreover, his parents did not own such documents and therefore could not verify their status as Americans. Nor did Bristow possess legal proof of his marriage to his wife of twenty years, with whom he shared "a baker's dozen of children."[2] Bristow feared that discussions about proof of citizenship, something the delegates to the state's Constitutional Convention might undertake, could call into question the legal status of current Oregonians such as himself. In April 1859 Bristow wrote to fellow delegate Asahel Bush, insisting that future legislation in Oregon needed to address and revise the specific language about citizenship verification. Bristow worried that requiring citizens to produce birth or marriage certificates would cause women like his own wife to "be called upon to prove she is an honest woman."[3]

Bristow's concerns about proof of marriage and propriety, as well as birth and parentage, point to larger debates and questions about the issue of citizenship in Oregon and within the United States during the early and mid-nineteenth century. Over the course of nearly twenty years (1841–59) elected officials in Oregon developed specific exclusions to both natural and political rights in their region, establishing a very narrow definition of citizenship there. They carefully crafted this definition around issues of parentage, nationality, class, and, especially, perceptions of race and gender. Early Oregon may not seem a likely place for evaluating the construction of race, gender, and citizenship in the United States during the mid-nineteenth century. But, in fact, these issues were central to Oregon politics, and Oregon's laws demanded the attention of the U.S. Congress on the eve of the Civil War.

The Oregon Country was a region over which several empires struggled for control during the first half of the nineteenth century. By the 1840s overland migration to Oregon from the United States had been initiated and was sustained by agrarian desires for land ownership and independence. But Oregon was already home to a very diverse population of numerous American Indian groups, French Canadians, British Canadians, and U.S. fur traders; Spanish, French, and U.S. missionaries; British and U.S. settlers; as well as immigrant laborers from Hawaii and China.[4] Not surprisingly, the representatives of these multiple nationalities and identities had varied interpretations of law and government. In time, as U.S. settlers came to dominate the population of this disputed territory, the territory's laws and policies also became dominated by U.S. settler views. U.S. claims to the region relied principally on settlement, but with a vast amount of land still unoccupied by U.S. immigrants, the security of Oregon could not be ignored, and the United States had to discuss both its existence and the laws that this settler colony in the Pacific Northwest was developing.

When the lower half of Oregon became a territory of the United States in 1848 (two years after the larger Oregon Country had been divided by the United States and Great Britain) and then a state in 1859, it did so during particularly turbulent times in America's history. Oregon politics only contributed to this turbulence: its exclusionary legislation restricted the rights of women, American Indians, Black Americans, as well as those of Chinese and Kanaka ancestry, and it forced the nation to focus on these issues, which became increasingly difficult to avoid as the 1850s progressed. Some of the legal exclusions present in the Oregon Constitution were not unique to Oregon, but the high levels of political, social, and economic tension coupled with Oregon's geographical placement in the West present an excellent vantage from which to consider the creation of citizenship through exclusionary laws on both the regional and national level. Despite Oregon's important position in the national narrative leading up to the Civil War, historians have not highlighted the fact that its provisional and territorial legislation and its proposed state constitution had impacted national events in the late Antebellum era. Oregon thus provides historians the opportunity to examine how political arguments and debates in the Far West had shaped national decisions on issues of slavery, immigration, land ownership, suffrage, education, naturalization, and ultimately, citizenship.

The Project

When I began this book, my intention was to understand how Oregon had passed, on the eve of the Civil War, a constitutional provision that excluded Black Americans from coming to or residing in the region.[5] With increasing sectional tensions over issues of race and slavery during this time, it seemed peculiar that Oregonians would potentially jeopardize their statehood application by including a provision sure to incite debate, if not violence, among members of Congress. As I learned about additional controversial policies brought forth by the Oregon Constitution, it seemed equally surprising that Congress had not denied Oregon's statehood application. These questions led me to consider how an understanding of Oregon's simultaneous independence from as well as dependence on the United States might be illuminated through applying the settler-colonial paradigm to it. Policies enacted by Oregon lawmakers from the time of their provisional government to the construction of their state constitution reveal a colonial identity among Oregon settlers, a regional awareness of the territory's colonial status, and the advantage Oregon had gained as a desired territory and then state. Moreover, I found that Oregon settlers had acted both through and alongside the colonization of the Pacific Northwest by the United States. Oregon settlers had established a settler colony with its own system of government and laws, enforcing these structures on the region's inhabitants (whether U.S. citizens or not). Finally, although settlers did sometimes report to the U.S. government, they did not necessarily adhere to their metropole's policies. Evaluating the process of settler colonialism in Oregon, therefore, provides a more comprehensive understanding of its exclusionary laws and the impact of that legislation.

This book examines the process of settler colonialism in the Pacific Northwest through the evaluation of Oregon's exclusionary laws on existing in the region, immigration, slavery, property ownership, education, suffrage, and naturalization between 1841 and 1859. When Oregon settlers established a provisional government in 1841, they in one sense officially founded a settler colony. Settlers initially re-created and enforced laws drawn from both the U.S. and British empires. After the Oregon Treaty in 1846, however, the region south of the forty-ninth parallel, west of the Rocky Mountains, and north of California became a colonial outpost of the United States. Although influenced by U.S. legislation, including policies from other emerging states of the West, Oregon's laws took on nuanced restrictions and new articulations when legislators there excluded specific groups from U.S. rights. With each step in the process toward statehood, Oregon reinforced the validity of its laws, even when those laws contradicted the U.S. Constitution or legal precedents established by U.S. states and territories. In 1849 Congress established Oregon's territorial government, adopting many of the Organic Laws created by Oregon settlers. With the admission of Oregon as a state in 1859, Oregon again carried legislation from its provisional government as well as laws specific to the needs of settlers, regardless of national interpretations and possible political and legal ramifications. Although statehood signified the final phase of Oregon's colonial status, the process of colonialism within the Pacific Northwest continued, and the influence of the laws created in the settler colony remained.

The construction of these Oregon laws, and the arguments surrounding their development, reified and institutionalized legal definitions and national perceptions of race, gender, and citizenship in the United States during the nineteenth century. Oregon's exclusionary laws either served as a supportive continuation of racial and gendered restrictions to specific rights or established a legal precedent for such restrictions, evidenced in other states' development of legislation throughout the remainder of the century. Additionally, Oregon's experience provides an American example of mid-nineteenth-century settler colonialism and demonstrates how a settler colony can impact an expanding empire.

Oregon

After a century of European sailors mapping and planting flags in harbors of the Pacific coastline, U.S. Captain Robert Gray "discovered" Oregon by sailing into and naming the Columbia River in 1792. A British vessel under Lieutenant William Broughton followed shortly thereafter and traveled even farther east to the lower mouth of the Columbia.[6] Spanish claims to the region, however, go back to the voyage of Columbus and Pope Alexander VI's decree, which granted Spain authority over the western section of the "New World." Spain's stronger claims rest with its settlements along the Pacific coastline throughout the eighteenth century, which covered the modern state of California.[7] France also complicated the story of Oregon's ownership, but its claims to the North American continent had ceased by the French Revolution. Russia's presence in the northwest (primarily the modern American state of Alaska) resided north of Oregon, but its interests of settlement farther south did not dissipate until the 1820s. Well into the nineteenth century, therefore, after foreign settlement had begun in Oregon, Spain, Great Britain, Russia, and the United States continued to claim and vie for control over the increasingly contested region.[8] Until 1846 lands identified as part of or connected to Oregon by one empire or another included areas up to the fifty-fourth parallel north, as far south as the thirty-seventh parallel north, and east of the Pacific Ocean coastline to the Rocky Mountains.[9] In total, this book addresses the region of the present day Canadian providence of British Columbia and the American states of Washington, Oregon, Idaho, and western Montana. Reflecting the transformation of Oregon Country into a U.S. territory and then state, however, the focus of the book follows the place identified as "Oregon."

Historiography

As the United States spread westward in the nineteenth century the American West became a stage where local lawmakers discussed and acted on national issues. Oregon joined this discussion on the eve of the Civil War, which is why this book uses Oregon and its inhabitants as the focal point in its evaluation of this era. Early to mid-nineteenth-century Oregon received much attention for its explorers such as Lewis and Clark, its fur traders, the overland trails that terminated there, its "pioneer" settlements, and its agriculture-centered frontier life. Although scholars have addressed immigration restriction and legal exclusions in the Oregon Country and the Oregon Territory, those discussions have focused on either the regional impact laws had on community development or compared the laws to policies in other developing regions of the West, such as California, Utah, and Nevada. Overall, historians have not sufficiently identified these policies as major influences on the formation of the Oregon Territory as part of the United States and then as a state, let alone viewed the laws as impacting the national narrative or federal policy.[10] This book focuses on how the settler colony's exclusionary laws had impacted settlement in the Pacific Northwest and the relationship between Oregon and the federal government, reflecting historian Daniel Richter's approach of "facing east" in order to understand the actions of Oregon settlers both separate from and in connection to external groups.[11] Instead of centering the evaluation from the perspective of

American Indians during the onset of colonization in North America, as Richter does, this book looks through the vantage point of settlers, with a focus on their laws before Oregon became a U.S. territory and then immediately following that transition. The events and laws are evaluated in the context of Oregon as a colonial space, making the focus simultaneously regional and national.

In the last forty years historians have periodically examined the U.S. West as a space where varied forms of colonization have taken place, although connecting the westward expansion of the United States to that conversation remains a contested issue among scholars.[12] Historians such as Thomas Hietala and Patricia Nelson Limerick have pushed the field to examine western expansion as a "variant of empire," arguing that U.S. settlement and the development of the West were premeditated rather than organic in nature. Hietala suggests that "the idealism of westward expansion embodied in the concept of manifest destiny persists because it helps to reconcile U.S. imperialism with an extremely favorable national image. The assumed benevolence and supposedly accidental nature of U.S. expansion are convenient evasion of the past."[13] Within the northwest specifically, historians Jeffrey Ostler and Gray Whaley have demonstrated the dramatic impact of colonization on American Indian groups, the restructuring of cultural, political, and social landscapes, as well as American Indians' relationships with the federal government as a result of colonization.[14]

This book has been written with the understanding that Oregon did not exist in a vacuum. The creation of settlements in Oregon by Europeans and U.S. settlers was not a natural extension, rather a calculated maneuver for their own self-improvement (whether economic, spiritual, or otherwise). The acquisition of Oregon by the United States was also not an organic process of expansion, but it was carefully negotiated and forcibly acquired through settlement, warfare, and the removal of American Indians native to the region. Moreover, the process came from the settlers themselves, who created a colony that was not, at first, directly aligned with a single nation-state or empire. Through the process of what scholars today recognize as settler colonialism, these Oregon settlers established and enforced a political and social structure of governance—one that resembled or mirrored structures from their various countries of origin—onto the land on which they had taken up residence.

In 1905 Joseph Schafer's article "Notes on the Colonization of Oregon" appeared in the *Quarterly of the Oregon Historical Society* (today the *Oregon Historical Quarterly*). Schafer addresses the process through which Great Britain and the United States had both attempted to claim and colonize Oregon. The term "settler colonialism" had not yet been in use, but Schafer concludes his article with the statement that regardless of the diplomatic negotiations between these rivaling empires, Oregon settlers "inaugurated the American era on the Pacific."[15] Schafer acknowledges the role of settlers in the settlement of Oregon, although he does not separate their actions from colonization itself. Settler colonialism and colonialism can coexist, and in the case of Oregon, settler colonialism operated within the process of colonialism. The two processes are different, however, as Lorenzo Veracini explains: "Whereas colonialism reinforces the distinction between colony and metropole, settler colonialism erases it."[16] Oregon settlers acted both on their own and for the empire, and they connected the colony to the United States. This created a different power structure than what would have been experienced by colonial occupants not under settler colonialism.

Australian geographer A. Grenfell Price's 1929 report "Experiments in Colonization" is credited as the first to discuss the influence and success of "settler-driven colonies," as he addresses the colonial developments of nineteenth-century Canada and Australia.[17] While other scholars continued to explore the role of settlers in empire and colonial schemes after Price's report, it would be another seventy years before Patrick Wolfe articulated the more current scholarly understanding of settler colonialism in *Settler Colonialism and the Transformation of Anthropology*.[18] Through the argument that settler colonization is a structure and not an event, Wolfe suggests that "settler colonialism is an inclusive, land-centered project that coordinates a comprehensive range of agencies, from the metropolitan centre to the frontier encampment, with a view to eliminating Indigenous societies. Its operations are not dependent on the presence or absence of formal state institutions or functionaries."[19] Wolfe's work remains foundational to scholars' understanding of settler colonialism as it applies to the global experience of colonialism as well as large population movements.

Within American history, the incorporation of settler colonialism into historical analysis has had two specific foci: the British American colonies and post–Civil War American Indian policies. Just as they have encouraged the study of "colonization" in western history, scholars have also called for an examination of settler colonialism that addresses the role of U.S. groups in carrying out federal policies. For example, historian Margaret Jacobs has compared the process of settler colonialism in the American West and in Australia through an evaluation of the role white women played in the forced removal of Indigenous children during the late nineteenth and early twentieth centuries.[20] Yet settler colonialism in the early to mid-nineteenth century, during the construction of western colonial societies and before the introduction of federal policies as well as the development of American states, still requires further evaluation.[21]

This book expands upon the research on colonialism, and especially settler colonialism, in the American West. It provides a particularly early example of settlers' roles within the process of U.S. colonization, including the efforts of women settlers—a group that was both inhibited by colonial structures and vital to the establishment and continuation of those structures. Moreover, as world historians such as Mrinalini Sinha and Donald Wright have demonstrated, "the direction of imperial influence flowed not just from the metropole to the colony but also in reverse."[22] The evaluation of Oregon settlers and their exclusionary laws provides a case study of how a settler colony had influenced the U.S. empire, something that is currently lacking in western history scholarship. Finally, an evaluation of settler colonialism in the American West allows for future comparisons of U.S. history with global systems.

This book also addresses some of the main themes of political history in antebellum America, including debates on congressional authority and states' rights, growing sectional issues over slavery and labor, as well as the evolving definition of U.S. citizenship. Alongside that work done by several western historians, political histories such as Michael Morrison's *Slavery and the American West* have long shown that once western lands had been brought into the Union, debates in Washington DC over the extension of slavery into them were a key factor in causing the Civil War.[23] But there is more to this story. What actually happened in those western lands—for example, political debates and the construction of laws within the region—was equally crucial in producing the impending crisis. Oregon legislators not only brought national attention to sensitive issues such as immigration, naturalization, suffrage, and slavery but also forced Congress to take positions on those subjects during the debates and through the acceptance of Oregon's territorial laws and then its state constitution. The issues of slavery and the rights of Black Americans or nonwhite immigrants became unavoidable topics of discussion for Congress and partisan groups as Oregon transitioned into statehood. Moreover, the ability of Oregon to carry exclusionary statutes and clauses from its provisional period into its territorial and state laws further challenged the actual authority of Congress over territories beyond the question of slavery, and it established earlier foundations for racially exclusive legislation at the state and federal levels.

Legal histories of the nineteenth-century American West tend to focus on water, railroads, and mining—all of which require an emphasis on land ownership and labor—but the capacity of the field allows for considerable expansion. Examining early western legislation provides a more comprehensive portrayal of how individual or cultural perceptions of race and gender gained the force of law. Historians such as Peggy Pascoe, Nayan Shah, and Katrina Jagodinsky utilize legal histories to evaluate specific pieces of legislation—such as miscegenation laws and immigration policy—and their connections to issues of gender, race, sexuality, and citizenship. Their work demonstrates the impact of laws on Americans' perceptions of race and gender; those constructed ideas, in turn, shaped America's legal system.[24] An evaluation of Oregon's exclusionary laws reveals complicated definitions and interpretations of race and gender in relation to specific political rights, furthering the understanding of how issues of race and gender were embedded within U.S. law. Ultimately, Oregon lawmakers used perceptions and discourses of race and gender to control access to rights in their region and to legitimize white males' political authority.

Methods, Definitions, Sources

This book employs critical discourse, gender, race, and colonial theory. Drawing from the theories of Michel Foucault on the historically specific roles of discourse in society and its function in connection to power relations, I have evaluated newspaper editorials and legislative minutes, among other forms of speech, as malleable discourses that not only are distributed by people but also can act upon people. Reflecting Joan Scott's discussion of gender as a category of analysis, and the application of gender analysis in American histories from scores of scholars in the past thirty years, I evaluate the use of "gender" as social meanings constructed from culturally perceived performative differences between sexes. Additionally, I evaluate gender as a discourse in political debates and legal documents.[25]

Unlike other categories in this book that draw from specific theorists and scholars, the use of race as an analytical lens comes from a wide range of historians who have informed my understanding of the construction of race.[26] Although race is inevitably connected to other issues, especially gender, historians such as Ibram X. Kendi demonstrate both how race distinguishes differences between groups of people and how racism has also been a way for a group to claim superiority over another as well as justify U.S. laws and colonial expansion.[27] In this book "race" represents the socially, politically, and legally created descriptions of groups, based on but not always predicated on physical appearance.[28]

And finally, my evaluation of settler colonialism reflects Patrick Wolfe's discussion of settler colonialism as an implementation of social and political structures by permanent settlers over native inhabitants. This is done in connection with comparative definitions of colonialism used in world history that emphasize the relationship between the metropole and the colony to reveal the development of the Pacific Northwest and how Oregon's laws impacted the U.S. federal government.[29] In the case of Oregon, and the definition used in this book, "settler colonialism" refers to the act and process of foreign settlers' spatial, political, and social colonization of Oregon (including its native inhabitants) both independent of and dependent on the U.S. empire. Furthermore, calling Oregon a "colony," as an aside, also reflects the language used by settlers when they referred to the region from the time of its provisional government to it becoming an American state.[30]

To effectively use specific terms, it is necessary that I provide clear definitions for main groups and ideas. In this book, the term "settler" means a person and a person's descendants who have permanently occupied a foreign land (i.e., space not of a settler's nation of origin). To identify this group as settlers is not to suggest that the region was unsettled, as American Indians had existed on the lands for generations before Oregon settlers arrived. Rather, it is to represent the ways in which this group had acted within the process of colonization. The term "colonist" can be substituted for "settler," but because these people were participants in settler colonialism in addition to colonization, this book uses "settler" exclusively. In connection to "settler" is the term "settlement," which refers to the intentional and permanent (or at least attempted permanent) occupation of a foreign land by settlers. The title of "American Indian" applies to all Indigenous communities on the North American continent and descendants of those groups that have existed on lands prior to European contact. When addressing a specific group, such as the Umatilla, the group name replaces the geographic indicator of "American"; they will therefore be identified as Umatilla Indians. An individual identified as a "citizen" is someone recognized by a nation-state as belonging to its populace. In the United States, someone can be recognized as a citizen by a specific state, but the same person is not necessarily viewed as a citizen in other states or by the federal government. "Citizenship," therefore, belongs to a citizen who enjoys all the rights and benefits provided by or protected by a government entity (whether state or federal). Not all citizens of the United States possess citizenship, just as not all citizens of Oregon possessed citizenship, because not all citizens had complete access to all U.S. rights.

Sources used in this book primarily consist of laws, bills, constitutions, legislative reports and debates, personal correspondence, speeches, and newspaper articles. Although all primary sources require contextual consideration, the political involvement of Oregon newspapers necessitates additional explanation. Oregon politics in the 1840s and 1850s predominately consisted of the Democratic Party and those who were arrayed against the Democrats—the Whigs, Republicans, Know-Nothings, and supporters of temperance. The Democrats themselves were somewhat divided, wavering at times between adherence to the national party line and the platforms put forth by their nominal leader, Asahel Bush, in his *Oregon Statesman* newspaper.[31] The parties that opposed the growing strength of the Democrats in Oregon—referred to here as Anti-Democrats—did not identify as a united group, but their attacks and rebuttals to the Democrats were similar. The Anti-Democrats projected their opinions through local newspapers, including the *Oregonian*, *Oregon Argus*, *Oregon Sentinel*, and *Oregon Weekly Times*.[32] Newspapers were a national platform for U.S. politics, and within the sparsely populated region of Oregon they served as the most effective medium for communicating political thought. The evaluation of these papers, in conjunction with other primary sources from the region, is necessary to understand Oregon's political culture as well as how lawmakers justified exclusionary legislation.

Organization

More often than not, Oregon's exclusionary laws intersected, whether through their legal definitions or in their construction. To understand the processes involved with the creation and implementation of each law, this book is organized thematically, allowing laws to stand apart from one another. Each chapter evaluates specific types of legislation through three lenses of analysis: settler colonialism, race, and gender. Chapters also conclude with a section addressing the immediate legacy of the main law in question prior to the twentieth century. The exception to this organization is chapter 1, "Oregon and the Making of a Settler Colony in the Pacific Northwest," which provides an overview of how Oregon became a colonized region and explains the process through which settler colonialism took shape. Colonization in the Oregon Country had begun much earlier than settlement or even U.S. involvement in colonizing the region. Settlers' presence and then permanent occupation shaped the evolving arguments empires used to claim authority over Oregon. The United States became the beneficiary of the foreign settlements, which impacted the relationship between the United States and the settler colony as well as how settlers established their own forms of governance and laws in the Pacific Northwest.

Chapter 2, "The Dispossession of American Indians and the Right to Exist," deals with the legal and physical dispossession of Indigenous communities from their homelands as well as the justifications made by Oregon lawmakers and U.S. officials for American Indians' removal. Reflective of U.S. colonialism across the continent, Oregon settlers occupied and claimed lands prior to treaties with American Indian groups. In the Pacific Northwest the process of foreign settlement had also begun before the United States had authority over the region, and it accompanied provisional laws regarding Indigenous lands and Oregon militias. The removal of American Indians from their traditional lands was connected to these provisional and then territorial policies, but it was driven by settlers' claims to land, racialized warfare, and the gendered portrayal of this history.

Chapter 3, "Understanding Immigration Restrictions through Arguments of Slavery and Labor," addresses how Oregon lawmakers restricted the immigration of Black Americans to the region and establishes connections between this legal exclusion and the issue of slavery. Oregon settlers created specific policies on the institution of slavery, but the issue of slavery had a widespread impact on Oregon laws as well as settlers' perceptions of race, labor, and states' rights. This influence was nowhere more evident than in Oregon's exclusion of Black Americans from coming to or settling in the region. By the time Oregon applied for statehood its lawmakers had continuously revised this exclusion as well as prohibited Black Americans from holding suits in an Oregon court. Oregon's laws restricting the rights of Black Americans contributed to increasingly contentious debates on slavery and labor and influenced national interpretations of citizenship.

Chapter 4, "Incorporated Definitions of Land Ownership," focuses on laws pertaining to property ownership, specifically land laws and those connected to the federal Donation Land Act of 1850. Land ownership and laws protecting property claims were important to Oregon settlers, but they also influenced Oregonians' relationship to the federal government. Not only did Oregon's land laws predate congressional involvement in the distribution and regulation of territorial land claims, Oregonians also ultimately introduced new property ownership policies that challenged national perceptions of gender roles and racial characteristics of citizenship. Additionally, Oregon land laws reveal the complicated role of women settlers as both actors in and subjects of the colonial process.

Chapter 5, "The Privileged Right to an Education," deals with Oregonians' perceptions of morality and miscegenation in relation to education laws. A broader understanding of how settlers and the federal government legitimized the settlement of Oregon emerges with an evaluation of connections between education and moral enlightenment. Although Oregonians developed education laws with specific exclusions, the availability of education in Oregon had to accommodate its diverse population, its unbalanced ratio of male to female settlers, as well as the religious foundations of many Oregon schools. Education laws influenced the national perception of race and gender in Oregon and reflected regional interpretations of class privileges.

Chapter 6, "Implications of Citizenship in Suffrage and Naturalization Laws," attends to suffrage laws and their connections with Oregon's position on naturalization. With the nation's elevated value of and specific exclusions to the right of suffrage, Oregon's laws both challenged racial restrictions and reified gendered understandings of U.S. citizenship. Oregon's suffrage laws also provided foundational arguments for other states' and territories' exclusionary laws, including policies that transformed the post-Reconstruction South.

As each chapter contains its own specific argument, the conclusion attempts to bring these exclusionary laws together to provide an overall meaning of their development and their influence on the nation. The conclusion also addresses the legacies of the three main themes in this book: settler colonialism, race, and gender. Further connections between Oregon's exclusionary laws and more modern legislation—for example, twentieth- and twenty-first-century applications of American Indian treaties, states' rights, the Equal Rights Amendment, access to public education, and naturalization policies can be made, but not in this book.

To understand the full weight of Oregon's statehood in 1859, it is necessary to look back at the initial formation of white settlement and to examine how the process of settler colonialism allowed for and contributed to legal exclusions in the Pacific Northwest. In contrast to histories depicting how the nation has impacted the region, viewing the development of the Pacific Northwest through the lens of settler colonialism demonstrates a transmission of legal influences from a colony to the empire.[33] The region that became Oregon has either participated in some of the most exclusionary legislation created in antebellum America or established legal precedents for similar restrictions. Oregon's statehood brought it within the folds of the metropole, but settlement in the region continued, as did the influence of those exclusionary laws. This book reveals how even a small colony of people can impact an empire with prejudicial policies.

LEVERAGING AN EMPIRE

CHAPTER 1

Oregon and the Making of a Settler Colony in the Pacific Northwest

It is not imaginable that . . . any European nation should entertain the project of settling a colony on the Northwest. This silence even now around is beginning to break and the sod that for ages had laid unturned is broken now by the red man's spade. Not long ere hamlets and towns shall be seen uprising on either hand. And the sway of the husbandman cheerfully chime[s] with glee of the school boys play. Not long ere the church bell to distance afar, its sounds shall extend o'er the land.

—Journal of Mary Richardson Walker, January 25, 1839

Mary Richardson Walker, shortly after her marriage to Elkanah Walker, accompanied a small group of missionary couples to the Oregon Missions in 1838. Walker consistently kept a diary, noting the group's travels from Maine across the "western territories" and through the Great Plains. Her group stopped for a time at a Waiilatpu mission in Walla Walla ran by Marcus and Narcissa Whitman before the Walkers, Ells, Smiths, and Grays went on to establish a mission at Tshimakain, near present-day Spokane, Washington. The missionaries were not the first foreign inhabitants of Oregon. After several empires had surveyed the region from the perspective of a ship's bow and through fur traders' reports, these missionaries joined colonization efforts that were decades in the making, but they arrived before many of the overland immigrants. Missionaries such as Walker provided a description of hopeful convergence, documenting an optimism that the land that lay before them was malleable and could naturally take shape into the form of their choice. As Walker's countless diary entries of frustration demonstrate, the realities of settling in this region (including the modern U.S. states of Washington, Oregon, Idaho, western Montana, and western Wyoming as well as the Canadian province of British Columbia) did not always align with this vision.[1] Nevertheless, by the early 1800s Oregon was a place that interested parties had longingly observed and the youthful United States had taken actions to colonize as its own.

As noted in the introduction, colonization efforts in the Pacific Northwest were put forth by multiple empires, namely Great Britain, Russia, France, Spain, and the United States. Although settlement was emphasized in diplomatic papers, establishing trade in Oregon was the first objective for European and U.S. officials. Periods of exploration correlated with attempted settlements, as competing empires understood they had a better chance of securing trade through and from Oregon, particularly of furs, if they could operate from within the region.[2] In many cases, groups involved in the northwest corner of the Pacific coastline used the words "colonize," "settle," and "occupy" interchangeably. Upon wanting to make lands the exclusive property of a state, the term "colony" became an identifier of the land in question. These empires applied this term to the Pacific Northwest regardless of whether they wanted complete control over the area's resources, intended to build permanent structures, or planned to extend the titles of their nations to that land.[3]

Those who developed foreign settlements in Oregon also referred to the region as a "colony." For example, in 1843 early settlers of the Willamette Valley called a meeting to discuss the security of their livestock and referred to the gathering as "a public meeting, of a number of citizens of this colony."[4] Between 1841 and 1849, when Oregon was formally organized as a U.S. Territory, settlers had used the language of "colony" in the meeting minutes of Oregon's provisional government and in the recorded proceedings of the initial territorial government.[5] Although the Oregon Emigration Society had identified itself in 1839 as "the people of Western America," the group's "Articles of Agreement" subsequently and continually referred to the settlement as a colony.[6] American missionaries who eventually became settlers did not view Oregon as a natural extension of the United States, either; rather, they saw it as a foreign place. Missionaries such as Mary Richardson Walker noted physical distinctions between Oregon and the United States; she explained in her diary that she had "Left the States," and on several occasions she stated that other missionaries had to make their way back to the "States."[7]

While these settlers recognized their settlement as a colony (evidenced in their government papers and personal writings), so too did the United States. In 1843 U.S. sub-agent of Indian Affairs Elijah White referred to immigrants' settlement in the Willamette Valley as a colony in multiple reports to U.S. Secretary of War J. M. Porter. White differentiated this colony from the homes and residences of American Indians and from missions and mission schools established in Oregon.[8] Although concerned about the proximity of the immigrant settlement to American Indian groups, White reported that "the settlers are actively and vigorously employed, and the colony in a most prosperous state."[9] Oregon was not yet under the jurisdiction of the United States when White penned the aforementioned passages, but U.S. agents employed by the federal government had worked in the region, and, as discussed later in this chapter, the United States viewed the increasing settlement of Oregon by U.S. immigrants as validation of its claims to the region. Ultimately it would be more than fifty years after foreign ships had begun entering Pacific Northwest inlets that Oregon became a "colony."

A colony represents a new sociopolitical organization created by invasion and generally existing within a region under the structure of colonization. A colony can contain inhabitants who are original to the region prior to colonization, are from the metropole of the colonizing group(s), or brought to the colony by the colonizing group(s).[10] In the case of Oregon, the colony included Indigenous peoples of the region, Kanaka and other Pacific Islanders brought to the region in connection with the fur trade, as well as U.S., British, French, Spanish, and Russian immigrants from their respective empires. Colonizing groups attributed the term "colony" to the entire Pacific Northwest, which explains this large inclusion of colonial inhabitants. Many of these foreign immigrants then became Oregon settlers. In fact, by 1860, just after Oregon had become a U.S. state, the Census documented that 43 percent of the region's inhabitants were foreign born, which included being born in areas in the unorganized West, such as Oregon.[11]

A majority of Oregon's foreign inhabitants at the end of the 1840s comprised of U.S., British, and French Canadian immigrants. The initial settler population of the Willamette Valley stood at fewer than 150 individuals in 1842 but grew to approximately 6,000 by 1845.[12] Foreign immigrants from the United States quickly outpaced other groups, with communities such as Oregon City comprised entirely of "American" inhabitants.[13] The settler population doubled in size according to the 1850 U.S. Census, although the Oregon territorial government only acknowledged 2,509 of those residents as qualified voters.[14] By 1855 the Oregon settler population had surpassed the estimated number of American Indians in the region.[15] Throughout this period of foreign immigration, the clustered settlements created their own laws and constituted a collective settler colony within the Pacific Northwest.

"Settler colony" is a term and concept that scholars have developed in relatively recent years. They have conceived it as different from "colony" even when the two coexist; settler colonialism can occur within the system of colonization. As a region that experienced structures of colonialism from multiple empires, Oregon as a colony and the Oregon settler colony saw different timelines. Oregon was eventually colonized by the United States once it came under U.S. jurisdiction through the Oregon Treaty of 1846, but settler colonialism had begun prior to this, when (primarily) British and U.S. settlers had established and implemented their own government systems and laws.[16] The Oregon settler colony would go on to include additional settlements by immigrant groups beyond the Willamette Valley, where it had first taken root, and institute its social and political structures over inhabitants of the region regardless of race or nationality.[17] When discussing Oregon during the early to mid-nineteenth century, the term "colony" could be substituted for the name "Oregon."

A region with blurring borders and individual settlements referred to as a "colony," this region will hereafter be called "Oregon" to simplify its identity and to properly follow the transition from "Oregon Country" to the specific settler colony developed by Oregonians.

This first chapter addresses the development of the settler colony and the eventual colonization of Oregon by the United States. This process not only required exhaustive negotiations over several decades with multiple empires but also demonstrates that Oregon had not been organically brought under U.S. jurisdiction simply because of the region's proximity to the empire. This chapter also explains that this process had coincided with the development of settler colonialism and highlights the kind of relationship between Oregon and the United States that resulted from these coexisting structures. While the following chapters address how settler colonialism in Oregon has fundamentally affected the relationship between Oregon and the U.S., this chapter establishes a foundation for that interaction as well as the groundwork of how Oregon's exclusionary legislation, established by provisional government laws, eventually impacted the United States.

Making Claims from Afar

The Pacific Northwest is the traditional homeland for thousands of Indigenous communities with numerous cultures (including multiple languages), political and economic practices, and several specific and unique groups within larger nations and tribes. Many American Indian communities of the region did not appear within European and then U.S. reports, nor are several Indigenous nations recognized by the U.S. federal government today. Although the population numbers of American Indians are wide-ranging depending on the source, certain regions such as the Columbia Basin Plateau were home to upward of 150,000 people prior to European contact.[18] Nevertheless, by the eighteenth century foreigners had begun to arrive on the lands of the following groups, as well as many other Indigenous peoples who had connections to the region through travel, trade, gatherings, and healings:

> Nez Perce Tribe, Yakama Nation, Spokane Tribe of Indians, Palouse Tribe, Kalispel Tribe of Indians, Colville Confederated Tribes, Confederated Tribes of Warm Springs, Cowlitz Indian Tribe, Osage Nation, Northern Paiute, Shoshone Tribes, Bannock Tribes, Confederated Salish and Kootenai Tribes, Confederated Tribes of the Umatilla, Wishram Tribe, Wasco Tribe, Shahala Tribe, Klickitat Tribe, Clackamas Tribe, Molala Tribe, Confederated Tribes of the Grand Ronde Community, Confederated Tribes of Coos, Lower Umpqua, and Siuslaw Indians, Modoc Tribe, Alsea Tribe, Confederated Tribes of Siletz Indians, Tillamook Tribe, Tualatin Indian Tribe, Clatskaine Indian Tribe, Clatsop Tribe, Kathlamet Indian Tribe, Taidnapam Indian Tribe, Kwalhioqua Tribe, Shoalwater Bay Tribe Chinook Nation, Confederated Tribes of the Chehalis, Nisqually Indian Tribes, Puyallup Tribe, Squaxin Island Tribe, Skokomish Tribe, Quinault Nation, Ho Tribe, Quileute Nation, Lower Elwha Klallam Tribe, Makah Tribe, Jamestown S'Klallam Tribe, Suquamish Nation, Steilacoom Tribe, Muckleshoot Indian Tribe, Duwamish Tribe, Snoqualmie Tribe, Port Gamble S'Klallam Tribe, Snohomish Tribe, Snoqualmoo Nation, Tulalip Tribes, Stillaguamish Tribes of Indians, Sauk-Suittle Tribe, Kikiallus Nation, Swinomish Indian Tribe Community, Upper Skagit Indian Tribe, Samish Indian Nation, Nooksack Indian Tribes, Lummi Nation, Marietta Band of Nooksack Tribe.[19]

Interactions between foreign groups and Indigenous peoples varied, but the presence of American Indians must be considered when evaluating the onset of European exploration along the northern Pacific coast and the absence of these Indigenous nations' voices in the diplomatic arguments of legal claims.

Empires interested in controlling Oregon were looking at the Pacific for financial gain. In the late eighteenth century the fur trade boomed across markets in China and India, and trading companies sponsored by a European state had begun monopolizing trade within specific regions. The substantial distance between Atlantic ports and the Asian markets limited U.S. merchants' participation in this growing trade. Oregon's Pacific coastline as well as the Columbia River's potential connection to internal waterways, however, led many U.S. merchants and ambitious fur traders to see the potential to be had in the colonization of Oregon. In fact, a large factor in New York merchant John Jacob Astor's establishment of the Pacific Fur Company at the mouth of the Columbia River in 1810 was to gain a more effective and thus more lucrative trade route to China.[20] The importance of Oregon in connection to trade was not lost on U.S. merchants, nor did it escape the attention of British and Russian merchants.

A growing European presence along the Pacific coast by the early nineteenth century also inclined the U.S. government toward the acquisition of Oregon. From the founding of the American Republic, the United States was serious about its claims to the Pacific Northwest and its desire to lessen European control over lands in North America. After war had commenced between France and Great Britain in 1793 European colonials literally spilled into U.S. settlements near the Mississippi River, and the United States' need to secure Oregon increased.[21] Although the developing national narrative would later describe the West as "open" to U.S. settlement, other empires had not only wanted to claim Oregon but also surrounded the United States by the beginning of the nineteenth century. The United States faced France from the west, Great Britain from the north, and Spain from the south. As a young republic, the United States was concerned about what advances by any of these European empires would mean for the security of the nation.[22] In addition to the economic opportunities available with the acquisition of the Pacific Northwest, territorial control through settlement of the region became another incentive for the United States to pursue control of Oregon.

In 1804 the U.S. government sponsored an expedition by Meriwether Lewis and William Clark to gather information on resources and landscapes in the Pacific Northwest. The Corps of Discovery, as Lewis and Clark's journey became known, took scrupulous notes, left numerous tokens from the U.S. government behind, and ultimately served as a way for the United States to justify jurisdiction over Oregon.[23] Following the publication of Lewis and Clark's travels, the U.S. Congress agreed that the occupation of Oregon was of increasing interest to the nation and began to create histories that detailed all "major" claims made to the region. Congress did this to legitimize U.S. claims to both the western regions of North America and encourage settlement in Oregon.[24] These reports ignored American Indians' centuries-long habitation of North America; rather, they focused on the United States' position in relation to European claims—many of which started with Spain.

The U.S. Congress began its calculated evaluation of Oregon's "ownership" with Spanish jurisdiction over the North American continent through the papal decree of "Inter Caetera" in 1493. It then described Spain's settlement along the Pacific coastline to "as high as the northern extremity of California," primarily in the form of Catholic missions more than two hundred years later, and addressed Spain's one-time brief control of Louisiana in the late eighteenth century.[25] A Select Committee in the House of Representatives, appointed to inquire about the colonization of lands along the Columbia River, concluded that Spain's "morbid thirst" for gold and precious metals was why Spanish settlement north of California had never been attempted. By 1795 the Spanish had, however, attempted and failed in three overland expeditions by the Company for the Discovery of the Nations of the Upper Missouri.[26] The United States conceded that Spain did have claims to lands along much of the Pacific coastline, though solely through the "right of discovery."[27]

A disagreement in 1789 between Spain and Great Britain over a post on Nootka Sound, known as the Nootka Dispute, challenged this same Spanish definition of sovereignty based on the right of discovery. Maquinna, "the principal Nuu-chah-nulth headman" of the Nootka Confederacy, had granted the British land to build a structure, but the Spanish, believing the land to be under their jurisdiction, seized the property.[28] The British prepared to go to war for this piece of land and argued that the issue really spoke to the larger questions of whether Spain had authority over the Pacific coast and whether the lands claimed by Spain but not occupied by it were still open for settlement. Meanwhile the United States situated itself between the competing empires and used this position to strengthen negotiations with Great Britain over lands near present-day Vermont and in the Ohio Valley, as well as with Spain over access to the Mississippi River.[29] Without the support of France, which was amid a revolution, Spain folded and compensated the British for their losses. The Spanish also declared that the Northwest Coast, or coastlines north of California but below the Russian settlements, was neutral for trade and temporary settlement.[30]

Ultimately the Nootka Dispute resulted in a change in perceptions about imperial claims. Previously the Spanish interpretation of sovereignty that had dominated international diplomacy argued that title was acquired through discovery, which included exploration and "acts" of possession.[31] The British definition maintained that evidence of occupation was necessary to demonstrate jurisdiction and title.[32] This latter definition became the dominant interpretation by competing empires in the Pacific Northwest by the beginning of the nineteenth century.

Spain's final retreat from the battle for Oregon came in 1819 with the Adams-Onís Treaty (or the Transcontinental Treaty). In addition to ceding Florida to the United States and drawing permanent boundary lines that recognized U.S. lands above the Sabine and Red Rivers and along the Arkansas River, the Spanish withdrew their claims to lands north of the forty-second parallel—from the western border of the Louisiana Purchase to the Pacific Ocean.[33] Technically the treaty acknowledged that Spain had ceded the land from the forty-second parallel to the forty-ninth parallel (through Oregon) to the United States. The U.S. government went on to cite this treaty in later negotiations for Oregon with Great Britain, but the British disputed both Spain's original claims to the region as well as U.S. claims through the Transcontinental Treaty.[34]

After establishing Spain's northern borders, the U.S. congressional recordings of land claims in the West generally focused on the holdings of France and Russia. The French empire claimed lands west of the Mississippi River, beginning with penetration of the river by French sailors as early as 1673 and later solidified by M. de la Salle's landing and settlement on the bay of St. Bernard on the west side of the Colorado River in 1685. Known as "Louisiana," recognized French claims stretched from "the Rio Grande del Norte, being the next great river to the west of that settlement, along the mountains of Mexico and New Spain west, as the western limits, and California as the eastern boundary."[35] By the eighteenth century the French had claimed their borders on the North American continent to reach as far east as present-day North Carolina and South Carolina, citing as evidence for this claim the successful commercial affairs of Anthony Crozat in the Gulf of Mexico.[36] Finally, according to this U.S. narrative, France's "sale" of Louisiana to Spain during the French Revolution was inconsequential, and the Louisiana Purchase in 1803 was cited as France's removal from claims to the Pacific Northwest.[37]

Russia's claims to Oregon, or more specifically the northwest coastline, generated some concern in the United States during the first decades of the nineteenth century. Russian claims, however, appeared more like declaratory bursts than a consistent assertion of ownership over the region. The two Russian stations on the Pacific coastline recognized by the U.S. government were New Archangel, near the fifty-ninth parallel north, and Bodega Bay on the coast of California, at the thirty-eight parallel north. Then in September 1821 a ukase (edict) of Tsar Alexander I claimed exclusive territorial rights to the Northwest coast along the Pacific, including not only present-day Alaska but also down to the fifty-first parallel north in Oregon.[38] When confronted by Great Britain and the United States over this claim, Russia asserted that its claims were based on "discovery, occupancy, and uninterrupted *possession*."[39] Russia claimed a continuous presence, citing the 1789 report by Spanish captain Haro that Haro had found a Russian settlement with approximately twenty families located somewhere near the forty-eighth or forty-ninth parallels north. This location was later identified by Haro as an error, and Haro noted that the correct location of the settlement was between the fifty-eighth and fifty-ninth parallels north, far north of Oregon. Within diplomatic correspondence U.S. officials also maintained that Russian claims were farther north, noting that during the Nootka Dispute "Russia explicitly disclaimed interfering with the exclusive rights of Spain to *beyond* Prince William's Sound, in latitude 61: and Vancouver, in 1794."[40] If Russia had acknowledged

Spain's sovereignty to the region below the Alaska Territory in 1790, it did not matter what lower settlement (regardless of its mistaken location) the Russians had previously "occupied"; U.S. officials asserted that Russia's previous actions had effectively relinquished its claims to Oregon. The Russo-American Treaty of 1824 granted Russia the right to trade along the coastline below the fifty-fourth parallel north, but a year later, Russia ceded all land south of its Alaska Territory to the United States and Great Britain—who had by that time established joint control over Oregon.[41]

Great Britain's claims to Oregon rivaled the duration of Spain's presumed ownership, as they began with the legendary exploits of English privateer Sir Francis Drake and extended well into the nineteenth century. Between Drake's controversial encounters with Spanish merchant vessels, the British claimed that in 1578 Drake had sailed in the name of Elizabeth I and made formal claims to the Pacific coastline from the thirty-seventh to the forty-eighth parallels north. The United States challenged this account, arguing that British claims that rested on Drake's voyages failed to reconcile with the fact that no settlement had been established within the area, which Drake had named "New Albion."[42] The U.S. diplomat to Great Britain under the Monroe Administration, Richard Rush, also questioned the legitimacy of this claim after the American Revolution, noting that the treaty of 1763, "of which Britain agreed to consider the Mississippi as her western boundary upon that continent," nullified any previous British authority over the region.[43] British diplomats did not accept this position from the United States and returned to charters issued by King James I in 1608, 1610, and 1611 for the colony of Virginia. The British argued that the seventeenth-century charters "were declared to embrace the whole extent of the country from thirty-four to forty-five degrees of north latitude, extending from sea to sea."[44] Countering the U.S. reliance on Spanish authority over North America to establish the transference of ownership in later treaties, the British pushed for the recognition of its earlier acts.[45] Nevertheless, the U.S. maintained that post–Revolutionary War treaties held greater legitimacy than previous exploration and fur-trading claims put forth by the British.

Drawing back to the Nootka Dispute, U.S. representatives cited 1790 as the point at which Great Britain had begun to recognize settlement as requisite for claims to land—using its occupation in a portion of present-day British Columbia against Spain's claims to the entire Pacific coastline.[46] Along that line of thinking, the British claimed to have possessed by 1822 structures created by the Hudson's Bay Company (HBC), which had reached the shores of the Pacific through overland travel in Canada from "latitude 54 30, north, longitude 125, west, and that in latitude 55 15, north, longitude 129 44 west."[47] The United States had also raised buildings in the Pacific Northwest prior to the two countries' negotiations in the 1820s, with the United States' greatest emphasis on Fort Astoria, established in 1811 by John Jacob Astor's Pacific Fur Company in the present-day state of Oregon. Although the U.S. company failed and was acquired by the Hudson's Bay Company only two years later, the fort still served as an important part of U.S. claims to the region. In fact, the restoration of Fort Astoria to the possession of the United States in 1818 became a point of contention in the Treaty of Ghent, in which the U.S. demanded and ultimately received its return.[48]

Even by the War of 1812 the United States had begun to view Oregon as "rightfully American."[49] U.S. ministers to the Treaty of Ghent assertively claimed that Oregon fell under the "natural dominion" of the United States and dubiously argued that the loss of Fort Astoria had occurred during wartime. Despite returning Fort Astoria to the United States, Great Britain did not accept the U.S. argument of natural dominion put forth by individuals such as Secretary of State John Quincy Adams. During negotiations with Great Britain, Adams openly speculated, "It is not imaginable that, in the present condition of the world, *any* European nation should entertain the project of settling a *colony* on the Northwest Coast of America; that the United States should form establishments there, with views of absolute territorial right, and inland communication, is not only to be expected, but is pointed out by the finger of nature, and has been for years a subject of serious deliberation in Congress."[50] Adams may have viewed Oregon as an inevitable part of the United States, but the developing colony was not under U.S. jurisdiction. Moving into a second decade of negotiations in Ghent, the British saw to it to remind the U.S. government of this fact.

Although the British were aware of the young American empire's expansionist ambitions, Great Britain wanted control of the Columbia River. The Hudson's Bay Company, which merged with the British Northwest Company in 1821, needed easy access to the ocean for its fur trade in Canada. The British viewed the forty-ninth parallel from the Rocky Mountains to the Columbia River and then down to the forty-sixth parallel (including all the river and land north of the river) as necessary for efficient trading. In addition to ownership of the Columbia River, the United States also wanted possession of the Puget Sound and its harbors, prompting diplomats to push for control up to the forty-ninth parallel, at the very least. Overall, the British government recognized the need to restore Fort Astoria based on the same argument that had restored them land in the Nootka Dispute (that those occupying the structure retained the claim for their government), but never recognized U.S. sovereignty over the region itself during the Treaty of Ghent.[51]

In a commissioner's meeting referred to as the 1818 Convention, an impasse between the two governments resulted in a somewhat vague and inconclusive decision. Technically, Great Britain and the United States decided on a joint occupation of Oregon, stating that "any country that may be claimed by either party, on the Northwest coast of America, Westward of the Stoney Mountains, shall, together with its harbors, bays, and creeks, and the navigation of all rivers within the same, be free and open for the term of ten years, from the date of the signature of the Convention, to the vessels, citizens, and subjects, of the two Powers."[52] In other words, while the convention made no decision on sovereignty, neither country could assume sole claim over lands in that region. Officials for these two empires believed that after ten years a more permanent arrangement could be found.[53] Those who wanted to settle in Oregon for trade, religious conversion, or even permanent settlement, however, did not recognize this ten-year agreement and settled in the region under the assumption that their country would support them anyway. As the following chapters demonstrate, these settlers also pushed their respective governments—who did not oppose their settlements—to take immediate action in the acquisition of Oregon.

Although the U.S. Congress had been discussing the settlement of Oregon for some time, by the 1820s representatives such as Congressman John Floyd of Virginia had pushed for the investigation of colonizing lands along the Columbia River in consecutive congressional sessions. The calls for action also came from the public, and newspapers increasingly covered discussions of Oregon settlement.[54] One inquiry from Congress into the acquisition of Oregon, however, not only made national papers but appeared in London newspapers as well. On April 6, 1824, U.S. Brigadier General Thomas S. Jesup responded to a request from Congress to report on "the expediency of occupying the Mouth of the Columbia River."[55] In his report Jesup evaluated Oregon and, taking a predominately military perspective, considered what benefits the United States might garner from owning this land. In addition to possibly preserving peace between the American Indian nations and any future settlement by U.S. immigrants, Jesup believed "the possession and military command of the Columbia [as] necessary not only to the protection of the [U.S.] fur trade, but to the security of our Western frontier." Viewing the position and holdings of the Hudson's Bay Company as the most immediate threat to occupying the Columbia River, the U.S. general suggested that three additional posts be established to "afford present protection to our traders, and, on the expiration of the privilege granted to British subjects to trade on the waters of the Columbia, would enable us to remove them from our territory, and secure the whole trade to our own citizens."[56] When Jesup's report reached British newspapers the public focused on this last suggestion and demanded that the British government confront the United States about removing its subjects and British business enterprises from Oregon.[57]

Secretary Adams had already instructed diplomat Richard Rush to reopen negotiations with Great Britain over the sovereignty of Oregon around the time Jesup's report reached England. The 1818 Convention had determined that the two empires would not broach the issue again until 1828, but pressure from the U.S. Congress and public to support settlement in Oregon prompted Adams and Rush to revisit the issue of sovereignty over the region ahead of schedule.[58] The British perceived this untimely approach by the United States as aggressive, and this made negotiations both uneasy and unproductive. Initially Adams had instructed Rush to call for the northern boundary between the two countries to be set at the fifty-first parallel north. The British Ministers, however, maintained previous arguments set forth in the Treaty of Ghent and the 1818 Convention. A frustrated Rush reported to Adams in 1824, "Neither my remarks nor my authorities, of which I have endeavored to present an outline, made the impression upon the British Plenipotentiaries which I was desirous that they should have produced."[59] The Monroe Doctrine of 1823 may have hardened the United States' interpretation of its authority over the Americas, but Great Britain was still very much committed to its Pacific Northwest forts and claims to the region.[60]

What had changed between the negotiations that culminated in 1827 and those held in 1818 was that the area of Oregon that both empires claimed became a smaller section of the region. Lands east of the Columbia River and below the forty-ninth parallel (namely today's Idaho and western Montana) had fallen into a "no-man's land" of sorts. Great Britain no longer argued for sovereign rights to these lands east and south of the Columbia River, but those lands remained part of Oregon, as the British did not recognize the region as a U.S. territory either. Maps of the region at the time (and still produced to this day) associated all lands west of the Rocky Mountains, and jointly controlled by the United States and Great Britain, as part of Oregon. The region that Great Britain and the United States tried to claim for nearly another twenty years and the region identified as "Oregon," however, were not the same.[61]

What remained clear was the fact that the United States and Great Britain were not willing to relinquish claims to the region between the Columbia River, the Pacific Ocean, and below the fifty-first parallel. Great Britain offered the United States an enclave of land on Puget Sound if the United States were to withdraw its claims to the Columbia River, but to no avail. Ultimately, the agreement reached in 1818 was extended

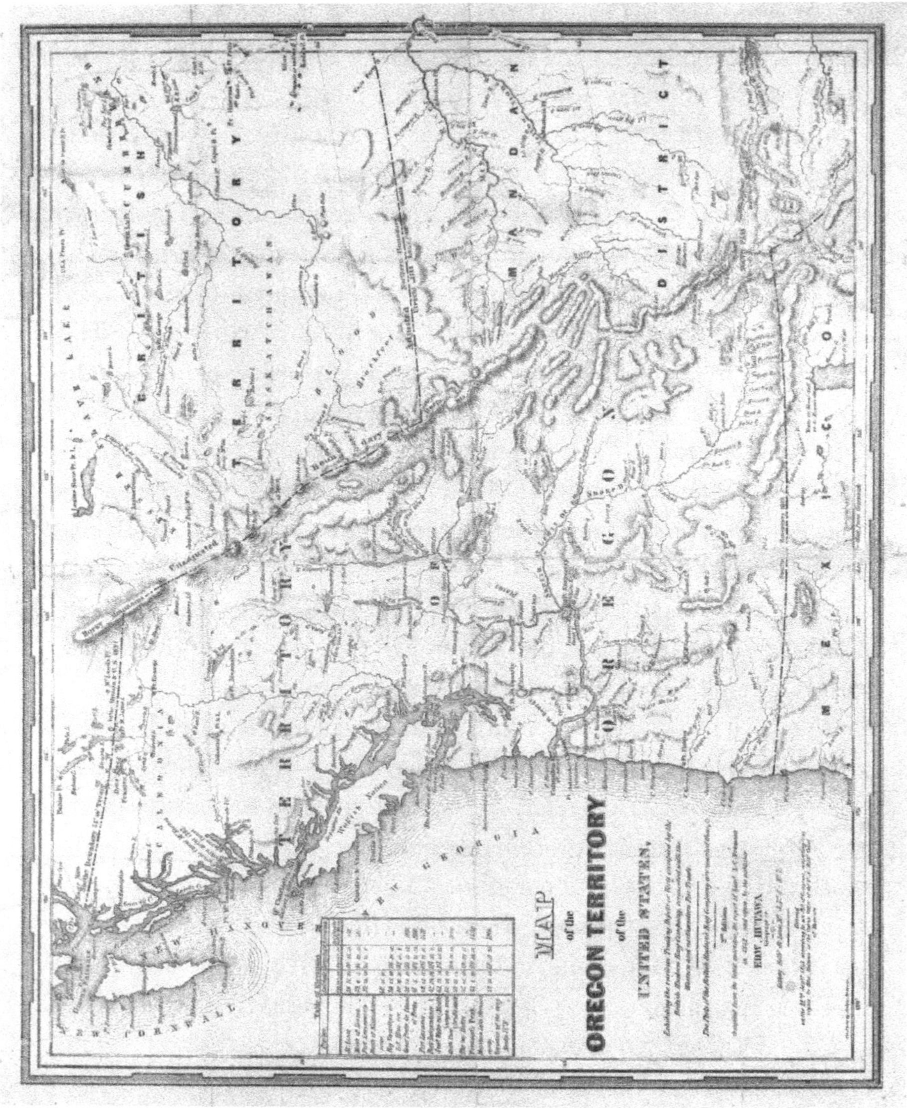

1. Map of Oregon Territory of the United States, 1843. G4240.1843.H87/MAP-086, Oregon Historical Society.

indefinitely. By the end of 1820s the claims the United States could make for Oregon, according to Great Britain, were limited to Captain Gray's "discovery" of the Columbia River in 1792 and its settlement with the construction and occupation of Fort Clatsop in 1805 and Fort Astoria at the mouth of the Columbia in 1811. As European and U.S. immigrants continued to settle in the region, neither empire extended its jurisdiction to Oregon.[62] These diplomatic negotiations between the empires, therefore, were part of the colonization of Oregon—but the process of settler colonialism had also commenced.

Occupying Oregon: Initiating American Colonization

Occupation by foreign settlers represented another phase in the colonization of Oregon and the most significant step for the United States toward westward expansion into the Pacific Northwest. By the 1830s Oregon had become occupied by settlers from, among other locations, Great Britain, Russia, and France, with the United States as the fastest-growing contributor.[63] Oregon settlers were colonists of a disputed region, and their presence became an effective method of occupying the region and thus claiming it for their respective countries of origin.[64] These settlers desired protection for the lands they awarded themselves as well as distance between themselves and the Indigenous communities that did not accept their foreign settlements. Oregon settlers also hoped that a nation would eventually bring them fully under its jurisdiction. In the meantime, a large group of settlers moved to create a temporary government among themselves officially known as the "provisional government." When constructing these legal structures, the settlers presumed that their new government would eventually transition to a system under a specific empire. Ultimately, the Oregon provisional government provided a needed structure to the region's multinational settlements, and because settlers used it to impose laws, it became the overarching authority over Oregon's inhabitants. Before the provisional government was established, however, other groups had served as colonizing forces and laid the groundwork for permanent settlement.

In the years following the Lewis and Clark Expedition, fur trading posts and forts began to appear across the Oregon landscape. The British Hudson's Bay Company and the Northwest Company emerged as early and consistent occupants in the Pacific Northwest, with the Northwest Company erecting the first foreign post along the upper Columbia and Lewis Rivers in 1807.[65] The British-controlled Salesh House, Kullyspell House, Spokane House, and Fort Nez Perces all went up within the first two decades of the nineteenth century. American traders with the Pacific Fur Company and Missouri Fur Company overlapped some of these spaces but attempted to counter British growth in the region with Fort Astoria, Fort Okanagan, and Fort Spokane.[66] American fur trading companies, hoping to capitalize on the success of the Lewis and Clark Expedition, tried to identify a commercial overland route. Yet even the failed Hunt Expedition of 1811–12, led by Wilson Price Hunt, did not discourage U.S. fur traders. Great Britain's dominant presence in Oregon, however, proved problematic for U.S. companies wanting to gain control of the Pacific Northwest market.[67]

Immediately following the 1818 Convention the U.S. government sent out (or at least recognized) several groups to survey Oregon for the construction of military posts and other forms of permanent settlement. The first U.S. immigrants able to occupy Oregon were those connected with the fur trade.[68] Following the path that many fur traders had taken in the century prior, hunters and entrepreneurs recognized Oregon's economic potential and the need for their own nation to secure such opportunities. In October 1828 the U.S. Congress received a memorial from the "Hunters of Oregon," comprising several individuals, including James M. Bradford.[69] After submitting a formal letter to the president, the memorialists informed Congress that they had formed a compact and union "for the purpose of hunting and trapping, trading with the natives, and a permanent settlement on the Columbia or Oregon river, within the limits of the United States." The following December the House of Representatives connected the hunters' letter to Bill No. 12, regarding the occupation of the "Oregon River" (the Columbia River). Of course, in 1828 the United States did not legally possess Oregon, let alone the land surrounding the Columbia River. Though the memorialists were aware of this fact, they vowed that their actions in Oregon would, in any case, be on behalf of the United States until the region fell under U.S. jurisdiction. Detailing the ways in which these hunters' occupation of Oregon would profit the United States, the memorial went on to note that "in their trade and intercourse with the natives," they would remove the fur trade from the hands of the British and place it "into the hands of citizens of the United States."[70]

The hunters' plans required that the United States give Great Britain a twelve-month notice for the termination of the countries' joint occupation over Oregon. The memorialists also warned Congress that sooner rather than later Great Britain would come to a similar conclusion about the wealth connected to the Columbia River as well as within Oregon, and they insisted that "the policy of Great Britain is, therefore, to possess the strongest points of control on this grand thoroughfare of commerce, as well as over every other commercial thoroughfare of the world."[71] The U.S. government could not sanction the actions of the memorialists, which included having a standing army around the Columbia River, but it could express a noncommittal agreement with the hunters' assessment of the situation. Moreover the U.S. could use the hunters' existence in Oregon in its future negotiations with Great Britain by noting the hunters' consistent presence as evidence of U.S. occupation.[72] Regardless of the nationality attributed to companies or individual hunters, the fur trade served as an economic function of colonization for competing empires.

Throughout the 1830s the British Hudson's Bay Company continued to control much of the region's fur trade and attempted, with the help of Iroquois traders, to exhaust fur pelts in the inland Northwest from the continental divide to the Snake River.[73] Preferring potential competition with Russian traders over the presence of U.S. companies, the HBC's Nisqually Fort began supplying the Russian-American Company in 1839.[74] Yet the more individual-based practices of U.S. companies made it difficult for the British to push them out entirely. This approach to the fur trade made manning a fort difficult for U.S. companies, which led locations such as Fort Astoria to employ a diverse staff, including British and Hawaiian fur traders.[75] U.S. companies' limited oversight of their fur traders also created problems for British relations with American Indians. U.S. groups such as those associated with Jedediah Smith attacked Indigenous communities—in that group's case, the Tillamook Indians—and soured existing and future negotiations between the HBC and American Indians.[76] Yet, regardless of how they had arrived in the region, some fur traders became the first Oregon settlers after choosing to retire and take up semipermanent residence. This growing foreign population diversified in the 1830s with the introduction of U.S. missionaries. And although the fur-trade companies did not benefit from this role, the HBC inadvertently assisted these U.S. occupants in also becoming settler colonists.[77]

Prior to the mass overland immigration of U.S. settlers, such as those who took to the Oregon Trail, the Hudson's Bay Company had helped American missionaries establish footholds in the region that eventually led to permanent settlements. Missionaries in the Pacific Northwest were dependent on Fort Vancouver for necessary supplies and specialized tools during the 1830s and through the 1840s.[78] It is unclear if the British company had fully realized the implication of its support for U.S. settlement, but some HBC employees opposed rendering this assistance to American missionaries. Hebert Beaver, the chaplain to Fort Vancouver, stated his concern about the presence of these missionaries near and at the fort multiple times to Benjamin Harrison, a committee member of the Hudson's Bay Company. In 1836 Beaver warned his employer, "It is to be regretted that American missionaries are so much encouraged here, for, independently of other motives, it is feared, that, [if] they, or their followers, become numerous, the interests of the Company will be undermined."[79] Beaver continued to communicate his concerns throughout his tenure at the fort, noting settlement developments such as abundant grain production by the U.S. settlers as well as speculating about the eventual threat this group would pose to Great Britain's trade with the Sandwich Island and Russian settlements.[80] The Chaplain also commented on the growth of U.S. settlements—at least initially associated with missions—noting, "Their's is a fast increasing and thriving colony, while our's here seems to be stagnated," and that these settlers (along the Willamette River) had procured six hundred and thirty heads of cattle from California in 1838.[81] Beaver knew of these activities because many American missionaries frequented Fort Vancouver at the invitation of the fort's chief factor Dr. John McLoughlin. Beaver complained to the Company, among his other concerns about the missionaries' practices, that these visits were a drain on the fort's provisions.[82] A financial drain they may have been, but Beaver's concerns foreshadowed a larger development at play. The Hudson's Bay Company had afforded American missionaries (and subsequently early settlers) the ability to gain a permanent residence in a region still disputed by Great Britain and the United States. As Beaver had feared, these missionaries served as additional colonizers and an imperial vanguard to U.S. claims to Oregon.

Missionaries such as the well-known and established Methodist minister Jason Lee presented Great Britain with a group of U.S. immigrants who not only intended to create religious institutions in Oregon but also actively supported the settlement of "like-minded" people. Lee and the Methodists had been expanding their occupation of the Willamette Valley since 1835. Once their plans had switched from converting Indigenous communities to making the valley their permanent home, their settlement opened trade between U.S. companies and these outlying imperial posts.[83] Under the direction of the Methodist Episcopal Church, a group from New York was inspired by the efforts of Lee and sailed via South America up to the coasts of Oregon to take up a missionary life. The group arrived in the present-day state of Washington in 1840, and it was sent to The Dalles station. According to the established Methodists in Oregon, The Dalles served as "an important location, not only for the influence it was expected the mission would exert upon the Indian tribes, but because it lay in the line of travel from the States to the fruitful valley of the Willamette; and it was hoped, therefore, that the emigrants might also be met, on entering the country, with the sound of the gospel."[84] The foothold U.S. missionaries had created for immigrants to settle in the region played a crucial role in the success of permanent U.S. occupation in the region.

"Spiritual salvation" was not the only thing U.S. missionaries in Oregon could offer. By the early 1840s the pace of immigration from the United States had dramatically increased, even though the region remained a disputed colony between the U.S. and Great Britain. Missionaries such as Marcus Whitman, who had lived in the region since 1836, served as guides for hundreds of incoming settlers between the Missouri River and the Willamette Valley.[85] In many cases arriving groups possessed a fraction of the goods, family keepsakes, livestock, and even individuals than they had started with back in the United States. This scarcity of supplies, let alone the absence of fully functioning settler "towns" in Oregon, left immigrants dependent on the forts and existing missionary groups. The New York missionary group in The Dalles reported of these incoming settlers, "They toil and privations of the overland route were, at this time, very great. . . . They were often very destitute, and, in most cases, taxed heavily the kindness of their Christian friends, who were not by any means abundantly supplied with the conveniences or even the necessities of life. But they made great exertions, toiling hard early and late, and sacrificing often their own little comforts, to aid the suffering."[86] Such provisions provided by the missionaries were deemed essential to many of the immigrants, but it was not the only source for obtaining resources. In fact, Lee loaned money to help new immigrants become established, and despite HBC policy, McLoughlin also extended credit lines to these U.S. settlers.[87] Reports from settler groups in Oregon would find their way back to the U.S. and inform future settlers of what awaited their arrival and how to establish permanence in the region.

The predecessors to Oregon Trail settlers, whose experiences occurred in tandem with the immigration of missionaries, were groups of U.S. settlers asking their government to form an official colony in the Pacific Northwest. Past claims, occupations, and settlements of Oregon had already made the region a colony, but potential U.S. settlers viewed this disputed area as a space that needed the designation of a U.S. colony. In February 1828 a group of U.S. immigrants requested from Congress land and aid "in forming a colony on the Northwest coast of the United States."[88] This group identified itself as "engaged in agricultural and mechanical pursuits" and asked for its government to "open this western wilderness to the skillful and preserving industry of civilized man."[89] What the would-be colonizers ultimately wanted, however, was for the U.S. government to grant them the right to live and form a government in Oregon, even though their nation did not have the power to grant such a request. By 1832 immigrant groups from Atlantic states were forming for the specific purpose of occupying a part of the Pacific Northwest.[90] The opinion that Oregon was within the United States' "natural dominion" had taken hold, and although the United States did not possess jurisdiction over Oregon, some settlers were determined to live there and make the land their own.[91]

The formation of emigration societies such as the Oregon Emigration Society, which left for Oregon in 1839, came with articles of agreement and other forms of documentation noting the group's intentions separate from its members' states of origin and uniquely constructed for the settlement of Oregon. Although historians have not counted the emigration societies' legislation as connected to Oregon's provisional government laws, these documents contain similarities to policies eventually developed by the Oregon settlers in the Organic Laws.[92] Similar to how English colonists had put piecemeal sections and ideas of English law together, Oregon settlers used British and U.S. laws as legal blueprints for their colony.[93] The difference between the groups that petitioned the U.S. Congress for land or for the colonization of Oregon and some of these emigration societies, however, was that the emigration societies did not recognize themselves as representatives of the United States. Rather, groups like the Oregon Emigration Society created constitutions that depicted themselves as separate from all other governments, even noting a pledge to defend the land they awarded themselves against the "claims of persons or governments whatsoever."[94] Oregon was a colony, but emigration groups and early settlers' construction of legislation also demonstrated a separation between the settler colony and any specific empire.[95] The settlers' laws were something the neither the United

States nor Great Britain controlled. Still, these policies by emigration societies and missionaries were not designed to apply to inhabitants outside of their immediate groups; therefore, the need for an overarching government system remained.

By the early 1840s, the growing number of Oregon settlers planning to make the region their permanent home had led many to believe they needed some sort of government for dealing with the increasing population. The death of Ewing Young, a prosperous settler with no heirs, in 1841 threw into sharp relief the fact that Oregonians lacked basic systems of government to deal with Young's three thousand dollars' worth of promissory notes left as common property to the community. Parties influential enough at the time to initiate a government remained the dominant employers of the region: the Hudson's Bay Company, the unorganized first settlers, as well as the missionaries—namely, the Methodists under Jason Lee.[96] Getting such a diverse group of people, including British Canadians, French Catholic fur traders, various European immigrants, and U.S. immigrants from both the Northeast and the South to elect officers was not a simple task.[97] Nevertheless, the floodgates for foreign immigration had been opened by decades of newspaper coverage on the occupation of the Pacific Northwest and by U.S. legislators such as Missouri Senator Lewis Linn, who argued for legislation that would award white U.S. settlers free land in Oregon.[98] With the appointment of officers and regularly scheduled meetings in 1843, the settlers created Oregon's provisional government and officially formed a settler colony.[99]

Oregon's provisional government passed laws pertaining to the establishment of courts, maintenance of a militia, regulation of land claims, and the existence of slavery, among several others. As mentioned earlier different groups of settlers existed in Oregon, but U.S. immigrants quickly became the majority and therefore the dominant group.[100] Nevertheless, as a disputed region, the provisional government did not directly associate with one specific empire. In fact, some of Oregon's earliest government documents specified future loyalty to whatever nation would eventually bring them under its jurisdiction, either the United States or Great Britain.[101] It was not until the Oregon Treaty of 1846 that the provisional government began associating itself with the United States. The settlements under the authority of the Oregon provisional government and south of the forty-ninth parallel thus became a U.S. territory with an already functioning government. This transfer of rule was not automatic. The provisional government continued operating under its own policies and elected officials until the United States created Oregon's territorial government in 1849. By the time U.S. appointees made their way to the Pacific Northwest, settlers had been creating and implementing their own laws for about eight years.

Even if settlers ventured to Oregon with the notion that they were doing so as U.S. citizens, prior to 1846 they had moved to a settler colony that existed outside of U.S. jurisdiction. Once Oregon was a territory, the United States maintained a steady eye on the West coast, as the nation understood the implications of bringing another free state or slave state into the union. The West presented multiple opportunities for either side to gain more representation for its cause, and many realized that whichever direction the West went would determine who controlled the government.[102] Whatever legislation Oregon settlers carried into the territorial government and adapted as a new U.S. territory would come under federal review. As the subsequent chapters address, several provisional laws brought under U.S. jurisdiction ran contrary to established policies and conflicted with constitutional amendments. Yet Oregon lawmakers consistently leveraged their location in the Far West and their role as colonizers to keep their controversial laws. Federal discussions of Oregon policies stirred during the acquisition of the region, the creation of the territorial constitution, and again with the Oregon state constitution elevated the influence of these laws within national debates and future policies.

Ultimately, the isolated beginnings of Oregon settlers and their legal structures, as well as the political context in which Oregon transitioned into a state, placed them in a position to influence the American empire. Several nations had vied for control of the region, and Oregon settlers helped the United States make claims to permanent occupation. Once representing a territory, Oregon lawmakers carried forward legislation that constructed a narrow definition of citizenship and reified perceptions of race and gender specific to the desires of the settler colonists. Oregon laws were challenged within the halls of Congress and on the floors of the Senate, as well as in national newspapers, but this occurred on both sides of the sectional division. Oregon settlers, therefore, retained significant pieces of their provisional laws up to and through Oregon statehood. The U.S. government's debate and eventual acceptance of Oregon's exclusionary laws in 1849 and 1859 legitimized Oregon's definitions of race, gender, and citizenship, allowing the former settler colony to impact national interpretations of issues such as American Indian removal, slavery, immigration restrictions, land ownership, education, suffrage, and naturalization.

CHAPTER 2

The Dispossession of American Indians and the Right to Exist

We have been willing to throw away the rest of our country and reserve the land lying between the forks of the Santiam—you thought it was too much. Then we agreed to take only half of it and to take in the Kallapooya beyond our south line, if they were willing—you thought it was too much. We then agreed to take this small piece between the Creek and north branch—you want us still to take less. We can not do it; it would be too Small; it is tieing [*sic*] us up into too small of a space.

—**Al-que-ma**, of the Santiam Band

Peter Burnett, an early Oregon lawmaker and future governor of California, reflected on the "privilege" of getting to live in the Pacific Northwest during the 1840s: "But, for the very reason that every human being has the right of domicile in the place of his nativity [Burnett argued] he is not, as a matter of right, entitled to a residence in another community."[1] Burnett maintained this position in *Recollections and Opinions of an Old Pioneer* to justify his original support of legislation to restrict Black Americans from the region. His confused scramble to defend a law that had fallen out of favor by 1880 takes on a different meaning if viewed from the perspective of American Indians in the Pacific Northwest.[2] Although Burnett and the thousands of immigrants that descended on Oregon in the mid-nineteenth century were both new and foreign to the land, the "community" he referred to did not include Indigenous peoples. Though the settlers engineered the systematic dispossession of American Indians from their traditional lands in the region, white Oregon settlers quickly viewed themselves as native inhabitants.

When Europeans and U.S. immigrants first began to settle in the Pacific Northwest, the lives of American Indians and structures of Indigenous communities had already undergone significant transformation. The introduction of the horse in the eighteenth century shifted migratory patterns, altered hunting routines, and moved groups beyond their traditional lands.[3] For example, equestrian Shoshone groups had pushed the Cayuse Indians south and out of the Blue Mountains prior to the Cayuse making contact with American missionaries.[4] Over the first decades of the nineteenth century the increased presence of European and American fur traders compounded these changes and altered Indigenous peoples' relationships with one another as well as their interactions with the surrounding landscapes. Waves of devastating epidemics such as smallpox and measles not only drastically reduced the populations of American Indians in the region, especially west of the Cascade Mountains, but also disrupted Indigenous people's life patterns. Ultimately an initial phase of dispossession, rooted in biological, ecological, and economic changes, took place prior to the Oregon Trail. Foreign settlement then accelerated and institutionalized this process.[5]

The dispossession of American Indians in the Pacific Northwest by Oregon settlers and the U.S. government removed thousands of Indigenous peoples from the lands and homes of their ancestors. This process of dispossession was not a succinct act of relocating American Indians; rather, it was a fragmented series of redefining where and how they could exist. Histories such as Whaley's *Oregon and the Collapse of the Illahee* demonstrate how American Indians in the region opposed this dispossession.[6] This chapter addresses how Oregon settlers and federal officials questioned, through action and discussion, American Indians' right to live in the Pacific Northwest.[7] In order to circumvent American Indians' rights to their traditional and cultural lands, Oregon lawmakers successfully pressured the U.S. government to legitimize their own unsanctioned land claims as well as negotiate treaties with Indigenous peoples and establish American Indian reservations. To justify the warfare against and removal of American Indians, Oregon settlers and U.S. officials created racialized and dehumanizing portrayals of Indigenous peoples in public records. Finally, Oregon settlers and U.S. officials attempted to reduce the presumed existence of American Indians in the Pacific Northwest by promoting the femininity of white settler women and minimizing the presence of American Indian women in newspaper and government reports.

Settler Colonialism and Dispossession Policies

The first foreign settlement in Oregon derived from the overlapping ventures of the Pacific Northwest fur trade and Christian missionaries. Both heavily relied on the existence and cooperation of Indigenous peoples for their operations to function, and both initially worked toward forms of coexistence, including living among the American Indians.[8] Ideas about the settlers' relationship with American Indians also changed for both groups over the early decades of the nineteenth century. While the British Hudson's Bay Company encouraged working with Indigenous peoples' social and political structures to ensure consistent trade relations, this was not the practice U.S. fur traders adopted. In recognizing the HBC's dominance over the region's furs, U.S. fur traders relied more on their own labor and deemphasized the connections provided through working with American Indians.[9] Meanwhile U.S. missionaries were struggling to demonstrate progress to missionary boards back in the States, and they began to question the need for their proximity to intended converts. By the 1840s Methodists at the Willamette Mission under the leadership of Jason Lee abandoned their missionary work and became permanent Oregon settlers.[10] These former missionaries were soon joined by disgruntled or retired fur-trade employees, and together with the first wave of U.S. immigrants they began to form their own provisional Oregon government.

By the time Oregon settlers arrived in the Pacific Northwest, centuries of legal justifications for acquiring lands from Indigenous peoples had been established. Beginning in the sixteenth century, English law cited various ideas based on a Christian purpose, rights of commerce, just war, conquest, and occupation of vacant lands to legitimize their seizure of domains from Indigenous peoples in North America.[11] The United States adopted many of these arguments to remove American Indians from the continent, as well as similar ideologies from other European nations that strategically dismissed the rights of Indigenous peoples.[12] Through Article 1, Section 8 of the U.S. Constitution, Congress held the power to regulate commerce with American Indians, and executive acts formalized U.S. relations toward American Indians.[13] The U.S. Supreme Court then helped institutionalize these federal policies. In *Fletcher v. Peck* (1810) the U.S. Supreme Court established that states could not interfere with contracts made to American Indian groups by the federal government, such as treaties. The court then affirmed that decision and expanded the concept of sole federal authority over Indigenous peoples in *Worcester v. Georgia* (1832).[14] In *Johnson v. M'Intosh* (1823) Chief Justice John Marshall argued in favor of the evolving interpretation that Indigenous peoples within U.S. territories did not own the land; rather, they only held the right of occupancy and therefore could only negotiate or sell lands with the U.S. federal government.[15] Quickly applying these decisions became necessary for the federal government to negotiate its authority and minimize the legal role of American Indians within the process of western expansion. Settler colonialism, however, had reached the Pacific coast prior to the arrival of the U.S. government's legal jurisdiction.

Oregon settlers may not have been versed in all the legalities related to British and U.S. colonization, but early Oregon lawmakers approached the creation of provisional land laws and regulated relations with the Indigenous peoples of the Pacific Northwest under the opinion that lands could be taken for the success of their colony. By 1843 the Legislative Committee of the Oregon provisional government had begun to establish such laws for the "purpose of mutual protection, and to secure peace and prosperity among ourselves."[16] Under "Laws of Land Claims," the committee laid out general requirements for "any person now holding, or hereafter wishing to establish," land claims, including required improvements toward and necessary length of occupancy on a claim. Article 3 of Section 1 implored colonists to recognize: "The utmost good faith shall always be observed toward Indians. Their lands and property shall never be taken from them without consent; and, in their property, rights, and liberty they shall never be invaded or disturbed, unless in just and lawful wars, authorized by the representatives of the people, but laws, founded in justice and humanity, shall, from time to time, be made, for preventing injustice being done to them, and for preserving peace and friendship with them."[17]

The committee acknowledged, theoretically, that Indigenous peoples held certain rights over their land and placed the power of negotiating for that property into the hands of the settlers. This ran contrary to both U.S. and British policies in the early 1840s that placed the power to negotiate with Indigenous peoples in the hands of the national governments, but at that time Oregon remained a colony outside of either empire's legal jurisdiction. Through the HBC, Great Britain extended a form of its judicial system to Oregon residents, but this did not fully extend its laws to the colony per their joint occupation agreement with the United States.[18] By 1842 Willamette Valley residents had also conversed with U.S. Agent of Indian Affairs Dr. Elijah White and expressed their wishes that he officially oversee issues with "claims that the aborigines of this country have" in the region, although such authority to create treaties would not extend to Oregon for another eight years.[19]

The provisional government's instruction in Article 3 to not take American Indian lands, except through just warfare, presumed that "unoccupied" land was not owned by Indigenous peoples and was therefore available to settlers, as defined by the committee. According to seventeenth-century English laws applied in North American colonies, vacant lands could refer to uncultivated or unused land and became property of the individual who transformed or improved upon them.[20] The interpretation of "unused" could vary depending on cultural understandings of cultivation. The camas fields of the Pacific Northwest, for example, provided vital foodstuffs for American Indians, but gathering practices dating back centuries may only last two weeks out of the year.[21] The U.S. government's interpretation of lands such as those fields being vacant served as an effective argument for dispossessing American Indians of their lands.

Some early U.S. state constitutions, such as North Carolina's constitution that predated rulings like *Johnson v. M'Intosh*, had recognized the authority of its General Assembly to purchase Indigenous peoples' lands on behalf of the public.[22] By 1843 the U.S. government had established that individuals could not purchase land from American Indians, and Oregon was not yet a U.S. territory at the time. Shortly before the ratification of the Oregon Treaty in 1846, the *United States v. William S. Rogers* decision expanded federal authority over all American Indian territories and asserted that "the aboriginal tribes of Indians in North America are not regarded as the owners of the territories which they respectively occupied. Their country was divided and parceled out as if it had been vacant and unoccupied land."[23] While the decision validated Oregon settlers' earlier possession of "unoccupied" lands and echoed their more recent Organic Laws (1845), Oregon lawmakers had created their own policy on acquiring lands and regulating "intercourse of the people with the Indian tribes," which reflected laws applicable to their situation rather than U.S. policy.[24] The continued encouragement of peaceful relations with Indigenous peoples became more difficult to enforce as wagon trains of immigrants began to pour into the Pacific Northwest and onto the lands of American Indians.

The Oregon Treaty formally placed the Oregon settlers and their colony under U.S. jurisdiction, but the appointment and placement of federal officials was slow and inconsistent during a crucial time in the relationship between immigrants and American Indians. In the summer of 1846 President Polk first addressed Oregon's situation and called for the extension of laws "regulating trade and intercourse with Indians" as well as the establishment of an "Indian agency, and subagencies" west of the Rocky Mountains.[25] Although Dr. White with Indian Affairs had served in the region, it was not clear to Oregon settlers whom they could immediately call upon to address the increasing difficulty faced in dispossessing American Indians of their lands.

In an editorial to the *Oregon Spectator*, M. M. McCarver spoke of his frustrations with the U.S. government on this matter, noting, "At the present there is no person in Oregon authorized by the American government to make present or counsel with these tribes in relation to them [*sic*] occupancy of their lands by the whites." Because the "right of occupancy by them has not been extinguished," McCarver noted, "they may . . . erect their wigwams before our doors."[26] The editorial acknowledges the right of occupancy held by American Indians and demonstrates Oregon settlers' realization that their claim to lands, whether just made or going on five years at this point, were tentatively secured and required legal intervention by the federal government.[27] Of course, this concern did not slow the flow of immigrants to Oregon, and public meetings continued to take place throughout the territory to discuss their hopes for the U.S. government to provide settlers with "grants of land."[28] Overall, Oregon lawmakers stuck to their Organic Laws and remained optimistic that the United States would validate their colonial land claims, but what might befall the territory before treaties were actually created remained uncertain.

Decades of foreign squatters as well as waves of epidemics had placed American Indians of the Pacific Northwest in a difficult if not unbearable position by 1847. The Cayuse War, identified as such after a conflict at the Whitman mission (Waiilatpu) resulted in the death of the missionaries, was not a surprise to Oregon settlers. Conflict between Oregon settlers and Indigenous peoples was an ongoing reality in the Pacific Northwest during the mid-nineteenth century, as the next section of the chapter will address. Increased tensions over land encroachments, unreciprocated use of resources, incompatible cultural practices, and the Cayuse Indians' desperate attempt to deal with the most recent round of "Old World" diseases had set the stage for what Oregon newspapers and U.S. officials came to describe as a massacre of U.S. citizens in November 1847.[29] This event fanned Oregon settlers' demands for U.S. involvement in matters of land possession and American Indian relations. While the U.S. ultimately provided military assistance, and

President Polk offered land bounties for service in the Cayuse War, the Oregon provisional government remained in operation during the conflict and raised the volunteer militias, many of whom already held land claims and increasingly viewed Indigenous peoples as barriers to their settlement.[30]

A week after the killing of the missionaries and the day before the Oregon legislature formally discussed the event, Governor of the Oregon Territory George Abernethy addressed Oregon settlers on the current state of their colony. While still "convened under the Provisional Government" the appointed Governor did not minimize his frustrations with the lack of U.S. federal involvement in the territory. He recognized that although the extension of U.S. jurisdiction was "hardly a doubt," the settlers remained "sadly disappointed" that it had not yet occurred. Among the list of issues Abernethy insisted the U.S. government needed to address were Oregon settlers' relations with American Indians and the need for "a fund set apart for treating with Indians."[31] Abernethy maintained that the relationship had become "every year more embarrassing," and despite having promised Indigenous people that they would be compensated for their lands, he explained that "[the latter] have been told this so often that they begin to doubt the truth of it." Indeed, years had passed since Oregon settlers began making such promises, and overland immigration to the region had continued. The conflicts this caused between Oregon settlers and American Indians, Abernethy argued, required an immediate remedy, something "of sufficient value to keep them quiet, until an agent arrive[d] from the United States." The message concluded with a discussion of property Oregon lawmakers believed to have been taken by Indigenous peoples. While they waited for U.S. assistance, the Governor instructed the provisional government that "appropriations should be made by you, sufficient to enable the superintendent of Indian affairs to take a small party in the spring and demand restitution of the property, or its equivalent in horses."[32]

By the end of 1847 Oregon lawmakers had viewed their relationship with the U.S. government as more theoretical than actual. Oregon settlers continued as they saw fit without federal support. In fact, Oregon lawmakers appointed commissioners to solicit funds "necessary to arm, equip, and support in the field, a force sufficient to obtain full satisfaction for the Cayuse Indian for the late massacre at Waiilatp[u], and protect the white population of our common country from further aggressions."[33] On December 11, 1847, the commissioners requested funds from Chief Factor James Douglas of the Hudson's Bay Company as well as the "Merchants and Citizens of Oregon," maintaining that "the citizens of the states and territories, east of the Rocky mountains, are justified in promptly acting in such emergencies." The commissioners argued that as a settlement under the authority of the U.S., "there appears no room to doubt that the lawful acts of the Oregon government will receive a like approval."[34] Governor Abernethy also called for volunteer militia, but Oregon lawmakers believed there was a need for funds to engage in war against multiple American Indian groups, as the focus of this warfare would not be isolated to those directly involved in the killings at Waiilatpu or to the Cayuse peoples in general.[35]

Oregon lawmakers then continued to seek aid from the U.S. government, with Speaker of the Oregon Assembly Robert Newell writing to the U.S. Senate and House of Representatives on December 29, 1847, pleading for "the guardianship and protection over this remote but beautiful and valuable portion of the United States."[36] Oregon lawmakers such as Newell believed not only in the eventual backing of the U.S. government in a war they had declared on American Indians but also that securing the newly acquired territory of Oregon was a priority of the federal government. The Mexican-American War no doubt occupied the U.S. government's focus at the time, but Oregon lawmakers were not wrong. The United States did get involved; the federal government eventually provided military and financial assistance to Oregon for waging its own wars on the Indigenous peoples of the region.[37] But before the United States established official Indian Affairs posts in the region, Oregon lawmakers had appointed their own.

In February 1848 Governor Abernethy appointed three "war commissioners" to "treat with the Nez [P]erces and other tribes of Indians" and to discourage Indigenous peoples north of the Columbia River from joining the Cayuse Indians in "hostilities."[38] Oregon lawmakers, still under the provisional government, took it upon themselves to name "Indian Affairs" officials within the Oregon Territory and authorize negotiations with American Indians.[39] Some Oregon settlers worried what this meant for Oregon settlers' claims to "unoccupied" lands. An Oregon settler identified only as "Theseus" questioned a reported proclamation by Superintendent of Indians Affairs H. A. G. Lee that land taken from the Cayuse Indians during the war would be granted to army officers "to settle and hold land claims." The author posed the question to his follow Oregonians, "Who ever heard of an Indian Agent giving charters or grants to settle a colony?," and he asserted that "the law creating the office of the Superintendent of Indian Affairs in Oregon does not express such a grant of Power, nor can it be implied."[40] Even though accusations about the abuse of power of the superintendent of Indian Affairs in Oregon during the Cayuse War would come about, especially in terms of the considerable funds spent, questions remained in Oregon over the legal acquisition of lands in the Pacific Northwest.[41] Oregon lawmakers continued to oversee land claims by settlers, and the Cayuse War demonstrated the need for formal treaties as well as U.S. intervention over Indigenous groups. Oregon lawmakers hoped to expand their settlement, but this required the further dispossession of American Indians from "desired" lands.

In August 1848 the U.S. federal government issued "An Act to Establish the Territorial Government of Oregon," and it limited settlers' acquisition of land "so long as such rights shall remain unextinguished by treaty between the United States and such Indians."[42] The act reflected U.S. policy that placed the authority to negotiate with Indigenous peoples on matters such as the acquisition of lands solely in the hands of the federal government. Unless Indigenous peoples' claims had been extinguished through a federal treaty, which had not yet occurred, Oregon settlers were not to take possession of American Indians' lands. The U.S. government wanted to prevent interference in future negotiations, but it seemed to overlook the history of Oregon settlers making land claims through their own provisional government. And while the act addressed the surveying of lands by the U.S. government, it did not address those existing land claims.[43] Furthermore, it would be several months before the United States appointed officials to the territorial government, meaning Oregon settlers had been operating under their own land laws and taking property from American Indians without compensation for six years by the time an official superintendent of Indian Affairs was appointed.

Joseph Lane became the U.S. governor of the Territory of Oregon and, therefore, the region's first ex officio superintendent of Indian Affairs in March 1849. Lane's first official encounter with American Indians in the Pacific Northwest that spring was a discussion with Indigenous peoples of the Willamette Valley. Arguably because of their location, these groups had faced the ramifications of foreign permanent settlement the longest and received the largest number of unsupported promises by Oregon settlers for the compensation of their lands and its resources. Lane reported to the Secretary of the Interior that the Willamette Valley peoples had become quickly discouraged that he was not prepared or able to provide such compensation at their meeting.[44] Instead, Lane continued the Oregon settler tradition of making promises to American Indians without the authority or funding to honor them. Nor did he curtail further foreign settlement; rather, within his first year as governor and superintendent of Indian Affairs, Lane urged Congress to create a treaty that would remove all American Indians from lands west of the Cascade Mountains to the east side of the range.[45]

In December 1849 Oregon laws continued to run contrary to U.S. policies, with the territorial government passing legislation that allowed them the power to negotiate with American Indians over lands "in the settled portion of the country in Oregon."[46] These actions further complicated agreements made by U.S. officials, such as Lane's "peace treaty," which promised to prevent further land encroachment with American Indian groups along the Rogue River.[47] Oregon congressional delegate Samuel Thurston attempted to explain the predicament U.S. officials faced, noting in his report to Congress that the settlement had reached fifteen thousand white settlers but that "the Indian title in a foot of land in that Territory has never been extinguished."[48] Rather than pointing out how Oregon laws violated federal policies, the U.S. federal government followed Oregon lawmakers' lead and prioritized securing Oregon settlers' land claims and encouraging further immigration to the region. Oregon lawmakers and federal officials viewed the treatment of American Indians' property as secondary, at best, to the settlers' occupation of Indigenous lands.

The creation of the territorial government technically included the first appropriation of funds for Indigenous peoples in the Pacific Northwest, but the U.S. government first appointed subagents and approved the creation of treaties through an act passed on June 5, 1850.[49] With this act—which came four years after the Oregon Treaty, three years after a provisional governor had requested it from Congress and almost two years after the territorial government had been created—negotiations with and the possibility of providing an official treaty to American Indians could finally commence in Oregon. Applying this act, however, became further complicated in September that year when Congress approved the Oregon Donation Act, which retroactively validated existing land claims and allowed for hundreds more claims to be made in the Pacific Northwest.[50] Although the previous congressional act had appointed three commissioners to begin negotiations of land secessions and the removal of American Indians to reservations, the United States had not yet established any treaties with American Indians in Oregon when land claims under the Donation Act began.

In the spring of 1851 three U.S. commissioners—John P. Gaines, Alonzo A. Skinner, and Beverly S. Allen—established six treaties with the "Willamette Indians." The American Indians recognized in these treaties included bands of the Kalapuya and Molala nations, which lived in desired settlement areas of the Willamette Valley and River. Unbeknown to these Indigenous peoples, Congress had dissolved the commissioners' position prior to the conclusion of their negotiations, and the treaties were never ratified.[51] This eventual fact did not prevent Oregon settlers from squatting on lands the treaties intended to open for settlement. Newspapers as far east as Vermont viewed these initial treaties as a "great relief, doubtless, of the numerous and fast increasing settlers there."[52] This would not be the last time a Pacific Northwest treaty was negotiated and signed by members of an American Indian group and then left unratified. Without a treaty Indigenous peoples lacked legal protection from dispossession through Oregon settlers' occupation of, if not their own violent removal from, the lands. Neither were American Indians compensated for such losses.

When the newly appointed superintendent of Indian Affairs—a position now separated from that of the governor of the Oregon Territory—Anson Dart began negotiations with American Indians, he faced the uphill battle of establishing any terms with groups that had witnessed years of abuses from Oregon settlers and their provisional government. Dart reported that the first group he had met with, the Clatsop Indians, "made long and loud complaints, at the injustice done them by the Government."[53] Ultimately, Dart would end up with thirteen treaties signed between September and October of 1851. These treaties, as listed in table 1, recognized groups of the "Chinook Indians," "Port Orford Indians," and the "Clackamas Indians," whose collective lands totaled around six million acres.[54] Again, these treaties were public news, broadcasted throughout Oregon as well as the nation; they too were not ratified.

Dart's thirteen unratified treaties faced a similar problem to the six made earlier by the U.S. commissioners in that the treaties did not remove Indigenous peoples from west of the Cascade Mountains—or rather, it did not remove American Indians from areas where Oregon settlers made land claims. The treaties had established reservations within a section of the groups' traditional lands, and although Dart made a lengthy argument for why this was necessary, Congress did not agree.[55] Additionally, a section of the proposed reservation for the Chinook Indians existed on a site claimed by Oregon settler Washington Hall, who asserted his having improved upon the land since 1845 and his future acquisition of a "Title under the Donation act of Congress to the Settlers of Oregon."[56] Rather than view this as an opportunity to formally secure millions of acres of land by ratifying the treaties, however, enough federal representatives did not believe the treaties met

Table 1. "Unratified" treaties with Pacific Northwest American Indians

GROUPS LISTED	NO. OF TREATIES	NEGOTIATED
"Willamette Valley Indians" Tualatin Kalapuya Lakmuit Kalapuya Santiam Kalapuya Yamhill Kalapuya Molala (bands of) Santiam Molala	6	April 1851 and May 1851 U.S. Commissioners John P. Gaines, Alonzo A. Skinner, and Beverly S. Allen (after their positions were dissolved by Congress on February 27, 1851)
Takelma	1	July 1851 U.S. Commissioners John P. Gaines (following a "Peace Treaty" in June of 1850 with Joseph Lane, superintendent of Indian Affairs in the Oregon Territory)
"Chinook Indians" (Tansey Point) Lower Band of Chinook Wheelappa Band of Chinook Waukikum Band of Chinook Konnack Band of Chinook Kathlamet Band of Chinook Quillequeoqua Band of Chinook Klatskani Band of Chinook Clatsop Naalem Band of Tillamook Lower Band of Tillamook	10	August 1851 Anson Dart—superintendent of Indian Affairs in the Oregon Territory (Appropriate Act of 1912 recognized initial treaties for the Tillamook, Clatsop, Nu-quee-clah-we-muck, Kathlamet Band of Chinook, Waukikum Band of Chinook, Wheelappa Band of Chinook, and Lower Band of Chinook)
"Port Orford Indians" Tototan (Rogue River) You-que-chae (Euchre Creek) Qua-tou-wah (Coquille) Ya-su-chah	2	September 1851 Anson Dart—superintendent of Indian Affairs in the Oregon Territory
"Clackamas Indians" Clackamas (included bands of the Kalapuya and Molala)	1	Fall 1851 Anson Dart—superintendent of Indian Affairs in the Oregon Territory

Tualatin Kalapuya	1	March 1854 Joel Palmer—superintendent of Indian Affairs in the Oregon Territory
"Coast Tribes" Coos Umpqua Siuslaw	1	August 1855 Joel Palmer—superintendent of Indian Affairs in the Oregon Territory

Source: Names of groups, treaties, and so forth are based on those listed in the titles of government records on negotiations with Indigenous peoples in the Pacific Northwest. Not all the American Indians involved in these negotiations were included in these documents, and some of the names were/are misspelled (with several of the records having different spellings in the same document). This table intends to capture as much accurate information from these records as possible and arrive at a better understanding of these negotiations, but it may still unintentionally represent misinformation. Information acquired for this table can be found in individual footnotes for respective negotiations. Names in parentheses represent groups that are directly connected to a treaty. See Vine, *Documents of American Indians*, 205, 206, 221–26; Coan, "First Stage of the Federal," 54–55, 75, 88; Fixico, *Treaties with American Indians*, 229; Lewis, "1851 Treaty Commission"; Beck, "'Standing Out Here,'" 6–37; Lewis, "Coast Indian Reservation." Also based on the official history provided by the Confederated Tribes of Coos, Lower Umpqua, and Siuslaw Indians on their Tribes' website: https://ctclusi.org/history.

the intended objectives of the 1850 act, and they ultimately sided with the Oregon settler's right to his land claim, forgoing the ratification of the treaties.[57]

Immigration into Oregon continued over the next two years despite a lack of ratified treaties, and Joel Palmer replaced Dart as the superintendent of Indian Affairs. Palmer was an early Oregon settler who had claimed lands under the Oregon provisional government and awaited formal U.S. ownership through the Oregon Donation Act. Palmer had fought in Oregon's volunteer militia during the Cayuse War against Indigenous peoples, some of whom he would negotiate with in removal treaties.[58] Although it was between "wars" at the time, the region experienced continuous conflicts between Oregon settlers and American Indians. When the Chetco Indians of southern Oregon, for example, resisted land encroachments from speculators, the settlers surveying the Chetco's land attacked the Indigenous peoples, killing fifteen and burning two villages. Surviving Chetco Indians sought legal justice, but the case was dismissed due to lack of "evidence"; the settlers' claims to the Chetco lands were processed, and the encroachment of newly arriving immigrants continued.[59]

After a conflict in the upper Rogue River Valley, a "peace treaty" was entered by Joseph Lane, representing the "forces of the Oregon Territory" and "Joe, principal Chief of the Rogue River tribe of Indians," on behalf of Indigenous communities under the latter's "jurisdiction."[60] This was the second time Lane had established a "peace treaty" with an Indigenous group in Oregon following a conflict. But the agreement with the Takelma Indians in June 1850, formalized by Territorial Governor John Gaines with a treaty a year later, had not been ratified.[61] In this instance, Palmer met with some of the Rogue River Indians only a few days after Lane's agreement, and on September 10, 1853, the groups signed a formal treaty.[62] Later that month the Cow Creek Band of the Umpqua nation also signed a treaty with Palmer, opening up sections of western Oregon for further settlement.[63] These treaties in 1853 were the first that Congress ratified in the Oregon Territory.

Ratification of treaties did not ensure peaceful coexistence between American Indians and Oregon settlers. Although they were agreed upon in the latter half of 1853, these treaties were not ratified by Congress until the following April, and the formal treaties were not proclaimed (made public) until February 1855.[64] The lag time between negotiations and ratifications followed years of Oregon lawmakers' unsupported policies toward American Indians, unsanctioned land acquisitions, and unratified treaties. Palmer attempted to explain as much in his annual report to Commissioner of Indian Affairs George Manypenny, stating, "experience moreover has taught us that the settlement of a country, prior to the extinction of the native title to the soil is, in most cases attended with serious difficulties and embarrassments to the Government, with annoyance and danger to the settler; and proves fatal to the best interests, the improvement and civilization, of the natives."[65]

Part of the difficulties addressed by Palmer was how American Indians with treaties did not have a permanent place to exist in; rather, initial reservations were both temporary and vulnerable to attack or encroachment by Oregon settlers. Treaties may have established reservations, but they did not dictate the actions of settlers in the Pacific Northwest.

The temporary Table Rock and Cow Creek Reservations were created at the end of 1853.[66] Discussion in Oregon focused on beginning the removal of treaty groups as soon as possible. Yet the dispossession of American Indians through removal treaties seldom accounted for Indigenous peoples' connections to the lands, seasonal life practices, or problems with the settlement of squatters on lands both newly ceded and within the reservations themselves. The U.S. government constructed Cow Creek near the South Umpqua River and located Table Rock at the north side of the Rogue River, but the government also found it necessary to construct forts, such as Fort Lane, to aid in this removal and the protection of American Indians from settlers. After three years of conflicts in and near the reservations, however, the U.S. government closed both sites and relocated American Indians to the Grande Ronde Reservation in northwestern Oregon.[67] Many of the Indigenous peoples at Cow Creek remained in the area, but without the reservation and promised support by the federal government, they became landless for the next century.[68]

By the mid-1850s the U.S. government had come to handle negotiations and establish American Indian reservations in the Pacific Northwest, but Oregon settlers' previous policies and continued actions influenced the overall process of dispossession. Congress had split the Washington Territory from Oregon along the Columbia River in 1853 and appointed Isaac Stevens as the Washington governor and superintendent of Indian Affairs. Together, Stevens and Palmer met with Indigenous peoples across the region and created five treaties in 1854. Four of these treaties—which involved bands of the Chasta, Scoton, Tekelma, Umpqua, and Kalapuya, in addition to the Rogue River Indians, Nisqually Indians, and Puyallup Indians as well as several other western Washington groups at Medicine Creek—were ratified by Congress within a year.[69] Although Palmer's treaty with the Tualatin Kalapuya was not ratified, the Indigenous peoples' lands acquired through these treaties greatly expanded "available" settlements west of the Cascade Mountains.[70] Settlers' occupation of these lands did not wait, and the temporary reservation at Calapooia Creek for northwestern Oregon treaty groups was abandoned by the U.S. government within two years. Conflict with Oregon settlers prompted federal officials to remove these American Indians to the Grand Ronde Reservation. More American Indians held ratified treaties, but the U.S. government quickly changed their terms to accommodate the actions of settlers.[71]

Treaty making continued in earnest by Palmer and Stevens, who established twelve treaties in 1855. Although Congress ratified the first of these in just a few months, the "Coast Indian Treaty" was never ratified, and the other ten were not ratified until March 1859.[72] Palmer was aware that not all Indigenous peoples had agreed with the terms or even acknowledged the treaties, explaining to the DC office that some felt "signing the treaty was averse to the will of the nation" and in at least one instance those who had signed were "denounced as traitors to their tribes."[73] By this point in the process of colonization, the presence of settlers was critical for Palmer and Steven's negotiations. Oregon and Washington settlers increasingly occupied American Indians' lands and threatened their property as well as their lives. Territorial governments, meanwhile, failed to hold settlers accountable for these actions. During treaty negotiations Stevens had promised to keep settlers out of the Walla Walla region prior to the removal of treaty groups, but he later encouraged settlement.[74] Thus compared to the alternative of being forcibly dispossessed of lands, a treaty did provide Indigenous peoples formal recognition by the U.S. government, including some compensation for lands and the chance to retain a section of their lands.[75] These removal treaties, listed in table 2, were less than ideal for American Indians and represented a means to an end. The U.S. government's priority remained supporting settler's land claims and developing the western territories.

Regional lawmakers' preference for immediately occupying lands rather than waiting for legal acquisition accompanied treaty making in the Pacific Northwest. Beginning in July 1855 Oregon newspapers ran notices of treaties with the Nez Perce, Cayuse, Walla Walla, Umatilla, and Yakama, all of which included dozens of bands and multiple

Table 2. Treaties with Pacific Northwest American Indians (prior 1860)

GROUPS LISTED	NO. OF TREATIES	NEGOTIATED	RATIFIED (Y/N)	DATE RATIFIED
"Rogue River Indians" Rogue River	1	September 10, 1853 Joel Palmer—superintendent of Indian Affairs in the Oregon Territory	Y	April 12, 1854 (not proclaimed until February 5, 1855)
"Umpqua-Cow Creek Band" Cow Creek Band of Umpqua	1	September 19, 1853 Joel Palmer—superintendent of Indian Affairs in the Oregon Territory	Y	April 12, 1854 (not proclaimed until February 5, 1855)
"Rogue River Indians" Rogue River	1	November 15, 1854 Joel Palmer—superintendent of Indian Affairs in the Oregon Territory	Y	March 3, 1855
"Chasta, etc." Chasta (Quil-si-eton and Na-he-ta) Scoton (Cow-nna-ti-co, Sa-cher-i-ton and Na-al-ye) Grave Creek Band of Umpqua (Takelma)	1	November 18, 1854 Joel Palmer—superintendent of Indian Affairs in the Oregon Territory	Y	March 3, 1855
"Umpqua and Kalapuya" Upper Umpqua Yoncalla Kalapuya	1	November 29, 1854 Joel Palmer—superintendent of Indian Affairs in the Oregon Territory	Y	March 3, 1855

GROUPS LISTED	NO. OF TREATIES	NEGOTIATED	RATIFIED (Y/N)	DATE RATIFIED
"Nisqualli, Puyallup, etc." (Medicine Creek Treaty) Nisqually Puyallup Steilacoom Squawskin S'Homamish Stehchass T'Peeksin Squi-aitl Sa-heh-wamish	1	December 26, 1854 Isaac I. Stevens—superintendent of Indian Affairs in the Washington Territory	Y	March 3, 1855
"Kalapuya, etc." Kalapuya (Confederated Bands: Tualatin, Calapooia, Chafan, Che-lam-e-la, Tekopa, Mohawk, Nin-ne-felly/Winnerfelly, Chemapho, Chepenapho, Yam Hill, Chelukimauk, and Santiam) Molala (bands of) Tumwater (Wah-lal-la and Willamette) Clackamas (bands of)	1	January 22, 1855 Joel Palmer—superintendent of Indian Affairs in the Oregon Territory	Y	March 3, 1855

"Dwamish, Suquamish etc." (Treaty of Point Elliot) Duwanish Snoqualmie Lummi Suquamish St-kah-mish Snoqualmoo Skai-wha-mish N'Quentl-ma-mish Sk-tah-le-jum Stoluck-wha-mish Sno-ho-mish Skagit Kik-i-aallus Swin-a-mish Squin-ah-mish Sah-ku-mehu Noo-wha-ha Nook-wa-chah-mish Mee-see-qua-guilch Cho-bah-ah-bish	1	January 22, 1855 Isaac I. Stevens—superintendent of Indian Affairs in the Washington Territory	Y	March 8, 1859 (four years after signing)
"S'Klallam" (Treaty of Point No Point) S'Klallam (Kah-tai, Squah-quaihtl, Tch-queen, Ste-tehtlum, Tsohkw, Yennis, Elh-wa, Pishtst, Hunnint, Klat-la-wash, and Oke-ho) Chimakum Skokomish To-an-hooch	1	January 26, 1855 Isaac I. Stevens—superintendent of Indian Affairs in the Washington Territory	Y	March 8, 1859 (four years after signing)
"Makah" (Treaty of Neah Bay) Makah (Neah Waatch, Tsoo-Yess, and Osett)	1	January 31, 1855 Isaac I. Steven—superintendent of Indian Affairs in the Washington Territory	Y	March 8, 1859 (four years after signing)

GROUPS LISTED	NO. OF TREATIES	NEGOTIATED	RATIFIED (Y/N)	DATE RATIFIED
"Wallawalla, Cayuse, etc." Walla Walla Cayuse Umatilla	1	June 9, 1855 Joel Palmer—superintendent of Indian Affairs in the Oregon Territory, and Isaac I. Stevens—superintendent of Indian Affairs in the Washington Territory	Y	March 8, 1859 (four years after signing)
"Yakima" Yakama (Confederated Tribes: Palouse, Pisquouse, Wenatshapam, Klikatat, Klinquit, Kow-was-say-ee, Li-ay-was, Skin-pah, Wish-ham, Shyiks, Ochechotes, Kah-milt-pah, and Sep-ap-cat)	1	June 9, 1855 Isaac I. Stevens—superintendent of Indian Affairs in the Washington Territory	Y	March 8, 1859 (four years after signing)
"Nez Perces" Nez Perce	1	June 11, 1855 Joel Palmer—superintendent of Indian Affairs in the Oregon Territory, and Isaac I. Stevens—superintendent of Indian Affairs in the Washington Territory	Y	March 8, 1859 (four years after signing)

"Tribes of Middle Oregon" Walla Walla (Taih / Upper D Chutes, Wyam / Lower De Chutes, Tenino, and John Day's River) Wasco (Ki-gal-twal-la and Dog River)	1	June 25, 1855 Joel Palmer—superintendent of Indian Affairs in the Oregon Territory	Y	March 8, 1859 (four years after signing)
"Qui-nai-elt and Quil-leh-ute" (Treaty of Olympia) Quinault Quileute	1	July 1, 1855, and January 25, 1856 Isaac I. Stevens—superintendent of Indian Affairs in the Washington Territory	Y	March 8, 1859 (four years after signing)
"Flatheads, etc." (Hell Gate Treaty) Flathead Kootenai Pend d'Oreilles (Upper)	1	July 16, 1855 Isaac I. Stevens—superintendent of Indian Affairs in the Washington Territory	Y	March 8, 1859 (four years after signing)
"Blackfeet" Piegan Blood Blackfeet Gros Ventres Flathead Nez Perce Kootenai Pend d'Oreilles (Upper)	1	October 17, 1855 Isaac I. Stevens and A. Cumming—U.S. commissioners	Y	April 1859 (four years after signing)
"Molala" Molala	1	December 21, 1855 Joel Palmer—superintendent of Indian Affairs in the Oregon Territory	Y	March 8, 1859 (four years after signing)

Source: Created by author from Kappler, *Indian Affairs*, 665–68, 669–84, 694–725, 740–41, 1049; Fixico, *Treaties with American Indians*, 230. Names in parentheses represent groups that are directly connected to a treaty.

other Indigenous groups. The notices, which ran in papers for nearly a year, informed readers, "By an express provision of the Treaty, the country embraced in the cessions and not included in the Reservation is open to settlement, excepting that the Indians are secured in the possession of their building and implements till removed to the Reservation."[76] Supported further by public announcement from Stevens, these notices encouraged settlement before the reservations had been built and compensation for lands provided. As stated in sections of the treaties themselves, the notices allowed settlers to claim lands "unoccupied" by treaty American Indians, an agreement similar to the policies Oregon lawmakers had established.[77] Thus, even with federal treaties the lands within American Indian reservations were still vulnerable to encroachment. Oregon settlers continued to operate under previous policies of land ownership, and the U.S. government supported these practices through federal land donations and treaties.

Four reservations were created in 1855 in connection to the treaties signed that year. One, along the Oregon coastline, closed within a year due to conflicts, and the rest were reduced by the U.S. government multiple times to accommodate further settlement and to open lands with desired natural resources.[78] These reservations were not a haven for the Indigenous peoples systematically removed from their lands. Rather, historian Ned Blackhawk pointedly describes them as "intertribal refugee centers where previously unrelated peoples joined together in diaspora."[79] As many of the 1855 treaties provided, the U.S. president retained the right to change and move reservations, including placing them "with other friendly tribes or bands."[80] This replacement referred to in the treaties, however, required American Indians to make long treks across the region—usually on foot and sometimes during the winter months—that removed them from their cultural lands into entirely different landscapes.[81]

Recalling his experience of being moved from one reservation to another, in this case from the Table Rock Reservation in the Rogue Valley to the northern Siletz Reservation, John Adams notes, "Pretty soon soldiers come again. That's the time they leave my old grandmother cause she can't walk. Maybe she die right there, maybe soldiers kill her. She cry plenty when my uncle take me away. Well, all time going round in woods. After while my uncle get killed. Then I'm lone."[82] If they survived the journey, American Indians at the reservations faced insufficient necessary provisions that were slow to arrive.[83] Once removed to reservations, if Indigenous peoples did not hold treaties with the United States, no annuity payments would be made, leaving some bands of American Indians—such as several at the Siletz Reservation—-prisoners rather than residents.[84] Moreover, according to reports by Oregon Indian agents between 1855 and 1856, most reservations wanted for basic supplies such as food and clothing, and many lacked even proper structures to shield American Indians from the elements. The conditions were bad enough that many Indigenous peoples would leave to find supplies, but such actions were construed by some officials as breaking the treaty.[85]

The 1855 treaties were the last set of treaties made with Indigenous peoples in the Pacific Northwest prior to the Civil War, and ratifications finally came a month after Oregon had become a state. The transition from intended coexistence between Oregon settlers and American Indians in the early 1840s had quickly given way to a removal policy that dispossessed thousands of Indigenous peoples of their lands. After years of conflicts with settlers, continuous unfulfilled promises for compensation of lands from Oregon lawmakers and then the U.S. government, many American Indians felt that the decision to leave their lands was a question of life or death. Although Indigenous peoples resisted removal, a man by the name "Cholcultah" from the Table Rock Reservation explained why he had agreed to leave his homelands temporarily: he had been told that "'if we go back the white people will kill us all.'"[86] As the next two sections explain, such sentiment, which this situation evoked, presented Indigenous peoples with the question of whether they wanted to stay on their lands or live, an ultimatum supported by the indiscriminate violence American Indians of the Pacific Northwest faced throughout the 1840s and 1850s. Oregon land policies and federal treaties, though ineffectively enforced, had successfully taken American Indians from their homelands. Conflict and warfare spurred by racialized portrayals of Indigenous peoples served as a violent support system for this removal process.

Race and Dispossession through Warfare

By the 1800s colonizing groups had been describing American Indians as different from themselves for several centuries. European racial perceptions and their use of differentiating or "othering" to socially and legally separate Indigenous peoples from their citizenry had influenced how U.S. officials portrayed and discussed American Indians from the onset of western expansion.[87] The racial specification of "white" had become more commonplace by the 1840s to distinguish between American Indians and settlers.[88] Descriptions such as "several affrays have taken place between the Indians and the whites" appeared in Oregon's earliest newspapers and drew a clear racial distinction between Oregon settlers and the region's Indigenous peoples.[89] Even national newspapers that Oregon settlers found too favorable of American Indians had by the 1850s used racial classifications to explain relationships in the region, such as the opinion of a Vermont paper that American Indians "evince a strong desire yet more to assimilate themselves to their white neighbors."[90] But another way to signify a difference between these groups was for Oregon settlers to describe American Indians as an "uncivilized" and "hostile" race.[91] Though this characterization was not unique to the Pacific Northwest, Oregon lawmakers and regional newspapers consistently portrayed American Indians as generally dangerous to explain the constant and often violent conflicts between Oregon settlers and Indigenous peoples as well as to justify both warfare against and removal of American Indians.

Perhaps no Pacific Northwest group's experiences demonstrate how Oregon and U.S. portrayals of Indigenous peoples had changed to defend warfare more clearly than that of the Nez Perce Indians. When fur-trade companies began to create posts in the Columbia Plateau, the Nez Perce Indians successfully negotiated stable trade relations with the Hudson's Bay Company, and they later adjusted for the more individualistic practices of American fur traders. The Nez Perce also developed a positive reputation among U.S. officials after hosting the Lewis and Clark Expedition on their return visit in 1805, which continued with the presumed success of the Spalding mission among the Nez Perce in the 1830s and 1840s.[92] Therefore, prior to the establishment of the settler colony, the work the Nez Perce had done to create good alliances seemed sufficient to ensure a positive rapport with Oregon lawmakers. Throughout the initial decade of the Oregon settlement, this held somewhat true, as evidenced in national newspapers such as a Boston editorial that described the Nez Perce as "making considerable progress in civilization" and demonstrating appropriate "attention to agriculture."[93] Even throughout the warfare between the United States and other Indigenous peoples in the 1850s, U.S. officials felt confident that the Nez Perce Indians remained allies to the federal government.[94] Yet the Nez Perce Indians still faced broken promises and unfulfilled agreements with the United States. Ultimately, the Nez Perce experienced years of conflicts with encroaching Oregon and Washington settlers, and their eventual removal to a reservation was fraught with misinformation and drastic changes to treaties. Once the Nez Perce began to reject the relationship and agreements offered by the U.S., the same federal government that had described them as "friendly" and "trusted" American Indians portrayed the Nez Perce as a "savage" enemy who could not exist with settlers and therefore should be eliminated in the Nez Perce War.[95]

As with the Nez Perce's experience, growth in foreign occupation of Pacific Northwest lands correlated with the increase in violence between American Indians and immigrants. Language used to note the racial differences of these groups and associate villainy with Indigenous peoples accompanied such conflicts. Reports from Oregon as early as the Lewis and Clark Expedition, for instance, included descriptions of American Indians as "rascals" and "rogues"—terms that Oregon settlers would come to use with frequency.[96] Violence had erupted between American Indians and fur traders west of the Rocky Mountains by the 1820s, and within a decade officials with the HBC, such as John McLoughlin, watched the dismissive actions and racist opinions of Oregon settlers toward American Indians with concern for future relations in the region.[97]

Alternatively, U.S. reports on the occupation of the Pacific Northwest continuously cited the HBC as making the American Indians hostile toward the Oregon settlement. In one such committee report from 1838, federal representatives maintained, "But a greater evil than this exists in the influence of the Hudson Bay Company exercises over the Indians, by supplying them with arms and ammunition, which may prove, at some future period, highly dangerous to our frontier settlement."[98] In the not-so-distant future the HBC and Great Britain would become less of a factor in regional relations, and only those relations maintained by Oregon settlers and American Indians would dictate the region's history of violence. Granted, all inhabitants were connected to conflict, but Oregon officials and regional newspapers predominately reported on acts allegedly carried out by Indigenous peoples to support their arguments for warfare against American Indians.

Conflict between American Indians and settlers that appeared in Oregon reports were usually a result of competition for land and resources. While violence over land claims occurred between settlers as well, as chapter 4 will address, Oregon settlers viewed the land where they built structures or attempted to farm as their own and saw Indigenous peoples' expectations for compensation of such use as an annoyance or even a criminal act.[99] The formation of an Oregon militia was not to address these conflicts, rather to wage "war" against animals destructive to the settlers' livestock. In part of the first "wolf meetings," Oregon lawmakers issued the formation of "civil and military protection of this colony" and their property.[100] American Indians were included in this call for fur bounties, but the provisional government identified them as racially separate from the armed settlers within the law and only paid them "one-half as much as the whites" for the furs.[101] Not long after this initial arming of Oregon settlers, the provisional government created the first "Militia Law."

According to Article 6 in the 1843 Oregon militia law: "It shall be the duty of each male inhabitant, over the age of sixteen years and under sixty, who wishes to be considered a citizen, to cause himself to be enrolled by giving his name to the proper officers of the militia, and serve under the same, except as are hereafter excepted."[102] The provisional government did recognize males with Indigenous mothers and white fathers as holding certain rights in Oregon, such as property ownership, and although American Indians were not specifically identified as potential militia members, some would serve as Oregon volunteers.[103] By the 1840s most state governments in the United States did not include a specific exclusion of American Indians to their militia laws, with the states of Indiana and Illinois being the only ones to list American Indians as an "excepted" group that could not report to or serve in a militia company.[104] In the Oregon militia, members were to provide their own "good rifle or musket," to report once a year for "company inspection," and to serve in a company of "mounted riflemen" under Oregon's one battalion.[105] The law also appointed and commissioned militia officers who could "order out the militia" in the case "of invasion or insurrection."[106] The militia law did not explain what constituted an invasion or insurrection, but it did create a group to carry out a war on behalf of Oregon settlers.

On March 4, 1844, Oregon lawmakers considered mobilizing the Oregon militia on the off chance that Indigenous peoples of the region would decide to retaliate for the killing of an Indigenous man. According to the Legislative Assembly, a "skirmish" involving Oregon settlers had resulted in the death of an Indigenous man, and although Oregon settlers who claimed to witness the event described the deceased as of "the vilest kind," they still feared retribution for his death.[107] For many Oregon settlers, communicating fears of American Indians was not new; rather, settlers had arrived in the region having already heard stories of "hostile" peoples in Oregon.[108] In the late 1840s legislative reports and newspapers described many examples of "difficulties" with American Indians, and these incidents typically portrayed Indigenous peoples as the aggressors or villains, even though the outcome was often the death of or injury to an American Indian.[109] For example, a local newspaper reported that an Oregon settler had killed an Indigenous man for stealing a bull. The man responsible for the killing, however, felt his situation had not been properly described, so he wrote a letter to the editor and provided his version of the event. His letter did not deny the murder;

rather, he argued that when confronted for stealing the bull, the American Indian had tried to attack him with a knife, and he had shot the man in self-defense. The Indigenous man, he maintained, was dangerous and had intended to kill him; therefore, the Oregon settler believed his actions were justified.[110] On what lands this bull had been kept were not mentioned, and there were no witnesses to the killing itself, but the altercation over who possessed the bull and how Oregon settlers described American Indians as dangerous to justify killing Indigenous peoples was reflected in numerous conflicts in the Pacific Northwest during the 1840s.

Discussion of the Oregon settlement's perceived vulnerability gained attention as the United States negotiated with Great Britain once again for authority over the region. Both U.S. representatives as well as Oregon lawmakers emphasized the need to secure the region to ensure the success of the settlement. During the summer of 1845 the Oregon Legislative Committee charged each county with determining what was necessary to prepare itself for the "peace and safety of the colony," such as specific defensive measures or military laws the county needed to prosper.[111] Meanwhile individual communities continued to create militia companies according to the provisional government's law.[112]

By the time the Oregon Treaty was signed in 1846, Oregon settlers were increasingly poised to address issues in their colony with an organized militia. The most pressing issue for the Oregon government at that time, however, was the ever-expanding settlement of immigrants on American Indian lands.[113] At the end of the Oregon legislature's session in 1846, lawmakers requested the U.S. government to address the need for treaties with Indigenous peoples in the region as "complaints made by Indians that they are encroached upon by whites" continued to surface, but they simultaneously noted the need for "better wagon trails to increase emigration."[114]

Immigration to Oregon in the 1840s soared, and so too did tensions and conflicts between Oregon settlers and American Indians. In his yearly message to Oregon, Territorial Governor George Abernethy addressed incidents in which American Indians had allegedly stolen items from wagon trains coming into the Pacific Northwest and urged lawmakers, "This should not be allowed to pass."[115] Abernethy continued, noting that immigration numbers to Oregon had increased with "four to five thousand souls" arriving in 1847 and that this only added to the urgency of securing "the future welfare and prosperity of Oregon."[116] Yet Abernethy as well as other Oregon lawmakers recognized the connection between increasing land encroachments and conflicts; he argued for U.S. intervention with the Indigenous peoples in the region, asserting, "Our relation with the Indians becomes every year more embarrassing. They see the white man occupying their land, rapidly filling up the country, and they put in a claim for pay."[117] But while the wheels of bureaucracy moved slowly toward the establishment of treaties in Oregon, the ramifications of invasive settlement without formal treaties and compensations had already come to a head.

In the summer of 1846, the Oregon government deployed a militia company to address "disturbances" between Molalla Indians and the white settlers "in the Molalla settlement."[118] At this point, Oregon lawmakers had decided the militia needed to resolve conflicts between American Indians and settlers. Treaties had not been established with Indigenous peoples in the Pacific Northwest, but the Oregon government began to address the unrest between the region's inhabitants as a defense issue, and Oregon lawmakers included areas occupied by missionaries as part of the settlement requiring defense. This fact became abundantly clear in 1847 when individual Cayuse Indians killed missionaries at Waiilatpu. Oregon lawmakers and newspapers labeled the killings a "massacre" and an attack on Oregon settlers from the first reports on the incident to validate a defensive response.

Some of the initial accounts of what became known as the "Whitman Massacre" derived from fur-trade officials at Fort Vancouver and Fort Nez Perce, who promised to safely secure other missionaries in the area from "the irritable of the Indian population" and "rescue" other settlers who were near or at the Waiilatpu mission.[119] William McBean at Fort Nez Perce attributed the conflict to the "fever and dysentery" that had plagued portions of the Inland Northwest, "especially at the Doctor's place [Waiilatpu] where he attended upon the Indians. About 30 souls, of the Cayuse tribe died, one after another."[120] According to McBean, the Cayuse Indians came to suspect Dr. Whitman of poisoning them, and that one settler by the name of "Mr. Rogers" claimed to have overheard the missionary's plan to slowly kill all of the Cayuse so that "not a soul would remain, when they would take possession of your [Cayuse] lands, cattle, and horses." McBean regarded this as only "Indian reports, and that no person can believe the Doctor capable of such an action, without being as ignorant and brutal as the Indians themselves." As with previous uneven and generally erroneous reports of conflicts in the region, McBean addressed the earlier deaths of American Indians but also described the Cayuse Indians as "brutal." His narrative focused on the death of settlers and portrayed the event as a "horrible butchery" by a dangerous group.[121]

Soon after the incident, Governor Abernethy (who was also the ex officio superintendent of Indian Affairs for the territory) insisted that the Oregon legislature must respond to the "horrible massacre committed by the Cayuse" with "immediate and prompt action."[122] The speaker of the Oregon Assembly, Robert Newell, implored the U.S. House and Senate for assistance against the Cayuse Indians, claiming that Oregon settlers were in great danger and that "the number of the white population of Oregon is alarmingly insignificant compared with the swarm of Indians which throng its valley."[123] In describing the continued presence of Indigenous peoples as a "swarm" in comparison to the "white population," Newell depicted a racial separation between the inhabitants of Oregon and portrayed American Indians as the region's potential aggressor. Meanwhile, the Oregon legislature agreed with the need to "raise arms."[124] Within a matter of days, the U.S. government received multiple requests from Oregon lawmakers for assistance in their conflict, which became referred to as the Cayuse War.[125]

Public reaction in Oregon reflected the sentiments of these early reports and quickly spread unfounded rumors of "hostile" Indigenous peoples throughout the upper Columbia River joining forces against the settlers. One such editorial claimed, without noting a source, that they had "received information that leads us to the belief that the Whites have abandoned the Dalles in consequences of the hostile bearing of Indians."[126] In an attempt to solicit funds for the settler war, the Oregon legislature capitalized on settlers' established and soured sentiments toward coexisting with American Indians by telling Oregon merchants that a lack of action by the militia against "repeated thefts, robberies, and murders of our fellow-citizens" had "emboldened" the Cayuse Indians in "the commission of the appalling massacre at Waiilatpoo [*sic*]."[127] The Oregon lawmakers maintained this message to the HBC and insisted that funds to support the militia's efforts in the Cayuse War were crucial to "obtain full satisfaction of the Cayuse Indians . . . and protect the white population of our common country from further aggression."[128] The HBC was not invested in this conflict in the same way that Oregon settlers quickly became; Oregon lawmakers therefore attempted to connect with company officials as fellow white inhabitants of the Pacific Northwest.[129] By 1848 the consistent message from Oregon lawmakers was that warfare was necessary to defend the Oregon settlement from "further aggressions" of American Indians.

When Governor Abernethy first raised an Oregon militia for the Cayuse War, he requested one hundred men to be stationed near the upper Columbia River. As soon as support for this war began to appear in Oregon newspapers, the governor called for more volunteers.[130] Abernethy proclaimed to Oregon settlers that "information has been received here which leads to the belief that the Indians have united, and the force ordered out in that case being insufficient, I therefore call on the citizens of this territory to furnish five hundred men." The escalated number of forces had come without proper funding, requiring Abernethy to ask Oregon settlers to provide provisions, but it continued the tone of urgency for the war from Oregon lawmakers.[131]

By the spring of 1848 reports from the field had begun to circulate, and though more men were called in to fight, many of the skirmishes between the Oregon militia companies and Indigenous communities resembled groups happening upon one another rather than planned battles or consistent pursuits. For example, an April report on the "battle of Tuchie" explained that a group of American Indians were located at a ford on the Touchet River, and when the Oregon volunteers under Captain Thompson decided to take the location, a fight ensued.[132] The following day a report was sent to Oregon newspapers that "Indians were erecting a fortification, with the intention of commencing hostilities against the whites," but upon further review it was determined that the American Indians were building a cow pen. Although the *Oregon Spectator* noted the error of this report, it still titled the article "Alarm!" and contributed to the increasingly hysterical public discussion of American Indians as a threat to the Oregon settlement.[133]

Altercations during the Cayuse War, even when they involved American Indians with no connection to the Cayuse, also reflected a self-appointed policing in Oregon by volunteers rather than an engagement in battles. Nevertheless, newspapers covered the events as part of a war. One such "war" report noted that Captain Felix Scott and Adjutant General A. L. Lovejoy "pressed the Indians so hard" when pursuing them for an allegedly stolen horse that the American Indians were forced to abandon "the stolen and two more of their own."[134] When a report emerged that "two friendly Indians had been killed, accidentally," at Fort Water, however, the newspaper carrying the story dismissed its authenticity, because a "Mr. Fleming" at the fort had not mentioned this occurrence in his recent report to the paper.[135] Selectively accepting reports on conflicts helped support the continuation of war, especially when the events did not play out as typical defensive warfare. The same newspaper published a report a few days later from Fort Waters that suggested more volunteers should be called into arms, yet it also noted that the Indigenous communities living in the area were "perfectly quiet—in fact they are terror-stricken, and skulk around rather than meet one of our people in the road."[136]

Oregon lawmakers and regional newspapers' continuous portrayal of a potential danger in the Pacific Northwest was ultimately effective and garnered their requested support from the U.S. government. President Polk informed Congress repeatedly that the settlement was in distress and at the mercy of "proud and powerful tribes of Indians."[137] Polk agreed with Oregon settlers' request for "aid" and called upon Congress to create a territorial government to provide Oregon the "authority to raise an adequate volunteer force, for defence and protection of its inhabitants."[138] Oregon already had volunteer forces, but up to this point Oregon lawmakers such as Abernethy could only promise the volunteers that the United States would eventually reimburse them for their service. Polk closed with the plea that any delay "may prove destructive to the white settlements in Oregon."[139] The creation of a territorial government to formalize military defense, he argued, was necessary to protect the white settlers in Oregon from American Indians.

Later that summer Senator Hannibal Hamlin from Maine admonished his colleagues for not properly acknowledging the supposed crisis in Oregon. Hamlin maintained that "savage hordes were committing depredations upon the whites" in the Pacific Northwest, with little action taken by the United States on their behalf.[140] The U.S. government went on to create a territorial government in Oregon and for the first time sent U.S. regiments of mounted riflemen into the Pacific Northwest.[141] The conflict moved into its second year, now with the assistance of the federal government, and Joseph Lane announced to the Oregon legislature, as the first territorial governor, that although "The Cayuse nation remains unpunished for the massacre at Waiilatpue [*sic*] . . . a fine regiment of troops, commanded by officers who have distinguished themselves in the service of their country, are en route for Oregon."[142] With help from the U.S. military, Lane asserted that "the whole tribe will be held responsible, until those whoever they may be, concerned in that melancholy and horrible affair, are given up for punishment."[143] Oregon officials had used alarmist and racialized portrayals of conflicts in the Pacific Northwest to justify warfare, and the formal involvement of the U.S. government supported their actions and helped Oregon's settler war continue for nearly another year.

In May 1850 a newly appointed judge, O. C. Pratt of the District Court of the United States for Clackamas County in the Oregon Territory, found five Cayuse Indian men (Tiloukaikt, Tomahas, Ishishkaiskais, Clokamas, and Kiamasumpkin) guilty of the murders of the Whitman missionaries and others. Oregon Marshal Joseph Meek carried out their execution on June 3, ending the Cayuse War almost three years after the killings at the Waiilatpu mission.[144] Many more than the five men had been killed in a war that settlers waged to punish those presumed guilty of killing missionaries, because the war had become an issue of defending the Oregon settlement. The killings at Waiilatpu mission were part of a violent experience in Oregon but discussing the event and potential conflicts helped justify warfare. For Oregon lawmakers, the war also supported further settlement, as the conflict had forcibly removed some Indigenous communities and increased settler claims to Cayuse lands.[145] The U.S. government supported Oregon's lawmakers' defense argument not merely because Oregon settlers had been killed by Indigenous peoples; rather, the protection of the settlement and the dispossession of American Indians coincided with U.S. colonization in the region. Depictions of American Indians being hostile aggressors was not the only reason for conflicts in Oregon, but it was a factor and helped justify future warfare.

With the creation of a territorial government, Oregon's militia became a formal standardized military unit across the region. One role the militia played during the Cayuse War, which persisted into the 1850s, was assisting emigrant wagon trains into and across Oregon.[146] As immigration to the Pacific Northwest continued and was further encouraged by the Oregon Donation Act, Oregon lawmakers found assistance by volunteer companies lacking in this capacity. Frustrated by reports of conflicts between new settlers and American Indians, Oregon politician Jesse Applegate demanded of Joseph Lane, Oregon's territorial delegate to Congress, "For the Love of God urge the Government the necessity for military protection to the country[;] if none is granted emigration, settlements, mining, and every thing [*sic*] else must stop, until the people rise and exterminate these red devils from our borders."[147] Tensions between Oregon settlers and American Indians had not simmered after the Cayuse War; rather, conflicts frequently occurred, and published reports of violence cited racial distinctions between the groups involved.

By the early 1850s Oregon lawmakers had begun to voice the opinion that all American Indians were potentially "hostile" and passed a law "to prevent the introduction of [additional] firearms among the Indians."[148] Superintendents of Indian Affairs Abernethy and then Lane requested the Legislative Assembly to "permit the sale of powder and lead to friendly Indians," but the distinction between friend and foe was made less often by Oregon lawmakers and regional newspapers.[149] Suspicion of American Indians even included the accusation that Indigenous peoples were susceptible to "feelings of hostility," and that for the safety of white settlers they should be kept separate from groups such as Black Americans.[150] Sensing the conflicts that lay ahead, and considering the "probability of bringing on hostilities with Indians now peaceable," Captain J. W. T. Gardiner of the First Dragoons suggested that "it would be better to leave the Indian unmolested."[151] But the removal of American Indians, whether as a result of conflict or in connection to treaties, was already underway.

The Pacific Northwest witnessed multiple wars between volunteer companies and American Indians from 1855 to 1858, including the Rogue River War, Yakama War, Puget Sound War, and Coeur d'Alene War.[152] Unlike the previous Cayuse War, justification for arming Oregon (and now Washington) settlers or for calling in the U.S. military was unnecessary, because they were already armed and present. Oregon lawmakers and local newspapers faced less of a need to justify warfare, because a level of formal conflict had continued to exist. Treaties were being made, but the dispossession of Indigenous peoples also occurred outside of these agreements and at the hands of militias and settlers. For example, following an altercation near a mining camp in the summer of 1855, in which the newspaper could only confirm the death of one white settler, a group of Oregon volunteers (including miners who joined in) were deployed to apprehend American Indians allegedly connected to the event and remove them from the increasingly populous mining area near the Klamath River. The newspaper article reported that in carrying out their objective, "The whites seem to be engaged in the indiscriminate slaughter—every Indian that falls within their reach is either shot down or hung." Though it acknowledged this violent result, the article still maintained the miners had been "sacrificed by the savages" who intruded upon their mining site.[153] The American Indians, according to the article, were a separate racial group that did not belong in the area.

The portrayal of Indigenous peoples as a threat to white settlement helped support warfare and also became connected to the argument for removing American Indians. Beginning in June 1855 local newspapers ran numerous stories on growing conflicts along the Rogue River, which were quickly labeled as the Rogue River War. One editorial claimed to assess "past and present indications" and determined that Oregon settlers "must have another general war with these savages, which must be a war of extermination in order for any thing [*sic*] like a lasting peace."[154] Removal via conflict was a violent process, and such "assessments" were not unique. Many letters and reports on the 1850s wars, especially those published by the *Oregon Argus*, included arguments for the "extermination" or "annihilation" of American Indians.[155] One early report by an Indian agent to the Oregon Territory, G. H. Ambrose, noted, "The settlers' patience has become exhausted; they are quite irritable . . . he gets peevish and angry, and embittered against the Indian race, and would about as soon shoot an Indian as eat his supper."[156] A letter to the editor described American Indians involved in the Rogue River Wars as having committed "savage barbarity" and being "foe[s] to the white man," and concluded that Oregon settlers' could not "do any thing [*sic*] with them but kill them off."[157] Through Oregon newspapers, settlers projected the savagery that they themselves practiced on the very people who were their victims.[158] Such portrayals of Indigenous peoples helped spur sanctioned and unsanctioned violence in the Pacific Northwest.

Oregon Governor George L. Curry made two proclamations for volunteer companies within a week of each other in October 1855, calling upon eleven counties to provide militia members.[159] Curry maintained that volunteers were needed to protect the Oregon Territory from "hostile" American Indians who had "combined" and "threaten[ed] the peace and security of the frontier settlements." His second message focused more specifically on calling for volunteer companies to fight against the Shasta Indians and the Rogue River Indians in southern Oregon, where a majority of reports about conflicts derived from, but the counties ordered to contribute volunteers were from all regions of the territory and made up both a "Northern Battalion" as well as a "Southern Battalion." These volunteer companies were not connected to the U.S. military; each man was therefore responsible for his own horse and arms, and each company had to appoint its own officers. These territory volunteers also reported to their own elected officers and to Governor Curry.[160]

There was limited oversight by the U.S. military when the removal of American Indians through warfare commenced in the Pacific Northwest.[161] In fact, First Lieutenant John Withers reported later that fall that although six Oregon volunteer companies had moved against the Yakama Indians and three were headed toward Fort Walla Walla, "They have refused to be mustered into the service of the United States." According to Withers, they continued to carry out campaigns solely as Oregon volunteers, but he doubted they could "supply themselves with provisions or clothing."[162]

What became evident in the 1850s wars was the limited attempt by Oregon lawmakers as well as U.S. officials to control armed forces in the region, as well as Oregonians' liberal interpretations of what constituted "hostile" acts. Major General John E. Wool reported on this uncontrolled situation, noting that despite formal attempts to bring the territory's forces under the U.S. military, Governor Curry "refuses to comply with the call, on the ground that Oregon volunteers would not serve under the command of the U.S. officers. In the meantime, he called out a much larger force, all mounted, whose operations were to be exclusively under the orders of the Territorial officers."[163] Oregon settlers responded to the call for volunteers, though they did not necessarily join a formal company when they took up arms against American Indians. Within days of Curry's proclamation, U.S. officials noted that "armed parties" that were neither Oregon volunteers nor U.S. military "had taken the field in southern Oregon, with the avowed purpose of waging a war of extermination against the Indians."[164] Accompanying such events were reports from Oregon lawmakers and volunteers that increasingly portrayed all actions taken by Indigenous peoples as "hostile" to support the violent removal of these communities.

With the 1850s wars underway, Oregon volunteers received instructions to regard all American Indians as the enemy unless individuals could prove otherwise.[165] Adjutant General Barnum told Oregon forces, "All Indians that may be encountered on the march will furnish unmistakable evidence of friendship, or be treated as enemies."[166] Following conflicts outside of Seattle, Washington Territory Governor Isaac Stevens called for volunteer companies to assist in the "prosecution of the enemy" and ensure that "the Indians now friendly may be prevented [from] joining them."[167] Presuming that American Indians, as one racial group, were potentially guilty of some offense added to alarmist reports in local newspapers and placed American Indians at odds with settlers regardless of the situation or location. This was compounded by exaggerated reports of how many American Indians had participated in conflicts, which tended to run contrary to numbers recorded by superintendents of Indian Affairs and Indian agents in the Pacific Northwest.[168] Several reports also stated it was hard to determine the number of Indigenous peoples involved in the wars because the American Indians had "carried the dead off with them in the night."[169] Depicting American Indians as a "hostile" group of unknown size that was different than and in opposition to settlers remained a part of how the wars were portrayed by Oregon and U.S. officials, though reports from the two groups varied in significant ways at times.

The U.S. military was certainly connected to, and several cases participated in, the warfare carried out against American Indians in the Pacific Northwest during the 1850s. Yet the reports from U.S. officials and the accounts of those connected to the Oregon volunteers (which sometimes included Indian agents) reveal different versions of the wars. This was especially true regarding how the wars progressed, where forces were deployed, and the acknowledgement of established treaties. When Pu-pu-mux-mux, a chief of the Walla Walla Indians, was killed in the fall of 1855, varying accounts emerged. Reports drawing on Oregon volunteers' accounts cited the earlier movement across the Columbia River by some Walla Walla Indians, including Pu-pu-mux-mux, as a "determination to join in the war."[170] Indian Agent R. R. Thomson then reported that this action was not received well by Pu-pu-mux-mux's son, and that he ultimately took part in the killing of his father.[171] Indian Agent Nathan Olney reported that after the presumed "hostile" action of crossing the river, Oregon forces had taken the group as prisoners and that Pu-pu-mux-mux, along with "eighteen to twenty" other Walla Walla Indians, had been killed by Oregon volunteers when they attempted to escape their capture.[172] Although Olney stated that Pu-pu-mux-mux had died at the hands of Oregon volunteers, he did not refute Thomson's report; rather, he defended the killings as necessary to protect the region from further hostilities. Echoing his letter to the *Oregon Argus* newspaper, Olney's report maintained, "The settlers in this part of the country are in the most imminent danger of being massacred without a moment's warning."[173]

U.S. Major General Wool and Superintendent of Indian Affairs Joel Palmer interpreted the situation and the actions of the Oregon volunteers differently. In his report the following January, Wool argued that the Oregon volunteers had made war on the Walla Walla Indians in the Washington Territory without cause and created more problems in the region.[174] Both Wool and Palmer maintained in multiple reports that Pu-pu-mux-mux's moving his people across the river had been within the parameters of their signed treaty and that the Walla Walla Indians had come to the Oregon volunteers with a flag of truce and asked for peaceful relations as well as offered restitution if such was called for by Oregon officials.[175] Wool and Palmer stated that Pu-pu-mux-mux was "barbarously murdered, scalped, and his ear and hands cut off, and these were preserved and sent to the friends of the volunteers in Oregon."[176] Wool noted that he had received much of his information from statements made by Oregon volunteers and printed in local newspapers. The volunteers had freely admitted to the violent mutilations and portrayed the event as permittable retribution for "hostilities."[177] Warfare intertwined with the violent removal of Indigenous peoples, and although some U.S. officials questioned the extent to which Oregon lawmakers and volunteers had incited and extended the warfare against American Indians in the region, the wars continued.

Reporting to Palmer on conditions along the Rogue River, where volunteer companies and local newspapers claimed American Indians had murdered numerous settlers, Indian Agent Edward Geary found, "The painful evidence is again before us that the initial acts in this bloody drama now acting there was by our own citizens."[178] Oregon lawmakers maintained the fault lay with Palmer's treaty negotiations; they requested he be removed from his position and for additional military assistance to aid the "defenceless inhabitants of this frontier" from a "horde of ruthless savages." The Oregon politicians were also angry that some lands included in Palmer's treaties pertained to lands that settlers had claimed or wanted. Oregon lawmakers worked to remove American Indians from lands occupied by settlers, and warfare was one of the ways dispossession occurred.[179]

Moreover, Oregon officials did not hide their desire to remove American Indians through warfare. In the beginning of 1856 General Wool reported, "It would seem, from the language of the Oregon newspapers, that the Oregonians are determined to make the most of the Indian war." Reflecting on the months of warfare Wool further suggested that "the governor had his forces raised, and something was to be done to justify the enormous expense and outlay in bringing them to the field." Full-scale warfare, Wool suggested, could have been avoided. After another surge of warfare in southern Oregon and reports of uncontrolled volunteer forces in both Oregon and California, Wool reported that volunteer forces were no longer necessary and that the "more than four hundred regulars, will . . . be all-sufficient to protect people" from future aggressions. In detailing the "extermination of the Indians" pursued by "white inhabitants, both in Oregon and northern California," Wool concluded, "Could the citizens be restrained from private war, I have no doubt peace and quiet would soon be restored."[180]

Though officials such as Wool denounced the actions of Oregon volunteers, U.S. and Oregon lawmakers saw the need for sustained warfare to secure the region for white settlement. Joel Palmer still prioritized the success of the Oregon Territory over peaceful relations with Indigenous peoples. Since war between American Indians and Oregon settlers was taking place, the cause of warfare in the region was inconsequential. Palmer reported that white settlers had instigated the violence, but the fact that war had commenced separated the settlers and himself from Indigenous peoples of the Pacific Northwest.[181] Palmer believed that warfare incited by some settlers endangered all settlers. Whether it was reports from U.S. officials or letters to the editor from an Oregon volunteer, American Indians were described as the enemy and a separate racial group throughout the 1850s wars regardless of the situation.

In March 1856 U.S. President Franklin Pierce recommended that Congress appropriate three hundred thousand dollars to address "Indian disturbances in the Territory of Oregon and Washington," which helped ensure the continuation of warfare in the Pacific Northwest.[182] Oregon officials would eventually request a much larger sum of money to cover the expenditures of warfare throughout the 1850s and cited their successful defense of a U.S. settlement against American Indians as justification for the cost.[183] American Indians still continued to live in the region, but reports from the 1850s wars promoted the idea that American Indians should only exist on future reservation lands removed from the proximity of settlers. Although U.S. officials had sought removal treaties in earnest, a majority of which were ultimately ratified by 1856, many recognized that years of improperly handled conflicts and wars could not be reversed by signed treaties. Removal of American Indians to reservations was a priority of Indian Affairs officials, but this had to take place while wars and treaty negotiations played out, which added to tensions and conflict between American Indians and Oregon settlers.[184] This included threats of violence and actual attacks on Indigenous peoples who held treaties with the U.S. government.

In one such incident, a group of American Indians in southern Oregon were traveling to a temporary reservation "where they expected protection from the whites," but were attacked by Oregon volunteers. Twenty-five American Indians were killed, yet despite these violent occurrences the U.S. military stationed in the region maintained that protection of American Indians was not their responsibility.[185] Following attacks in northern Oregon, Palmer reported to General Wool that the "war of extermination by our citizens against all Indians" had prompted the removal of American Indians from Fort Lane and those near the Umpqua River. They were removed with such haste that the temporary coastal reservation had yet to officially open when the American Indians arrived.[186] Attacks on American Indians at or en route to reservations established an additional level of violent removal and helped fuel the wars that would continue to rage in the region. Indian agents requested military escorts for the removal of Indigenous peoples, but the U.S. military ultimately decided that such assistance fell under the responsibilities of territories' superintendents of Indian Affairs.[187] And despite promises by officials such as Governor Stevens to groups of Colville Indians and Spokane Indians that he held a "determination to protect Indians who were friendly," the 1850s wars pulled dozens of American Indians groups into warfare regardless of their locations or their connections to treaties.

Between 1846 and 1858 Oregon lawmakers and regional newspapers portrayed American Indians as a "hostile" race to justify warfare against and the violent removal of Indigenous peoples from the Pacific Northwest. Whether reports out of Oregon suggested American Indians and settlers could not live in the same areas or revealed settlers' arguments for the "annihilation" of Indigenous peoples in the region, violent dispossession through warfare accompanied removal treaties. U.S. officials did not always agree with the methods used by Oregon officials and volunteers, and Congress would aggressively question the financial cost of the wars, but once the settlers had engaged in warfare, their governments supported them. Acts of violence against American Indians, even when deemed regrettable by some, were incorporated into the general narrative of how the Oregon settlement grew and American Indians vanished from areas of settlement. Remaining on or even near their traditional lands in Oregon was no small task for Indigenous peoples, and gendered recording of this history further manipulated explanations of how American Indians were dispossessed as well as their continued existence in the region.

A Gendered Existence

As with other marginalized groups in Oregon, the use of gendered epithets and creation of sex-specific laws impacted the lives of American Indians from the first arrival of foreigners throughout the colonization of the Pacific Northwest. This was particularly apparent when it came to the portrayal of Indigenous women. Initially foreign immigrants perceived the role of American Indian women, and their bodies, as beneficial to settlement. Much of the land first acquired by white settlers was through marriage to American Indian women; the children of these unions were included in the first generation of permanent settlers, and the white fathers as well as their sons had access to the first set of Oregon rights. As settlement continued, however, interracial unions became less acceptable in the colony.[188] By the late 1840s American Indian women were no longer seen as providing access to the goals of colonization; rather, they were portrayed as both separate from Oregon settlers and different from white women, if recorded at all. Furthermore as scholars such as Audra Simpson demonstrate, Indigenous women's bodies have historically represented not only their people but their lands; thus their very presence became an obstacle to foreign settlement.[189] As removal treaties and conflicts engrossed the Pacific Northwest, Oregon lawmakers and local newspapers' gendered and exclusionary portrayals of American Indian women helped further justify settler warfare against Indigenous peoples and reduced their presence in the regional narrative.

Women's identities in antebellum America were heavily connected to their roles as wives and mothers, and their service in those roles defined their womanhood. To describe a woman during the mid-nineteenth century as a wife or mother, therefore, was to recognize her embodiment of proper feminine attributes.[190] Although race most certainly played a role in how women were portrayed, reports on settler conflicts in Oregon reflected a heightened distinction between women in the region, which connected white female settlers to appropriate gender roles and diminished or entirely removed a feminine identity from Indigenous women.[191] For example, reporting on a conflict between American Indians and settlers that had resulted in a series of arsons, Indian Agent G. H. Ambrose took the time to note the impacted settler households and identified the woman of each home as "Mrs.," whether connected to a "Mr." or noted independently.[192] That same day a letter to the editor explained that a white settler woman identified as a "Mrs. Wagner" had died as a result of warfare along the Rogue River, but the letter also reported the killing of an American Indian community, including "fifteen women and children."[193] The one white settler woman the letter referenced was given a title and a surname, and the loss of her daughter was noted, yet it was unclear how many American Indian women had died, as none was individually identified; rather, they were grouped with "children" as part of the casualties.[194] Identifying white settler women as wives and mothers was common in warfare reports in Oregon, and this consistently portrayed white female settlers as embodying proper womanhood.

Throughout the years of warfare, Oregon newspapers not only portrayed white settler women as appropriate wives and/or mothers but also depicted these women as heroines of the settlement. Whether white settler women died as a result of warfare or survived some sort of "attack," their experiences were romanticized to convey extraordinary feats and sacrifice. One of the first white female settlers in Oregon depicted as a heroine of sorts was Narcissa Whitman.[195] As one of the missionaries killed at Waiilatpu in 1847, Whitman was described by newspapers as an "amiable wife" and "accomplished lady."[196] Further identified as "Mrs. Whitman," newspapers as well as territorial and federal reports noted her work in the colony for the American Board of Foreign Missions, and some national papers even suggested she had been shot while inside the mission yet still tried to escape despite her injury.[197] Articles and reports from Oregon depicted Whitman's experience as a tragedy, but they also highlighted her qualities as a woman, and she appeared with the title of "Mrs." in the list of the honored deceased.[198]

Stories of courageous white settler women filled Oregon newspapers and reports by Oregon officials during the 1850s wars, and tales of how women identified as "Mrs." had escaped death bolstered the narrative that such women were both feminine and heroic representatives of their settlement.[199] In the fall of 1855, a "Mrs. Harris" was reported to have survived with her daughter even after their house had been attacked and her husband killed.[200] In another account from Fort Hall, a "Miss Grace Clark" miraculously survived an alleged encounter with individuals identified as Shoshone Indians despite being "shot through the body and wrist" and then "thrown over a precipice to die." According to the story, her attackers then "rolled stones over her," yet somehow she still managed to escape and find her way to Oregon City. But this was not where Clark's story ends. Though she had been shot, thrown off an embankment, and stoned, she evidently went through this while safeguarding her femininity. The tale of Miss Clark concludes with her marriage to a white male settler and the two taking land for a farm near the Willamette River.[201] Clark's story and ultimate transformation into the wife of a settler captures the idealized and gendered narrative of white female settlers. Of course, most settler women were not depicted as heroines; rather, stories such as these appeared in Oregon newspapers alongside calls to arms that focused on the need to protect white women and children from American Indians for the good of the settlement.

As the previous section of this chapter demonstrates, encouraging Oregon settlers to fight for the success of their settlement was an effective approach to raising militias. Women were not only part of the settlement but also essential actors in its literal future, and calls to arms would therefore generally insinuate that white female settlers were in danger of hostilities from American Indians.[202] During a meeting of "Oregon Riflemen" in the spring of 1848, the militia group expressed its "deep sense of gratitude to the ladies of Oregon City, and the Willamette Valley" and then vowed "in all that becomes the patriot woman, we, in our turn, pledge ourselves, that so long as their safety or favor is at stake, to protect and defend it to the utmost of our abilities, while life remains."[203] In equating the ongoing warfare with the protection of white female settlers, these volunteers provided justifications for fighting in the Cayuse War. And while pledging to prevent violence from befalling white female settlers, reports of attacks on white women and children further encouraged warfare.

Reports from Oregon and federal officials during the 1850s wars depicted acts of violence toward women and children from all sides of the conflict. When these reports and local newspaper articles addressed white women and children, the groups were portrayed as "innocent," "defenseless" victims.[204] The accounts argued that an injustice had been done, referred to the events as a "massacre," and implied the act was an affront to the settlement itself. It was not uncommon in antebellum America for people of a region to entwine the security of its space with the protection of white women, especially when a situation was connected to issues of race and colonization. Some states, such as southern slave states, adopted policies directed at the defense of white women, although they generally lacked evidence of such policies' necessity.[205] Oregon newspapers and reports interpreted the possibility of white female settlers being in danger as sufficient evidence to act on. Interestingly, even when reports were based on scenes after the fact, the Oregon stories would still identify white women as having possessed proper feminine attributes such as motherhood. In one report of an attack on an emigrant train near Fort Boise, the source maintained that some of the charred human remains were children who had been "burnt alive before the eyes of their mother, who was lying nearby."[206]

A California newspaper then reported that news of this specific attack had "created great excitement among the whites, and two volunteer companies of sixty men each, were quickly raised to follow and chastise the perpetrators of the deed."[207] Identifying the remains as those of a mother and her children, therefore an affront to white settler women and the settlement, elevated the severity of the attack and helped justify a military response. In stark contrast to the reports of violence toward white female settlers in Oregon, accounts that portrayed the death of American Indian women included limited pieces of information and minimal association with womanhood.[208]

A vast majority of the published accounts that depicted American Indian women in the Pacific Northwest prior to the Civil War came from the perspective of non-Indians, whether fur traders, missionaries, settlers, or Indian agents. While Europeans had associated the language of inferiority with the term "squaw" and then applied this name toward American Indian women as early as the seventeenth century, one of the first printed examples of this term being used as an epithet was in Oregon during the mid-nineteenth century.[209] In his widely circulated publication "A Plea for the Indians," John Beeson denounced the violent actions of Oregon settlers against the American Indians and berated settlers' inability to "recognize the right of humanity" in those they referred to as "buck" or "squaw." Beeson maintained that these terms were used to dehumanize American Indian men and women, noting that the American Indian, "by being spoken as a brute, is cast beyond the pale of a common humanity—where the killing of him ceases to be murder, and no atrocity is considered cruel or unjust."[210] By the time readers in the East consumed Beeson's work, early Oregon settlers had been using the term "squaw" to describe American Indian women for two decades.

As early as 1838 Oregon missionaries such as Mary Richardson Walker recorded American Indian women as "squaw[s]" in their journal entries rather than by name, title, or even "woman" or "wife."[211] This identification was evident in newspapers outside the Pacific Northwest as well, with depictions of Oregon often emphasizing the diversity of its inhabitants, such as one noting that "many of the English have squaws for wives."[212] Throughout the series of wars in the region, reports involving American Indian women, regardless of circumstances, would also include the term "squaw." For example, after Oregon volunteers had set fire to the homes and stores of Rogue River Indians, U.S. General Wool reported on the devastation and, upon removing the surviving American Indian women and children from their homes, explained, "The squaws and children are now at this post suffering severely from frozen limbs."[213] Wool did not provide the number of American Indian women included in his report, nor did he identify if any of these children belonged to the women.[214] This term also appeared in direct reference to targeted violence against American Indian women. Assuming the title of "Squaw Hunters," some Oregon volunteers and individual settlers tasked themselves with capturing and then raping and/or murdering Indigenous women.[215] The perceived acceptability of violence toward American Indian women, which increased with the continuous escalation of conflicts in the region (though it had its roots in abuses carried out by American missionaries), commonly accompanied war reports in the Pacific Northwest.[216]

As addressed in the previous section, numerous reports from Oregon and U.S. officials in the 1850s wars describe targeted violence by Oregon volunteers and their uncontrolled killings of American Indians, including women and children. Within those reports, sometimes the only indication that Indigenous women had been among those killed are references from officials that claim the violence had occurred "without respect to age or sex" or had been carried out against "both sexes."[217] When the report focused on American Indian women and children exclusively, these events were described in terms such as "butchery" or "murder" and portrayed as separate from sanctioned warfare, or explained as a result of how the "settlers' patience had become exhausted."[218] Within accounts of attacks on Indigenous peoples more generally, however, American Indian women were "killed" or "dead."[219] Military officials did not explicitly identify American Indian women as combatants, yet Indigenous peoples were perceived as threats, and those killed were generalized to such an extent that the distinction of being a woman was not always made or recognized. Regardless of whether these omissions were intentionally made, they excluded Indigenous women from the narrative and minimized their deaths. The reports that listed "women" as among those killed provided the fullest extent of details within published accounts on the killing of Indigenous women. This held true even when American Indian women had the largest number of casualties in a given attack.

In the fall of 1855, reports on the killing of American Indians filled correspondence from Joel Palmer and Indian agents assigned to the Pacific Northwest. Some reports made no note of whether Indigenous women or men had been killed, using instead the language of "whites had killed," followed by "three Indians" or "while in the Yakama country—some five or six Indians killed."[220] In one of the more horrific scenes described, Oregon volunteers led by Captain Smith attacked two separate bands of Rogue River Indians, and of the twenty-seven reportedly killed—though they noted that "quite probably several more were killed whose bodies were not found"—only eight of the dead were listed as men.[221] The report states that the Indigenous women had been shot, with at least "two women floating down the river," but in speculating as to why American Indian women had been disproportionally killed, the report suggested, "The attack was so early in the morning, it is more than probably that the women were undistinguishable from men."[222] Though Oregon newspapers also described this event based on the report, the Indigenous women killed that October morning were not given names, and whether they were mothers, daughters, or wives was not included in the narrative.[223] Generalizing them as part of the American Indians that Oregon settlers were at war with, reports on the warfare denied Indigenous women connections to their femininity and womanhood and helped normalize violence toward American Indian women.

Erasing distinctions between Indigenous men and women was evident beyond Oregon reports of "casualties" in warfare. Providing a "statistical table" of the "bands and number of hostile Indians," Indian Agent Ambrose included the numbers for men, women, boys, and girls of nine different bands of American Indians. U.S. officials applied the blanket label of "hostile Indians" to all individuals in these Indigenous communities, including women and children, and tables such as this also provided a quantitative glimpse of the impact of warfare within these groups. According to Ambrose's calculations, the Indigenous men and women significantly outnumbered their children, with boys and girls only representing 33 percent of the populations. The smallest group was Indigenous girls, who were only 14 percent of the populations.[224]

Reports from Oregon and federal officials also portrayed the taking of American Indian supplies as specific to warfare, noting in one case that volunteers had come upon a large group of American Indians and had "broke up some large caches of Indian provisions, taking away ten mule-loads of store, and destroying about twenty more."[225] Although it was possible these twenty or more supply stores had been only used by American Indian groups engaged in warfare, it was perhaps just as possible that they had been supplies of an Indigenous community with women and children. Not including Indigenous women as a part of a American Indian group, even when women were present, would have been in keeping with warfare reports.[226] Oregon officials viewed Indigenous groups in motion as particularly suspicious and presumed that large groups moving through areas—movement usually connected to traditional migration patterns, such as from the Columbia River into the Cascade Mountains—as evidence that a nondescript group comprised "hostile Indians."[227] American Indian women did not appear as a specific group in narratives such as these, even though their presence was possible, nor were they individually identified in relation to the existence of Indigenous peoples at U.S. forts.

Even when groups of American Indians were being held at a U.S. forts, the information recorded by Indian agents on Indigenous women did not increase. When reporting on the population at Fort Lane in October 1855 the Indian agent only listed male American Indians over the age of twelve, even though other officials had noted that women and girls were also present at the fort.[228] Nor were American Indian women particularly safer at a fort; as a report from a Father Josette explained, a group of American Indians who had attempted to leave Fort Water during the Cayuse Wars had been attacked by Oregon volunteers, who forced the Indigenous men to "escape, leaving their women and property in possession" of the militia.[229] During the 1850s wars Joel Palmer reported that a group of Umpqua Indians temporarily moved and awaiting a reservation on the coast had been attacked by "a body of lawless banditti and put to death—men, women, and children."[230] Moreover, Palmer and other officials recognized that attacks by Oregon volunteers toward American Indian groups with treaties undermined the treaty removal process.[231] This reality at U.S. forts prompted many Indigenous peoples to leave or try to return to their homes. Reporting on the "flight of the Indians from this place" in November 1855, Lieutenant

John Withers described "about fifty men" attempting to flee north into the Cascade Mountains.[232] Later in the same letter, Withers noted that whole families accompanied those men, which was why he believed their escape during the winter months would fail and force them back to the fort. He seemed to have only mentioned that families, including women, were a part of this exodus in order to explain why he thought the American Indians would return.

Although reports from Oregon underrepresented the presence of Indigenous women and minimized the impact of warfare on their lives, the treaty process institutionalized this process of erasing American Indian women from the narrative. Representation was problematic in U.S. treaties with American Indian groups of the Pacific Northwest all around, but Indigenous women were notably excluded from this process. Even in groups of Indigenous peoples such as the Chinook Indians, who wanted their women present at treaty negotiations, American Indian women were not included and not permitted to participate.[233] This exclusion of women was not dependent on timing or what warfare ensued. When Anson Dart negotiated a treaty with "bands of Wheelappas and Wuilleque-oquas," just two adult males of the group remained, and although several Indigenous women belonged to these bands, only the marks of the two males appeared on the treaty.[234] Indigenous women's presence in sections of treaties that discussed acreage appointed to the American Indian groups was also wanting, with language such as "person" or "head" of the family acknowledging those who could own property. Although the lack of specification with "person" seems possibly inclusive, the term "head of the household" in Oregon remained connected to males until the late nineteenth century.[235] The use of "his" and "he" throughout the treaty also highlights the inclusion of Indigenous males rather than Indigenous females. Finally, each of the ratified treaties signed in the Pacific Northwest before the Civil War includes only signatures from American Indian men, with the language of "his x mark" accompanying each male name.[236]

Throughout the warfare of the 1840s and 1850s Oregon and national newspaper articles as well as official reports portrayed the experiences of white settler women as possessing properly feminine attributes. These experiences were set in contrast to the depiction of Indigenous women. The main difference lay in how their experiences were recorded and how violence against American Indian women was described, if noted at all. American Indian women were attacked, removed, and killed, yet they remained a consistent group in the region despite what the local accounts suggested. Issues of race were intimately connected to the gendered portrayal of women in the Pacific Northwest, as it cast white settler women as a group to be honored or protected while diminishing the role and existence of Indigenous women. Overall, these gendered depictions helped justify settler warfare and established a historical narrative that minimized violence against American Indian women and excluded both their social and political participation.

Still Existing

Warfare in the Pacific Northwest did not end with Oregon's statehood in 1859. The region witnessed more wars and became home to the "last Indian War," the Nez Perce War. Treaty discussions and changes continued to take place throughout the rest of the century, although most of the treaty making in the region had concluded prior to the Civil War.[237] Dispossession of American Indians through treaties (those after Oregon statehood are represented in table 3), as well as through warfare and settler encroachment also persisted, which in multiple cases led to the breaking of treaties and, typically, more warfare. Conflicts after the Civil War, such as the Modoc War of the early 1870s, however, involved a much greater presence of the U.S. military, their trained forces, and federal financing. And while early warfare in the Oregon settlement had taken the lives of many Indigenous peoples, the "Indian Wars" launched under President Ulysses Grant's "Peace Policy" amplified this legacy of carnage against American Indian communities.[238] Violent removal and dispossession of Indigenous peoples remained part of the regional landscape.

Nevertheless, American Indians' fight to retain lands, culture, and legal authority successfully ensued because dispossession was never

Table 3. Treaties with Pacific Northwest American Indians in the 1860s (post Oregon statehood)

GROUPS LISTED	NO. OF TREATIES	NEGOTIATED	RATIFIED (Y/N)	DATE RATIFIED
"Nez Perces" Nez Perce	1	June 9, 1863 C. H. Hale—superintendent of Indian Affairs, and Charles Hutchins and S. D. Howe—U.S. Indian agents for the Territory of Washington	Y	April 17, 1867 (four years after signing)—supplemental and amendments to the Nez Perce's 1855 treaty
"Klamath, etc." Klamath Modoc Yahooskin Band of Northern Paiute	1	October 14, 1864 J. W. Perit Huntington—superintendent of Indian Affairs in Oregon, and William Logan—United States Indian agent for Oregon	Y	July 2, 1866 (not proclaimed until February 17, 1870)
"Snake" Walpapi Band of Northern Paiute	1	August 12, 1865 J. W. Perit Huntington—superintendent of Indian Affairs in Oregon	Y	July 5, 1866
"Middle Oregon" Confederated tribes of middle Oregon	1	November 15, 1866 J. W. Perit Huntington—superintendent of Indian Affairs in Oregon	Y	March 2, 1867—supplemental to 1855 Treaty
"Eastern Band Shoshoni and Bannock" Eastern Band of Shoshoni Bannock	1	July 3, 1868 U.S. commissioners	Y	February 26, 1869

"Nez Perces" Nez Perce	1	August 13, 1868 Nathaniel G. Taylor—U.S. commissioner	Y	February 16, 1869 —amendments to 1855 Treaty

Source: Created by author based on Kappler, *Indian Affairs*, 843–1020.

completed in the Pacific Northwest.[239] As recently as 2019 the Yakama Nation used their 1855 treaty to prove an exemption from a Washington tax regarding the importation of motor fuel across state lines. U.S. Supreme Court justices determined that the 1855 treaty's language of the "right, in common with citizens of the United States, to travel upon all public highways" permitted the Yakama Nation to carry their products on U.S. roads but did not hold them accountable to the tax.[240] The phrase "in common with," the court argued, would not have meant in 1855 that general legislation applied to all citizens, but the 1855 treaty did protect the Yakama Nation's right to use the roads, and that tax would burden this right. This decision cited another case with the Yakama Nation, in which these Indigenous peoples became exempt from fishing licenses in Washington because the 1855 treaty included the right to fish.[241] Although imperfect and in many ways incomplete, the same 1850s treaties used to remove American Indians from their traditional lands continue to be used by these Indigenous peoples to protect their lands, communities, and rights.

How American Indian women have been described or excluded from portrayals of female experiences or as Indigenous peoples within mid-nineteenth-century treaties and warfare is a legacy that continues today. Although vitally important within Indigenous communities and key to the first white Oregon settlers' establishment of permanent residence, American Indian women and their roles within their communities were quickly minimized within the general narrative. American Indian women have fought these descriptions and stereotypes, and many have not only found recognition for their contributions and individual experiences but also reached social and political authority within their communities over the past century.[242] Oregon settlers and U.S. officials' effective erasure of American Indians from the narrative and dissociation of Indigenous peoples from regional lands, however, has been followed by a long history of violence against Indigenous women that has gone overlooked and underreported.[243]

In many ways this part of the Oregon settlement story underlies all that follows, because the right to exist connects to the other rights that Oregon lawmakers carefully constructed and restricted. The next chapters will address American Indians in relation to rights beyond treaties and conflicts, within the context of legislation applied to the increasingly diverse Pacific Northwest. It remains necessary, however, to remember this piece of the historical puzzle in order to properly situate U.S. and Oregon officials' claims to authority in the region, to understand the chaos behind the seemingly controlled development of a territorial and then state government and to adequately appreciate actions taken by settlers separate from and supported by the United States. Moreover, observers of the past should realize that though the displacement of American Indians was not fully achieved, the attempt devastated Indigenous communities.

CHAPTER 3

Understanding Immigration Restrictions through Arguments of Slavery and Labor

> But this bill proposes to exclude negroes from our Territory, and prevent them from settling in our borders. Are numbers of them coming here? Which way are they coming, by land, or by sea? Do we hear the noise of their approach? Do we hear the bugle notes? No sir, they are not coming. This bill is the apple of discord—the firebrand thrown in to distract us, and disturb our domestic tranquility. It is the work of politicians. It is a thimble-rigger's game—now you see the littler joker—now you don't! The main object is concealed, but once in a while shows itself.
>
> —Delazon Smith, "House," *Oregon Statesman*, January 20, 1857

A "disgraceful riot" occurred between Oregon delegates during the territory's Constitutional Convention in 1857.[1] Upon the proposal to gag discussions on slavery and allow the people of Oregon to vote on the issue in addition to the state constitution, "members (pro-slavery) rose to their feet with flashing eyes and distended nostrils, and with frantic eagerness shouted, or rather yelled forth their disapprobation of the resolution." Combinations of "bowie, knives, dirks, and pistols were drawn," multiple delegates were wounded by pistol shots, and one "free-state democrat" was stabbed in the abdomen. Proslavery politicians hurled "scurrilous attacks . . . bitter invectives . . . [and] the most infamous calumnies were bandied by the reckless border ruffians, who seemed to revel in their native element." Free-state delegates, attempting to flee the chaos, threw themselves from the hall's windows or rushed the narrow stairway. Not until the riot had spilled into the streets and the marshal, sheriff, and Salem's City major (with assistance of the city band) had confronted the politicians did the violence cease.[2]

The *New York Tribune* writer who reported this event asserted that the riot would likely lead to a proslavery majority in the Oregon Constitution, a fear he knew many of his readers shared.[3] Slavery in Oregon had been under discussion and of concern in national papers as well as within congressional sessions since the creation of the Oregon territorial government in 1848. Of course, this article portraying the effect of slavery on Oregon politics was distinctively different from other national accounts, because this article was the work of fiction. The violent Oregon riot between proslavery and antislavery delegates that the *New York Tribune* reported never occurred.

To dismiss this source would be unwise. The article, though demonstrating the questionable ethics of the New York paper, reveals the centrality of Oregon politics and its debates on the national stage of events during the mid-nineteenth century. This fabricated story, perhaps more reflective of occurrences in Kansas from just a few years earlier, draws on several issues identified in national politics at the time: the expansion of slavery, the building tension between states that allowed slavery and those that did not, and the understanding that popular sovereignty could be used by both sides of the slavery debate. Historians such as Joanne Freeman demonstrate that the atmosphere in Washington DC was not just tense but "on the edge" of violent chaos when Oregon applied for statehood.[4] Slave states maintained a watchful eye on Oregon, taking solace in the fact that some of Oregon's political leaders had been originally from southern states or were Democrats with proslavery leanings. Additionally, three free states had entered the Union since the time Oregon had become a territory, and the divisive issue of who had the authority to regulate slavery had grown more complicated by the time Oregon drafted its own state constitution in 1857.[5]

Within Oregon itself, the issue of slavery remained connected to several regional issues but always associated to legislation that excluded free Black Americans from coming to or settling in Oregon. Lawmakers and community leaders entwined debates over slavery and the immigration restriction of Black Americans, both legally and politically, since related policies had first emerged under the provisional government and it remained advantageous for white settlers to establish racial barriers in the region.[6] Although Oregon was not the first to construct a law excluding an entire group of Americans (discussed later in this chapter), the question remains: How did Congress accept a state constitution with such a provision on the eve of the Civil War? The settler colony's occupation of the region, coupled with the timing of sectional divisions and Oregon's balance of prohibiting slavery but having a Democratic majority, all allowed Oregon to keep its laws.

Oregon's immigration restriction of Black Americans derived from and became a contributing factor to local and national debates over the issue of slavery. An evaluation of political discussions on slavery provides an avenue for understanding both the construction of Oregon's immigration restriction of Black Americans as well as the acceptance of such a law by the federal government. This chapter addresses how Oregon legislators, through a focus on free and enslaved labor as well as the radicalization of abolitionism, used racial and gendered arguments to construct laws for immigration restrictions. Furthermore, it demonstrates how debates over slavery and the immigration restriction of Black Americans reified definitions of gender and race as applied to legal rights and political participation.

Settler Colonialism through Slavery

As addressed in chapter 1, Oregon politics developed according to rules prescribed by foreign settlers, with many of their ideas for societal guidelines coming from their nations of origin. Although groups of American Indians remained the largest population of inhabitants during Oregon's early settlement period, settler colonialism began once foreigners had established their provisional government and attempted to control the legal structures within the region that settlers then identified as their own. Oregon settlers used laws to define and wield their presumed authority within the region.[7] From its beginnings, however, this far-removed settler colony did not escape the issue of slavery, and newspapers from both the United States and Great Britain drew connections between slavery and their nations' control of Oregon.

Amid congressional debates addressing western expansion and growing national interest in Texas, U.S. newspaper articles speculated on how far the United States would have to go to secure the northwest region currently held under joint occupation with Great Britain. Some reports maintained that the regional foothold achieved by the Hudson's Bay Company supported British control and influence throughout Asian markets. Citing this presumed stake in the region, U.S. newspapers further speculated that the nation's acquisition of Oregon would require war with Great Britain.[8] Although overshadowed by the Mexican-American War within the historical narrative, the potential for war between the United States and Great Britain was quite real. In fact, British Prime Minister Sir Robert Peel deployed a warship to the Pacific Northwest upon news of U.S. President Polk's inaugural address in 1845, in which Polk proclaimed that Oregon would become part of the United States.[9] Within Oregon, individuals such as John McLoughlin, previously with the HBC, expressed the belief that there was a higher likelihood of a war between the United States and Great Britain than between the United States and Mexico in 1845.[10] Yet some U.S. newspaper articles shifted the discussion from U.S. disputes with the British over Oregon to the alleged involvement of Great Britain in the African slave trade.[11]

U.S. abolitionists and politicians, especially leading to and following the War of 1812, accused Great Britain of continued involvement in the slave trade even after the Slave Trade Act of 1807. These arguments focused on the authority Great Britain wielded on the seas over other nations' vessels and the implied correlation between imposing its will upon foreign ships and the continuation of the slave trade.[12] Playing on U.S. fears of British tyranny and the vulnerable nature of a young democratic nation, politicians again rallied social and political support for an aggressive approach to the acquisition of Oregon.[13] Antislavery politicians such as Caleb Cushing also berated the federal government for its inaction in Oregon and insinuated that Great Britain threatened

America's right to its "natural boundary," the Pacific Ocean. Cushing, along with other expansionists, argued that freeing Oregon from British "enslavement" would provide U.S. merchants with access to desired Asian markets.[14]

By the 1840s Oregon settlers had agreed with this economic evaluation and further believed that their settlement created a doorway to the markets in the Pacific. In fact, Oregon settlers were so confident of their market advantages that editorials brushed aside voices to the contrary, even when the concerns came from the same Pacific trading partners Oregon held up as examples of its economic prowess.[15] The exaggerated opinions of Oregon settlers were important to this phase of settlement, because although U.S. newspapers and politicians such as Cushing were primarily trying to encourage western expansion in general, the arguments that connected Great Britain's claims to the Pacific Northwest with the institution of slavery also played up the value of Oregon.[16] In this case, correlating slavery with Great Britain's claims to an economically advantageous Oregon also supported the process of settler colonialism. The more the United States desired the region, the greater the control Oregon settlers possessed over their settlement, including its policies.[17] Among the many policies Oregon lawmakers would create within the provisional government, which the United States would eventually accept as part of the territorial government, Oregon settlers developed their own laws related to slavery.

The Oregon provisional government first adopted a law prohibiting slavery in 1843.[18] This law reflected the language of the Northwest Ordinance (1787), and although Oregon fell outside the region addressed in this federal act, many Oregon settlers interpreted it as prohibiting slavery in all new territories.[19] Although influenced by U.S. legislation, this law was not a replica of U.S. policy. Oregon lawmakers constructed legislation specific to and in the interests of those who had settled in the colony, which remained outside of U.S. jurisdiction. Furthermore, as with an abundance of laws adopted within the early United States, similarities existed between British and U.S. policies on slavery.[20] While the popular narrative about western expansion and the treatment of slavery in the

West may have suggested that Oregon had been organically brought into the fold through its adherence to the Northwest Ordinance, U.S. authority was not passed into Oregon through its usage. In fact, given the uncertainty of which nation would extend its jurisdiction over the region in 1843, settlers had initially pledged their allegiance to both the United States and Great Britain in provisional government records.[21]

Then on June 26, 1844, the Oregon provisional government passed the "Lash Law," its first piece of legislation prohibiting Black Americans from residing in Oregon. According to the law, slaveowners had three years to remove enslaved individuals from Oregon, or the enslaved individual would be freed. Upon acquiring his/her freedom, however, the Black American was to leave the region or be subject to a punishment of twenty to thirty-nine lashes.[22] How exactly someone would determine that a Black American man or woman living in Oregon had been enslaved, the law neither explained nor considered. Thus, all Black Americans were subject to this legislation whether they had resided in the region or were new immigrants to Oregon. Although the law would be revised multiple times, it existed under the provisional government and the territorial government, and it was finally incorporated into Oregon's state constitution. The longevity of this restriction reveals the settlers' desire to exclude Black Americans from Oregon. Moreover, the attempted removal of Black Americans within the growing settlement effectively accompanied colonizing efforts to promote white agrarian authority in the region by drawing an actual racial barrier around the colony.[23] Details on how Oregon officials were to remove Black Americans became more specific as the immigration restriction law evolved.

Oregon lawmakers revised their legislation on slavery in December 1844 by removing the Lash Law and replacing it with the punishment of servitude. This change followed objections to the harshness of lashing free Black Americans who failed to leave Oregon, deciding instead that the justice of the peace could apprehend and "expose such free negro or mulatto to public hiring."[24] The winner of this public auction was then responsible for removing the person indentured to them within six months after services rendered. Thus, forced servitude was the punishment for Black Americans' continued existence in Oregon.[25] The connection between slavery and the expulsion of free Black Americans from Oregon would continue, but after the 1844 law these two issues no longer shared legislation.

In 1845 the settlers passed one more piece of legislation on slavery prior to the Oregon Treaty, and before Oregonians came under the legal jurisdiction of the United States. The Organic Laws of Oregon again used similar language to the Northwest Ordinance and prohibited slavery in the settler colony. To suggest, as many antislavery U.S. congressional representatives did, that Oregon's provisional laws fully embraced and carried the Northwest Ordinance into the region is to disregard the potential influence of British law. In fact, the British had outlawed slavery for nearly a decade by the time Oregon settlers formed the Organic Laws.[26] Arguably Oregon lawmakers were privy to both sets of policies, as Great Britain had extended its jurisdiction over British fur-trading forts in the region, and a substantial number of U.S. citizens were familiar with the national Constitution during the Antebellum era.[27] It remains difficult then to determine with absolute certainty the influence of the Northwest Ordinance on Oregon lawmakers. Regardless, the Organic Laws were uniquely the making of Oregon settlers and demonstrate a continuation of previous provisional laws.

Oregon had operated under its own slavery laws for three years before the United States and Great Britain ratified the Oregon Treaty. Meanwhile, the outbreak of the Mexican-American War and the subsequent territories acquired in the Treaty of Guadalupe Hidalgo thoroughly questioned the legitimacy of the Missouri Compromise and its applications.[28] Congress ultimately applied the Missouri Compromise to the acquisition of Texas, but both the formation of the Oregon Territory and the statehood of California would sidestep and retire the federal policy. This, in part, was a result of how debates on slavery in territories during the late 1840s developed at the federal level. Although general arguments addressed the issue of state rights, these became more of a disagreement about how Congress could use its recognized authority over territories to rule on the existence of slavery. One side, predominately representing slaveholding states, argued that Congress could force U.S. territories to permit slavery, whereas the other side insisted that Congress could (if desired) prohibit slavery in a territory.[29] Before Congress could apply anything to Oregon, however, it needed to establish Oregon as a formal U.S. territory.

Reflecting the position that Congress could prohibit slavery in territories, Senator John Milton Niles of Connecticut questioned why the United States would change a law that a new territory had already created and presumably enforced. Niles argued that Oregon had proved capable of creating its own laws, including one that prohibited slavery, but he also noted that Oregon was not a sovereign nation, nor did its provisional government serve as a sovereign power. Therefore, Niles insisted that Congress needed to extend its jurisdiction over the territory to formally enforce Oregonians' slavery-prohibiting law. Given the timing of the Oregon Bill and the failing authority of the Missouri Compromise, antislavery politicians such as Niles wanted his colleagues to recognize Congress's power to prohibit slavery even in the case that a future territory would likely exclude the institution themselves.[30] Through such a perspective, Oregon served as an example for this argument, but federal politicians also used Oregon to support the other position on Congressional authority that allowed for slavery.

South Carolina Senator John C. Calhoun built on the proslavery argument in the Oregon Bill (1848) debates when he cited several articles within the U.S. Constitution to defend his position that Congress had the power to dictate laws for a territory. Calhoun argued that a territory restricting slavery denied slaveowners a right honored by their home states, and that the territorial law was therefore in violation of the constitutional amendment that granted citizens of all states equal rights.[31] Proslavery representatives furthered this argument by proposing an amendment that would prohibit the territorial government from passing laws that could "be so construed as to authorize the prohibition of domestic slavery in said Territory, whilst it remains in the condition of a Territory of the United States."[32] Congress did not accept this amendment, but the opinion that Congress could dictate territorial laws on slavery continued.

Another approach Calhoun took during the Oregon Bill was to argue that each individual state of the union was financially responsible for the acquisition of Oregon. As the creators of its western territories, the states, Calhoun argued, should be able to control—through their congressional representatives—laws applied to territories. Calhoun insisted that the Louisiana Purchase and the Lewis and Clark Expedition had only been possible through a common fund that the states financed and, therefore, each state was "under every aspect . . . full contributors to all."[33] But not all proslavery politicians agreed with Calhoun's belief that Oregon owed the nation a debt.

In fact, Senator Thomas Hart Benton of Missouri composed a letter to the people of Oregon asking for their patience, as they must continue to govern themselves without assistance from the federal government while divisions within Congress prevented the passage of the Oregon Bill. Benton commended Oregonians on their ability to settle into and secure the region for the nation, and he assured readers that he had supported the speedy acquisition of Oregon since the Convention of 1818 and would continue to do so. Although a slaveowner himself and notoriously short-tempered when it came to the issue of slavery, Benton also pleaded with the Oregon settlers to maintain their prohibition of slavery. Benton recognized Congress's resistance to the expansion of slavery, the levels to which antislavery politicians would go to prevent slavery, as well as the low likelihood of slave labor being successful along the Pacific coast.[34] Benton then concluded his letter with the hope that he should live long enough to see "an emporium of Asiatic commerce at the mouth of your [Columbia] river, and a stream of Asiatic trade pouring into the Valley of the Mississippi through the channel of Oregon."[35] U.S. politicians who supported the immediate acquisition of Oregon did not see the settlement as owing the United States for previous financial backing; rather, they depicted Oregon as aiding the nation in its settlement and providing future economic opportunities to the entire country.[36] Oregon was a necessary addition—therefore, whatever was required to secure Oregon's entry, even if it meant prohibiting slavery, should be done.

Meanwhile antislavery congressional representatives had a vested interest in ensuring that Oregon would eventually enter as a free territory. Politicians such as Daniel Webster were quick to point out that in recent years the nation had gained five slave states (if one included Texas); meanwhile not one free state had joined the union.[37] Although not a new state, the addition of a territory brought with it its future federal representatives. Senator John H. Clarke of Rhode Island echoed this sentiment, citing the fact that even though the northern territories had lost land during the Oregon Treaty, the nation had gained more southern territories than expected with the acquisition of Texas.[38] This desire to balance congressional power between partisan groups did not go unnoticed by proslavery politicians, which is why several Democrats ultimately did not challenge the growing opinion that peace within the union would require the admittance of free territories such as Oregon.[39] Oregon's law restricting slavery from the colony, therefore, continued with the settlers into the territorial government.

Following the passage of the Oregon Bill in 1848, President Polk took the unusual step of addressing the nation to explain why he had approved the bill. Although presidents sometimes found it necessary to explain to the public why they had vetoed a significant bill, Polk felt compelled to defend his decision to approve the Oregon Bill, stating, "Questions occasionally arise of such transcendent importance, as to cast all those of mere party character into the shade. But one such can now be agitated in the country; and this may endanger our Glorious Union. This question is Slavery. And so, the occasion arose for this demonstration."[40] Polk maintained that had Oregon been geographically positioned below the line designated in the Missouri Compromise and prohibited slavery, he would have vetoed the bill, because that would have run contrary to the Compromise.[41] Congress, however, did not cite the Missouri Compromise among the dominant reasons for establishing Oregon as a territory. Nor did many newspapers accept Polk's position about the application of the Compromise. In fact, one North Carolina paper refuted Polk's argument as irrelevant, stating that Oregon did not fall under the territory designated in the Missouri Compromise, as it was not part of the Louisiana Purchase. The Oregon Bill, the author maintained, "stands on its own bottom."[42]

Discussion of dissolution had occurred within the halls of Congress by this time, but many of the federal representatives wanted to extend jurisdiction to Oregon and accept its entrance as a free territory given Oregon's location and its existing laws.[43] The congressional allowance for Oregon's provisional laws prohibiting slavery, moreover, provided a trial run for western settlers to decide on the matter of slavery for their own regions. The U.S. federal government went on to ratify five different treaties with American Indian groups in the Pacific Northwest between 1854 and 1855 that included specific articles outlawing slavery, further supporting Oregon's existing policies.[44] The Kansas-Nebraska Act of 1854 later institutionalized this process for U.S. territories (identifying the concept as popular sovereignty), but congressional debates over Oregon's entrance as a territory had raised this issue years earlier.[45] Oregon did not deal with neighboring states or territories rushing in to influence its territorial laws on slavery, but neither did Congress truly challenge Oregon's own laws on the matter.

The way Congress treated Oregon laws on slavery during the Oregon Bill impacted discussions on California's statehood. California was a territory that had never established a territorial government due to controversy over the Missouri Compromise and its connection to acquisitions from Mexico. Therefore, California went from being under military rule directly to its application for statehood in 1850.[46] Debates over Oregon's slavery laws in the decade prior had created a precedent for how the federal government could treat other Far West territories, which was primarily how Congress could sidestep the Missouri Compromise. Again, the Oregon Bill had required Congress to renegotiate the 1787 Northwest Ordinance to allow the continuation of Oregon's provisional law. This application expanded the eighteenth-century act to the west prior to California statehood, but debates over Oregon's slavery laws not only impacted the way in which Congress addressed

California's existence as a free state but also influenced congressional debates over immigration restriction in Oregon's state constitution.

By the time Oregon applied for statehood in 1858 its lawmakers had created, amended, and institutionalized restrictions to the settlement of Black Americans in the region. The settler colony and then territory joined only a small number of states with such legislation, and only Missouri had included this exclusion in its state constitution prior to Oregon's immigration restriction laws.[47] Florida joined other Atlantic Southeast slave states in prohibiting Black sailors from leaving their vessels while harbored in their states' ports, but then further granted its general assembly the power to "prevent free negroes, mulattoes, and other persons of color, from immigrating to this State" in the Florida state constitution.[48] In 1848, four years after Oregonians had prohibited the presence of Black Americans in their region, the state of Illinois revised its state constitution to include instructions for future legislative sessions to create a law that would exclude free Black Americans from immigrating to or settling in their state. As a free state, Illinois also connected this revision to the restriction of slavery. Democrats in Illinois had conceded that slavery would not be permitted within their state, but proslavery lawmakers successfully included this required "future" restriction of free Black Americans despite their colleagues' objections that it violated the federal constitution.[49] Sharing language with Oregon's provisional laws, Virginia later revised its constitution in 1851 to include a provision that required all Black Americans freed from slavery to leave the commonwealth within twelve months of their emancipation, or they would forfeit their freedom and be enslaved once again.[50]

Oregon may not have been the first to prohibit Black Americans from its borders, but the longevity of Oregon's exclusionary legislation is important to understand. Oregon presented Congress with provisional laws that restricted the presence of Black Americans during their admittance as an organized territory; Oregon then passed subsequent laws in 1849 and 1854 as a territorial government. Finally, Oregon carried this legislation into its statehood application.[51] California lawmakers had considered adopting legislation to restrict Black Americans' entry into

Table 4. State constitution immigration restrictions (prior 1860)

Specification	STATE	SLAVE / FREE	YEAR	ORIGINAL / REVISION	INCLUDES "FREE" TO IDENTIFY BLACK AMERICANS
Connected the exclusion of "negroes and mulattoes" to slavery	Missouri	Slave	1820	Original	Yes
	Florida	Slave	1845	Original	Yes
	Illinois	Free	1848	Revision	Yes
	Oregon	**Free**	**1849**	**Territorial Constitution**	**Yes**
	Indiana	Free	1851	Revision	No
	Virginia	Slave	1851	Revision	No
	Oregon	**Free**	**1859**	**Original**	**Yes**
	Kansas	Free	1861	Original (proposed 1857)	Yes
	Total (States) = 7 **Total** (Territories) = 1				

Source: Created by author based on ratified constitutions; Swindler, *Sources and Documents*.

their future state in 1850, but ultimately abandoned the policy in fear of jeopardizing their statehood application.[52]

The federal government had helped institutionalize Oregon's provisional laws each time it allowed Oregon to bring such legislation into U.S. jurisdiction—as a territory and then as a state. Congress was aware of Oregon's laws restricting the immigration of Black Americans, but multiple states implemented similar legislation only after Oregon had become a territory. Finally, when Oregon drafted its state constitution, Congress was forced to converse about Oregon's laws on slavery and the immigration restriction of Black Americans, because the territory would be up for admittance as a new state.

Contrary to the Oregon Bill discussion, both local and national newspapers ran stories on the probability of Oregon entering as a slave state during the Oregon Constitutional Convention in 1857. The fact that Oregonians were asked to vote (separate from the vote on the constitution itself) for or against slavery as well as for permitting or prohibiting Black Americans from living in their future state fueled national coverage of the convention. Even though former Whigs and Republican delegates also represented Oregon and were collectively referred to as the Anti-Democrats, the region was home to a powerful Democratic Party with members who were in the newspaper business, appointed to courts, and holders of territorial offices.[53] With a Democratic proslavery majority among Oregon politicians, the attention newspapers gave to Oregon's constitution also revealed the influence that Oregon's presence as a slave or free state would have on the nation.

Drawing on articles published in Oregon or, more commonly, those printed in California, national papers began publishing potential voting statistics for both special provisions. Overall, newspapers from northern states demonstrated a concern that either Oregonians would approve slavery in their state or Democrats in Congress would shoot Oregon's statehood application down if it voted against slavery, in addition to prohibiting Black Americans from moving to Oregon. Editorials viewed the provisions as connected, noting that restricting both would be seen by proslavery representatives as closing the door on the possibility of slavery being brought to the new state.[54] One Philadelphia paper even noted "the extraordinary character of this constitution," because Oregon's entrance as a state would come with controversy regardless of how Oregonians voted.[55] For this reason, it is necessary to understand the connections between the immigration restriction provision and slavery. The *Dred Scott v. Sanford* decision may have undercut the constitutional argument for why Black Americans should be allowed to live in Oregon by the end of the 1850s, but that very decision was controversial primarily because of its connection to slavery, and the national debates surrounding Oregon's statehood highlighted this fact.[56]

In the end, Oregon applied for statehood as a free state, with a Democratic majority, and it restricted the immigration of Black Americans to its future state. Congress again approached Oregon's application with the desire to maintain a balance of power. California had become a state in 1850, and Congress had achieved a temporary balance between partisan powers through the Compromise of 1850, including the revised Fugitive Slave Act. By the time Oregon applied for statehood, however, the state of Minnesota and the territory of Kansas had threatened to offset the number of representatives in favor of the free states.[57] This situation enabled Oregon to submit controversial laws such as the restriction of Black American immigration into its state, because Oregon benefited from both sides of the partisan divide—Oregon would be both a free state and led by Democrats.

When debating Oregon's statehood, several representatives quickly disregarded objections to the Oregon constitution itself, arguing such opposition purely arose from a partisan divide rather than the restriction of Black Americans from the future state.[58] An editorial from the *Mississippian and State Gazette*, for example, echoed the arguments of proslavery Oregonians that federal representatives opposing the immigration restriction of Black Americans were only doing so to oppose slavery. The editorial continued that these would-be abolitionists and "Negrophilists in Congress" felt Oregon's decision ran contrary to their doctrine of "equality of the races."[59] This proslavery argument also connected to Supreme Court judge Benjamin B. Curtis's 1850 ruling that a state could prevent immigration to itself when that threatened the security of a state, such as free Black Americans moving into a slave state.[60] By associating opposition to Oregon's immigration restriction with abolitionism, the Mississippi newspaper appealed to proslavery advocates in Congress, firmly connected Oregon's provision with the support of slavery, and suggested their opponents embraced extremely polarizing ideas of racial equality. Because of this earlier position, primarily made by Democrats, Republicans who wanted to vote Oregon's admission down fought accusations of placing their party over the nation. Such representatives tried to maintain that they opposed the admission because of the unrepublican or unconstitutional nature of the Oregon constitution but faced accusations that their arguments only contributed to the growing sectional tensions.[61]

The timing of Oregon's application for statehood aided its passage. Oregon may have brought in laws fraught with questionable provisions connected to slavery, but it served as a desired and less problematic new state in comparison to other regions during a tumultuous time in

U.S. history. Debates regarding slavery did arise and are discussed in later sections. Yet, the federal government did not at any point in its transition from a settler colony to a state infringe on Oregon's laws on slavery or the immigration restriction of Black Americans. In granting Oregonians authority over their laws in this manner, the federal government also allowed Oregon laws to influence the adoption of similar restrictive legislation in other states and territories. Laws constructed by a settler colony were legitimized with each step toward statehood and given authority within a state constitution.

Constructing Race and Class through Slavery and Immigration Restrictions

One of the first discussions about Black Americans living in Oregon was in relation to the Pacific Northwest becoming a colony for free Black Americans in 1829. Individuals such as Henry Clay, aware of U.S. claims to the region, rejected this idea and argued that Oregon would ultimately connect to the rest of the United States, thus undermining the purpose of removing free Black Americans from the States.[62] Once foreign settlement in Oregon had commenced, discussions to exclude Black Americans, whether free or enslaved, in the region were consistently incorporated into early provisional legislation. The construction and implementation of laws regarding slavery and immigration restriction became a way for Oregon lawmakers to racially define the region as well as hone their legal interpretations of labor and individual rights.[63] Policies on slavery and immigration were bound to attract national attention and warrant an evaluation from Congress, but the specific exclusions and racial qualifications not only set Oregon's laws apart from those of other territories and states but also influenced legislation in other parts of the nation.

Although Oregon was home to both free and enslaved Black Americans by the 1840s, with approximately 112 individuals identified as "blacks and mulattoes" in 1850, these populations remained very small in comparison to those existing in the South or even in midwestern states like Kentucky.[64] A large population of Black Americans, however, was not necessary for race to become an issue in Oregon politics. Slavery laws brought about far-reaching implications regardless of how many enslaved people existed in a region. Oregon laws were also not simply formalities performed by legislators. Slavery existed in Oregon even after the provisional government had prohibited the institution, after Congress had extended the Northwest Ordinance to the territory, and after the territorial government had passed antislavery legislation. One example of this was the *Holmes v. Ford* case.

In 1844 the Holmes family traveled with slaveowner Nathaniel Ford to Oregon. While the parents, Robin and Polly Holmes, were freed by Ford in 1850, their surviving children remained enslaved. According to Oregon law, the enslavement of the Holmes family and the continued enslavement of their children should have ended upon their arrival to the region. At the very least, all members of the family should have been freed following the first trial regarding their enslavement. Although presumably a clear situation, it was not until 1853 that Judge George A. Williams awarded the Holmes children their freedom due to a lack of legislation supporting slavery in Oregon.[65]

In the United States, policies toward slavery had a history of being connected to laws that restricted Black Americans from coming to or living within a specific region. Missouri was the first state to include a provision in its constitution about prohibiting free Black Americans from residing in the state, but its 1820 constitution stated that future legislators should create this restriction. Missouri wanted to control the presence of free Black Americans, which was a practice many slave states would adopt in relation to their laws on slavery.[66] This was especially true after groups began attributing slave insurrections to the involvement of free Black Americans. Events such as the Nat Turner Rebellion of 1831 solidified this association between the presence of free Black Americans and slave insurrections.[67] At the time Congress was debating the creation of Oregon's territorial government; however, Missouri still had no such law.[68] Meanwhile Oregon's provisional governments had legislation restricting the immigration and settlement of Black Americans on the books.

Oregon lawmakers and community leaders also continuously associated Black Americans in the region with slave labor. Within Oregon's political discussion, Black Americans became somewhat synonymous with slavery or slave labor. This association racialized Oregon's perceptions of labor and cast Black labor as inferior to white (free) labor. Connecting Black American labor to slavery further separated Black Americans from Oregon's definition of citizenship and ultimately helped support the institution of slavery by promoting arguments made by "enslaving interests."[69] During the congressional debates over both the Oregon Bill and Oregon statehood, some representatives took the position that slavery could be permitted where it "naturally exists" or where crops viewed as ideal for slave labor could take root. This position seemingly placed the decision on where slavery could expand more on location than on federal ruling.

Senator John Middleton Clayton of Delaware, for example, argued that slavery could not thrive in Oregon and asserted that the territory was a region "which no one imagines can ever be slaveholding."[70] But slavery did exist in Oregon, and as evidence of slaves being freed throughout the 1850s in Oregon demonstrates, slavery had continued.[71] Representatives based their arguments on assumptions about labor and a person's ability to thrive in a region, much of which relied on racial theories put forth by individuals like Samuel Stanhope Smith.[72] These claims asserted that peoples of African descent (whether enslaved or free) could only live in certain climates. By the time Oregon lawmakers were drafting policies about slavery and the restriction of Black Americans from the region, theories such as polygenesis had gained popularity and promoted the idea that racial groups evolved separately and could not be improved or diminished by the environment.[73] Due to the variety of these theories presented in discussions about Oregon's immigration laws, it is likely that both generations of racial theories had influenced Oregon lawmakers' discussions and decisions.

These eighteenth- and nineteenth-century perceptions about race played out in Oregon politics throughout the 1850s. Each time Oregon settlers debated whether the race of a laborer determined that person's ability to labor, they also discussed racial groups' ability to exist within the territory. In one editorial from the *Oregon Statesman*, the author addressed the debate of foreign immigration versus the migration of Black Americans to Oregon. Arguing that "One good German is worth more than fifty negroes, to a neighborhood," the editorial further suggested that Black Americans did not understand the idea of freedom and therefore could not effectively participate within a community.[74] The author did not distinguish between free Black Americans and enslaved individuals, treating the two groups as one and the same. Drawing connections to adaptability, the author continued, "black and Celt-Saxon races are not fit to inhabit together . . . their disposition, color, and capacity forbid it."[75] The editorial argued that Black Americans would not prove as helpful in Oregon as European immigrants, but also that Black Americans were not fit to make a life among white races within Oregon.

Building from these ideas of race and the ability of groups to adapt, another Oregon editorial focused on the climate of Oregon and its supposed effects on Black Americans. The author, convinced that slavery would not be successful in Oregon due to its seasonal weather, insisted that Black Americans would not be able to perform as laborers in the region or do so without considerable cost to the employer: "It is a well demonstrated fact that a cold Sambo can neither move nor work briskly. It is a well demonstrated fact that a sick Dinah is the most worthless of all detangled property. Out door [*sic*] laborers could go not part of the year without good shoes or boots. Every thing [*sic*] becomes so dry and hard and sharp in the summer that bare feet cannot go it."[76] Again, the editorial made no distinction between free Black Americans and enslaved individuals; rather, the focus remained on a specific race's inability to labor in Oregon based on the alleged inability of Black Americans to adapt to its climate.

Oregon politicians such as Delazon Smith, who supported the institution of slavery, still insisted that slavery would not work in the region and claimed that "God and nature—climate, soil, and everything considered render it impossible." Although soil can dictate what sort of crops thrive in a region, Smith's objections to slavery working in Oregon still focused on the racial element of this equation. Moreover, if slavery remained illegal in Oregon, proslavery politicians such as Smith did not want the region opened up to free Black labor.[77] Oregon politicians and community leaders who argued against the effectiveness of Black American labor in Oregon extended this sentiment to both free and enslaved Black Americans, because they based their arguments on racial theories that supported their desire to keep jobs and authority over the region in the hands of white laborers.

Although Black Americans technically have the same likelihood of surviving the climate of the Pacific Northwest as white Americans, the social climate in Oregon was another matter. In fact, Black American immigrants carefully chose where to settle in the territory upon arriving there. George Bush, a Black American who migrated to Oregon via the overland trail in 1844, ultimately settled his family north of the Columbia River in what would become the Washington Territory. Bush did not attempt to claim a settlement in the Willamette Valley, the most densely settled part of the entire region, in large part because the Oregon provisional government had passed legislation to prevent the immigration and settlement of Black Americans. Bush chose, instead, to place some distance between his family and the white settlers of Oregon. The Bush family went on to do quite well in the region and assisted in the development of settlements within the Washington Territory.[78] Race may have become a defining factor in debates over who could labor in the region, but multiple Black Americans who settled in Oregon proved these biased assumptions incorrect.

When Congress formed Oregon's territorial government in 1848, bringing in Oregon's prohibition of slavery, the territorial constitution approved by Congress did not include the immigration restriction of Black Americans. Oregon lawmakers, however, wanted to prevent the presence of free Black Americans, and they successfully reinstitutionalized the policy later in 1849 and throughout the 1850s regardless of who objected.[79] During the debates over Oregon's Donation Land Act of 1850, Congressman Joshua Reed Giddings of Ohio proposed to strike out the racial specification that only "white" citizens could claim a land donation. Oregon's congressional delegate Samuel Thurston quickly objected to this proposal, arguing that in Oregon "the people themselves had excluded" Black Americans from entering their territory and "trusted that Congress would not introduce them in violation of their wishes" by encouraging further settlement of that specific group.[80] Oregon, Thurston asserted, did not want Black Americans in its territory regardless of whether they could be considered citizens. But with each reintroduction of or change to this law also came objections by some Oregon lawmakers.

Oregonians who opposed the immigration restriction law but wanted to avoid the issue of slavery approached the debate by addressing the region's need for laborers. One particular group of white petitioners approached the territorial Council and House immediately following the passage of the law in 1849 and requested its repeal. The petitioners argued that Black Americans living in Oregon had proven themselves "industrious and civil . . . Having no knowledge of this law, some of them have spent their all by purchasing property, or entering into business to gain an honest living."[81] Questioning whether Black Americans represented the group that Oregon settlers should be concerned about, they further explained that "injustice" had been done them "by more unworthy, and despising men lodging complaints against them under this law." The petitioners asserted that the exclusionary law, directed at a specific racial group, not only ignored the contributions of this group to Oregon but also dismissed "honest and industrious men" solely on account of their race.[82] Among the petition's signatories was Thomas Dryer, the editor of the *Oregonian* newspaper, who would become one of the more outspoken residents against slavery and the exclusion of Black Americans.[83]

Labor provided an avenue to discuss objections to the immigration restriction of Black Americans, but the fact remained that the law focused on Black Americans. The ability of an American to migrate to the Oregon Territory, therefore, became a right defined by race. In racializing the right of a citizen, Oregon racialized its definition of citizenship as well. Limiting the rights of a group recognized as U.S. citizens in other states ran into objections, but the conjoining issues of race, labor, and citizenship remained an active discussion at the national level.

Despite the continuation of this law and all the subsequent debates accompanying it, Oregon courts rarely enforced the removal of free Black Americans from Oregon. One of the only times this occurred took place on August 26, 1851. U.S. Marshal Joseph L. Meek arrested Oregon resident Jacob Vanderpool under the 1849 law prohibiting "negroes and mulattoes" from coming to or settling in Oregon. A white resident had identified Vanderpool as a "mulatto" and brought charges against him for illegally residing in Oregon City. Attempts had been made to enforce this law in the past, but petitioners or outright community support had prevented the courts from ruling on the matter.[84] Unfortunately for Vanderpool, the course of the accusation, arrest, trial, and conviction took only six days, and the three witnesses his attorney brought forth could not dissuade territorial chief justice Thomas Nelson from ruling against the Black Oregonian.[85]

During the trial Vanderpool's attorney, A. Halderbrook, brought to light five objections to the validity of the charges made against his client. Among these objections was that the Oregon law that prevented Black Americans from coming to or settling in Oregon violated the second and sixth articles of the Northwest Ordinance, which recognized "all the singular rights, privileges, and advantages granted and secured by which, the said Vanderpool an inhabitant of this Territory is entitled to enjoy."[86] As a resident of the territory, Vanderpool was technically protected under the Ordinance, which Congress had approved a year before the territorial government reinstituted the immigration restriction law. Yet Judge Nelson, and by extension Oregon, ignored the authority of the Northwest Ordinance and expelled Vanderpool from the Territory.[87] Oregonians would not extend to Vanderpool or other Black Americans wishing to migrate to the Oregon Territory the rights protected by the federal government. Oregon courts, founded on earlier provisional government laws, chose to uphold the racial qualification for living in Oregon.

Oregonians' debates over the admission of Black Americans into the territory also addressed the presence of other nonwhite laborers, especially those of Chinese descent. During a legislative session in January 1855, House Representative David Logan proposed to include the word "Chinese" wherever "negroes and mulattoes" occurred in the bill. Logan, however, claimed he had intended to kill the bill in question, as he believed laborers of Chinese descent then living in Oregon were an "intelligent and virtuous class of citizens," and other legislators who shared this opinion would strike such a bill down.[88] Logan further argued that if immigrants were "enterprising, industrious and rich people, let us, then, instead of preventing, invite their capitalists to come here; let us place no barrier to their free ingress—but let us rather let them come and populate our valleys, and level down our mountain side." Like many Anti-Democrats in Oregon, however, Logan did not necessarily support Black Americans' being in Oregon; rather, he insisted that the passage of this law would remain a "dead letter on our statute books," as he did not believe that the small population of Black Americans who might migrate to Oregon warranted a law prohibiting their presence.[89]

Representative J. F. Gazely also supported the presence of Chinese laborers in Oregon, at least initially. Upon being accused that he was favorable to Chinese immigrants in general, Gazely quickly amended his statements to include that the individuals of Chinese descent in Oregon were "the lower classes of that nation."[90] As addressed in later chapters, some Oregon laws did specifically exclude individuals of Chinese descent, such as in land laws and in voting restrictions. As laborers in Oregon were still in demand during the 1850s, however, nonwhite laborers continued to find support among community leaders.[91] In other words, although Oregon politicians continuously connected Black American labor to slavery, other nonwhite groups in Oregon were not associated with slavery and therefore not included in the immigration restriction laws.

Most Oregon lawmakers recognized the need for laborers in their territory, prompting representatives such as Delazon Smith to focus on this necessity. Smith argued that Black Americans were not only needed laborers in Oregon but also "made better servants than white people."[92] Smith implored his colleagues that the need for Black American labor was great, as there was "no class so destitute of 'help,' as the Yankees call it, as the wives and mothers of Oregon." As many proslavery politicians in Oregon conveyed earlier in the territorial government and went on to negotiate during the Constitutional Convention, Smith recognized that the law restricting Black Americans from coming to or settling in Oregon would effectively shut the door on future options for slave labor. Likewise, Robert Ladd of Umpqua proposed to amend the bill preventing "negroes and mulattoes from coming to or residing in Oregon" by exempting enslaved Black Americans. It was Ladd's intention to ensure that the law did "not affect persons coming here with their slaves."[93] His argument demonstrated how some Oregonians were opposed to free Black American laborers but not necessarily the presence of enslaved Black Americans. The combination of arguments for and against the immigration restriction used race or racial institutions to make their case, effectively racializing the ability to have rights in Oregon. As the 1860s approached and national tension over the issue of slavery increased, Smith, Ladd, and others took greater precaution when discussing the matter.

When Oregon delegates gathered for the Constitutional Convention in 1857, they decided not to draft a provision on slavery. Rather, as noted above, they had the people of Oregon decide on it as a separate initiative when the constitution itself came up for a vote. The debate on slavery in Oregon was not over; rather, the delegates agreed they would not directly deliberate on whether Oregon would permit or prohibit slavery as a state. And although this would also become a separate vote, delegates debated at length on whether Black Americans would be permitted in Oregon. These debates then provided Oregonians with an avenue with which to discuss slavery and slave labor. Oregon legislators and local newspapers, therefore, intentionally interjected their opinions on slavery into their discussions of the immigration restriction law both throughout the convention and leading up to the people's vote on the state constitution. From the beginning of the convention, Oregon politicians hijacked the debate over the restriction of Black Americans and continued to associate Black American labor with slavery, thus further racializing Black Americans' labor and entwining their presence with the institution of slavery.[94]

Section 35 of Article 1 in the Oregon State Constitution of 1857 states, "No free negro or mulatto, not residing in this state at the time of the adoption of this constitution, shall come, reside or be within this state."[95] Initially the provision provided no language indicating whether this applied to free or enslaved Black Americans.[96] Some proslavery delegates seized the opportunity to vote the exclusion down, thus potentially allowing slaveowners to bring slaves into Oregon. Oregon legislators such as Delazon Smith argued that "he was opposed to the bill because it prohibited all n—s bond as well as free from coming here."[97] Other Democrats, such as Asahel Bush, announced their intentions to vote down a free-state constitution if Oregon did not accept the immigration restriction, as they did not want any Black Americans in their state if slavery were not allowed.[98]

The support for slavery in Oregon complicated these debates on many levels. Even if delegates did not endorse using slave labor in the region at that given time, some wanted to retain that option for the future. Delegate Asa Lawrence Lovejoy, for example, did not believe that Oregon was geographically positioned to accommodate the successful implementation of slave labor given its climate and proximity to "British Possessions on the north, the Indians on the east, and free State on the south."[99] He declared that he would not argue for slavery in Oregon but objected to the distinction between free and enslaved Black Americans in the provision. Lovejoy insisted "that a negro is not a 'negro' in the sense the word is used in this bill . . . [he] is not a 'person,' but in every respect a chattel . . . [that] the master can take anywhere he may choose, in any of the Territories, provided that there has been no legislative enactment prohibiting slavery." Lovejoy equated slavery with Black Americans and understood this exclusion as restricting present and future slave labor. Moreover, he rejected the idea that a Black American in Oregon was "an independent being" or could be identified as something different than "chattel."[100] Lovejoy identified all Black Americans laborers as slave labor.

By affixing labor to a race, Oregon delegates were also able to connect these discussions about slavery with established concerns about the intersection of labor, class, and race. During the Antebellum era definitions of labor focused on one's ownership of their labor. People who ran farms or companies controlled their own labor and managed the labor of their employees. Employees, however, still owned their own time, because the person they worked for had to compensate employees for their time. Slave labor eliminated the employee in this equation, because enslaved individuals did not own their time; therefore, they did not own their labor.[101] Once slave labor had become equated with Black American labor, white American laborers began interpreting the connections between themselves and Black American laborers—regardless of their slave status—as an insinuation that white labor was enslaved. To avoid such insinuations, working-class men encouraged the racialization of labor, because it allowed them to socially position themselves above Black men of the same socioeconomic background.[102] Mid-nineteenth-century labor, therefore, took on racialized elements that also conveyed a lower, degraded class.

At the national level, some federal representatives questioned the value of labor performed by Black Americans in the Pacific Northwest. Senator John Adams Dix of New York argued, although he conceded that slave labor could be productive for a short period of time anywhere in which the institution was carried, that Black American labor was fundamentally less effective than white American labor. Dix identified the fact that Black Americans were a group with restricted rights and limited connections to governing bodies as a reason why he believed Black American labor was less beneficial to a state. As a degraded group of laborers, this argument maintained, Black Americans threatened to degrade labor itself.[103] Senator Daniel Webster of Massachusetts echoed these sentiments and explained that his opposition to slave labor was "that it put free white labor in dispute; that it makes labor to be regarded as derogatory to the character of the free white man, and that the free white man despises to work . . . where slaves are employed."[104] Webster identifies the type of labor he is specifically critiquing to be slave labor, but his comparison of it to free white American labor does the same thing that Dix's argument did—it places the types of labor in racial opposition to each other. These federal representatives identified slave labor, a degraded form of labor, as something someone of the Black race does; free labor, the more respected form of labor, belonged to the white race.

Although many of these northern arguments on how slavery led to the degradation of labor appeared in the discussion of labor in Oregon, in the West, the southern argument that slaves in the South lived a better life than did the poor laborers of the North fell upon deaf ears. Proslavery southerners used this argument to battle the rising influence of abolitionists in the nation, who continued to reveal slavery as brutal and inhumane. Within the debates on labor in the West, however, this southern argument lacked an audience because it insulted the propriety of white farm labor.[105] The West and developing territories of the Midwest differed from the established Atlantic states in this way. Oregon wanted laborers, and it did not want to diminish the respectability of laboring white men. Even those who wanted Black Americans to come to Oregon to provide needed labor focused their arguments on how this specific group could fill "basic labor" needs, or jobs seen as menial.[106] Oregon legislators who argued for the presence of Black Americans, therefore, continually backed their opinions with the statement that the workers of such basic and less desirable jobs would not be in competition with white American laborers.

One of the main approaches Oregon delegates took during debates on the immigration restriction of Black Americans at the Constitutional Convention was to address the effect that slave labor would have on free labor in Oregon, including on a laborer's livelihood. In an editorial directed at young men of Oregon, the author warned that if Oregonians were to allow slave labor within their future state, free laborers would be "compelled to compete with slave labor" and "the price of labor would be cut down to a low figure, forbidding forever the hope of realizing either wealth or competence."[107] As with other examples in Oregon, the author equated Black American labor with slave labor, thus not only arguing against slavery but also depicting the labor of Black Americans as inferior to white labor.[108] Furthermore, the author argued that the class structures found in the South would accompany slave labor, ensuring that members of the laboring working class "are poor and kept under, while the other [slaveowners] are free, independent, and prosperous."[109] In other words, slave labor would degrade free laborers to a lower class and elevate those owning the slaves.

Continuing the argument that slave labor in Oregon would create a new class structure, another editorial added that only a small portion of white Oregonians would be able to "purchase negro stock," thus "enabling him who owns the colored stock to live at his ease, and perhaps to look down with scorn upon those who chance to be in poorer circumstances than himself."[110] The very presence of slave labor, the author believed, would not only reduce the respectability of white laborers by creating a class of nonlaborers above them but also place white laborers alongside of Black laborers, thus challenging the white settlers' racial claims to rights in Oregon. Delegate Leander Holmes echoed this argument within the halls of the convention, stating that "the poor, honest white man's labor should be made disreputable that his occupation should be disgraced, that all who by the sweat of their brow eat the fruit of their tool, should be placed side by side and equally yoked with the black serfs of Africa."[111] Holmes maintained that Black labor, regardless of its conditions of servitude, would reduce white laborers to the standing of those enslaved.

Attacking the position of Asahel Bush—editor of the *Oregon Statesman* and general spokesman for the Oregon Democrats—the *Oregonian* editor Thomas Dryer insinuated that Bush's support of slavery and the immigration restriction of free Black Americans revealed the Democrats' desire to degrade white labor in Oregon and place themselves as slaveowners above working-class Oregonians. Dryer asked his readers, "Are the free white laborers of Oregon ready and willing to sell themselves into a bondage worse than that of a Russian serfdom?"[112] Although Dryer compared free labor to being a serf in Russia, he distinguished his audience as "free" and "white" to address the negative effect that slave labor would have on the propriety of labor in Oregon. If slave

2. Thomas Dryer, neg. no. 341, Oregon Historical Society Research Library.

labor were to take hold in Oregon, whether through a vote for slavery or against the immigration restriction, white laborers would suffer a fall within the social hierarchy and be equated with Black laborers. The issue of slavery deeply impacted Oregon's debates on the immigration restriction of Black Americans, and it continued to racialize labor and challenge the racial construction of class.

Despite these labor arguments, supporters of slavery still existed in the region as Oregon moved toward its statehood application. Amid the Constitutional Convention, an article from the *Occidental Messenger* expressed the concern that excluding Black Americans from coming to Oregon would prohibit any future existence of slavery in the state.[113] Unlike earlier arguments along these lines, however, this article focused on how this immigration restriction would prevent the migration of white southerners, as they would be unable to bring their slaves with them.[114] This argument rested, it would seem, on the assumption that following statehood Oregonians would allow slavery to continue regardless of its free-state status. Perhaps unsurprisingly, this assumption did find support in the territorial government. As early as December 1857, Oregon legislators operating under a territorial government began laying a legal foundation to "protect the rights of persons holding slaves in this Territory."[115] In a manner of speaking, these legislators wanted to create a loophole for slavery in Oregon—which was possible. The free state of California passed a law in 1850 protecting the property of slaveowners in cases where the slaves had existed in California prior to its statehood.[116] Just in case, some Oregon lawmakers tried to ensure that slave property would be protected under territorial law before Oregon became a state.

To further protect the possibility of slavery existing in the free state, the constitutional provision prohibiting Black Americans from coming to the state ultimately specified that Oregon would exclude "free" Black Americans. The inclusion of the word "free" provided Oregonians with the opportunity to, technically, bring in and have enslaved Black Americans in Oregon. Again, while voters decided to prohibit slavery, Oregon lawmakers continued to seek legal protection for possessing existing or new slaves in the region. Proposed bills for the protection of slave property, for example, were presented to the territorial assembly all the way up to Oregon's admittance as a state. Ultimately, Oregon never passed legislation to protect slave property.[117] But this embattled discussion over slavery and the labor of Black Americans in Oregon demonstrated Oregonians' overall objection to the presence of Black Americans (free or enslaved) in their future state and willingness to construct a legal racial barrier to ensure the region remained in the control of white Oregon settlers.

Even with a Democratic majority, the objection to the presence of Black Americans as a group won out. The *Oregon Statesman* provided further evidence of this sentiment by proclaiming, immediately after Oregonians had approved their constitution, "Oregon is a land for the white man and refusing the toleration of negroes in our midst as slaves, we rightly and for yet stronger reason, prohibit them from coming among us a free negro."[118] Thus, passing their state constitution, Oregonians voted to prohibit both slavery and Black Americans from coming to or settling in their state. Congressional debate over Oregon's statehood addressed not only these constitutional provisions and their connection to slavery but also how they conflicted with federal or other states' laws.

By 1859 states such as Massachusetts and New York extended certain rights to Black American residents that were not recognized in other states. Moreover, some states prohibited free Black Americans from their borders.[119] Oregon, however, was the first one to apply for statehood with a constitution that explicitly restricted a group (recognized as citizens in another state) from entrance into its state.[120] This meant that Oregon's constitutional exclusion of free Black Americans provided Congress with the opportunity to debate this type of state restriction toward a class of citizens. Engaging with this discussion, Congressman Charles B. Hoard of New York argued that "the free negroes and mulattoes of the United States are not trespassers upon the soil of the country, to be hunted down and driven from it as wrongdoers." Imploring his colleagues to consider what Oregon's exclusion of Black Americans could mean, Hoard asked, "Can we deny them a home and all the rights of humanity in the land of their birth? . . . If free negroes and mulattoes are to be hunted down like demons in the free States, and driven from their borders like lepers, what else are we doing but driving them into slavery."[121]

As chapter 4 discusses, the Oregon constitution additionally excluded Black Americans from the right to own property or to hold a legal suit in Oregon. Congressman Hoard addressed these restrictions to Black Americans in Oregon, but he also connected the state's immigration restriction to slavery.[122] Not shying from the issue, Hoard declared, "I have been told that the section against free negroes in the Oregon constitution was placed there by free-State men to prevent the adoption of a slave constitution." Hoard suggested that "if it is necessary, anywhere in the United States, to indorse and adopt such monstrous and revolting doctrines as this section contains, to get rid of slavery, I think it is high time that we should abandon all further opposition to that institution." Although Hoard was not a supporter of slavery, he attempted to elevate his disdain for Oregon's immigration restriction by noting, "I do not believe that there can be found, in all the constitutions of the slave States combined, so much inhumanity and rank injustice as this single section of the Oregon constitution contains."[123] Hoard maintained that Oregon's immigration restriction provision, which stripped Black Americans of their rights, offered a fate worse than enslavement. Building on his objections to Oregon's provision, Hoard also argued for a nationwide abolition of slavery to prevent free states from enacting such a law. Whether this was a clever way to introduce a debate on the abolition of slavery or whether Hoard sincerely believed that Oregon's prohibiting Black Americans from coming to or settling in its region was worse than slavery is hard to tell.

Hoard's connection of the severity of slavery to Oregon's exclusionary laws, however, also brings to light the important issue of citizenship, as he further stated, "I protest against the right of any State to deny any free-born American, who is guilty of no crime, the right to be, that is the right to exist, in the land of his birth."[124] Similar to the debates in Oregon, this argument on the floor of Congress equated the provision preventing free Black Americans from entering Oregon with slavery. But unlike the Oregonians, at the national level this comparison was also used by antislavery politicians to demonstrate how Oregon was not just restricting a group from migrating to Oregon but also denying Black Americans rights as citizens.[125]

The Oregon state constitution's more liberal policies toward naturalization, which are addressed in chapter 6, aroused concerns from northeastern representatives who took issue with the extension of rights to white foreign men despite the granting of limited rights to natural-born Black Americans. One Boston newspaper cited the "political inconsistency" with Oregon's laws, stating that Black Americans were "deprived of almost all civil rights."[126] A Wisconsin newspaper listed the number of representatives who had pledged to vote against Oregon statehood "principally on the ground of the free negro clause in the Constitution."[127] This group of representatives highlighted Oregon's exclusion of Americans based on that group's race. They focused not on the issue of slavery but rather on the contradictions between Oregon's laws and the U.S. Constitution. Yet, despite objections to the constitutionality of Oregon's exclusion of Black Americans from coming to or settling in the region, Congress admitted Oregon as a state in 1859.

Oregon's debate over the immigration restriction of Black Americans and its connections to slavery reified its regional definitions of labor, class, and individual rights. Oregon's admission into statehood then institutionalized those definitions and challenged national perceptions of citizenship. Again, Oregon's application to statehood was the first time Congress was able to discuss a possible state constitution that directly excluded a group of Americans from coming to or living in a state. Such opportunities would become more common in the latter half of the nineteenth century, but Congressional approval of Oregon's prohibiting the presence of Black Americans in the state served as a precedent for later race-based exclusionary legislation.

Constructing Gender through Slavery and Immigration Restrictions

As with most national discussions by the 1840s, debates over slavery in Oregon were never far removed from discussions about abolition, race, or citizenship. To combat their opponents, advocates of slavery would associate abolitionists with being radical, dangerous to the preservation of the Union, and irrational. In the process of radicalizing abolitionists, proslavery politicians associated any politician who did not support the institution of slavery with abolitionism regardless of whether that person identified as an abolitionist. In several ways, the term "abolitionist" became a derogatory epithet, which proslavery politicians used to discredit their opponents.[128] The following section demonstrates how Oregon Democrats used and furthered the political radicalization of abolitionism to emasculate male Anti-Democrats and delegitimize women's participation in politics during debates over the exclusion of Black Americans from Oregon. Examining the process in which politicians used racial and gendered terms while constructing legislation not only reveals how those laws became defined by gender but also demonstrates how these specific terms and arguments reified social perceptions of gender—including perceptions on which groups should have access to political authority.

Gendered epithets found their way into Oregonians' discussions about the immigration restriction of Black Americans and slavery from the onset of those issues in Oregon. Critical of the first law that prohibited Black Americans from coming to Oregon, John Minto insinuated that Peter Burnett, his colleague and an initiator of the legislation, had "represented the just fears of girlhood and womanhood of slaves fleeing for life and liberty" in supporting such a law.[129] Minto associated Burnett's motivation for the law with a female response to fear but noted the common concern that free Black Americans could encourage a slave revolt against their masters. Whether such a connection made sense was irrelevant, because Minto employed this language to insult Burnett by associating him with a fearful woman or girl. Minto attempted to emasculate his political opponent and call the validity of Burnett's legislation into question.

Oregon lawmakers were not alone in the usage of gendered epithets to debate their laws on slavery and immigration restrictions. During the Oregon Bill in 1848, Senator John Milton Niles of Connecticut scolded his colleagues for allowing Oregon to bring its provisional laws on slavery into a territorial government. Niles argued that Congress had intentionally avoided giving a definitive answer to the extent of congressional power over territories because this allowed Oregon to change its policies, meaning Oregon could eventually apply for statehood as a slave state. Niles accused his fellow senators for being "unmanly" by not addressing the issue at hand; rather, they were "shrinking from the duty which [Niles believed] we owe to our country."[130] Niles attempted to emasculate his colleagues for not settling the slavery question in Oregon or in other territories. Overall, the usage of gendered epithets in debates over these Oregon laws reveals an abundance of male politicians' attempts to feminize their opponents to challenge the latter's credibility and their right to participate in politics.

The use of gendered epithets in political discourse reaffirmed the idea that manhood and womanhood were the opposite of each other. In the mid-nineteenth century, men were considered a group that could (potentially) be politically enfranchised, but women were viewed as a group that lacked political authority. Therefore, to insinuate that a man possessed female attributes was to connect a male politician to a group with limited, if any, political enfranchisement. The lack of public authority associated with womanhood made any association with women an insult for male politicians. And when womanhood became a political epithet, this further enforced the exclusion of women from U.S. politics and political authority.[131]

Moreover, the increased political involvement of disenfranchised groups such as women and Black Americans by the 1840s put pressure on the group then controlling the nation's political structures—white men. In fact, social and political organizations (separate from partisan groups) of white men during the Antebellum era intentionally excluded women in their public reports in order to restrict women's association with these groups and to diminish women's access to the public sphere.[132] Gendered epithets, therefore, became a way for white American men to redefine the boundaries of political rights and to keep those currently disfranchised but seeking rights at bay.[133]

The cultural perception of gender roles in the mid-nineteenth century cast women as the enforcers of good behavior and preservers of men's morality. However, once a woman stepped into the public realm—which included politics—she had to carefully negotiate her role as a woman. In some ways, women had to accept nonpolitical identities even if they were active within specific partisan groups. Women could safely engage in politics so long as they remained within the acceptable and conservative realm of female partisan activities, such as hosting benefits or picnics, appearing at rallies dressed in their Sunday best, or creating anthems for a specific candidate. Participation in radical groups, such as the abolitionists, became associated with fanatical actions deemed inappropriate for respectable women.[134] Therefore, calling a woman a fanatic or a similar radicalized term was to insult her womanhood.

Nevertheless, women's involvement in partisan politics, especially through movements such as abolition, had gained significant ground by the time Oregon became a U.S. territory. Many arguments made by women about abolition were also connected to issues of gender equality, which ultimately laid the foundation for the women's rights movement in the late nineteenth century. Yet, as women's influence in the abolitionist movement grew, derogatory gendered language from proslavery groups and politicians also increased, and abolition groups became associated with being both radical and feminine.[135] Through the development of this political discourse, women's presence in politics became necessary for and used in the development of these gendered political epithets.

Associating a male politician or community leader with being an abolitionist or a fanatic (many times the two were not presented as mutually exclusive) became a way to both radicalize and feminize one's opponent. In fact, calling someone a fanatic became a more subtle way to form connections between womanhood and abolition or antislavery sentiment. Senator Niles of Connecticut, again voicing his frustration during the Oregon Bill debates, asserted that the proslavery contingency had successfully painted its opponents as radicals, stating, "They are called fanatics—Abolition fanatics! . . . I have known cases in which the cry of the 'mad dog' has led to the rejection of men in these halls who did not really belong to that proscribed class." Niles further insisted that if accused of being abolitionist, "No[t] one of them can receive office under this Government, any more than though he had been convicted of treason against it!"[136]

Because fanaticism had become equated with being impulsive and irrational, among other meanings, politicians who called other politicians fanatics implied that the latter could not control their emotions. Gendered perspectives of the time inequitably separated character traits and behaviors between the sexes, assigning the quality of "rationality" to men and therefore the opposite—irrationality and emotionalism—to women. If a politician charged his opponent with being a fanatic, the accusation also contained a gendered component that insinuated his opponent had conducted himself irrationally, like a woman. Again, because women lacked the political authority granted to men, suggesting that a male politician possessed female traits not only challenged his manhood but also threatened his authority within the public sphere.[137]

Whenever politicians (namely Republicans) attempted to turn this radicalization of antislavery sentiment against those who used it, they faced formidable opposition from Democratic politicians, who had been perfecting their language in defense of slavery since the national rise of abolition. For example, Senator John Parker Hall of New Hampshire, dissatisfied with the discussion of slavery in Oregon, asked his colleagues in 1850, "Does this disturbance come from firebrand Abolitionist[s]? Not at all sir. It comes from this very sensitive quarter of the Union so prone to cast reproaches against everybody who introduced this subjection of abolition, as they are pleased to call it, and who, the moment it is withdrawn, bring it in themselves!" Upon Hall's insinuating that proslavery politicians were perhaps the emotional group in this equation instead of the supposed abolitionists, Senator Henry S. Foote of Mississippi quickly jumped to the South's defense. Foote's exclamation delivered a stream of insults so vile that the Senate's reporter did not record all of Foote's speech; rather, the reporter transcribed a few phrases, noting where he had chosen to leave gaps, and finally stated that Foote had spoken forth "in the most unmeasured terms of abuse."[138] In spite of these seldom attempts by Whigs and eventually Republicans to turn the radical and gendered epithets of abolition or fanaticism against the Democrats, these epithets remained an effective tool for proslavery politicians to besmirch their opponents up to the Civil War.

By the 1850s the heightened tension surrounding slavery in Oregon was evidenced by the fact that even some Democrats had become wary of political opponents accusing them of being abolitionists. Proslavery politician and Oregon judge Matthew Deady informed his friend Asahel Bush, editor of the *Oregon Statesman*, that a rumor was circulating around the territory suggesting that Bush was secretly an abolitionist.[139] Such an accusation would not only have significantly damaged Bush's reputation as a prominent Democrat with significant pull in his party but also lessened his credibility as a male politician. Bush, however, was a general target of Anti-Democrats in Oregon, who consistently associated him with the institution of slavery. Likely unbeknown to Bush's opponents, their discussions and articles about Bush's supporting slavery prohibited any such rumor about him being an abolitionist from taking root.[140]

The connection to abolitionism found its way, not surprisingly, into the discussion about the immigration restriction of Black Americans as well. Questioning why the debate had become such a controversial issue, Democrat Delazon Smith opposed the immigration restriction of Black Americans but laid the blame for why this bill had created divisions within Oregon politics at the feet of abolitionists; he noted, "This subject by which, by agitating it, merely enables fanatics and fools to blaze away at the Legislature." Smith continued that he himself "was not an abolitionist. . . . He did not countenance fanaticism and fools; nor [would] he go about hammering chains."[141] Smith attempted to paint groups opposed to slavery, or even the presence of Black Americans, as being unfounded and irrational with the sole intention of creating problems. This sort of accusation was another way to both radicalize and emasculate supporters of the exclusion.

National coverage of Oregon politics that used epithets involving radicalism and gender went neither unnoticed nor ignored by Oregonians. Reprinting an article from the *New York Tribune*, the *Oregon Statesman* referred to the New York newspaper as a "fanatic abolition sheet" and suggested that both this paper and the *Washington City Era* were "suffering" from a "sore perplexity" over the issue of slavery in Oregon.[142] Both East Coast newspapers cited took the position that Oregon would apply for statehood with a constitution that allowed for slavery (and perhaps excluded free Black Americans) due to the strong influence of proslavery politicians in the region. Slavery and the presence of Black Americans was most certainly a prevalent issue in Oregon at the time. Although these newspaper articles did not overemphasize this fact, coverage such as the fake report on a violent riot during the Oregon Constitutional Convention provided Democrats with the ammunition to dismiss this growing national discussion of slavery in Oregon as unfounded and tied to abolition.[143]

The *Oregon Statesman* also questioned the actual influence abolitionists would have on Oregon's application for statehood. For example, one editorial noted that the "'Bleeding Kansas' agitation is too rich a lead and promise too favorable a result for the black hypocrites to abandon it."[144] The author further accused non-Democrats of irrationally stirring up issues about slavery ahead of Oregon's statehood. Attempting to radicalize opponents of the Democratic Party, the editorial not only associated Anti-Democrats with having emotional reactions that led to their making irrational decisions—neither of which were perceived as masculine traits—but also identified this group as Black.[145] Effectively, this editorial doubled down on its attack on Anti-Democrats by connecting them to multiple characteristics and groups perceived as different from enfranchised Americans.

During Oregonians' debates over the immigration restriction of Black Americans there were more obvious ways to associate a politician with a specific gender, such as insinuating that a man who participated in a (supposedly) female-dominated movement was less of a man as a result. As women's participation in abolition and temperance movements increased, so too did the association of those organizations with women. These associations did not necessarily hurt the organizations themselves; the *Oregon Argus* newspaper still provided considerable space in its paper to record both temperance and abolition meeting minutes, many of which included female members.[146] Nevertheless, opposition to abolition was strong in Oregon, and Democratic politicians routinely used the presence of women in the abolition movement to challenge male participants' political authority. In addition to accusing someone of radicalism, when a male politician called another male an abolitionist, the accuser was also insinuating that the abolitionist practiced politics with women—a nonpolitical group. Because women, as a disenfranchised group, were not seen as holding political authority, the validity and public nature of their organizations' activities was questioned. This gendered insult became more direct when the accusers identified the supposed abolitionist as also being a woman, further defining "female" as a political epithet.

For example, a meeting by Congregational and Presbyterian ministers in Salem to discuss the issue of slavery and the Kansas-Nebraska Act of 1854 was identified by the *Oregon Statesman* as a "'weak lot of sisters' as were ever congregated." Further suggesting that the ministers had no business involving themselves in politics, the author continued, "In the old States can always be found a class of young men, (it is sometimes hard to determine which sex they are of,) who conceive that they can be useful at the pulpit, and without the self-respect, spirit, or manhood to help themselves, they get some old or young ladies sewing society to pass them through college, and, in the course of time, they come out 'ministers,' with about as much capacity to preach as have the zealous old dames who contribute their picayunes to 'educate' them."[147] The author suggested not only that the ministers were dependent on female groups for receiving an education necessary for their chosen profession but also that they lacked the manliness necessary to carry out a lifestyle or occupation that would validate their manhood. The author, therefore, simultaneously acknowledged the necessity of women in assisting a young man to become a minister and denounced the minister's manhood due to that association. The article, then, not only called the ministers "young ladies" but also supported the idea that women should not have access to political discussions. Speculating on why these questionably male ministers thought they could discuss politics was an attempt to associate those men with women, whom the author of the article had removed from the realm of politics and cast in opposition to political enfranchisement.

Taking gendered epithets in political debates one step further, Oregon politicians as well as white males across the nation insinuated or directly referred to their opponents as "old women" or "grannies." Within antebellum politics, one of the earliest uses of gendered epithets that implied a man was an aged woman appeared in the *Maryland Gazette and Political Intelligencer* in 1820. Here the author, angry about the cost of holding Congress and its inability to pass bills, entitled his article "Notes to Granny Gray."[148] The article contained a perplexing list of costs and bills waiting for congressional approval but associated congressmen and their inability to make decisions with their being old women. Twelve years later, a Vermont newspaper attacked the male editor of a competing paper, referring to an article the opponent had written about a Whig convention as the work of "Granny Walton."[149] Although the Vermont author may not have purposely associated a report on Whigs with the insinuation that its editor was a "granny," starting in 1836 the Whigs became the focus of such gendered epithets in connection with General William Henry Harrison's presidential campaign.

During Harrison's run for the U.S. presidency in 1840 the Democrats and supporters of incumbent President Martin Van Buren latched on to a story from Harrison's military history in the War of 1812. The story connected Harrison to the act of wearing a petticoat in an attempt to pass as a woman and escape from American Indians who were attempting to take Fort Meigs. According to Whig supporters of Harrison, the story derived from a remark made by Harrison about what he would have done if the war had forced them to surrender the fort. When informed that a group of American Indians intended to seize him upon the surrender, Harrison, out of frustration with British general Henry Proctor, had supposedly replied, "Then the General Proctor can be neither a soldier nor a man. But if it shall ever be his fate to surrender to me, his life shall be protected, but I will dress him in a petticoat, and deliver him over to the squaws, as being unworthy to associate with men."[150] Citing this report, which was also loaded with gendered meanings, Harrison supporters insisted that the gendered slur that Democrats employed had actually originated from Harrison's insinuating that another man was a woman. Nevertheless, Democrats spun the story to imply that Harrison had either voluntarily donned a petticoat in anticipation of surrendering the Fort or that he was told that he would be dressed as a woman upon his surrender. This story evolved into one identifying Harrison as "Granny Harrison."[151]

Whigs attempted to embrace the gendered epithet of "old granny," which Democratic papers printed in large quantities, by arguing that an older, wiser man was better than the inexperienced youth "whose beard had not sprouted at the time of the last war" who attacked him.[152] They also ran articles that overused the word "granny" in an attempt to demonstrate its ridiculousness and defend Harrison.[153] As the election of 1840 approached Democrats did not hold back from equating the Whig candidate with being a granny, even dropping his name and purely referring to Harrison as "Granny."[154] Harrison's supporters witnessed the results of their hard work with his presidential victory, but they also continued to read about "Granny Harrison" until his death shortly after taking office.

Historians have generally attributed the usage of "granny" against William Henry Harrison to his older age when running for president. Harrison's association with older age likely found inspiration from the growing younger wing of the Democratic party, whose members not only viewed themselves as the preservers of Jefferson's America but also those capable of rebuilding their party. Identifying themselves as the "Young Americans" by the 1840s, this wing of the Democrats associated age with antiquated European principles, a conservatism that did not support reform or aggressive western expansion, as well as mindsets that were easily corruptible and therefore illogical.[155] Harrison's association with being an old woman came before the emergence of this group but not before the age-centered ideas behind it. By the 1820s both Whigs and Democrats had used rhetoric to support the younger members of their party given the growing absence of the Founding Fathers, who were by then dying off. Whigs, in fact, championed the argument that it was the youth's responsibility to salvage the nation and its constitution from the prevailing arrogance that controlled the federal government.[156] Originating as a shot at the Democrats' control over the presidency, this language was adaptable, and by the 1840s election it was available to whatever cause found it useful. Moreover, as historian Yonotan Eyal has pointed out, Democrats throughout the nation appropriated the Young American movement for their own specific purpose.[157]

Within national politics, the usage of "granny" to invalidate one's political opponents significantly decreased after the 1840 presidential election, especially after the death of President Harrison. By 1844 most gendered epithets had also lost their traction due to the growing acceptance of women's participation (at least within gender-specific capabilities that did not challenge social roles) in partisan politics by both the Whigs and the Democrats.[158] Scholars also point toward the weakening of the Second Party System in the late 1840s and into the early 1850s as another reason why gendered slurs had become more uncommon, as the presence of three parties complicated the delivery of such gendered insinuations.[159]

In Oregon, however, the use of gender- and age-based epithets continued throughout the 1850s and into the Civil War. Part of this may have stemmed from the fact that while Oregon had multiple partisan groups, the Democrats possessed such a majority that the rest of the political groups (referred to here as the Anti-Democrats) collectively opposed the Democrats, which created something similar to a two-party system in Oregon.[160] Another factor was the malleable nature of the Young American movement. Oregon Democrats appropriated the idea and language of the "Young Americans" to question those in opposition to slavery and legitimize their own arguments in the debate. This insinuation of a generational divide with gendered connotations took on a partisan identity, much in the way an age division emerged in the post-Reconstruction South and in the years leading up to the Spanish-American War.[161]

Moreover, the use of the term "granny" in Oregon politics during the 1850s in relation to the immigration restriction of Black Americans and the issue of slavery may correlate with the fact that politicians and community leaders had actively sidelined women's participation in Oregon politics. Evidence for this includes newspaper articles that noted women's participation in political meetings—regardless of whether women had been present—to invalidate the meetings and their groups' political platforms.[162] Again, using the presence of women in Oregon politics to emasculate men involved with them also discredited women as legitimate political participants (or as people with political authority).

Reporting on a meeting identified as a gathering of abolitionists in Albany, an *Oregon Statesman* article described the participants as "old grannies." Although it was quite possible that the meeting had been about abolition, the meeting's attendance list contained the names of men, and the author later noted that none of the "men" on the list were subscribers to their newspaper. The group had asked if the newspaper would print the minutes of its meeting, to which the author replied, "It is decidedly icy of these n—struck *dames* to ask the Statesman to public their stale fanaticism." Regardless of whether this group of men identified as abolitionists, the articles insinuated that these men were females infatuated with Black Americans and associated them with fanatical actions. The article continued, "they ask us to fill our column with a batch of Fred Douglasism, which the sensible men who patronize and sustain this paper don't wish to see."[163] Here the author places the actions of the group in opposition to those who subscribed to the newspaper, with subscribers being "sensible" and not wanting to read about meetings that the author had deemed nonsensical. This article leaves the group in question with very little information to identify them as white male politicians and community leaders. Rather, the author attempted to strip these men of their social and political authority by associating the group with several things that suggested just the opposite, according to contemporary gendered and racial perceptions.

By contrasting women with sensible or valid political participation, Oregon politicians further separated women from gaining social acceptance for not only their presence in politics but also their right to have a political voice. The insinuation that a man was an old woman expanded this exclusion of women from politics and associated older women with being socially as well as politically useless. Women's femininity held meaning, and their beauty was associated with femininity. An old woman, or granny, had presumably lost her youthful and beautiful face, thus part of her femininity. She had become, therefore, not even a pretty face spouting political rhetoric that partisan groups could use to gain the moral foundation that her feminine womanhood would have provided. The rise of the middle class redefined cultural understandings of women's position within the home, as the use of house servants for domestic chores and even childrearing became more acceptable. Finally, the transition between "natural fertility and parity specific fertility" after the American Revolution provided women with more control over when they had and stopped having children. Within this dynamic, an older woman with grown children and who was beyond her childbearing years had even less of a role within the household. In working-class homes, an elderly woman could become a financial burden, if not destitute and relegated to alms homes entirely.[164] Regardless of the actual reality of older women in antebellum society, the lowered perception of their usefulness provided politicians and political leaders with a counterimage to that of the effective male politician. Older women became the ultimate version of perceived uselessness within the political realm; therefore, the insinuation that a man was a granny could symbolically undermine both his credibility as a man and his being effectively competent at his duties.[165]

Newspaper battles between Anti-Democrat Thomas Dryer, the editor of the *Oregonian*, and Democrat Asahel Bush, editor of the *Oregon Statesman*, raged during the 1850s with a focus on age and gender epithets. Responding to Dryer's recent editorials on divisive partisan politics in the region, an *Oregon Statesman* article depicted him as "a garrulous granny whose brain is crazed by the presence of an idée which gives perpetual motion to her tongue." The writer, likely Bush, likened the *Oregonian* articles to Dryer's "rejoicing himself thereat somewhat after the manner a pullet cackies over her first egg, and then sets up a huge cry of danger, and begs the people not to wreck a ruin everything by organizing political parties."[166] The *Oregon Statesman* article associated Dryer with being a granny and insinuated that he was mentally enfeebled as well as incapable of formulating logical ideas about Oregon politics without becoming emotional in the process. In challenging the validity and rationality of Dryer's political arguments, the *Oregon Statesman* article supported the argument that women were irrational beings unfit for public discussions, thus demeaning their political presence and invalidating women as political participants.

Another example of this political discourse by the *Oregon Statesman* came from a report on an antislavery meeting, held by recognizable politicians, this time identified as "thirty-two other old ladies of both sexes!" The author, Democrat Delazon Smith, insisted that the group drew connections between local issues and slavery that unnecessarily agitated the people of Oregon. He further suggested that this specific group in question would like Oregonians to "abandon your present views, denounce the administration, the Union, the Constitution and the democratic party, and go over your soul, body, breeches, newspaper, types in all, to the one idea, abolition fusionites [*sic*]."[167] Smith connected this antislavery group with being "old ladies" and insinuated that not only were their members' actions problematic for Oregon and the preservation of the Union but also that they irrationally gave themselves over to these concepts. Again, this both challenged the authority of the group in question as political participants as well as damaged the social perception of women in politics and their role as political participants.

During the presidential election of 1856 between Democrat James Buchanan, Republican John C. Fremont, and Whig Millard Fillmore, the *Oregon Statesman* kept close tabs on the discussion of the election by other regional newspapers, particularly articles composed by Thomas Dryer of the *Oregonian*. Addressing Dryer's coverage of the election and support of Fremont, the writer suggested, "The Oregonian goes in boots and breeches, and suffers itself to become terribly alarmed for fear that Mr. Buchanan, if elected, will force slavery into Oregon. The old lady is so much exercised on that account that we suspect she lays awake nights."[168] The *Oregon Statesman* article would have needed only to insinuate that Dryer of the *Oregonian* had acted emotionally toward the presidential election and the issue of slavery to connect Dryer with perceived female characteristics of the time. Rather, the article associated Dryer and his ideas toward slavery with being an aged woman in an attempt to further invalidate Dryer's arguments in the *Oregonian*. In using older women as an epithet, the article also perpetuated the idea that women's involvement in politics was ineffective and invalid.

While Oregon applied for statehood, its U.S. neighbor to the south—California—began reflecting the tendencies of Oregon's political debates through its own usage of "granny" as an age and gender epithet. Again, national politics had employed gendered slurs that included the insinuation of a male politician's being an old woman, but Oregon carried this language throughout the 1850s, well past its popular usage along the Atlantic coast. The California newspaper the *Daily Evening Bulletin* adopted this gendered epithet to discredit a competing newspaper, the *Daily Alta California*, by referring to that newspaper or its editor as "Granny."[169] Although the connection between the newspaper's coverage and the insinuation that this was the work of a granny did not relate to either the issue of slavery or Oregon, the usage still reflected the language employed by Oregon Democrats. Because California had become a state nearly a decade before Oregon, the assumption within the historical narrative has been that California's policies and politics had influenced Oregon's. Californian reports on Oregon usually supported this idea. In fact, upon Oregon's passage of its state constitution, California newspapers identified Oregon as its beloved "younger sister," suggesting that Oregon had finally "overcome her maidenly coyness and timidity" and commending the people of Oregon for passing a law preventing the immigration of Black Americans to their future state.[170] Oregon's law and debates over the immigration restriction of Black Americans as well as slavery, however, predate California legislation. Those policies and, arguably, Oregon's debates and usage of age and gendered epithets, therefore, influenced California politics. California may have referred to Oregon as a young maiden, but its own gendered political discourse likely stemmed from Oregon politicians' long-standing arguments.

Why did Oregonians continue the usage of gendered epithets throughout the 1850s? In part, the tension surrounding the issue of slavery and laws that connected to it, such as the immigration restriction of Black Americans, gave Oregon Democrats a political atmosphere that allowed for such rhetorical weapons. Another contributing factor could be the fact that Oregon politics were quite exclusive, and white male politicians worked hard to disassociate nonwhite males and females from political agency. But an evaluation of other laws that specifically reference women requires further analysis, as the subsequent chapters do, to better understand the exclusion of women in Oregon politics during the 1850s. Nevertheless, women and perceived feminine traits were placed in opposition to political participation and manhood during debates on slavery and immigration restrictions. Women were consistently cast as the opposites of those with the political rights of U.S. citizens. Overall, in debates on slavery and immigration restriction Oregon politicians used women, negative portrayals of female characteristics, and age to invalidate their male opponents' arguments and perpetuate the social belief that women did not and should not possess political authority.

Legacy of Slavery and the Immigration Restriction

Shortly after Oregon had become a state the authority of the Democratic Party in the region began to wane, and like the national party, the group itself grew divided. As if predicting such an event, Massachusetts Congressman Eli Thayer urged his Republican colleagues during their debate over Oregon's statehood to accept Oregon as a free state regardless of its provisions, insisting that the region would surely transform from a Democratic majority to a Republican state. Thayer had been thoroughly chastised by northeastern representatives for his support of Oregon's statehood due to the immigration restriction of Black Americans. By September 1859 and Oregon's election of Republican David Logan to the House of Representatives, opinions toward Thayer had quickly changed.[171] The power dynamics between partisan groups in Oregon may have undergone a transformation with Oregon's admittance as a state, but its laws did not. In fact, not until 1926 did Oregon repeal the law that restricted Black Americans from coming to or settling in the state. This was fifty-eight years after the Fourteenth Amendment to the U.S. Constitution formally recognized Black Americans as citizens.[172] Oregon's tradition of restricting Black Americans from their rights as citizens remained with the state through the development of Jim Crow legislation, which further institutionalized race-based legal restrictions that Oregon had helped establish.

The restriction of Black Americans from coming to or settling in Oregon remained one of the more specific exclusions within the Oregon Constitution. And the continued legacy of this law can still be seen today in the proportionally low numbers of Black Americans who live in the state of Oregon.[173] And as other chapters discuss, this immigration restriction also influenced other Oregon laws that went on to impact exclusionary legislation of different forms and those in other states.[174]

By the 1870s, however, Oregonians' reflection on their earliest laws excluding Black Americans from the region had adopted a more critical position than had existed during the creation of that legislation. A comprehensive history of Oregon by settler William H. Gray asserted that the first law addressing the restriction of Black Americans from Oregon "was one inhumane act passed by this Legislative Committee, which should stamp the names of its supporters with disgrace and infamy."[175] Gray focused his discussion on the role played by Peter Burnett in constructing the law, noting that "Burnett's bill [referred to as the Lash Law] made it a crime for a white man to bring a negro to the country, and a crime for a negro to come voluntarily; so that in any case, if he were found in that country and he was guilty of a crime, and punishment and slavery was his doom."[176] Gray continued that "to the honor of the country" the law was never enforced. Although the full implementation of this law remains unknown, Oregon territorial records reveal that a small number of Black Americans (including Vanderpool) had been removed from the region under this law. If Oregon officials did carry out this law, it likely occurred prior to 1880, because after that the population of Black Americans in Oregon grew from approximately 487 to about 19,000 in 1900.[177] Nevertheless, Gray also failed to acknowledge that when he penned these reflections, the immigration restriction remained on the books and Black Americans still possessed no legal recourse in Oregon.[178]

In terms of slavery in Oregon, despite continued efforts to pass a law to protect slave property immediately before and following Oregon's statehood, legislators never legally allowed slavery to exist in the region. Unlike California, where such laws found enough support, Oregon's admittance as a state came on the eve of the Civil War, and support for the Union ultimately overwhelmed any desires for slavery that continued to exist.[179] Arguments linking race to labor, however, prevailed and were primarily related to Chinese immigrants or descendants of Chinese immigrants.

Within the Oregon Constitution, those identified as "chinamen" and not currently residing in Oregon were restricted from holding "any real estate or mining claim, or work any mining claim therein."[180] Although initially limited to the exclusion from owning a mining claim, as the century progressed those of Chinese descent who worked in the mines began to be taxed by Oregon, as its laws attempted to remove this group of laborers from the mining professions entirely.[181] In order to justify these laws, Oregon legislators and newspaper editorials began labeling the labor of Chinese descendants as degraded in comparison to labor by white Americans. This was similar to how they had identified the labor of Black Americans in the 1840s and 1850s. In addition to the descriptions of being "lazy" or a "nuisance" to progress, those of Chinese descent became targets during strained labor conditions with accusations that they, "as foreign people," drained Oregon of "its wealth" and took jobs from the "industrious white people."[182] These sentiments would eventually lead to further labor exclusions in Oregon and ultimately the federal Chinese Exclusion Act of 1882.[183] Although not commonly linked, the language used against the Chinese in post–Civil War America directly reflects Oregon's older arguments about Black Americans. Those of Chinese descent faced their own exclusive legislation, as later chapters address, but the similarities between the treatment of Black American labor and the labor of Chinese descendants demonstrate the racialization of labor in Oregon and its continued effectiveness in restricting groups from occupations as well as from living in Oregon.

The usage of gendered epithets within Oregon politics lessened after statehood, predominately because the language had been applied to accusations against supposed abolitionists. Abolitionists as a group, just like proslavery politicians, dissipated in Oregon once the Civil War had broken out and the region had taken the side of the Union. As a tool of rhetoric, however, gendered insults such as the term "granny" continued to find an audience throughout the nineteenth century. A Vermont newspaper article in 1860 depicted President James Buchanan as a "granny" who either struggled to hear the cry for popular sovereignty from the people or simply failed to recognize the meaning of popular sovereignty.[184] Divisions within the Republican Party also utilized age and gendered epithets to invalidate their opponents' arguments, with one Boston newspaper referring to the "Constitutional Union Party" as the "Granny-dears" incapable of restoring peace to their party.[185]

As mid-nineteenth-century Oregon politicians demonstrated, for a gendered epithet to effectively invalidate an opponent's opinion or actions, the gender being invoked needed to be perceived as opposite of that group which possessed political authority. While books can be written on how gendered epithets placing women in opposition to men were used throughout the twentieth century, this chapter brings to light the continued usage of this discourse in antebellum America. And although social and political perceptions of women have drastically changed in the country since the mid-nineteenth century, gendered epithets are still used within U.S. politics.[186]

In summary, Oregon laws and subsequent debates on slavery and the immigration restriction of Black Americans took on nuanced perceptions and legal definitions of citizenship, race, labor, and gender. Tensions surrounding issues related to slavery allowed a restriction of Black Americans' political rights to transition from the Oregon provisional government into territorial legislation and finally into the Oregon Constitution after additional discussions by Congress. During the 1840s and 1850s, Black Americans straddled the classifications of citizen and alien, as federal law did not explicitly recognize Black Americans as citizens and several federal court cases during that time backed state laws that denied Black Americans rights possessed by citizens.[187] Ultimately, laws restricting Black Americans from Oregon played a role in this evolving definition of citizenship and the institutionalization of race-based legislation.

CHAPTER 4

Incorporated Definitions of Land Ownership

Marriageable women (they are marriageable at 12 or 14) are rather scarce. It would be a fine thing for the country, and equally so for the ladies, to import Lowell or some other feminine burgh. They would draw better than the gold mines ever did, and give much better satisfaction.

—**Asahel Bush**, "Women and Taxes in Oregon," *Milwaukee Daily Sentinel*, March 28, 1851

On January 7, 1851, gunshots rang out near the town of Salem in the Oregon Territory. Witnesses say they watched as a riderless horse sprinted up Waldo's Hill by William Kendall's property, before they found William Hamilton (who leased the land) lying in the road some distance away, unconscious, bleeding, with pitted wounds in his chest. Hamilton died later that evening, and authorities arrested and tried Kendall for murder. Three months later, the courts found Kendall guilty of murdering Hamilton based on witness testimonies and a review of the coroner's report. Kendall's motive for the murder came down to a dispute over a land claim.[1]

After acquiring an Oregon land claim through the Donation Land Act, Kendall had moved to California in the summer of 1850 and leased his land to Hamilton for a period of two years. Leased land claims were not unheard of, and because federal and territorial governments were slow to issue patents, general disputes over land claims and property lines in the Oregon Territory were a common occurrence between 1850 and 1862.[2] Kendall later returned to his Oregon claim before the lease expired, but he and Hamilton had several disagreements on how to deal with the property now occupied by both men.

Neighboring landowners observed the men's dispute over the course of a few months, witnessing on at least two occasions Kendall threatening the "health" of Hamilton and his brother John.[3] During one such confrontation Hamilton remarked, "[You] think I am afraid of you?," with Kendall responding, "God damn you, you had better be for no man can live, that lives on that claim." Kendall also confided to neighbors his desperate need to regain the land from Hamilton and his growing frustration with Hamilton's unwillingness to break the lease. Kendall took Hamilton's inaction as an affront to his rights as the landowner. Hamilton's death and Kendall's murder convictions were the result of this challenge to property rights.[4] Both of these men participated in an early phase of white settlement in Oregon.

As the Hamilton and Kendall dispute illustrates, securing land was critical to the colonization of the West. Owning land in Oregon—even if only a provisional government independent from a sovereign nation could sanction such ownership—became an important indicator of a settler's social and political position in the colony. Property ownership laws and disputes accompanied expanding colonialism and directly impacted the formation of citizenship in the American West. Specifically, Oregonians restricted the right to own property or real estate in the region, one of the basic principles of natural rights for a U.S. citizen. The land laws established in the settler colony of Oregon then went on to influence territorial laws, the first federal land act in a territory, and the Oregon state constitution. This chapter addresses how Oregon land laws opened new avenues to land ownership while simultaneously reinforcing racial and gendered limitations for women, nonwhite immigrants, and "half breed" American Indians. It further demonstrates that Oregon's land laws impacted the federal relationship with western lands and engrained the issues of race, gender, and class into national discussions about property ownership and citizenship.

Settler Colonialism through Land Laws

A group of Oregon settlers, serving as the provisional government's first Legislative Committee, drafted and adopted various laws for the settler colony in the summer of 1843. Among these policies was the "Law of Land Claim," which intended to serve the settlements "until such time as the United States of America extends their jurisdiction over" Oregon.[5] Oregon settlers had been creating policies for themselves since 1841, at which time U.S. politicians such as Senator Lewis Linn of Missouri promoted land donations to people willing to emigrate to the Pacific Northwest, but claims over the region remained disputed between the United States and Great Britain.[6] The settler colony did not have formal treaties to validate land allotments to settlers, but Oregon lawmakers constructed guidelines for what they defined as a land claim as well as how to officially record, preserve, and maintain such claims.[7] This first provisional law also addressed the ownership of land in Oregon in a fairly inclusive fashion by allowing "any person now holding or hereafter wishing to establish a claim to land" to make such a claim.[8] Nonetheless, within a year the settlers felt compelled to revise their land law to include clear and exclusive specifications for sex, age, servitude, and marital status, thus limiting access to land ownership in Oregon.

The "Act in Relation to Land Claims" of 1844 identified a future landowner as being "male," "free," and over the age of eighteen.[9] Although some of the first wagon trains to migrate overland to Oregon carried with them a small number of enslaved individuals, the inclusion of the word "free" also served as a signifier of "white" in most cases.[10] In fact, many northeastern and western states amended laws in the mid- and late nineteenth century to include the word "white" where they had previously used "free" as an indicator that the law pertained to white individuals.[11] These amendments in the East were prompted by the growing number of free Black Americans prior to the Civil War, but after the abolition of slavery, the term "free" no longer drew a racial distinction as it had in the early nineteenth century. Oregon lawmakers' replacement of "free male" with "white" had occurred years before this became a growing trend in the United States, as well as before many states made this transition.[12] As with other examples of settler colonialism, Oregon laws reflected those constructed by the empire, whether laws by the United States or Great Britain. Oregon lawmakers also developed legislation, however, with little to no counterparts. Oregon's application of land laws was specific to the region, and it served as a component of settler colonialism for an awaiting empire.

The Oregon Treaty of 1846 put the region squarely under the sovereignty of the United States. The fact that Oregon settlers had been establishing a permanent occupation of the region aided its transition to a territory, because Oregon had a system of government in place with connections to the United States.[13] For example, while debating the Oregon Bill (the creation of the Oregon Territory) the U.S. Congress discussed connecting its bill to the creation of territorial governments for California and New Mexico. These other territories, however, did not necessarily share the same demographics as Oregon. While a growing number of U.S. and British immigrants were colonizing Oregon and establishing a government in likeness to U.S. structures, California had only more recently received permanent settlers from the United States. New Mexico, a new acquisition from another nation, had few U.S. settlers to speak of but a large contingency of American Indians.[14] Oregon certainly had a diverse population, but those who were constructing laws and communicating with the United States were white U.S. immigrants or European immigrants. Senators such as John M. Clayton of Delaware, therefore, believed Oregon to be more appropriately "entitled" to a self-run territorial government with its own delegate to the House of Representatives.[15] Oregon's presumed whiteness, however incorrect, privileged its transition to a territory.[16] Although the U.S. representatives overwhelmingly desired Oregon as a new territory, discussions about what Oregon had specifically provided to the nation by creating a government and colonizing the region would appear in later debates about the Donation Land Act for the Oregon Territory.[17]

The United States did not formally establish the territorial government in Oregon until March 1849, meaning that the provisional government remained active and continued to produce legislation for a time despite its still precarious authority over the inhabitants of the territory.[18] In February 1849 Oregon legislators adopted a resolution that restricted the provisional government from sanctioning the purchase of "wild lands" or establishing treaties with Indigenous communities for the purpose of acquiring their lands.[19] The resolution did not possess language to indicate the difference between the lands claimed by settlers and those designated as "wild lands," but the phrase suggests the provisional government recognized that not all lands in the region were the same and that limitations existed as to what lands settlers could technically claim under the land laws. Nevertheless, Oregon settlers had been granting themselves land according to their own policies for several years by this point and had even developed a provisional land office in 1845 to oversee claims made prior to the Oregon Treaty.[20]

Oregon settlers' access to lands within their territory was further challenged by claims made by the Hudson's Bay Company to areas it had occupied prior to and during the Oregon Treaty. In the treaty, the United States acknowledged that the British company had undefined "possessory rights" to lands that fell within the boundaries of the U.S. territory. In addition to requesting clarification on the rights of the Hudson's Bay Company to lands in Oregon, settlers took the position that the region had been decidedly "American" prior to the Treaty and, in some cases, rewrote the narrative of the settler colony's political formation to support this claim.[21] In one newspaper article, an Oregon author asserted that the U.S. and British settlers not only disagreed over the creation of a government but had developed separate structures altogether. The author failed to reconcile this with the influence and participation of British Canadians such as John McLoughlin in the formation of some of the settlers' first political meetings in the region.[22] Regardless of whether this oversight was intentional, what remained clear was Oregon settlers' determination to make land ownership in Oregon a restricted right.

Immediately following the Oregon Treaty, Oregon lawmakers passed an act in December 1849 "providing for the extinguishment of the Indian title to the lands in the settler portion of the country in Oregon."[23] American

Indians had actively engaged in and participated with the settlers during the early colonization of Oregon. Such participation allowed Indigenous communities the power to negotiate some early control of lands important to their groups and cultures. As the settler colony grew, American Indians adapted, but soon Oregon settlers wanted and forcibly took lands still occupied by Indigenous communities.[24] Oregon congressional delegate Samuel Thurston told Congress that without proper treaties with Indigenous communities the Oregon settlers were "comparatively trespassers upon the soil."[25] Thurston acknowledged the dispossession of American Indians from their lands in the region, but he also asserted that those actions were necessary to secure lands for Oregon settlers. By the end of the 1840s the settlers' land claims remained disputed at best or, as Thurston described, virtually nonexistent. Despite this complex web of legalities, the Oregon land laws in place were enforced by its settlers. A portion of these laws created by the settler colony would be absorbed by the empire in the territorial government, and they would retroactively find authority through the enactment of the Donation Land Act.[26]

Before Congress established the Donation Land Act, however, federal representatives had debated at length over the parameters of such a law and contemplated the implications of bestowing donations to one area over another. As mentioned above, one of the questions that arose during debates over the Donation Land Act was why Oregon settlers deserved such a generous land policy. Senator David Levy Yulee of Florida proposed to strike out the fifth section of the act, which granted future settlers in Oregon land donations, and asked his colleagues why Oregon was not placed upon the same footing as other territories or states in the encouragement of settlement: "Why turn the tide of emigrants to that Territory alone. . . . If you say it is desirable that the Pacific shore shall be populated, then why not give it to California?"[27] The state of California had swiftly moved past the stage of being a new territory and into eligibility for statehood, and it did not lack incentives for immigration. Oregon attracted settlers as well, but even southern Oregon's gold booms did not detract from the alluring draw California had over U.S. as well as foreign immigrants.[28]

Moreover, Oregon remained a potential ally to both sides of the growing partisan divide in U.S. politics. Although Oregon had entered as a territory that prohibited slavery, many of Oregon's political and social leaders were Democrats.[29] Oregon's future loyalty (i.e., congressional votes), therefore, remained within reach to both sides of the isle. Yet Oregon's sparse population, coupled with its location next to other empires (mainly Great Britain), meant that more Americans were needed to secure the region.[30] Senator Thomas Hart Benton of Missouri felt Oregon settlers had already assisted the United States in this capacity, insisting, "Its settlers [are those] who will improve and defend the country, and who in all time to come will furnish defenders not only for their own State, but for the service of the country." Benton further argued that Oregon settlers deserved large land donations because they had been responsible for the successful colonization of the region, asserting, "It was their occupancy which forced the decision of the question from which diplomatists and statesmen had been shrinking . . . the pioneers of the West went and took possession, and their taking possession forced the decision of the question upon the country." According to Benton, Oregon settlers had "conquered it from the savages" and then "conquered it from Great Britain . . . and they are entitled to the gain."[31] U.S. representatives such as Benton believed that Oregon was important to the future of the nation and its settlers were owed for the work they had done to provide for such a future. Land donations were a way to ensure the protection of the region and repay Oregon settlers for "their services."

The settler colony of Oregon may have enforced U.S.-like policies, but the territory had not experienced a direct legal connection with the federal government for most of its existence. Texas Senator Samuel Houston explained that although Oregon had been a "bone of contention" since his appointment to Congress, "Oregon has been for years without the benefit of any protection from the Government."[32] It was time, Houston believed, for Oregon to take a more central place within the perspectives of Congress. Not only did Oregon gain federal support for the continuous "pains" an infant government in the West experienced—especially regarding conflicts between itself and Indigenous communities—Oregon's position also allowed its existing laws to influence the application of a federal act.[33]

The U.S. Congress, at the continuous urging of Oregon representative Samuel Thurston, created the Donation Land Act in 1850 to ensure that lands in Oregon would become public domain, that white U.S. settlement would continue, and that requirements and allowances for land claims would be clarified. This act was the first federal land donation law, and it symbolized the merger of the federal government with western lands and with territorial laws. The Donation Land Act also granted authority to land claims previously issued by Oregon's provisional government. Finally, the adoption of inclusions for white settlers' Indigenous wives and their male children—as well as specific racial exclusions, discussed later in this chapter—came from established Oregon laws.[34] By allowing its land laws to work within a federal policy, Oregon influenced future interpretations on settlement and U.S. access to land in the rest of the empire.

The Donation Land Act ultimately opened Oregon up for large-scale settlement. Many settlers may have been in favor of the act and the additional land it would open for settlement, but not everyone felt further land acquisitions were necessary. One Oregon settler from Astoria expressed as much to a Cleveland, Ohio, newspaper and focused on the forced removal and relocation of Indigenous communities. The author believed that the new land ownership policy would attempt to remove several coastal groups to east of the Cascade Mountains, which would effectively be "equivalent to destroying them." Noting that Oregon was still sparsely populated, the author questioned if the removal of American Indians from lands was necessary.[35] Of course, this type of sentiment faced the more popular opinion and misconception in the United States that American Indians did not practice land ownership in a similar manner to white settlers. This counter-opinion maintained that the native inhabitants did not view land as important or vital to their existence, or at least not in comparison to Oregon settlers.[36] In reality, all parties attempting to live in Oregon held strong convictions toward land ownership. In some cases, those feelings led to altercations, even between settler colonists—as was the case in the 1851 murder of William Hamilton.[37]

Settlers sought land as, among other reasons, a way to begin a new life. The ownership of land also automatically provided a profession through farming. Not all settlers who made land claims devoted their lives solely to cultivation, but it was a way to start a career in Oregon. Because land held such economic and personal promise, it was also something people protected with force if necessary. Due to the informal nature of land claims prior to the Donation Land Act and the confusion surrounding mass claims once the law came into effect, property lines tended to become blurred. In fact, some Oregon settlers carried with them into the Pacific Northwest ideas of "tomahawk law," wherein simply girding trees could demonstrate the boundaries of someone's lands.[38] The property-line confusion was especially true if one of the parties involved had moved away at some point. One of the first land laws in Oregon even permitted persons with land claims to "remedy forcible entry and detainer against intruders, and action of trespass against trespasser[s]."[39] Applying this legal allowance, some Oregon settlers took the enforcement of land laws into their own hands. An altercation over a land claim between A. M. Short and Dr. David Gardner near Fort Vancouver in the spring of 1850 resulted in the death of Gardner and his servant, a Kanaka man (whose name was not given). Both parties believed they owned the land claim, and when a fight erupted over this disagreement, the Kanaka man somehow found himself between the two so-called owners; he was shot and killed by Short.[40]

Settlement of the colony did not become easier, nor was there less violence, once Oregon had become a territory. The process of settler colonialism employs social, cultural, and legal policies from the empire in combination with the colony's own unique requirements, which came to represent the formation of Oregon land laws. When U.S. colonization and settler colonialism worked in tandem, the region's inhabitants included in the right to own land, let alone the people whose rights were protected, became narrowly defined. A Klickitat man by the name of Dick Johnson was killed by white settlers for his farmland in the

Umpqua Valley in 1858; because the only witnesses to the murder were American Indians, the murderers were never charged with the crime, but they did successfully receive a land claim for Johnson's property.[41] The construction of laws remained complex, and in the case of Oregon, violent protection of land ownership became another element of that process. While Congress debated the Donation Land Act, an argument over a land claim near Fort Vancouver between a "half-breed" and Mr. Jenkins (listed as a wage master employed by the government) turned violent. Although both men claimed to be the proprietor of the land and house located on the disputed property, the person who actually owned the claim was living in California.[42] Under Oregon laws, however, the "half-breed" in this account (though not granted a name) would have a case if his father were white.

In 1850, the Donation Land Act adopted the language of "white males" and "half-breeds"—men with white fathers and Indigenous mothers—to identify which groups of men were eligible for a land donation claim.[43] This federal identification of eligible landowners reflected the existing laws of Oregon's provisional governments, and the continuation of such language to exclude specific groups from land ownership not only played out for the duration of Oregon's territorial years but also made its way into the state constitution. The influence of policies constructed under Oregon's settler colony in territorial, federal, and state land laws therefore demonstrated the ability of exclusionary land ownership policies to serve as an instrument of settler colonialism. Moreover, the fact that a federal law reflected the policies of the settler colony provides an example of a colony impacting an empire. How exactly Oregon's land laws influenced and changed national discussions of land ownership is further demonstrated by the evaluation of racial and gendered classifications within the land laws.

Racial Definitions through Land Laws

Landownership in the United States has a long history of being exclusively accessible to people with money. With property came access to political systems and the power to construct laws. Although most landed men were careful not to alienate the vastly larger group of nonlanded men, those without property were dependent on landowners for political representation.[44] This is why the connection of land ownership to other rights, such as suffrage, resulted in such a narrow definition of who could possess those rights. Once land ownership became more accessible, however, stricter qualifications for the right to own property began to emerge, more so in the American West than elsewhere.

As Oregonians addressed the specifications for land claims and property ownership in their settler colony and then territory, states such as New York reminded Oregon settlers of the precarious nature of rights without definitive exclusions. The *Oregon Spectator* shared a report in 1849 that a man by the name of Gerritt Smith had passed away and left his large New York estate—containing several parcels of land—to a group of free Black Americans. The *Spectator* noted that around three hundred Black American men had become voters in the state of New York through their inheritance of Smith's land. The state of New York required a holding of land or assets of a specific value for a man to secure the right of suffrage. Thus, a Black American man with sufficient funds or land holdings could become a legal voter in the state.[45]

Lineage also became a way through which nonwhite Oregon settlers could acquire a land claim, but who specifically could claim inheritance became defined by law. As noted above, Oregon's first land laws restricted land ownership to "free males," and in 1845 the provisional government included a specification of lineage, stating that "all male persons over the age of eighteen years old, being a descendant of a white man shall be deemed lawful to hold a land claim."[46] With this additional language, a racial specification not only became a fixed component of Oregon's land laws and made the right to own land a "white right," but it also represented how the miscegenation that uniquely defined early Oregon had complicated the region's legal structures.

Intermarriage between white settler men and Indigenous women was accepted during early immigration to the colonial settlement of Oregon. Prior to the wagon trains of the 1840s, approximately 70 percent of marriages performed in Oregon were between white men and Indigenous women, and "half-breed" children were the byproduct.[47] While issues of miscegenation in education laws, access to suffrage, and immigration restrictions are discussed in other chapters, the Oregon land laws initially granted a specific group of mixed-race males rights to land ownership in the settler colony. Early Oregon legislators were quick to protect the rights of white fathers, and they did so through the inclusion of the lineage specification. After the Oregon Treaty, however, Congress's jurisdiction over Oregon included the temporary use of statutes from Iowa, including a land policy that restricted land ownership to "white males," which conflicted with the language about lineage previously accepted in Oregon.[48]

An editorial by "a correspondent" in the *Oregon Spectator* took direct issue with the land claim's exclusion of nonwhite Oregon settlers, arguing that "this would cut off many worthy citizens, whose interest, it is to be feared, has not been fairly represented to our government." The author did not say whether he had been referring to Black Americans, Kanaka immigrants, or men with Indigenous mothers. Nevertheless, lineage was a concern; as the author continued, some "liberal" politicians had evidenced their support of these citizens "regardless of the mere circumstantial difference of birth." In appealing to sympathies for this group of nonwhite citizens in Oregon, the author was reflecting the racial exceptions that had been made in Oregon and the settlers expected Congress to accept.[49] Oregon's early land laws, therefore, although possessing exclusionary language about race, were quite particular about who did receive the right of land ownership—men who had white fathers. Long-time settlers such as John McLoughlin also argued that the right to own land by men with a white father and Indigenous mother ought to be maintained in order to keep such individuals from living among American Indians and further straining relations between Indigenous communities and the Oregon settlers.[50] In Oregon, white fathers' rights were upheld even when Oregon's land policy became entwined with a federal act.

Oregon's land laws were always national in the sense that the policies of the settler colony both reflected and influenced the empire. But the federal government's involvement in the creation of the Donation Land Act brought to light deep fissures over issues of race within the United States. From the onset of Congressional debates over the land donations, representatives struggled with Oregon's allowances for men of white fathers and Indigenous mothers but restricted all other non-white men from land claims. As addressed in chapter 3, proslavery representatives tended to conflate any question on the rights of Black Americans or a state's control of slavery with the volatile issue of "negro equality." Politicians fanaticized this subject in a fashion similar to what was done to abolitionism, thus making it synonymous with disunion. This association made accusing someone of promoting "negro equality" an effective tool, because it made whatever argument a representative accused of promoting such a view a dead letter.[51]

Nevertheless, Congressman Joshua Reed Giddings of Ohio confronted the issue of "negro equality" in the summer of 1850 to question why the Oregon land grant act prohibited donations to nonwhite men, such as free Black American men, whom other states recognized as citizens. Giddings went so far as to insinuate that some Black Americans seeking land in Oregon could have been descendants of "Founding Fathers," asking "with what consistency, not to say gratitude, disciples of Jefferson could consent to keep Oregon from those whose veins coursed the blood of Thomas Jefferson." If Giddings's intention had been to gain the attention of the House, his speech was indeed successful. When Congressman Charles Magill Conrad of Louisiana accused Giddings of stating that Black men were better than white men, Giddings simply replied that "whites were quite as good as the blacks."[52]

Although Giddings's approach was somewhat extreme for his time, his opposition to a racial exclusion in Oregon's land laws raised the issue that classifications of race not only protected a specific group's right to land ownership but also determined which races would not have access to a central right of citizenship—the right to own property. Although with different intentions than representatives such as Giddings, Congressman Thomas Bayly of Virginia interpreted the exclusion of nonwhite men from land donations as effectively "excluding free blacks from citizenship."[53] At the time, few states extended basic political rights to their Black American populations, and in the 1850s none granted Black Americans access to all the rights of a U.S. citizen. The Donation Land Act, therefore, drew national attention not only because it made a land donation a "white right" but also because it stood as a federal law that explicitly excluded "nonwhite" men from land ownership, and thus access to full citizenship. Again, the federal land donation with a restriction of nonwhite males from land ownership came seven years before the *Dred Scott v. Sanford* decision. This racial exclusion within the Oregon Donation Act established a racial restriction to U.S. citizenship and a federal precedent for the Homestead Act to follow.[54] The inclusion of "American half-breed Indians" as potential landowners in the federal land grant act also demonstrated a specific influence from Oregon land laws.

Building from Oregon's recognition that males with white fathers and Indigenous mothers could enjoy the same rights as "white males," the Donation Land Act extended the right of a land donation to "American half-breed Indians." This differed from Oregon law only in the fact that it included the specification of "American."[55] The reason for this change in language was to clarify the difference between a man with a white father and an American Indian mother, and the descendant of a Kanaka woman or mother from the Sandwich Islands.[56] This specification came at the insistence of the Oregon settlers, or, more directly, from territorial delegate Samuel Thurston. During the debates over the Donation Land Act, Thurston informed the House of his opinion that people of the Pacific islands were of "a race of men as black as your negroes in the South, and a race too that we do not desire to settle in Oregon."[57] The provisional and then territorial governments of Oregon had passed immigration exclusion laws prohibiting the entrance or settling of Black Americans, and although Kanakas and other groups of immigrants were not included in this exclusion, some Oregon settlers still held animosity toward their presence in the territory. Legislators again resolved that dilemma through the adoption of Oregon's "half-breed" language and the requirement of having a white father. Lawmakers maintained that this allowance for "half-breed" men preserved the white father's property rights.[58] Being a descendant of a white man, therefore, was requisite for land ownership; this held true for white immigrants as well.

The Donation Land Act continued Oregon's use of a racial qualification and established a precedent for Oregon policies toward white immigrants. As long as the white male immigrant "made a declaration according to law, of his intention to become a citizen," he could claim land in the Oregon Territory under the federal act.[59] This allowance—especially the ease with which a foreigner could acquire the rights of a citizen—continued within Oregon laws and drew considerable concern from Congress during Oregon's application for statehood. But during the debates for the Donation Land Act representatives were concerned about the inclusion of white foreign men. Proslavery politicians, for example, felt that the racially specific restriction to land claims highlighted how Oregon did not equally observe the "right to own property." The territory prohibited slavery; therefore, Oregon forbade property in the form of slaves. One Mississippi newspaper objected to the inclusion of white foreigners in Oregon's Donation Land Act, stating, "A foreigner has many rights in any of the territories of the United States over a native born citizen of one of the Southern States."[60] A white southern man could obtain a land donation, as could a woman if married to a white man. This author's problem was not with the racial classification in the right to own land; rather, the author opposed the fact that noncitizens also had access to this right, whereas slaveowners' perceived right to own property in the form of slaves was not allowed in the territory. Ultimately, southern representatives were more supportive of the act's racial classification of land ownership than concerned with including white foreigners in the land donation. With a portion of western states sharing this sentiment, the Donation Land Act gained congressional approval.[61]

The racial specifications in Oregon's land laws reflected the desire to keep nonwhite populations from resources and rights in the region. A simple way to eliminate competition was to exclude nonwhite groups from gaining one of the most important footholds in a developing settler colony—land.[62] Another way to ensure that land would not be available to those legally excluded was for lawmakers to expand the definition of land ownership for white men. In addition to allowing foreign white men the opportunity to hold a land claim, in December 1851 the Oregon territorial government proposed an amendment to the Donation Land Act that lowered the legal age requirement for white men from twenty-one years of age to sixteen. The territorial government further charged its congressional delegate with obtaining "from Congress an extension of said act so as to provide that all white male American youth . . . shall receive a donation."[63] Moreover, the Oregon legislator also proposed to include "white American females" over the age of eighteen and orphans of "white parents" as eligible for a land donation.[64] Although Congress did not accept any of these proposed amendments, these additional qualifications maintained the requirement of being white in Oregon land laws. These proposals also demonstrated that Oregon leaders at least presented themselves as open to expanding the "white right" to land ownership. That being said, the actual laws enforced in Oregon and the debates of land ownership during the Oregon Constitution suggest this inclusion still possessed narrow qualifications.

Oregon lawmakers carried the policies of the Donation Land Act into the debates over land ownership during the Oregon Constitutional Convention in 1857. Again, legislators focused on the race of the potential landowner but also debated how to extend land ownership rights to foreign white immigrants without breaking from the policy that land ownership was the right of U.S. citizens. In other words, legislators had to decide how they could exclude nonwhite Americans but allow an opening for foreign immigration. Oregon politicians answered this question by streamlining the process to naturalization through the ownership of land, thus making landowning white foreign males U.S. citizens.[65]

When the Bill of Rights committee for the Oregon Constitutional Convention presented the first draft of Section 31, it stated, "Foreigners who are or may hereafter become residents of this state shall enjoy the same rights in respect to possession, enjoyment and descent of property as native-born citizens."[66] The term "residents" presented a departure from the requirement in many states that immigrants must become citizens before they could own land in the state. In a national context, the Whig side of the naturalization debate argued that foreign immigrants were not automatically loyal to the United States upon their entrance into the country and therefore should not achieve full access to citizenship until living in the country long enough to build such loyalty. Oregon Anti-Democrat Thomas Dryer echoed this sentiment when he moved to replace the word "residents" with "citizens."[67] Representing the Democrats' position, Lafayette Grover opposed this limitation to "citizens" under the argument that white foreigners would only continue settlement of the region, thus helping secure lands for the nation. Grover scoffed at policies such as those in Massachusetts, which required twenty-one years of residence before any eligibility for naturalization.[68]

To bridge the gap between these opposing viewpoints over naturalization, Democrat Perry P. Maple moved to modify the section by including that only foreigners "who has declared their intention of becoming citizens" could hold property, a move similar to what Congress had done with the Donation Land Act.[69] Maple's motion, however, failed. In dropping the requirement that someone declare his intentions of becoming a citizen, Oregon moved away from the federal land grant policies and into a position of maintaining one of the most liberal policies toward foreign immigrants and land ownership in the nation. Moreover, because the section also associated having the right of property ownership with being equal to U.S. citizens, this land policy granted the right of citizenship to white foreign immigrants.

Oregon lawmakers also drew very specific classifications for which immigrants qualified as potential landowners in the state constitution. Early in the debate over property ownership within the Bill of Rights, Matthew Deady brought the requirement of race into the discussion of foreign immigrants' transition into citizenship. Even though Oregon legislators had cut out the federal contingency about declaring one's intention to become a citizen, the continuation of a racial qualification was quickly applied through the addition of the word "white" before the word "foreigners."[70] This addition, though seemingly simple and reflective of past policies, fundamentally altered which groups of immi-

3. Matthew Deady, neg. no. 9806, Oregon Historical Society Research Library.

grants this inclusive legislation applied to—only immigrants associated with the white race. Access to the right of land ownership in Oregon, now connected to citizenship, became exclusively a "white right," and this disqualified nonwhite foreign immigrants from becoming citizens.

This chain of events should not be misunderstood as a matter of interpretation, because Oregon legislators took Section 31 one step further. Following the sentence that granted white foreigners residing in Oregon the right to own land as enjoyed by U.S. citizens, the section continues, "And the legislative assembly shall have power to restrain and regulate the immigration to this state of persons not qualified to become citizens of the United States."[71] This section not only made it impossible for nonwhite foreigners to own land but also granted the state government the right to restrict foreign immigration; in Oregon's case this meant all immigrants not eligible to become citizens, therefore all nonwhite immigrants. Through the Naturalization Act of 1790, the U.S. federal government had restricted the right of naturalization to white foreigners, but it did not prohibit nonwhite foreigners from immigrating to the country. By connecting property rights to the process of naturalization as well as the ability to emigrate to the state, Oregon's land policies unprecedentedly restricted foreign immigration through a racial specification. Oregon's restriction of free Black Americans from entering its territory and then state may have reflected other western statutes, but restricting nonwhite foreign immigrants was a first for state exclusions and preceded the first national immigration restriction (the Chinese Exclusion Act of 1882) by twenty-three years.

Of course, nonwhite Americans were not exempt from this racialized policy of land ownership. In addition to the immigration restriction preventing Black Americans from coming to or settling in the state, the Oregon Constitution prohibited the same group of Black Americans from holding any real estate in Oregon. Concerned that Black Americans could take part in land speculations from other states, Oregon legislators felt the need to add this prohibition to the thirty-fifth section in the Bill of Rights.[72] Oregon, however, was already home to Black Americans who owned real estate when Oregonians ratified their constitution. For example, Abner Hunt Francis owned a mercantile store in Portland. Francis held his shop throughout the period when numerous debates over property ownership occurred and continued even after territorial officials had arrested his brother O. H. Francis under the immigration restriction law.[73] Similar to how the resistance of slaves on southern plantations demonstrated political activism against slavery—whether through running away or slowing down work production, among other methods—free Black Americans' resistance to leaving a territory and then a state that continued to enact laws depriving Black Americans of basic rights was also a form of political resistance.[74] Abner Hunt Francis further proved his resistance to the oppressive policies by writing to an abolitionist paper about Oregon's many exclusionary laws.[75]

Regulating property ownership was also a way to limit a group's participation within local economies.[76] In order to exclude Chinese immigrants and Chinese Americans from rights in the region, Oregon legislators specifically restricted those of Chinese descent from holding real estate. Regardless of their origins of birth, or the races of their fathers, those of Chinese ancestry were barred from being property owners under Article 15, Section 8.[77] These exclusions of entire nonwhite groups made it very clear that if one wanted to come to and own land in Oregon, one had to be identified as white.

The racial exclusions and language for land laws in the Oregon Constitution did not escape criticism during congressional debates over Oregon's statehood. One of the main objections to Oregon's constitution in connection to land ownership restrictions was the exclusion of Black Americans from filing or maintaining suits in an Oregon court. In Section 35, after the language that prohibits Black Americans from entering or residing in the state of Oregon as well as excludes them from owning real estate, the Bill of Rights states that this group shall also not "make any contracts, or maintain any suit therein."[78] As mentioned above, racial specifications in land policies had started to appear in new and western states' statutes, replacing the wording of "free males" with "white males," especially after the use of such language in the Donation Land Act. Excluding a group from the right to file suit in a court, however, was not common. Congressman Charles J. Gilman of Maine addressed this significant point when he informed his colleagues there was "not a slave state in the Union that denies the free colored man access to her courts."[79] As true as this may have been, given the fact that even the most densely populated slave states allowed slaves to file suit through someone recognized as a citizen, the opposition to Oregon's exclusion mainly came from northeastern representatives.[80] When Gillman further explained that in the State of Maine, a Black American was "more than a person; he is a citizen," and that many "compare favorably with those whose skin is whiter," his sentiments hit a wall of western indifference when Clement Vallangiham of Ohio stated, "It is not so in the West."[81] Oregon, like other territories and states in the U.S. West, not only brought about new perspectives of race to national debates but also provided new policies of exclusion to influence those discussions.[82]

By 1859 the question remained as to whether Congress had the power to make Oregon or any state change its state laws. Furthermore, some representatives who opposed Oregon's exclusion of Black Americans from the right to own land and file suit in state courts returned to the question of whether a state can deny the rights of citizenship to someone identified as a citizen in their state of origin. Observing that this provision was "injustice and oppression incarnate," John Bingham of Ohio protested that the adoption of Oregon's constitution would exclude "eight hundred thousand of the native-born citizens of the United States" from the state of Oregon, defying Article 4, Section 2 of the U.S. Constitution.[83] Oregon did define land ownership as a white right and in doing so restricted the rights of groups recognized as citizens in other states. But the constitutional contradiction this presented at the federal level was ultimately not viewed as significant enough to deny Oregon statehood.

Congress approved Oregon's statehood with its racial exclusions to land ownership and the right to file suit intact. As with the immigration restriction provision that managed to find acceptance among Congressmen, timing was important for Oregon. Tensions over the state's ability to regulate slavery, the growing sectional divisions within Congress that made each side seek alliances with new states, as well as the strong apprehension toward discussing the legal rights of Black Americans (let alone passing policy on the subject) granted Oregon settlers the ability to hold more sway in national politics than they would otherwise have been permitted.[84] This influence primarily existed in the form of Congress allowing Oregon to possess exclusionary legislation that extended citizenship to white foreigners while stripping the rights of a citizen from nonwhite Americans. Overall, the federal government validated Oregon's laws, making them something that other territories and states could cite as precedents to their own racialized exclusions.

Gendered Independence through Land Claims

To be an independent person in the early to mid-nineteenth century meant that a man was not dependent; he owned his own labor and his own property, and he had dependents (including a wife and children) under his care.[85] Identifying women as dependent allowed men to not only equate independence with the male sex and place the sexes in opposition to each other but also use "independent" as a gendered term to determine one's level of masculinity. If a male was not independent, he lacked sufficient masculinity and became associated with femininity. Demonstrating features of masculinity, such as political participation and the claiming of rights and resources, placed him in a position of power over others who lacked such holdings, thus making him independent.[86] Landownership, therefore, became legally identified as male and necessary for the perceived manliness of a man, because it represented a state of independence. Landownership allowed someone to possess an asset that he/she controlled. Specifically, settlers with land claims could farm their property, as well as lease, sell, and live on the property as their own landlord. Many Oregon settlers sought out these luxuries of independence, and the specifications of Oregon's land laws for white settlers allowed this specific group the opportunity for both personal and economic independence.[87]

Under the law of coverture, a woman was legally represented, or "covered," by a male family member, who was generally her father or husband. Upon marriage, a woman's personal property fell under the authority of her husband.[88] After the birth of a child within the marriage, the husband "assumed the status of 'tenant by courtesy' over his wife's real estate and with it the right to rent out those lands, cut timber on them, or otherwise collect profits from them until they passed to her heirs."[89] Laws pertaining specifically to protecting women's property had gained support throughout the country (including Oregon) by the time of the Civil War, but the power structure of property ownership did not significantly change with the addition of these laws.[90] Nevertheless, land claims in the name of a wife or widow still permitted women some level of independence during the Antebellum era, even if only economically rooted. In Oregon, this independence for women was not without patriarchal strings that maintained and reinstitutionalized white males' control of Oregon lands.

Scholarship addressing the inclusion of women in Oregon land laws usually focuses on the Donation Land Act, yet settlers drafted policies pertaining to women while the Oregon settler colony was still under joint occupation by Great Britain and the United States. The Oregon Emigration Society's "Articles of Agreement" of 1839 serves as one of first examples of not only a land law applied to Oregon but also the first proposed inclusion of women as property owners in the American West. The emigration society specified that married men would receive six hundred and forty acres, single men over the age of sixteen would receive three hundred and twenty acres, and "every single female of sixteen years of age or upwards, one hundred and sixty acres of land."[91] The significance of this policy was the fact that the land granted to women did not require that the women be married to male settlers. It should also be pointed out that some of the earliest examples of women's property laws pertained to married women exclusively. This settler society, however, did not provide land to married women in connection to their husband's land; rather, single women were the only females who could own land. It would initially appear that this policy contradicted the strongly perceived idea of western expansion as a familial enterprise with the father as the "homesteader."

A popular gendered construction for men in the early to mid-nineteenth century, referred to as "communal manhood," centered on the idea that a man needed to be at the center of his household to adequately serve his community. In the case of the Oregon Emigration Society, this meant that the communal man needed to settle on land and cultivate it for the purpose of reconstructing a community.[92] Furthermore, under Jefferson's republican idea of the yeoman farmer and his expansion to the West, women's role was to be subservient to the men who could perpetuate the idealized form of U.S. life—the agrarian lifestyle.[93] Land ownership lessened the necessity for a single woman with her own property to marry a man and become his dependent. In fact, a landed single woman could theoretically avoid that relationship altogether if that were what she chose.

The Oregon Emigration Society and its members, however, were not as radically progressive as it would first appear. Section 3 of the "Articles of Agreement" stated that within the hierarchy of the settler society, "each member of the society, and all members of his family . . . in all respects whatsoever, conform himself and his family to the rules, regulation, and direction" of the elected officers until the time that the Oregon Emigration Society constructed a constitution.[94] The male pronouns and their possessions are hard to miss, demonstrating that the nucleus of this atomic settler society was a father-led family. To whom did the single woman holding her own land claim report in this hierarchy, then? Presumably, the single woman with land reported to the patriarchal leader of her family and was expected to marry and preserve the family unit, perceived as necessary for the society's success.[95]

In 1845, the same year that the Oregon provisional government passed a law specifying that males eligible to claim land must be descendants of white men, Oregon settlers acknowledged widows of landowners as having the "same privilege as others in this act specified."[96] States, including newly formed ones, had begun adopting land laws specifically addressing property held by married women and widows. For example, Texas had a constitutional provision that recognized property brought to the marriage or inherited afterward as a woman's separate property.

Table 5. State constitution property ownership provisions (prior 1860)

SPECIFICATION	STATE	SLAVE / FREE	YEAR	ORIGINAL / REVISION	EXEMPT FROM HUSBAND'S DEBTS
Identified women as separate owners of property	Texas	Slave	1845	Original	No
	California	Free	1849	Original	No
	Michigan	Free	1850	Revision	Yes
	Oregon	Free	1859	Original	Yes
	Kansas	Free	1861	Original	No
	Total (States) = 5				

Source: Created by author based on ratified constitutions; Swindler, *Sources and Documents*. Kansas had proposed in all three of its constitutions (Topeka Constitution of 1855, Leavenworth Constitution of 1858, and the Wyandotte Constitution of 1859) that women have separate property ownership.

The specific language used in the 1845 Texas law appeared (with small differences) in the constitutions of California in 1849 and Michigan in 1850 as well as the proposed Wyandotte Constitution for the territory of Kansas in 1859. Oregon's territorial laws in 1850, after the Donation Land Act, also granted married women the right to half of a land claim, and this continued in Oregon's state constitution.[97] I address these similarities not only to point out that these western populations had crafted similar laws to protect women's property over the course of fifteen years, which reflects a regionalized perspective on the topic, but also to highlight that Oregon had not been brought into this fold until after the Donation Land Act.

Before the federal policy, Oregon had not been on course with the more liberal laws protecting women's property, because those enacted by the provisional government did not recognize women's right to land claims unless these women were widows of landowners. Protecting the property of married women in Oregon became directly connected to the significant expansion of land claims through the Donation Land Act and the desire for settlers and the federal government to protect property from land speculators and creditors. Ultimately, women's right to property ownership in Oregon became more of a legal space to hold or transfer property than their individual rights. This is not to suggest that women were inactive participants in the settlement of lands in Oregon but that women's roles became ingrained in the very process of settlement, serving patriarchal and colonizing structures. In other words, the settlement of Oregon could not have been done without women, even though women would not reap the full benefits of their labors for many years to come.

The Donation Land Act of 1850 granted white male settlers and male "half-breed Indians" above eighteen years of age as well as white foreigners who declared their intentions to become citizens 320 acres of land if single and 640 acres if married. Half of the donation available to a married couple was to be held by the wife as her own property.[98] This act was the first time that the federal government had recognized women as separate entities, insofar as they could hold land claims under their own names and not just as heirs to the property.[99] Both the federal government and Oregon legislators wanted to encourage settlement of lands in Oregon. Because a married man could receive twice as much land as a single man, congressional representatives and Oregon's political organs (namely its newspapers) placed great emphasis on why potential landowners should ensure that they were eligible for the largest portion of land donations possible and, therefore, why getting married was in their best interests.

Oregon congressional delegate Samuel R. Thurston wrote to various newspapers across the country to provide a simple explanation of the numerous requirements for a land claim under the proposed Oregon Land Bill (which became the Donation Land Act). Out of all the sections of the bill, Thurston highlighted those pertaining to how much land a married man would receive.[100] Granted, the amount of land a man could receive was likely of great interest to potential settlers, but it also set a tone for the Donation Land Act that emphasized marriage as a means to acquire more land. Thus, campaigning efforts for the land bill, and then encouragement for filing land claims after the bill had become a federal act, focused on marriage as the optimal goal for land ownership.

Oregon newspapers kept settlers on their toes about deadlines for the Donation Land Act, including prodding nervous young men to find wives before the cutoff date in December 1851. In one such editorial, the author explained that the development of several land claims was slow going because the bachelors were too preoccupied with trying to find wives, adding that this had created "the greatest buzzing at this time among the bachelor portion of the lords of the soil, ever witnessed in any country." The author sympathized with these bachelors, noting that "they have but four months grace allowed them for courting and marrying. It is all right; we wish every mother's son of them may be well suited, and that, too, in time to take advantage of the most liberal allowance guarantied in the bill."[101] The drive for single white males to receive the full amount of land available removed any romantic notions about marriage, or even marriage as a necessity for procreation; rather, it made marriage entirely about acquiring land.

Of course, editorials such as this did not acknowledge that half of the land donations the would-be husbands received legally existed as their wives' separate property. The legal and cultural perception that her land would become his land, and thus fall under the authority of the husband, prevailed throughout this mad dash to obtain a wife. In fact, white Oregon men married to Indigenous women were able to claim the married persons' acreage due to the interpretation that legal authority remained with the white husband.[102]

Asahel Bush, editor of the *Oregon Statesman*, perplexed a Wisconsin newspaper with his letter suggesting that Oregon needed to import single women. Bush identified single women as being worth more than gold in his territory and maintained that the higher ratio of men to women in Oregon made finding a wife in order to claim the land donation for married couples nearly impossible.[103] The sex ratio imbalance did ultimately result in a much higher number of single male claims in the first years of the Donation Land Act, though not from a lack of trying.[104]

One newspaper editorial reminding single males that the deadline to obtain a married man's donation was approaching insisted that single women should do their part in pushing these shy bachelors into matrimony. The author explained that these ladies should "wear the most winning smiles, and encourage the timid young man to nerve himself up to the sticking point, and boldly declare his desire to possess another half (section)."[105] Women, therefore, were charged with not only providing single men with this additional land donation as their wives but also helping men assert their independence and manhood by getting them to "nerve himself up" and get married, so the men could claim the full land donation. Women were the key to settlement in Oregon and apparently also drivers of the settlement whenever nervous single men were involved.

The stigma and repercussions for men unable to secure a wife also evidenced the preferential treatment of married men in Oregon land ownership. An Oregon settler by the name of Isaac Peet had been widowed before the Donation Land Act and was unable to find another wife within the time frame allowed by the land policy. In addition to not being able to acquire the full land donation, Peet felt that Oregon was inhospitable to his plight due to his marital status. Peet, therefore, advertised the sale of his land and property, as he planned to "leave the country."[106]

Peet's old age may have been a factor in his inability to remarry, but youth could also be a drawback in obtaining land donations. An editorial to Oregon's congressional delegate in the summer of 1851 proposed that young men be allotted land claims "under a different tenure from those having families." The author explained that it was unfair to deny young single men the full acreage of a land donation, because the lack of land would stunt their independence. Young men who had to help their fathers farm the family lands were placed at a disadvantage for cultivating their own claims, and this prevented them from becoming independent men. Those still tied to their family farms were also less desirable as potential husbands to the already limited single female population. The author insisted, therefore, that young single men be able to claim the same amount of land as married men, under the assumption that the young men will eventually get married.[107]

Again, land ownership provided an avenue for young men to acquire their economic and social independence, and marriage to a woman was the only route for a young man to claim the full land donation. Having a wife, therefore, was the only way a man could achieve this most coveted level of independence. And if for some reason this "shotgun" approach to marriage in order to acquire land donations did not work out very well, Oregon did adjust its divorce laws during this time to increase the legal causes for divorce to nine possibilities in the eyes of the territorial court.[108] In the event that the wife associated with a land donation died, the legal resolution of her property would become a much more complicated process.

Under the Donation Land Act, a widow, if a resident of the Oregon Territory before the enactment of the land act, could still claim a donation of 320 acres, and that land would pass to her children or heirs upon her death.[109] Individuals like Agnes Courtney, widowed after immigrating to Oregon in 1845 with her husband, made such a claim for herself and her six children.[110] The federal act did not address, however, the availability of land donations to widows who had arrived after the enactment of the law but within the specified time period and according to the other qualifications. The restriction of widows' rights became a great concern to Oregon legislators, who proposed multiple amendments to Congress that would expand the time frame for widows to claim a land donation.[111]

The preoccupation with women who were made widows en route to Oregon or shortly after arriving did not stem from a sense to protect women's property rights; rather, it came more from a fear of too many people becoming dependents on the territorial government. Therefore, Oregon legislators connected policies for orphans with almost all their proposals to Congress pertaining to widows' land donations. Both orphans and widows were potential dependents on the territory, but land donations would allow them, at the very least, somewhere to live or something to sell and thus retain a form of economic independence. But as a group of people who were on the cusp of becoming dependents, their authority over the land claim became precarious, with several requirements and qualifications.[112] Furthermore, a civic obligation within the United States was to not be a dependent on the state, and it was not culturally acceptable for white women to partake in forms of labor—even in the American West, where that was nearly impossible to avoid. In order to keep white widows, or at least widows of white men, from the degrading their status by laboring, Oregon lawmakers argued that a land donation would allow the widow to keep her social standing and not become a dependent on the state.[113] Congress did not accept these amendments.[114] Nevertheless, control of the lands remained important, and protection of heirs' rights and their fathers' authority over those inheritances required careful language.

Settlers who wanted the maximum amount of land from a land donation in Oregon placed a high importance on the exact property rights that a married man, his wife, his widow, or the heirs of his widow would hold. According to sections 8 and 9 of the Donation Land Act, a widower with children from his deceased wife could marry again, with his new wife receiving a donation adjoined to his claim and his children (the deceased wife's heirs) receiving their mother's donation. This meant that a widower could not only still acquire the full land donation if he had remarried within the qualifications of time in the act but also potentially have lands under his authority from three separate donations: his own, his second wife's land, and the land of his children (if minors) from his first wife.[115] The property of a married woman and that of a widow's heirs both symbolized potential independence for these respective persons, but the authority of a husband and father ultimately made those persons dependents. Granted, once of age, the legitimate heirs of a widow could choose to do what they pleased with the land donation from their mother. If the heir were male, he could manage the land as his own. If the heir were female and married, the land would stay in her name, but it would then also fall under the authority of her husband. For the head patriarch of Oregon households, however, a problem arose when it came to family debts and land donations. Oregon lawmakers had to figure out how to protect married women's property from their husbands' debts not only during her lifetime but also in relation to her heirs' inheritance.

Industrialization in America had a profound effect on the ownership of land, as land became a marketable commodity. Politicians nationwide advocated the loosening or expansion of property, which allowed more land to enter the market, and those with money could then control commodities such as land. Additionally, business speculations increasingly grew as a byproduct of industrialization. In reaction to this speculation, landowning fathers began wanting to protect property given to their daughters upon marriage from their husbands' possible financial failures.[116] Land allotted to a married woman was made in conjunction to the land donation of her husband, and she was only allowed such a donation because she was married. By making women economic dependents of their husbands, the law still recognized husbands as those with the authority over land claims taken by married couples.[117] Even if the husband had lost his land claim to debt, the family—under the authority of the father and husband—would still have the land that was under the wife's name. This was because the construction of distinct laws that separated a woman's property from her husband's property made the land under her name legally exempt to creditors. The land remained in the wife's name, and authority over the property remained with the husband. Thus, arguments behind the legalities of women's property ownership were heavily embedded in white men's struggle to control their assets and privileges as well as in offering a solution to inheritance problems.

Although the original Oregon Land Bill that Samuel Thurston brought to Congress had contained a section that addressed the rights of married women to property and its protection from their husbands' debts, the final Donation Land Act did not include this section.[118] Shortly after the enactment of the federal land grant, Oregon legislators quickly worked to construct territorial laws that would address this shortcoming. Bills exempting married women's land donations from the debts of their husbands flooded the chambers of Oregon Council, mirroring other western legislation aimed at protecting farm families from land speculators trying to buy property out from under indebted families.[119] Within a year Oregon legislators had passed a law requiring that land donations obtained through the Donation Land Act under the name of a married woman be accrued to "the sole and separate use and control of the wife, and such interest in be made subject to or liable for the debts or liabilities of her husband, whether contracted before or after the passage of this act."[120] But

Oregon departed from other western legislation in one important aspect: the definition of "tenant by curtesy." Unlike other land laws that provided protection for married women's property rights, Oregon allowed a husband curtesy: the right to manage and control his wife's property regardless of whether the marriage had produced a child.[121] This provisional law did permit married women or widows to possess a degree of legal rights over their land donations that women had not previously experienced in Oregon, but it also came with more rights given to the husbands of those women as well.[122] In 1854 the territorial government repealed the section that protected married women's property but retained the curtesy section, placing further emphasis on the fact that women's property rights were governed by an expanding patriarchal structure and were used to strengthen that structure. Oregon legislators did reassert the protection provision in the state constitution, but delegates seriously questioned whether the "use and control of the wife" over her land donation was necessary to or in the best interest of the state.

In September 1857, Oregon delegates to the Constitutional Convention partook in a vociferous debate over Section 5 of Article 15, which secured "married women property inherited, bequeathed, etc., in their own individual right."[123] Numerous Democratic delegates, including George H. Williams, Matthew Deady, and W. W. Bristow, wanted to strike the entire section out, arguing that Oregon laws pertaining to dowry sufficiently addressed this issue. By 1857 Oregon legislators no longer connected land laws to the Donation Land Act. Having a wife, therefore, no longer secured larger land claims, and less land was now available for ownership. Nevertheless, supporters of the provision such as Democrat Reuben P. Boise insisted that "it was simply declaring that the property of the wife could not be taken to satisfy the husband's debts, and could not be taken from her without her consent. It was the doctrine of the civil law." Why had support of women's property rights wavered? Some delegates claimed they feared any division of land between husband and wife would become problematic for familial relations.[124] Lest they had forgotten, legislators had claimed the very opposite in 1851 when they passed a territorial law to protect women and their families from creditors. What had changed between then and the Constitutional Convention (in addition to growing competition over land claims) was the growth of women's rights across the nation, which also occurred in Oregon through land claims.

Although most achievements in legal rights during the mid-nineteenth century seem subtle compared to more modern conceptions of women's equality, they were significant changes to U.S. gender roles and cultural perceptions of their time. For instance, five single women from Oregon (Delilah White, Mary Center, Jane Pugh, Mary Canada, and Sally Goodman) had successfully claimed land donations between 1853 and 1856.[125] Although they were not legally eligible recipients, these women were awarded patents to their land claims by 1862 due to clerical confusion at the land office, making them independent owners of land.[126] Men may have needed women to claim the maximum land donation, but evidently, some women did not need men to settle and establish a life on a land claim.

Drawing on arguments about the sanctity of the family and marriage, Oregon delegates associated the protection of married women's property with women's rights and the assumed effects of those rights on a happy home. Not shying away from his objections to the state of the times, George Williams asserted, "In this age of woman's rights and insane theories, our legislation should be such as to unite the family circle, and make husband and wife what they should be—bone of one bone, and flesh of one flesh." Imploring his colleagues to consider what individual rights for a husband and a wife meant, he argued, "The provision of our donation law giving the husband and wife separate and distinct estates in the land claim had been the cause of much domestic trouble and many divorces in this country." Williams then suggested that these separate rights would cause a negative chain reaction, noting, "If we [delegates] established this provision, we must provide laws by which the husband and wife can sue each other." Matthew Deady shared this opinion, adding, "He would not make two persons of the husband and wife—it only tended to family alienation and jars."[127]

The concept of viewing husband and wife as one entity both legally and culturally was not uncommon. As mentioned before, the practice of coverture designated the wife as possessing a civic identity only through her husband and allowed him a level of control over the wife's property.[128] Land laws may not seem capable of altering gender roles or moving women out of the domestic sphere into the public sphere, but owning land did allow women to exist as separate legal entities and within the political world of men, as evidenced by Oregon land laws.[129] Thus, a constitutional provision that continued the practice of protecting married women's property would assist such women in achieving a level of independence. The same patriarchal structures that permitted husbands and fathers authority over women's property continued in Oregon, but the growing hesitation by legislators to construct laws recognizing women as separate owners also demonstrated a concern that such land ownership had granted some women individual rights over land.

Meanwhile, some delegates did not see this constitutional provision as threatening men's authority over land. Oregon lawmakers such as Anti-Democrat David Logan associated married women's rights with a mother's social obligation. Logan believed that a mother needed to "have the power to preserve her property to support herself and the education of her children" if her husband were not "prudent and thrifty."[130] Democrat Delazon Smith also dismissed claims that divorce resulted from familial disputes over property ownership, stating, "It was not separate and distinct property which caused divorces; it was the want of affection—the want of marriage of the heart." The convention reporters then recorded Smith as asserting, "He [Smith] was for the provision as it was" and that he would protect a married woman's "property from dissipated or mercenary wretches." Seemingly different from his and other delegates' discussions of rights during the rest of the convention, Smith was also attributed to have stated, "He was for a woman's rights and was not afraid of her having too many. She had been long denied her just rights."[131] It appeared that the discussion of property ownership had taken an about-face.

While Smith rejected the unromantic notion that land claims and personal rights were at the heart of a marriage, as had been suggested during the wife/land grab of the early 1850s, Smith's support of women's rights contained a familiar connection to previous policies on married women's property—protecting said property from outside sources, be they creditors or land speculators. Despite additional language in support of women's rights, the issue over property rights was still a matter of preserving property connected to men's assets. These "dissipated or mercenary wretches" who could potentially take a married woman's property also threatened land that either her husband had authority over or that she had received from her family. The fact that delegates such as Smith encouraged women's rights may reflect a changing cultural perception of legal rights, but Oregon land laws remained rooted in patriarchal structures.

In the eyes of wealthy fathers with daughters, the "wretches" Smith referred to could also have meant a woman's debt-ridden husband. The convention's debate over protecting married women's property connected to an earlier concern of landowning Oregon fathers about protecting the land passed to their daughters. Democrat Fredrick Waymire posed this very issue to his fellow delegates when he asked, "How many men had already in this country married girls, used them a year or two, spent all their property, and put off to the states?" Waymire insisted that this could and must be prohibited, further stating, "If men married for money they ought not to have control of it. Every day they lived together they lived in adultery, for he married the money and not the girl." Waymire also expressed personal concern about a man marrying "a daughter of his, with a large band of cattle, and skin her, and leave her."[132] Legal protection of women's property, like that held by his daughters, was necessary to prevent the loss of property held in a woman's name.

The Donation Land Act and its larger allotment for married couples assisted in the settlement of Oregon, but it also prompted numerous marriages for the sake of acquiring land donations. The fear that Waymire had expressed about whether his daughters would find or had found husbands who did not love them but rather planned to squander their property remained a concern for legislators after the federal land act. States addressed this issue with laws that permitted wives to legally separate their property from that of their husbands. A Louisiana law in 1808 even required this separation of property to appear in a public notice.[133] Likewise, Oregon lawmakers saw the need for a provision to protect married women's property. This opinion became a general consensus among the convention delegates, and they amended the property provision to include that "the property and pecuniary rights of every married woman at the time of marriage, or afterwards, acquired by gift, devise, or inheritance, shall not be subject to the debts or contracts of the husband, and laws shall be passed by the legislature for the registration of the wife's separate property."[134]

Although a success for women's ability to retain economic control of their inheritances in the face of their husbands' debt, the provision did not break down the patriarchal structure of Oregon land laws. Married women could become landowners with their own separate claims, but authority over the use of these claims remained with their husbands.[135] During the congressional debates over Oregon's statehood application, Oregon representative to Congress Joseph Lane laid to rest any question of this when he quickly dismissed the interpretation that married women could take claims in Oregon. As with many Oregon legislators, Lane argued that married women only held claims through the act of being married to white males with a land donation.[136] Married women's property, therefore, was dependent on being married to white males, and the protection of their property stemmed from concerns about the protection of white men's property in the form of an inheritance. Without control of property beyond that which was negotiated with a male patriarch, the Oregon constitution excluded women from full access to the right of property ownership, the social perception of independence, and the political identity of citizenship.

Repercussions of Land Laws

In the 1880s relatives of individuals who had taken land claims began publishing memoirs, journals, and stories of these early settlers, now identified as "pioneers." Although those renditions of the overland Oregon Trail and the hardships of homesteading would go on to influence subsequent generations' understandings of settler colonialism in the U.S. West, the western nostalgia for the initial settlers who had claimed land had begun to occur even while the Donation Land Act was still in effect. In a newspaper obituary titled "Another Pioneer Gone," published in 1855, the author describes the romanticized adventures of this deceased westerner, how he had come to the West in 1846, and how his legacy was in being a "public spirited and [a] useful citizen."[137] Popular memory of U.S. settlement had quickly woven an image that could incorporate a settler who had only lived in the West for nine years. Although this type of memorialization moved fast, settler colonialism played out in Oregon land laws just as quickly. Once such settlement had become a part of the United States' colonial process, westerners began reappropriating the history of their settlement and redefining their roles as colonizers by labeling themselves "pioneers."[138]

During the congressional debate over Oregon's statehood in 1858 and 1859 U.S. representatives tended to connect specific arguments on Oregon's statehood with the "duty" Oregon settlers had performed by colonizing the region in the first place. This association was then accompanied by the argument that expansion was not only the nation's duty but also its legacy as a great empire. Representatives who supported the admittance of Oregon, its constitutional exclusions and all, argued that Oregon's admittance would add to this legacy. Congressman Alexander H. Stephens of Georgia even explained to his colleagues, "At this time the area of our Republic is greater than that of any five of the greatest powers in Europe all combined; greater than that of the Roman Empire in the brightest days of her glory; more extensive than were Alexander's dominions when he stood on the Indus, and wept that he had not more worlds to conquer. Such is our present position; nor are we yet at the end of our acquisition."[139] From the perspective of the twenty years preceding Oregon's statehood—during which time Oregon land laws had helped colonize the Pacific Northwest region—the United States had won a war with Mexico, settled northern boundary disputes with Great Britain, acquired six new states, and held multiple territories. Stephens viewed Oregon as an additional piece of the empire, but Oregon remained an active entity, and as the product of settler colonialism Oregon and its laws continued to influence this growing empire.

Decades after Oregon had become a state, other states continued to discuss Oregonians' racial exclusions to land ownership, including real estate, established by Oregon's state constitution in 1859. A Kansas editorial speculated that a "wild-eyed fanatic who promised to enforce them was elected Governor . . . [and that] he screamed 'nullification!' every time a free n—was allowed to squat on his domain." The specific language choice of "fanatic" notes the author's disdain for the law, but it also questions how such a law had remained active in Oregon. Questioning the effectiveness of this exclusionary law, the author asked, "And what was the result? Go ask the free n—s in Oregon today [1882] who are holding real estate, making contracts and maintaining suits in direct opposition to the State constitution and laws."[140] Following decades of investing a great deal of time and effort into constructing exclusionary laws about property ownership, Oregon had not consistently applied the restriction. Regardless of Oregon's perceived lack of enforcement for property laws, the legacy of Oregon's exclusionary policies was a matter of who else acknowledged their legitimacy and accepted their racialized foundations.

Amid the contentious environment in the country after the passage of the Chinese Exclusion Act in 1882, non–West Coast papers were quick to point out the questionable continuation of the thirty-year-old Oregon law, which excluded citizens of Chinese ancestry from owning real estate. One New Orleans paper noted a sizeable real-estate investment in Portland made by an Oregonian of Chinese descent by the name of Seid Black. The author explained that this was unique to Oregon, not because those of Chinese descent did not have the funds to invest in the city but because Oregon's longstanding laws had prevented such investments.[141] This brief statement on Oregon's exclusion to property ownership demonstrated that Oregon's laws hurt Oregonians themselves. Nevertheless, this exclusion to property ownership was only one of the first exclusionary laws specifically applied to those of Chinese ancestry in Oregon. Moreover, this property law exclusion, constructed in the mid-nineteenth century, compounded Oregon's restriction of nonwhite foreign immigration and provided the discourse and legal precedent later echoed in the construction of the Chinese Exclusion Act. Oregon's racialized exclusion to property ownership—as well as its labor restrictions, addressed in chapter 3—ultimately influenced federal immigration policies for the next century.[142]

Regarding married women's property, Kansas followed Oregon and its fellow western states in the practice of constructing legislation that protected wives' property from husbands' debts. Kansas, however, also permitted married women "their equal rights in the possession of their children."[143] This specification allowed for new interpretations of the tenant rights of curtesy, because the Kansas provision granted wives rights over their children, thus questioning the authority husbands had over family property upon the birth of a child. Laws pertaining to the protection of married women's property in Oregon appeared in state statutes in 1866 and 1872. In 1866 Oregon legislators finally created the actual registry for married women's property as required by the state constitution in 1859. Oregon had participated in the national construction of married women's property rights since the Donation Land Act, but Oregon did not stand out for being progressive in comparison to other participating states. Regardless of the state's very active groups of women suffragists, which included Abigail Scott Duniway and Clarina Howard Nichols among their members, Oregon's property laws continued to favor the authority of white men into the twentieth century.[144]

Ultimately, land laws applied to Oregon between 1839 and 1859 demonstrate that land ownership was a mechanism of settler colonialism and a white right, as well as inherently male though dependent on the participation of women. Moreover, Oregon's land laws did not occur in a vacuum. In fact, they influenced other territories and states in the process, whether through the construction of similar laws or by bringing new articulations of racialized and gendered arguments into discussions about the settlement of lands, land ownership, and U.S. citizenship.

CHAPTER 5

The Privileged Right to an Education

Although gathered from the various portion[s] of the Union, the Americans in Oregon are one people. A prevailing desire to educate, to refine, to moralize and ennoble the rising offspring of these hardy and industrious pioneers of the "far west," is every where [*sic*] conspicuously manifested.

—"Society in Oregon," *Oregon Spectator*, September 3, 1846.

Mary and Maria were girls with English fathers and Indigenous mothers who came with their families to Oregon in 1841. Their fathers, employed by the Hudson's Bay Company, married Cree women while stationed in Canada along the Red River. Soon this Canadian settlement became densely populated, and the two families decided they would move to the Willamette Valley in search of more space and greater economic opportunity. After arriving at the Methodist mission located at The Dalles, Mary (age eight) and Maria (age eleven) were left in the care of the missionaries at the Sabbath school while their parents continued west.[1]

According to missionary records, while they were pupils at the Sabbath school both Mary and Maria converted to Christianity and obtained limited reading proficiency. Mary's father returned after ten months to bring the girls to their settlement in the Willamette Valley, though the missionary noted that the father "did not obtain pardon of his sins."[2] Although Mary and Maria had white fathers, the two became subjects within a recording of "heathen conversions," or reports pertaining to the presumed conversion of Indigenous peoples to Christianity, which simply referred to the girls as "half Indians."[3] The girls' fathers were also not distinguished as different from American Indians of the area other than the single mention that the men were English. In fact, when Mary and Maria left the Sabbath school, the missionary remarked, "Thus clearly and most providentially were these littler wanderers in the wilderness prepared to return to their paternal roof."[4] Even though Mary and Maria came from white fathers and the "wilderness" to which they were returning was a white settlement in the Willamette Valley, their racial identities remained nonwhite. The story of Mary and Maria reflects many Oregon children's experiences, and mission schools that focused on Christian conversions were the first available forms of U.S. or European education in the region. All children, whether white or Indigenous, who sought instruction during this earlier phase of settler colonialism found it under the roof of religious institutions.[5] Over time the population of the Pacific Northwest changed, and with this shift in demographics came debates over who had access to an education and what type of education would best serve Oregon children.

During the mid-nineteenth century education became a pillar of American society, but it was not largely viewed as a right; rather, it was seen as a privilege constructed and maintained by a community group or government. Access to education came with rules and restrictions, which meant lawmakers had to decide who could have the privilege of an education. Part of the reason why some western immigrants viewed education as a privilege and not a right came from the fact that education—or school systems deemed acceptable by European or U.S. standards—in areas under settlement often came into being through the service of a religious group. Missionaries found education a necessary component of conversion and believed those receiving an education benefited from the instruction. Pupils, the missionaries believed, had the privilege of receiving this education and potentially of being converted.[6] Once settler communities levied taxes on their inhabitants to develop and maintain educational systems, however, both the goal of an education and the power structures behind education changed. Inhabitants of the community had a right to schooling in the same way they held a right to other services developed and maintained by the city, county, territory, or state. Education, therefore, became a right even in the sparsely settled Far West and despite the prevailing perception of education as a privilege.

Much of the discussion around establishing education systems in Oregon became rooted in the process of colonization and U.S. justification for settlement. Taking focus away from economic and political arguments, some promoters of overland immigration to Oregon insisted that U.S. settlement was a means to enforce moral conditions in the West. In one Oregon editorial, a settler boasted about the region's morality, stating that Oregonians "feel unfeigned pleasure in announcing to the world, that the social, moral, political and religious state of society in Oregon, is at least as elevated and enlightened as can be witnessed in any of the territory or frontier settlements east of the Rocky Mountains." The author continued that among Oregon settlers there was "A prevailing desire to educate, to refine, to moralize and ennoble the rising offspring of these hardy and industrious pioneers of the 'far west,' is every where [*sic*] conspicuously manifested." Promoters of Oregon settlement, such as the aforementioned author, believed that Oregon served as a continuation of the "moral enlightenment" found in the United States. Through the settlement of Oregon and subsequent education opportunities, this colonial outpost was brought into the social and cultural fold of the nation.[7] This perspective emphasized Oregon as a colony that benefited from U.S. settlement as well as echoed the moral obligation that settlers had to Oregon, in much the same way that support for missionary efforts had done and would do.

Education policies in Oregon had to address the needs of those living in the region, but lawmakers also negotiated how education should be established and for whom it was available. The mission schools, the early colonists' arguments about securing moral settlements, and the reality of miscegenation within the region all had long-lasting effects on education in Oregon. This chapter addresses how education laws and arguments about morality helped perpetuate the process of settler colonialism in the West and shaped Oregon's perception on the role of religion in education. It further reveals how miscegenation between white Oregon settlers and American Indians (as well as Kanaka immigrants) had influenced the role of race and gender in the right to an education. Finally, it demonstrates how the issues of religion and class defined both access to and control over education in Oregon.

Settler Colonialism through Morality and Education

Part of the discourse used by the United States in the colonization of the West reflected the belief that the United States would improve the land with its physical presence and potentially enlighten the Indigenous communities by introducing American and Christian cultural practices. Arguments about moral improvement, therefore, became a way to legitimize the settlement of the West.[8] The basis of these moral arguments reflected ideals of the Enlightenment. Progress, it was perceived by many in the U.S., embodied the basis of human betterment, and this extended to advancements in western expansion.[9] Furthermore, as historian Nayan Shah demonstrates, Enlightenment ideals empowered those with access to liberties and protections granted by a government while providing "rampant justification for inequality and the subordination of those" viewed as not benefiting from the ideas of Enlightenment, therefore those "deemed incapable of self-rule."[10]

Sub-Agent Elijah White, for example, reported to U.S. Secretary of War J. M. Porter in 1843 that settlement by U.S. immigrants in connection with missionary activities not only benefited U.S. claims to Oregon but also did much "in advancing civilization, temperance, literature, and good morals, saying nothing of the evils that must [have] arisen in this lawless country in the absence of all moral restraint."[11] Oregon settlers and national commentators viewed the education of the youth (whether white settler children or Indigenous children) as a vehicle through which to improve the region's morality. Oregon lawmakers' use of morality arguments and subsequent construction of education policies both supported the process of settler colonialism and laid a foundation for Oregon's treatment of education as a right within its territory and then state.

As discussed in chapter 1, missionaries served as one of the first waves of European and U.S. colonization in Oregon during the nineteenth century. Although the buildings established by missionaries were not always permanent, the construction of missions and the attempt to conform Indigenous peoples to the mission's culture and social policies (generally involving an education system) helped initiate what soon became a lasting process of settler colonialism. By the mid-nineteenth century numerous denominations of Christian missionaries had found their way to Oregon; among them was a large contingent of U.S. Methodists led by Reverend Jason Lee.[12] National newspapers noted this movement, with one New York editorial reporting that two sizeable groups of mission families, geared to bring Christianity to Indigenous communities of the Pacific Northwest, had left Boston for the Methodist mission along the Columbia River in the summer of 1838. This particular group also served as "reinforcements" for current missionaries in the region.[13]

The U.S. missionaries were not alone. European missionaries continued to arrive in Oregon with both religious and educational prerogatives as late as the 1840s. For example, an Ohio newspaper explained that Belgian nuns had embarked on a mission to Oregon with the intention of providing moral assistance to the people of Fort Vancouver, which predominately comprised "Canadians and Indians."[14] Which religious group would achieve the moral high ground in Oregon was still unclear as overland U.S. settlement began. Moreover, this religious movement to Oregon coincided with the imperial struggle between the United States and Great Britain over ownership of the region. U.S. politicians as well as Oregon settlers drew connections between morality and the perceived American culture to insist that their presence would bring enlightenment to the region. The establishment of mission schools laid the groundwork for arguments about morality in the acquisition of Oregon.

Supporters of Oregon settlement promoted the efforts of early missionaries and the advancement of Christian education in the region. Oregon editorials described the work of individuals such as Hall J. Kelley (an early businessman who attempted to develop a colony on the Columbia River) as having helped in the "planting on the northwest coast of America, the vine of Christianity, and the germ of civil freedom." One article maintained that these groups were "anticipating the formation of an American settlement" and therefore had brought educational systems founded in Christian morals in "preparation for the colonization of Oregon." Oregon settlers' depiction of missionary development in the region had merged the goal of conversion with the need for education to portray U.S. settlement as a natural extension necessary for the "founding of a new republic of civil and religious freedom on the shores of the Pacific Ocean."[15] Moral benevolence, this perception argued, was the foundation of U.S. colonization in Oregon from which schools would be created.

Once education was rooted in arguments of moral enlightenment, the construction of schools could be conceived and requested outside of missions. And upon the development of the colony, Oregon settlers began to view education as necessary to establish a permanent foothold in the region, thus seeking out communal and governmental involvement in education systems to ensure a future with educated occupants capable of continuing prosperous settlements.[16] Oregon education systems were developed to maintain physical settlement, first through missionary structures and then within the creation of communal or government-run schools.

When Oregon became an American territory in 1846, settlement by U.S. immigrants had been underway for many years. Controlling lands remained important to the colonial development of the region and further solidified both the settlers' and U.S. authority over the unrestrained region.[17] Soon, however, some settlers became concerned that this emphasis on land was detrimental to other elements of a successful society, especially its education. Oregon settlers began bringing this issue to light, with one editorial noting, "Of all the evils which threaten to trouble us, there is not a greater than the want of a disposition in our people, to educate their children." Yes, securing the lands of Oregon was necessary and demonstrated that the region was in the possession of the settlers, but—as the author of the editorial expressed—"On the other hand, with all that is justly ours, with the whole continent at our command, and our children growing up in ignorance, of what benefit would it be to us?"[18] Settlers feared that the absence of an education system in each community and within the reach of Oregon children meant that all the work to settle the region would have been for naught. Education, they believed, would provide permanence and successful longevity to the settlement.[19]

The Oregon Emigration Society's "Article of Agreement" of 1839 asserted that agrarian settlement accompanied goals of moral enlightenment. The Society stated that "the country west of the Rocky Mountains affords very many facilities for the exercise of Christian benevolence, in civilization of the Indians, for the accumulation of wealth by agriculture and commerce"; settlers believed that their settlement of the region would be mutually beneficial for both the settlers and Indigenous communities, whom the settlers believed would be civilized by their society's "establishment of government."[20] This argument of moral improvement existed in the minds of people beyond those physically occupying Oregon, and groups such as emigration societies helped reinforce arguments about morality the U.S. government had cultivated in its claims to the Pacific Northwest decades prior.

As early as 1811 John Quincy Adams, then a U.S. diplomat to Great Britain, expressed his view that the western regions of the North American continent should be brought into the fold of the United States, "For the common happiness of them all, for their peace and prosperity."[21] Adams believed that U.S. systems of governance would uplift inhabitants of the Far West and argued that the occupation and settlement of Oregon would bring about structures necessary for the moral enlightenment of the region. By 1846 Adams—the former president of the United States and acting Congressional representative—had further urged his colleagues to take immediate action toward the acquisition of Oregon, insisting that the United States had a moral duty to U.S. settlers in Oregon to end the joint occupation agreement with Great Britain and force England to act on the matter. At this time, with the country already engaged in diplomatic issues along the border between Mexico and Texas, U.S. politicians feared that attempting to take Oregon would only result in war with England.[22] At the very least, Adams pleaded, the U.S. government should extend its laws to those settlements that lay outside of the disputed lands (those east or south of the Columbia River) in order to protect these footholds that supported U.S. institutions.[23] Oregon had become a land secured by settlement, and U.S. politicians defended this settlement through arguments of moral improvement via the creation of U.S. structures.

Various members of Congress had supported the formal occupation of Oregon by the 1840s, arguing that such territorial additions were morally beneficial to western lands and their inhabitants as well as to the people who would go to Oregon and build a democratic society.[24] For example, Massachusetts Congressman Joseph Richardson viewed western expansion as a moral duty of the federal government and saw U.S. settlement as "an extension of the blessing of civilization, of freedom, and happiness, to the human race."[25] Missouri Senator Thomas Hart Benton described western settlers as "children of Adam" who continued to spread civilization across the globe. Benton further asserted, "American yeomanry perceives this to be their country . . . [and they] expect to perpetuate a race of free men, worthy to uphold the independence of their country, and to advance the glory of the American name."[26] When settlement grew to the point at which colonial leaders created a provisional government, some Oregon settlers became concerned with preserving the region's moral authority and looked to education for the answer.

Among other policies the provisional government wanted to secure once the United States held jurisdiction over Oregon were laws that provided "liberally for the education of the rising generation."[27] Mission schools had only supported small portions of settler children, because the goal of Christian conversion required these institutions to focus on the education of Indigenous children. As the colony developed, so too did the Oregon settlers' desire to create educational services separate from the mission schools. The nearly three-year delay by the United States in creating a formal territorial government in Oregon, however, prolonged the development of public schools. Oregon provisional governor George Abernethy addressed this issue in his "Message of the

Governor" in 1847, pledging to bring the need for education in Oregon to the attention of Congress. Abernethy argued, "School districts should be formed in several counties, and school-houses built. Teachers should be employed by the people, I have no doubt, and thus pave the way for more advanced institutions."[28] Oregon settlers had high expectations for education and, it would seem, for the role of the government in providing access to that very education.

In 1849 the territorial government of Oregon established a system of common schools to provide settlers' children with an education. Praising the Legislative Assembly for its work on the school law, one editorial explained that Oregon was in dire need of an educational system to protect its impressionable youth. The author argued that because "This Territory is very peculiar[ly] situated; and to no people in the world is education more important." The editorial continued that though the region had been "Exposed to all the ingredients and facilities of vice, our safety will be found in the enlightenment of our people." For such salvation, the author insisted that Oregon lawmakers should "Let the youth of our Territory receive a thorough and liberal education, and much will have been done to secure them against intemperance and kindred vices." The editorial even suggested that Oregon settlers sought out and valued education more than national contemporaries, and that, "animated by these enlightened views on the subject, we [Oregonians] only need an efficient system to secure to us."[29] The school systems established by Oregon lawmakers, however, had to operate without the donation of school lands from the federal government for two years, until Congress passed an act to create school lands for both the territories of Minnesota and Oregon.[30] As with several other laws that Oregon carried into the territorial and state government, the educational structures in Oregon predated federal involvement. Regional education policies reflected perspectives about moral integrity that Oregon settlers had embraced as necessary for the future development of their colony and that Oregon believed it was particularly poised to enforce.

Politically speaking, not all Oregonians felt that the U.S. government possessed the moral principles represented in Oregon, and concern about the moral authority of the U.S. federal government became more pronounced after the Oregon Treaty of 1846.[31] Addressing the existence of political slander within national politics, an Oregon editorial suggested that the region held a greater moral foundation under its provisional government than what it would obtain by becoming a U.S. territory. The author argued that prior to the extension of U.S. laws and politics over Oregon, "each one felt an interest in his neighbor's prosperity, and as far as in him lay was willing to promote it—when party and national spirit was not manifested; then Oregon was a land of liberty." Under their own laws, the author believed, Oregon settlers did not fall to the folly of those "whose minds are as uneducated as their own vocabulary, and as deep as the black on their shoes."[32] The United States may have acquired Oregon, in part, to secure the morality of the West, but some Oregon settlers maintained that the moral nature they had established was superior to that experienced in the rest of the nation.

Moreover, Oregon lawmakers felt they could use their provisional government and its laws to enforce moral conditions upon settlers. One Oregon editorial insisting that the formation of the government was necessary for settlement in the region questioned why Oregon's Organic Laws, "founded upon just principles," would require alterations. The author insisted, "The people of Oregon being of different nations, and in a land over which no power exercised exclusive sovereignty—their number increasing, and their interest bringing them in collision to adjust disputes, punish crimes, or keep the peace—found it absolutely necessary to establish some rules, by the observance of which they could live together in peace and harmony."[33] Oregon settlers had established a government and laws to address their own needs, not just those reflective of the empire. Those structures, many settlers believed, were to secure a settlement guided by Oregon lawmakers' interpretations of democratic morals.

Part of why Oregon legislators attempted to defend the moral image of Oregon was to validate their self-made government system and laws. Oregon settlers hoped that questioning the authority of a "morally upright" colony would prove challenging, if not impossible.[34] In his letter to President Millard Fillmore, the newly appointed Oregon governor John P. Gaines explained that the foundations to and context of Oregon's provisional legislation made it a necessary addition to the development of territorial laws. Gaines suggested that Oregon settlers had proven themselves to the nation because they had successfully existed on "the great extent of coast and still more extended frontier, constantly exposed, [despite] the great distance from Washington and the difficulty of rapid communication." Due to the fact that Oregon settlers had been placed in such a position, the colony had been forced to construct its own policies. Gaines continued that the federal government should grant "their brethren who are located on the extreme western border of our great republic" liberties in their legal and governmental dealings, rather than constraining them to Congressional approval.[35] The distance between Oregon and the nation's capital was an important part of Gaines's evaluation of why Oregon's provisional policies needed to be carried into the territorial government. Gaines emphasized that fact that though the laws Oregon settlers passed had been made outside of U.S. purview, the settlement had aided the nation, and Oregon should therefore receive certain considerations from Congress for its provisional laws.

Although discussions about making Oregon a U.S. territory placed a premium on the moral advancements that came with the nation's acquisition of the region, many U.S. representatives did not view Oregon as possessing superior policies or structures, especially when it came to its exclusionary laws.[36] The region's laws preventing Black Americans from immigrating to as well as owning property or filing a suit in Oregon found considerable objection at the national level. And while some Oregon lawmakers, especially Anti-Democrats, questioned the integrity of those who wanted to exclude Black Americans from political rights in Oregon, these arguments did not focus on the morality of the region.

Despite the reality of the region's laws and practices, Oregon legislators attempted to protect the image of moral integrity the settlers had bestowed upon themselves while they conducted the Constitutional Convention. One of the methods Oregon delegates employed when debating laws that restricted the rights of Black Americans was to associate republicanism with acts of humanity. Addressing the provision to restrict Black Americans from coming to or settling in Oregon, Anti-Democrat Thomas Dryer described the proposed exclusion as "anything but liberal, humane, democratic, or republican." But Dryer was careful not to claim that Oregon possessed these characteristics; rather, he placed these unsavory exclusions at the feet of the Democrats and suggested that adopting such a provision would weaken the humanity of Oregon.[37] Furthermore, William Watkins explained to his colleagues that while he appreciated the goal of keeping Black Americans from taking up residence in Oregon, he feared the provisions were unrepublican and that leaving this group no legal recourse in the future state would damage Oregon's moral image. Watkin further stated that he felt compelled to vote against the constitution, asking his fellow delegates, "Could anything be done to prevent the negroes migration hither, and at the same time not stultify every sentiment of justice and humanity, I should not oppose it, but I cannot purchase it at the expense of our good name abroad."[38] Preserving the image of Oregon, he believed, was more important than his desire to exclude Black Americans from the region.

While Oregon lawmakers may not have implemented policies reflective of the moral nature they believed their settlement embodied, Oregon legislators tried to disassociate the region's more controversial laws from its moral image.[39] Not all members of the U.S. Congress, however, shared this opinion about Oregon. Representatives who opposed Oregon's exclusion of Black Americans from specific political rights questioned the morality of such policies as well as those who supported them. In fact, Congressman Clark B. Cochrane of New York went to the extent of characterizing Oregon's treatment of Black Americans in its proposed constitution as "refined inhumanity" and "venture[d] to affirm, that in point of needles and gratuitous barbarity, it is without a parallel in the whole history of civilized States."[40]

Defending his territory against accusations that Oregon's constitution contained unconstitutional and immoral provisions, Oregon territorial delegate to Congress Joseph Lane insisted that the House should recall what Oregon settlers had provided the nation. According to Lane, prior to Oregon becoming a U.S. territory, "the enterprising men who were there took care of the American right to the soil, organized a provisional government in 1841." Lane proclaimed that settlers had "established missions and settlements there . . . A provisional assembly was appointed to watch over the general welfare . . . In 1843, a regular provision[al] government in a healthy condition." Contrary to Congress's questioning of Oregon's morality, Lane explained his preference for the settler colony's government, noting, "There was order and happiness, and I felt that it was a pity to disturb the government."[41] Lane effectively depicted a utopian society based on American principles and serving U.S. interests in the West. Even representatives such as Charles Gilman of Maine, who greatly opposed Oregon's restrictive provisions, acknowledged this "service" and suggested that Oregon settlers had "gone there to lay the foundation of a State on the western slope of the Rocky Mountains."[42] Interestingly, the language used by Congress to explain the benefits derived from Oregon settlers—both for the nation and for the "civilization" of the region—suggested the result was predetermined. These discussions depicted past actions by Oregon settlers as if they had known the colony would eventually become a state in the Union.

Oregon's history of acquisition had become a story of moral endeavors and the extension of U.S. democratic systems rather than a narrative of chaotic and brutal settler colonialism. Kentucky representative John Stevenson, for example, provided a speech for Oregon's admittance to statehood that supported this false perception and even asserted that the acquisition of Oregon was necessary for the continuation of the nation. Stevenson insisted that "to expect that this Union can be kept alive and perpetuated without the attachment of every section of the country" was akin to expecting that bringing a man "into a church and showing him the ten commandments engraved upon tablets of wood or stone" would make him "a Christian." Representatives such as Stevenson connected ideas of organic expansion to destined acquisition and argued that denying Oregon its statehood also kept the nation from being complete. "I stand by this Confederation," Stevenson continued; he proclaimed to his congressional colleagues, "one of the proudest votes I shall ever give will be that which I shall give in favor of the admission of Oregon."[43]

The admission of Oregon as a state in 1859 represented another stage in the colonization and settlement of the region. Oregon and federal legislators argued that the region and its settlers perpetuated Enlightenment ideals associated by Congress with the government structure of the United States. In doing so, both groups were able to justify the settlement and acquisition of Oregon. The position of Oregon as a desired colony, territory, and then state permitted the region leniency on the exclusionary laws it bore. Arguments of morality, however, could not hide the complicated reality of Oregon's settlement. Oregon lawmakers' development of education laws and the influence of miscegenation on definitions of citizenship revealed such imperfections as well as the colony's dependence on Indigenous bodies.

Race, Gender, and Miscegenation in Education Laws

Fur-trade marriages, sometimes referred to as marriages *á la façon du pays* (in the manner of the country) and generally misunderstood as monetary exchanges for wives, became commonplace in the Pacific Northwest during the eighteenth and early nineteenth centuries. Such marriages usually resulted in the birth of what were customarily referred to by settlers as "half breed" children.[44] The population of the Hudson's Bay Company's Fort Vancouver distinctively reflected these relations, as many employees developed relationships with American Indian women from neighboring Indigenous communities. Even the fort's officers married Indigenous women, including its chief factor Dr. John McLoughlin, whose wife, Marguerite Wadin McKay McLoughlin, was born to a Cree mother and a Canadian father.[45] The frequency of miscegenation, or mixed-race relationships, does not suggest that those connected to the fur trade did not hold racial biases of their own.[46] As missionaries began to enter Oregon, however, racial biases toward American Indians became more distinguished.

Evaluating the practice and acceptability of miscegenation in Oregon demonstrates how the goal of conversion and missionaries' perceptions

4. Marguerite Wadin McKay McLoughlin, neg. no. 707, Oregon Historical Society Research Library.

of race had brought forth the initial establishment of European and U.S. school systems. The treatment of race within these mission schools not only reveals how Oregon settlers would continue to view the education of "half breed" children but also explains how Oregon lawmakers viewed the racial qualification for the right to an education, more generally. The Hudson's Bay Company established the first of these educational institutions at Fort Vancouver, which brought Indigenous children in from across the region, including seven American Indian boys from the eastern Columbia Plateau.[47] The schools were initially facilitated by officers of the fort, and in 1836 Chaplain Herbert Beaver became the school's formal headmaster. Although short-lived, Fort Vancouver's education system portrayed how mission schools in Oregon drew racial distinctions between missionaries and those they educated. Within the fort, all the children received the same education whether they were children of American Indian or Kanaka women.[48] Beaver focused conversion efforts toward all "nonwhite" children and associated all children with Indigenous mothers as being nonwhite; thus, he believed they were students in need of spiritual salvation regardless of their fathers' race.[49] This early region-specific application of the "one-drop" rule influenced missionaries' perception of race and miscegenation in Oregon.

Beaver's reaction to miscegenation in the fort further defined racial differences between the missionaries and those they worked with. Among Beaver's numerous objections to Fort Vancouver was the number of mixed-race fur-trade marriages and the fact that many marriages were never sanctioned by a church or state. Hoping to redress what he identified as "illegitimate marriages," Beaver requested to perform a marriage between McLoughlin and his wife, and he aggressively encouraged other mixed-race couples to have church marriages as well.[50] McLoughlin refused, and Beaver retaliated by writing several reports to the company's headquarters about McLoughlin's unsanctioned marriage to a nonwhite woman. In making these reports, Beaver attempted to challenge McLoughlin's social status by questioning the validity of his marriage and referring to Marguerite Wadin McKay McLoughlin as racially inferior.[51] Although Beaver claimed concern about upholding the institution of marriage, the fact that McLoughlin's marriage did not abide by British or church customs was not at the heart of his issue. Beaver would not have approved of the McLoughlins' mixed-race relationship regardless of how they were married, nor would he have viewed the marriage as equal to one between two white individuals. In fact, Beaver's reports to London expressed his view that himself and his wife Jane were in an elevated social position at the fort because they were both white. Beaver tried to legitimize and grant his own marriage greater social authority at the fort by racializing the McLoughlins' marriage and defining it as immoral and illegitimate.[52]

U.S. missionaries coming into Oregon in the 1830s also held specific ideas about the race of American Indians and mixed-race relations. Joining other missionaries appointed by the American Board of Commissioners, Mary Richardson Walker and Elkanah Walker set out for Oregon in 1837. When documenting the trip and recording her work as a missionary Mary Richardson Walker diligently attributed titles to women she discussed, except when the woman was not white. Early in her overland immigration, for example, Walker referred to her female colleague Mary Dix Gray as "Mrs. Gray," such as when she recorded in the spring of 1838, "Mrs. Gray and myself found entertainment at Rev. Mr. McCoy's."[53] When addressing a married white couple, Walker assigned both the man and woman titles, as she did in an entry in August 1838, stating, "Found Mr. and Mrs. Spaulding, Mr. and Mrs. Gray had gone to Walla Walla."[54]

But in August 1838 Walker noted, "Mr. Connor's wife gave birth to a daughter. She followed camp about thirty miles," and the following day mentioned that "the squaw came into the camp with her child in her arms about ten o'clock."[55] Connor, a white man, received the title of "Mr.," and the entry connected a wife to him. It was not until the second entry that Walker revealed the wife to be an Indigenous woman. Rather than recording a name for said woman, Walker referred to her as "the squaw." Walker did not perceive American Indians as qualifying for the same titles that her white missionary colleagues deserved. Although she acknowledged that Connor had a wife, Walker did not extend her the courtesy of possessing a name or the title of "Mrs.," thus devaluing the Connors' relationship regardless of its marital status. Both prior to and following this event Walker noted several instances when "half breed children" were present and referred to individual unnamed women as "half blood."[56] Although Walker did not directly speak against miscegenation within her journal entries, she treated those whose race reflected the act of miscegenation the same as those identified as American Indians, without a name or title recorded. Walker's perceptions of race exemplify a pattern generally found among missionaries: the belief that even people with a white parent were not themselves white.[57]

U.S. missionaries also racialized American Indians' capacity to learn or perform acts attributed to Christian behavior. In some instances, Pacific Northwest missionaries depicted the bodies of American Indians as something that could be both colonized and controlled. As mentioned earlier, missionary efforts to convert and subsequently educate Indigenous communities in Oregon served as a process of colonization, but this also included having American Indians conduct themselves in ways that reflected what the missionaries believed to be acceptable moral lifestyles. Missionaries encouraged American Indians to adopt American and European practices, including specific methods of farming, house care, and parenting.[58] This could take the form of missionaries bringing American Indians into a mission household to provide a labor or service and *learn* from the missionary family how to conduct themselves. Within a missionary's household, American Indians' actions were monitored, adjusted, controlled, and always recognized as being different from actions conducted by the missionary family.[59]

How Indigenous bodies appeared at public events also concerned these foreign settlers. Dr. Elijah White expressed to the U.S. Secretary of War his concern that Indigenous women's bodies were not properly covered and therefore inappropriate for attendance at religious services put on by local missionaries. Feeling compelled to aid in the "improvement and reformation" of the Indigenous women, White gathered money to purchase "various articles of manufacture, in order to get them clothed comfortably to appear in church." Evidently White perceived the American Indian women as needing to cover their bodies in different attire before they could attend the religious service and receive the mission's gospel. White enlisted "the cheerful co-operation of the mission ladies in instructing them [on] how to sew and make up their dresses." The female missionaries obliged and assisted in this attempt to control Indigenous women's bodies by changing the women's clothing to reflect Christian cultural practices. White concluded this section of his report by noting his "happiness to see some twenty of these neatly clad [American Indian women] at divine service."[60] Although "improvement and reformation" was the goal, the U.S. federal agent and the missionary women had distinguished the bodies of Indigenous women as culturally different from their views of acceptability, and tried to changed them to the settlers' perceptions and lifestyle.[61] This change of wardrobe did not change how White and the missionaries viewed these Indigenous women; these women were still identified as American Indians. Rather this interaction further distinguished differences between the settlers and Indigenous peoples.

The opportunity for Indigenous communities to adopt the missionaries' lifestyles sometimes gave way to serving the mission as laborers.[62] In an 1838 journal entry Mary Richardson Walker recalled the household of Narcissa and Marcus Whitman at the Waiilatpu mission (near present-day Walla Walla, Washington). This mission house comprised several American Indians performing chores and, in Walker's eyes, resembled more the "house of a Southern planter than a Christian Missionary."[63] The Walkers themselves employed several American Indian children to help with seasonal responsibilities or to assist the family for a time after the birth of a child. Although missionaries such as the Walkers and Whitmans depended on such labor, a common complaint was that American Indians were intruding on the missionary families' personal space. Missionary families such as the Whitmans and Walkers asked Indigenous men and women to provide intimate services but also attempted to create space between the house servants and the family. One way for missionaries to create this separation was to distinguish racial differences between the groups and define racial spaces.[64]

When white Oregon missionaries identified acceptable or appropriate contact between American Indians and missionary families, they consistently elevated their families above the Indigenous communities. For example, while the Walkers were visiting the Whitman mission, an American Indian woman that served in the house breastfed the Walkers' son Cyrus. Mary Richardson Walker on one occasion noted, "I am glad my babe can be supplied with milk though it comes from a black breast."[65] Walker allowed the Indigenous woman to breastfeed her son and thereby provide a service for her family, but she also recognized and noted her concern about the racial difference between the woman and that of her family. Fears of moral "contamination" from the breastmilk of nonwhite women had gained prominence in the United States, and by the mid-nineteenth century groups of medical professionals discouraged mothers from having "strange women" breastfeed their children.[66] Nevertheless, the use of a wet nurse continued within the Whitman household, and Walker accepted this practice. Though the proximity of bodies was necessary for an American Indian woman to breastfeed a white child, distance was established by noting the racial difference between the two individuals.[67] Such racial distinctions and desired separation between Indigenous communities and missionaries was necessary to define differences between mixed-race individuals and white settler families. As with arguments for the settlement of Oregon, the missionaries interpreted their position as spiritually benefiting American Indians, noting specific differences they saw between themselves and those they tried to convert to Christianity to justify this relationship.

Reflecting this approach to identifying race in Oregon, the Oregon Emigration Society set out in 1839 to develop its own education system for its settlers. The emigration society's "Article of Agreement" specified that in addition to providing "one common school for every fifty children," the organization would establish "a manual labor school for the benefit of the Indian children."[68] Similar to the Methodists' Willamette mission, the schools were to be segregated, with the white children attending the common schools and American Indian children sent to a labor school focused on agricultural education.[69] The society, however, made no mention of schools or qualifications for children with mixed-raced parents; thus, the lack of a racial distinction was itself a racial classification that children were either "white" or "Indian." Several sections later the "Articles of Agreement" also stated that "civilized Indians" were eligible to receive "all the rights and immunities of citizenship and no distinction whatever shall be made by law on account of color."[70] Although the Oregon Emigration Society did not define the qualification of a "civilized Indian," the provision demonstrated a different interpretation of race from that used in Oregon mission schools and by missionaries. According to this group of Oregon settlers, there were at least variations of Indigenous individuals, and certain characteristics other than race ought to define those differences.

The demographics that awaited Oregon settlers of the 1840s remained unclear, if not completely speculative, east of the Rocky Mountains. The *New York Tribune* published a letter in 1842, which it claimed to be an extract from an Oregon letter, that addressed the diverse population of the Pacific Northwest and the amount of miscegenation that existed in the region. According to the letter Oregon's non-Indian population comprised approximately seventy-five French Canadians previously employed by the Hudson's Bay Company as well as fifty U.S. immigrants in dispersed groups. Of these settlers, the letter continued, about "one hundred and twenty-five to one hundred and thirty male inhabitants . . . are married to Indian women."[71] If all these numbers are accurate, simple arithmetic would suggest that all adult male Oregon settlers were married to American Indian women. By 1842 the ratio of white males to white females remained quite unbalanced, but white women did live in Oregon, and more were emigrating to the region each spring.[72] Though not exactly representative of the actual demographics in the region, the letter reflected U.S. perceptions of Oregon's population as overland settlement commenced.

Miscegenation was a reality in the Pacific Northwest, and many of the early U.S. settlers had mixed-race families. In 1840 alone twenty-five of the thirty-six marriages recorded by Oregon officials were unions between white men and American Indian women.[73] Although scholars such as Adele Perry have demonstrated that empires employed "non-recognition" practices to sidestep the complication of mixed-raced children in their colonies, the period of joint occupancy in Oregon between the United States and Great Britain allowed white settlers to determine their own policies for this regional population.[74] Once the white male settler population had grown, the group not only took over systems such as education but also altered the treatment of "half breed" children with white fathers. Furthermore, many of these white fathers had gained access to lands through their Indigenous wives' cultural and ancestral authority, and bringing children of these unions under settler laws further removed Indigenous claims to the region.[75] Oregon legislators, therefore, had to reconcile with the fact that if the settler colony's laws were to protect white men's rights, such legislation would also have to protect the rights of their children.

Discussion on the importance of education among Oregon settlers existed from the very formation of the provisional government. A report by the Legislative Committee in 1843 recommended that the judiciary establish certain laws in the settler colony; it included an article stating, "Religion, morality, and knowledge, being necessary to good government and the happiness of mankind, schools, and the means of education shall forever be encouraged."[76] Although such statements were representative of Oregon settlers' desire for an education system, the provisional government had failed to establish schools in Oregon up to that point. A year later the Legislative Committee recognized the settler colony's position between empires but asserted that "we may now be unknown as a state or power . . . But, in order to carry this important measure, and arise to that distinguished station, it becomes the duty of every citizen of this country, to take a deep interest in its present and future welfare." The committee maintained that education in the region should not be delayed—"[as] yet we have the advantages . . . of attaining, at no distant day, to as conspicuous an elevation as any state or power on the continent of America."[77] Establishing education systems continued more slowly, but Oregon legislators interjected the need for schools into bills, reports, and proposals throughout Oregon's time under a provisional government.

The legislative assembly in Oregon also became more direct about this need for an educational system and changed its language from eloquent statements of hope to statements citing it as the "duty of the legislature" and mentioning that "education demands your attention."[78] As a growing region with changing landscapes—whether demographically or physically through increasing settlement by U.S. immigrants—Oregon faced the need to establish numerous institutions, including jails, roads, and a formal land claim office. Private and generally nonsecular schools—addressed in the next section—had begun to replace mission schools, but community and government-ran schools were absent when Oregon became a U.S. territory.

In 1849 the territorial government passed an education law that established schools throughout Oregon where populations and tax revenue could support the institutions. The law specified that the schools "shall be open and free to all children between the ages of four and twenty-one."[79] It made no qualification of race, nationality, or gender for access to an education. Schools were to be aware, however, of each student's lineage. The Oregon law required that teachers keep attendance of students, including "the names of their parents or guardians."[80] This could appear as standard documentation, but the revised education law of 1854 dropped this section and only specified that the schools were available to the "children and youth of each [district]."[81] Perhaps it became undesirable to identify parents in a formal record; no discussion was noted, but the 1849 law was the last time Oregon lawmakers required the recording of students' lineage in the territorial government.

The proposed education article in the Oregon Constitution continued the practice of not including specifications for the types of children allowed to attend the common schools. Ultimately, Oregon delegates simply identified students as "children." The lack of specifications, however, became a focus for delegates during those debates. Delegates such as David Logan pushed for restrictions and moved to include the word "white" before "children." Logan argued that without such racial qualifications in it, the education article "could wring in a n— or an Indian under the provision as it stood." And each time the word "children" stood alone in the article, such delegates pushed for restrictions. John W. Watts, for example, maintained that the article did not fully restrict nonwhite children from attending said schools, so he moved again to include the word "white" in a section different from the one Logan had opposed.[82] Part of delegates' insistence for a racial qualification stemmed from their concern that Black American children would receive the same access to an education as white American children would—or, as other legislators feared, the two races would receive an education at the same schools. Focusing on this possibility, Matthew Deady pointed out that the Ohio constitution had failed to specifically restrict Black American children from entering its common schools and that this had resulted in Ohio admitting "negroes into their schools."[83] Finding this fact and its potential occurrence in Oregon troubling, Deady supported the amendment to include a racial specification to the right to an education.

Always concerned that the Oregon Democrats would bring slavery into Oregon if at all possible, Thomas Dryer questioned his colleagues' full intentions in adding the word "white." Dryer argued, "He saw it sticking out that we were to have slavery here, and he wanted that gentlemen should have an opportunity to educate their own children."[84] Insinuating that Democratic delegates wanted to preemptively exclude Black American children to prepare for the possibility of slavery existing in Oregon, Dryer not only argued that all children of "gentlemen" (including Black American men) should receive access to education but also drew out the very contentious subject of slavery. As discussed in chapter 3, Oregonians later voted on whether their state would allow for slavery and the settlement of free Black Americans as part of the constitution's final passage. Yet, Black Americans already resided in Oregon, and delegates such as William H. Farrar felt that it was necessary to create a provision specifying what access Black American and Indigenous children would have to education in Oregon.[85]

The education of American Indian children in Oregon had already established a precedent based on the specific demographics of Oregon.

Missionaries had treated both American Indian children and "half breed" children as the same, and Oregon settlers incorporated all children into the first common schools to accommodate the children with white fathers and American Indian mothers. Supporting this established precedent, delegate John S. White opposed the racial specification amendment, arguing, "There were many half-breed children in his county" and that these mixed-race children had white fathers who possessed rights as citizens in Oregon. Agreeing with White and recognizing the ramifications of denying the right to an education to children with a voting parent, delegate John C. Peebles added that "there were many voters in his county whose children had Indian blood—half-blood or less. They paid taxes, and their children ought to enjoy the benefits of common schools."[86]

Miscegenation created a unique scenario within Oregon when it came to the rights of white men and their children. As addressed in chapter 4, the male offspring of white men could claim property, which initially granted them access to some rights of citizenship. Restricting a child with an Indigenous mother from the right to an education, therefore, would deny the white father (and citizen of Oregon) the right to send his child to a state-sponsored or public school. While Oregon settlers had struggled with the definition and treatment of race within their laws since the beginning of the provisional government, the rights of white men remained protected.[87]

Even Oregon delegates who vociferously opposed nonwhite children receiving the same education as white children would not question white fathers' rights. Overall, the adoption of a racial qualification faced more opposition than support, and the right to an education was opened to all children to accommodate the reality of miscegenation and its connection to the rights of white men. The final version of Article 8, "Education and School Lands," only distinguished in Section 4 that students were "children residents."[88] Had Oregon included a racial specification within its education article, it would have joined Louisiana as the only state to restrict the right to an education in its state constitution. Another region with a long history of miscegenation, Louisiana had revised its constitution in 1852 to specify that "free public schools" were only open to "free white children."[89] At about the same time that Oregon became a state in 1859, Kansas legislators debated an amendment to the state's constitution that would have excluded Black American children from attending state schools. But, as in Oregon, the amendment ultimately failed.[90]

Much of the role miscegenation played in Oregon's education laws was lost in national discussion of such legislation because the nation lacked an understanding of these local debates. Nevertheless, national papers still addressed the issue of miscegenation in Oregon when it applied for statehood. A New York newspaper article, for example, addressed its distrust of Oregon Democrats and the proposed state's position on slavery, noting, "Quite a number of the leading Lane politicians, lead as they brawl against 'Black Republicanism' and miscegenation." The New York author continued that such Oregon politicians viewed those issues "as much the same thing, hav[ing] already, according to some of our Oregon letters, provided themselves with Indian wives. Very likely they may find satisfaction in completing patriarchal establishments by the addition of Indian slaves."[91] Many national papers viewed Oregon's territorial delegate to Congress, Joseph Lane, as the leader behind Oregon's proslavery sentiments and the Democratic Party's dominance in the region. As addressed in chapter 3, Oregon politicians (along with other Democrats of the day) attempted to invalidate arguments against slavery by associating antislavery opinions with abolition and even suggesting that those against slavery loved Black Americans and encouraged miscegenation. National politicians also used this tactic on Oregon politicians, but they either did not recognize the role miscegenation in Oregon played or chose to use this role to further insult Oregon politicians by reducing mixed-race relationships to a system of Indian slavery. Regardless of intent, the nation (or rather, those not settling in Oregon) did not view miscegenation or the resulting mixed-race children in the same light as Oregon lawmakers did.

Discussion about gender and its connection to miscegenation also made its way into the construction of Oregon's education laws. Unlike the transference of enslaved status through the mother in U.S. slave states, the racial identities of children in early Oregon came from their fathers. Under the settler colony's policies and social practices, the child would potentially be identified as "white" if the father were white and the mother were American Indian—and sometimes Kanaka or other Indigenous peoples from the Sandwich Islands.[92] Oregon lawmakers never gave this specific distinction its own law, but Oregon legislation consistently listed "mulattoes" and persons of Black American ancestry as an excluded nonwhite group, whereas "half breed" persons with white fathers received certain advantages and rights in Oregon. This difference in racial classification derived from the prejudice toward Black Americans in Oregon, but it also connected to the fact that Oregon settlers accommodated offspring deemed the result of white settlement.[93] White men were initially able to access land through marriage to Indigenous women, and the highly disproportionate ratio of white men to white women in Oregon prior to the 1850s made such mixed-race couplings acceptable.[94] In fact miscegenation laws restricting marriage between a white person—man or woman—and a person with "more than one-half Indian blood" in Oregon did not come about until 1866.[95] Prior to the Civil War Oregon lawmakers viewed miscegenation between Black and white settlers as neither necessary nor beneficial to the settlement of Oregon. Indigenous mothers of "half breed" children in Oregon, however, did not benefit socially or politically in the same way that their children (possibly) could.

If both settlers and specific Indigenous communities recognized the union of a white man with an American Indian woman, the Indigenous woman might retain a respectable social status or at least indifferent respect from the two groups. But in Indigenous communities the social position of the mixed-race child was at greater risk than the status of the American Indian mother. If a specific Indigenous community did not recognize the union as fulfilling its cultural requirements, such as a bride price, then the woman would not be seen as married and her children considered illegitimate or parentless. If an Oregon official did not document the union, then the settler colony could view the child as illegitimate, too; if the white father claimed the child, then the child would be at least socially legitimate. The American Indian or Kanaka mother, however, was unlikely to receive social acceptance from the Oregon settler community regardless of the union's marital status or the perceived race of her children. According to Oregon settlers, she would not be viewed as a citizen of Oregon, nor would she possess rights as such.[96]

Regarding Oregon's education laws, American Indian or Kanaka mothers of mixed-race children represented both the racial and gendered qualifications for the right to an education. Only the father's racial identity could extend rights within Oregon's settler community to his children; the mother's racial identity could not, as she did not possess rights outside of those granted to her white husband. In 1854, as Oregon lawmakers dealt with legal entanglements associated with the Donation Land Act, Chief Justice C. J. Williams ruled that white male settlers married to Indigenous women were eligible to claim the land donations available to married couples. Defending his decision with the explanation that Indigenous women were not themselves eligible as settlers—rather, they were eligible as wives to settlers—the judge further noted, "Congress must have known that many of the early settlers of Oregon had married Indian women; and if it had not intended to place men so married upon the same footing with other married men, why did Congress not say so?"[97] Thus, the Donation Land Act included Indigenous wives in order to protect their white settler husbands' rights to full land claims. Oregon legislation, backed by a federal law, recognized that white settler husbands could extend their rights as citizens to their American Indian wives, but the nonwhite wife could not exercise those rights herself.[98] A white wife, in contrast, could technically hold property in her own name.

Questions of inheritance for the estates of unmarried women further revealed the legal perception of women's rights in Oregon as well as how those rights could extend to their children. Addressing a bill "relative to executors, administers, &c.," Oregon legislators debated (and ultimately passed) a provision that would prevent "an illegitimate child" from being "the representative of his mother, from inheriting any part of the estate of her kindred, either lineal or collateral." Objections to illegitimate children becoming their mothers' heirs focused on the opinion that extending such rights to illegitimate children would become "another inducement for the production of illegitimate children" and would place these children "no matter what cast of color—upon the same footing as children born in wedlock." Apart from emphasizing the perception that illegitimate children were social outcasts, the Oregon legislators regarded this as a race issue and objected to the idea that "a little half breed or mulatto" could "claim to inherit their property, as the illegitimate offspring of a female relative."[99] The very fact that the children were mixed-race and connected to a female's inheritance played a part in their illegitimacy, as Oregon had accommodated white men marrying American Indian (or sometimes Kanaka) women, but laws did not recognize or defend unions between white women and any nonwhite men. If such mixed-race unions were illegitimate, then any children as a result of said unions were also illegitimate.[100] Legal debates on the rights of Oregon mothers reflected the settler colony's debate over the meaning of citizenship and revealed lawmakers' willingness to change mothers' access to rights as the conditions of the colony themselves transformed into those of an American state.

Oregon legislators' discussions on women's inheritance to mixed-race children demonstrated how these lawmakers perceived mothers as simultaneously guilty for the existence of mixed-race children and legally separate from such children. Despite La Fayette Grover's pleas not to punish illegitimate children for "the parent's crime," Reuben P. Boise laid the blame for why illegitimate children existed in Oregon at the feet of their mothers by suggesting, "They seem to be a distinct race, or rather, the commencement and origin of a new race. Without ancestry—a father whom they are not able to find or recognize, they seem to have but one connecting link with their kind—their mother."[101] Oregon lawmakers did not hold fathers accountable for illegitimate children; rather, they viewed such children as lacking "ancestry" and thus without a legitimate family altogether. By the mid-nineteenth century U.S. laws increasingly identified illegitimate children as connected to the mother, rather than the father, which absolved white fathers of parental responsibilities to mixed-race children.[102] But in removing any connection between the illegitimate children and the families of their parents, Oregon legislators denied mothers' authority over their mixed-race children as well. The Oregon laws maintained that illegitimate children were "heretofore considered as having no claim upon their mother's kindred, as having no relationship to or connection with them whatever."[103] In other words, the mother of mixed-race illegitimate children did not hold rights to her children on her own; she only had those obtained through her family members (or male relatives) who actually possessed legal rights. Illegitimate children could not access the rights of their mothers, because these Oregon laws did not recognize these mothers as possessing rights as individuals.[104]

A white father's citizenship may have allowed his children to claim access to various rights, including the right to an education, whereas a mother's status could not, but women were necessary for an educational system to work in Oregon. Regardless of how Oregon settlers viewed the rights of mothers or felt females should be educated; Oregon women became necessary components of education in the region because they served the important role of teachers. Granted, men could also be teachers, but the region did not need single white males in the same way that it needed single white females. Single white females who could serve as teachers and become wives and mothers were by far the more desired immigrants of the day. White women in Oregon, therefore, helped perpetuate the process of colonization by bringing education to the region and serving as mothers to future generations of settlers.[105]

Advertisements, articles, and public discussion followed the immigration of missionaries and educators to Oregon, and as early as 1840 national papers began highlighting the role of white female teachers. Discussing the Whitman mission and the steady occupancy of Indigenous students, an Ohio newspaper reported that throughout the winter of 1840 Narcissa Whitman taught lessons to an average of ten scholars. Her husband Marcus Whitman only accompanied her when the numbers of students warranted it.[106] As many missionaries came over as married couples, the mission schools utilized the females available in a similar manner to how male teachers were used. When settlement in Oregon by white settlers increased only a few years later, however, the need for more female teachers emerged.

The Oregon Institute, one of the first U.S. school systems established in Oregon by the Methodist Mission Board, created segregated departments for male and female students and found it appropriate for teachers to be of the same sex as their students. An Oregon author identified only as "An Observer of Things" reported to the *Oregon Spectator* in 1846, praising C. A. Wilson, a teacher and leader of the female department at the Oregon Institute, for her work with Oregon's white daughters. The article insisted that Wilson's "qualifications for teaching and conducting a school, are of the first order; and in a country like this, where so much depends on the correctness of principles employed and inculcated in the education of our daughters, and in the formation of their character, we consider her eminently useful in this department, and hope she may continue."[107] Female teachers also taught male students, because women made up a large portion of teachers for rudimentary education in the United States during the mid-nineteenth century. Arguably, however, the larger numbers of female teachers in Oregon was the result of the region needing women. Much rode on the success of white women in Oregon, and, therefore, many in Oregon viewed not only female teachers but also education for girls as necessary for the longevity of the region.[108]

The education of females in Oregon, many settlers believed, meant an educated mother, a money-conscious wife, and an honorable, independent family. As one Oregon newspaper article explained, "Without knowledge, no wife is truly [a] wife—no mother truly [a] mother. In unveiling the feminine intelligence the laws of nature, we need not seek to make our daughters physicians or astronomers, but to invigorate their faculties by the discipline of science—to prepare them to partake the idea[s] of their husbands, the studies of their children."[109] Oregon settlers generally promoted the idea of women having an education, but they wanted this education to focus on the needs of these women's future husbands and children. In fact, many articles described the education of females as essential to what it meant to be a wife and mother.[110] Further suggesting that Oregon settlers should not fear educated women, the author continued that "it will only render them more worthy of the name."[111] Private female-only schools that supported this idea of women's education also emerged during the 1840s. Courses such as those offered in the Mrs. N. M. Thornton School focused on an "English education," including needlework and watercolor painting.[112] The increased support for women's education also coincided with the settlers' need for teachers.

The Board of W. P. Education reached out to Oregon's Congressional Delegate Samuel Thurston in the summer of 1850 for more information about the region's need for teachers and to learn how the educational organization could support them. Among other questions, the Board asked Thurston the extent to which the demand for teachers exists in Oregon. In his reply letter, Thurston asked the Board to "bear in mind that the country is almost entirely destitute of Teachers," noting that while finding teachers was already difficult, it was nearly impossible to locate white female teachers, "from the fact that the female is much less than the male population." The Board also asked of Oregon, "What compensation may be expected by well qualified female teachers, taking in consideration the patronage they would likely obtain there?"[113] Oregon settlers paid a much higher rate for nearly all laborers, professional or otherwise, than the rest of the nation, and Thurston assured the Board that teachers would be more than adequately compensated for their work.[114]

Thurston believed Oregon could provide additional incentives to the high salaries for female teachers—Oregon had many bachelors. Attempting to describe this "compensation," Thurston explained that "it now frequently happens that when a young lady arrives at qualification for the work of teaching, she very soon exchanges such a situation for one more congenial—the sphere of married life . . . [therefore teachers] will not need to return home to secure a permanent and attractive partnership." Thurston insisted that all new white female teachers would find ideal prospects for husbands in Oregon and that "They will not find it difficult to enter upon such of one in Oregon with young gentlemen, who are at once moral, wealthy, intelligent and enterprising." In sending white female teachers to the region, it would be interesting to know if the Board had felt it was acting as an educational institution or providing some sort of mail-order-bride service. Thurston's closing statements would not have helped this confusion, as he stated unapologetically, "We have among us the resources, the wealth, and the enterprise; and we want ladies—the moral, Christian, intellectual ladies."[115] Nevertheless, Thurston's answer to the organization reflected both Oregon's need for teachers as well as Oregon males' rather desperate desire for wives.

Interest in bringing education to the Far West remained active within the northeastern states, and organizations such as the American Board of Education created the Society for Promoting Popular Education in the West with the specific intent to establish schools in Oregon and California. The American Board of Education sent a group of female teachers from Vermont to Oregon in 1851—much to the delight of Oregon settlers, according to newspaper editorials—but many wished that the number of female teachers had been much larger.[116] The author of one editorial relayed his single friend's request that the female teachers be "young and rosy cheeked," and "that if their service should not all be required as teachers, he is in town, perhaps."[117] Oregon needed all the teachers it could collect, but white female teachers potentially filled the additional need for wives in Oregon, which made their presence and the organization's willingness to send such teachers of greater importance.

White female teachers represented such desired additions to Oregon that even Samuel Thurston took it upon himself to escort five teachers (Misses Lincoln from Maine, Gray from Vermont, Smith from Lima, as well as Wand and Miller from New York) to Oregon when returning home from Congress. A New York newspaper noted that this group of young women had contributed to the "two hundred and four ladies as teachers . . . sent to the new States and Territories of the West and South west" by the Society for Promoting Popular Education in the West.[118] The future Oregon teachers' escort, however, died en route on April 9, 1851. Thurston may not have arrived home, but his constituents felt he had helped to ensure that Oregon received these coveted female teachers and potential Oregon wives.[119]

The request for white female teachers in Oregon and continued desire for more women persisted throughout the 1850s. In fact, Oregon settlers began to place emphasis on the number of daughters arriving with each wagon train as overland migration from the U.S. increased. One newspaper editorial noted the higher number of daughters than sons within a new group and explained that this fact was of much interest to the young men of Oregon.[120] The article went on to note, "Many of these girls, we are informed, are of sufficient age and size for the matrimonial market. We shall expect to receive frequent specimens of wedding cake during the coming winter."[121] Although such sentiments appeared to restrict the roles of females in Oregon to those as wives and mothers, the overall need for white women demonstrated the important position females played in the settlement of the region as well as their valued contributions as teachers.

A white female teacher new to the region not only provided an education to the children of the territory but also became a white wife who helped increase the amount of land claims Oregon men could obtain, which more firmly placed land in the control of white settlers. The entwined nature of race and gender in the development of education in Oregon reveals the region's progression through settler colonialism and its eventual identity as a state with a racialized and gendered definition of citizenship.[122] If female Oregon settlers, however, were to contribute to future generations as teachers and raise their sons to adequately compete with their eastern counterparts, Oregon would have to address the need for college courses, if not the development of universities altogether.

Class and Religion in Education

Religion, whether through the efforts of missionaries or in connection with arguments of morality, had a constant presence in the discussions of the Oregon settlement. As addressed earlier, mission schools established the first European or U.S. educational systems in the region. Although the focus of a Christian education remained after the missionaries had mostly abandoned the field, the purpose of the schools eventually moved from solely the conversion education of American Indian (including "half breed") children to providing "moral guidance" to white settlers' children. As the population of Oregon settlers increased, however, funding from the provisional government and the territorial government for education became slow and generally insufficient. Additionally, business philanthropic involvement in Oregon education was still a few decades down the road at the time settlers began calling for schools in the region.[123] Religion-based education, therefore, dominated Oregon schools, and its schools remained the largest institutions even when Oregon became a state.[124] Overall, private schools played an important part in the formation of education systems in Oregon and permitted legislators to delay the development of free common (public) schools.

Technically the children of missionaries, as the first children of Oregon settlers, received an education from the mission schools alongside Indigenous children—or were taught by the same instructors, at least. The desire for more than a rudimentary education led some missionaries and white occupants of trading or military posts to send their children back to institutions in the United States. Mary Richardson Walker noted in the summer of 1838 that Methodist Reverend Jason Lee, along with several young men, had stopped at her mission on their way from Fort Vancouver en route to the East Coast. Lee was escorting the boys into the United States to receive a formal education.[125] One of these young men was William Cameron McKay, the step-grandson to Dr. John McLoughlin. When the time came for McKay's education to continue beyond what was available in the mission schools of Oregon, he traveled with Lee to the United States.[126]

By the early 1840s communities comprised of Oregon settlers had slowly formed. The goal of early Oregon settlers to acquire enough land to cultivate created considerable physical space between each settlement and left these communities loosely knitted together. Although these communities desired schools, it was not until the U.S. Congress had established a territorial government in Oregon that settlers began collecting revenue from the sale of selected land plots in each township; they then applied those funds to the development of an educational system. When it appeared to Oregon settlers that no action was taking place in this regard, petitioners requested to know what had happened to those land sales designated for the development of schools and further urged Oregon legislators to enact direct taxation to support common schools. The petitioners, including Oregon's former provisional-government governor George Abernethy, believed that there was "a present and urgent need of free schools," and a "necessity which will be constantly increase"; therefore, immediate action was required from Oregon legislators to establish and maintain a public educational system.[127] But gaining traction on the establishment of public schools was a difficult task, as evidenced by the multiple bills that crossed the desk of the territorial government.

In 1849 alone three education bills pertaining to the development of common schools in Oregon entered the House and Council of Oregon's territorial government. Each specified guidelines for a proposed school district structure and measures for taxation, as well as specified that the schools should be "open and free to all children between the ages of four and twenty-one years" of age.[128] The first of these education bills included the restriction that schools would only be free and open to children "whose parents or guardians . . . [were] taxpaying citizens." This section was stricken when introduced to the Council, and such a specification would not appear again in Oregon's bills or laws for public schools.[129] Oregon's first education law as a territory did emerge from these bills and debates in 1849, but even after Oregon legislators had enacted the policy, Oregon lawmakers failed to enforce the collection and/or management of the funds. This left the region still dependent on religion-based private schools.[130]

Part of the inactivity toward developing schools supported by the school districts' respective communities throughout Oregon came from the fact that several private educational institutions did exist, and many settlers felt such institutions provided necessary spiritual guidance to the region's youth.[131] As early as 1843 Elijah White, sub-agent of Indian Affairs, sent a report to Secretary of War J. M. Porter noting at least four private schools existed in Oregon: the Tualatin Plains school run by a Reverend Clark, a Roman Catholic mission school under the instruction of a Mr. Blanchet, the Indian Mission School established by the Methodist Mission Board, and a school "sustained by the citizens, and kept at the falls of the Wallamet [*sic*]."[132] The focus of these early schools remained on the education of Indigenous children, but these institutions also demonstrated the transition from mission schools to private education in Oregon.

One of the schools White had listed in his report was the Indian Mission School located in Portland. Established in 1842 and focused on the conversion of American Indian youth, the school also boarded students at the facility to promote full immersion into Christian culture. Within two years, however, the school had lost nearly all of its students, as "A fatal disease carried away many of the children, others ran away, and some were stolen by their parents until but a few were left."[133] During this time the Methodists had also founded the Oregon Institute in Wallace's Prairie, which continued to thrive and catered to white settler children. Seeking a better structure and location, the Institute's trustees bought the failed Indian Mission School, moved the Oregon Institute into the Portland building, and continued to grow its private institution for white settler children as overland settlement increased.[134]

The last school White mentioned was likely the school in Oregon City created by Sydney W. Moss in 1843 and housed within his hotel to educate the children of Mrs. Richardson, who had been widowed during her family's overland immigration to Oregon. The schools served the children of Oregon settlers, but in 1853 Moss notified the territorial government of his intentions to support a formal public school in Oregon City; Moss pledged to provide the schoolhouse and to board the teachers. But the territorial government failed to follow through, and it let the motion to create a public school in Oregon City die. The need within the community remained, however, so the following year Oregon legislators passed a law creating a school district in Oregon City. The law allowed the Oregon City council to collect tax revenue in support of a school, which became operational by 1855 and gave control of school operations over to the council. Between sixty and eighty students attended the Oregon City school within its first year, and additional tax was collected to support children from outside the school district who wanted to attend.[135] Private schools run by religious groups had certainly existed in Oregon by the 1850s, but free local schools controlled by parents and community leaders were in demand. Supporters of common schools also maintained that such institutions could reach a larger number of children, thus expanding access to education in Oregon.

Oregon settlers who believed that "education should be common to all classes; placed within the reach of the whole community; the high and the low, the rich and the poor" and praised the Oregon legislators for passing an education law in the territory, however, did not reject the focus of nonsecular schools.[136] Instead, legislators and petitions from the public continued to connect the moral growth of the region to an educated populace. Furthermore, the separation of private and public schools did not suggest that morality and religion were mutually exclusive in Oregon education. Their differences lay in funding, because public schools were supported by tax revenue, whereas the private and religiously operated institutions could charge tuition and control their schools according to their own rules. Since the control private schools wielded included who could attend, access to these institutions was further restricted.

Although public education allowed community members more control over the school system and educational process, it also came at a cost and time involvement that not all settlers were willing to sacrifice. Criticizing Oregon settlers' preoccupation with the material advancements to be achieved in the region, one Oregon editorial suggested that settlers had been too "absorbed in such worldly matters as 'going to the mines,' opening farms, building houses and barns . . . that some of them we fear have sadly overlooked the great necessity of giving their offspring such an education as will prepare them honorably to bear the burthens [*sic*] of the government."[137] The author went on to note that private educational institutions had served Oregon and provided the youth with moral guidance, but still called Oregon parents and legislators to action in developing permanent school systems in every community for all Oregon children. Moreover, the article and others like it emphasized a different importance to education than mission schools and private institutions had. Some Oregon settlers viewed public education (more reflective of East Coast schools and colleges) as necessary to create informed citizens and political leaders in addition to upholding or perpetuating moral enlightenment.[138]

During the mid-nineteenth century organizations such as the Society for the Promotion of Collegiate and Theological Education at the West (or the Western College Society) focused their efforts on bringing a Christian education to the West. Although the schools that these groups developed were concentrated in the states just west of the Appalachian Mountains, much interest in the education of the Far West, as noted earlier, came from religious groups in the East.[139] The emphasis on schools that groups such as the Western College Society developed provided a collegiate education that would create future ministers for the group and for the region. Appealing to moral obligations felt by New England members of the Western College Society, in 1859 the president of the private Pacific University in Oregon, S. H. Marsh, sought financial assistance for the completion and maintenance of his western college. Marsh explained, "Oregon is isolated, and can have no recourse to colleges at the east. The population is agricultural. The churches of New England origin are few and weak. Still, the ministers and teachers for that section must be educated there." A Vermont newspaper editorial shared these sentiments and promoted the Oregon college, further noting that "such efforts to build up genuine New England Colleges at the West, are among the noblest of our day."[140] By this time numerous groups had created private nonsecular schools and colleges in Oregon; therefore, President Marsh suggested a heightened need to ensure that his specific school could compete with those of other denominations.

In 1853 Oregon received its first private college—Willamette University, formerly the Oregon Institute—through the support of the Methodist Mission Board and chartered by the territorial government. The development of colleges spoke to the growing need for higher education in Oregon, and in 1858 the territorial government chartered three additional private colleges: Corvallis College, established by the Methodist

Episcopal Church South; the Union University Association of Eugene; and the Baptist College at McMinnville. Although the first two of these schools later became state universities (Oregon State University and the University of Oregon, respectively), all colleges in the region at the time of the Oregon Constitutional Convention were private institutions.[141] Thus, as Oregon approached its application for statehood, it possessed only private colleges. Restrictions to such institutions included acceptance into the college but also affordability.

When Oregon delegates broached the subject of university funds at the Constitutional Convention, they were asked to decide whether Oregon should immediately request to create a state university or let "the fund lie idle."[142] Rather than directly resolving the issue, however, Oregon politicians expressed their opinions as to whether they wanted a state university in their future state. One concern generated during these debates was how the Oregon legislature could control the presence of a religious element within a state university. Other western states, such as Wisconsin and Ohio, had included sections in their state constitutions that specifically restricted religious groups from being affiliated with or having any authority over their states' common schools.[143] Although discussion over the influence of specific denominations arose during several states' development of their constitutions, most did not explicitly restrict religious groups from their school systems; rather, they presumed that as the schools were public institutions, only the state and respective school districts would have authority over the schools.[144] But some Oregon delegates feared that a state university would fall under the control of a church instead of the state itself.

Operating under the assumption that Congress would approve funding for a university in Oregon, debates over the constitution's education article addressed the role of religion and religious organizations at a university. Admitting that he was not an "admirer" of public education in general, Oregon delegate Matthew Deady questioned the sectarian nature of a state university, arguing, "A state university would be under the care and control of the dominant religious denomination of the country, acting through public sentiment. Thus the whole people would pay taxes to support a really, though not nominally, sectarian school." Deady maintained, "[This has] been the history of other state institutions, and it would be of ours. . . . And if the state appropriated a school fund, let it be drawn by the various sectarian schools, in proportion to the number of scholars they had, and let those of no religious profession draw their proportion."[145] Deady suggested to his colleagues that private institutions already available in Oregon could address the educational needs of the region; therefore, any funding granted by Congress should be offered to those private schools as well as any public systems that might be created. Of course, without state and local government support no public schools would emerge, and private schools would continue to be the main source of education in Oregon. Deady continued that people should simply choose between the religious denominations to select schools for their children. This position and opposition to funding a state university when private colleges already existed disregarded the concerns that other delegates had about the cost of private schools.

Drawing on concerns about the separation of church and state, W. H. Watkins speculated whether Oregon's government could realistically keep religious groups from controlling the region's schools, specifically its universities, regardless of what the education article specified.[146] Moreover, Watkins feared a dominant religion could take control of an Oregon state university, as had occurred in other states, noting, "The state university of Indiana was as completely under the control of the Methodists as though the conference elected its officers and teachers. And although we had forbidden the expenditure of public money for any theological institution, let us establish a state institution here, and it would run into sectarianism in spite of us. The Massachusetts university was a bigoted theological institution."[147] Oregon's own history of educational systems being governed by multiple religious groups and denominations throughout the region probably guaranteed that this would not be the case, because no one dominant religious group existed in Oregon. Nevertheless, up to that point religious groups had controlled Oregon's colleges, which made several delegates hesitant to pass an education article without restricting religious groups from a future state university.[148]

Meanwhile, other Oregon delegates such as Thomas Dryer attempted to fend off accusations against Harvard and other private educational institutions of the East and support the establishment of a state university regardless of potential influence from religious groups. Dryer insisted that "New York's [state] universities had flourished" and that "children wanted to know more than was taught in common schools," but Oregon "had no university but what was under [the] control of some of the religious denominations" at the time. Mr. Boise furthered this opinion by suggesting that a university dominated by a specific denomination was still better than no university being available to Oregon youth; he asked of his colleagues, "shall we have a state university, or shall our children go uneducated in the higher branches?"[149] Delegates who combated the position that religious groups might take control of Oregon's public schools ultimately brought the issue back to whether Oregon wanted a university. As became apparent during debates about access to a university, the argument against religious involvement was not without precedent, but it also supported arguments about not wanting to provide a state university for Oregon's youth in general.

By the time Oregon delegates were debating the education article of the Oregon Constitution, the region had established a history of avoiding the development of a public university. A territory creating a public university would have been unusual, but Oregon had also existed as a territory for ten years and functioned under a governing body for nearly a decade before that time. In other words, Oregon settlers were in a better position than most to establish such an institution but had repeatedly failed to do so. In 1851 the Oregon territorial government requested from Congress a donation of lands to build upon and develop a university, but also enough lands to sell for necessary revenue to maintain a university. The lands that Oregon settlers requested, however, were lands claimed by Dr. John McLoughlin.[150] As a result, McLoughlin and the territory became entangled in a legal dispute over the lands; these lands were eventually granted to McLoughlin's estate, as discussed in chapter 6. Thus in 1854, still without a public university, the Oregon settlers petitioned the territorial government to request different lands from Congress for this purpose. The House of the territorial government received the petition and sent it to a committee, but once the committee had reported on the bill, it was quickly laid on the table and dismissed.[151]

Even when a law to develop a public university had been successful, Oregon settlers did not follow through with the schools' establishment or their maintenance. For example, the territorial government passed a law in 1851 to develop a university in Marysville (later Corvallis). After the law had made its way through the House and Council, however, little else was discussed on the matter until the university was moved to lands in Jacksonville four years later. Once the university had been moved to Jacksonville, Oregon legislators passed a bill to "prevent the expenditure of money [for the university] until April, '56."[152] Debates surrounding this last bill focused on transferring the money designated for the university into the common school fund, which observers correctly interpreted meant the end of a public university's taking shape in Jacksonville.[153] Yet, these ineffective struggles to establish a public university still demonstrated that some Oregonians continued their support for a public university.

To better understand these debates, it should also be noted that Oregon lawmakers as well as delegates to the Constitutional Convention consisted of individuals who could afford to send their children to private institutions or public colleges on the East Coast. Religion had plagued debates about what would happen to a state university, but those supporting its existence in Oregon focused on another issue: the access to an education afforded to specific classes. Oregon legislators had to reconcile with the fact that not having a state university in Oregon would limit how many Oregon children had access to a college-level education. Moreover, the question arose as to whether the failure to establish a state college was restricting Oregon children from the right to an education.

When Oregon applied for statehood, many states had not included a section within their constitutions' education articles that specifically addressed instructions for creating a university. In fact, by 1857 only North Carolina and California had noted the creation of a state university in their constitutions.[154] Several states, however, included the words "free" and "open" within their education articles, which placed emphasis on the fact that children of their states should have complete and free access to public schools.[155] Although it did not specifically explain wealthy residents' access to education, the state of Missouri included the statement that "the poor shall be taught gratis" to eliminate any restriction to an education.[156] Overall, schools were to be available to all children and to be seen as both a necessity and a right. Rhode Island's constitution stated as much when it noted that an education was "essential to the preservation of their rights and liberties" and that the state needed to "secure to the people the advantages and opportunities of education."[157] Thus, education not only protected a person's rights as a citizen but also was a right itself that the government was to secure. Many Oregon settlers agreed with this sentiment and viewed education as both a solution to problems of inequality and something required for a prosperous region.

For example, one Oregon editorial viewed "classes of society" as "destructive to human happiness" and urged settlers to see education as a way to prevent this problematic element from emerging in their region. The article continued that if Oregonians were to "Educate the mass, and the distinction of wealth will not be seen," and thus divisions that might jeopardize democratic principles would not become a problem for Oregon's future generations. Finally, the author acknowledged the fact that public education came at a cost but maintained that "the labor of our hands will not be lost, but on the contrary, our children will bless us, and our children's children will revere our memory and become a blessing to the world."[158] Oregon had a diverse population, but several articles throughout Oregon's time as a territory pointed toward the idea that class divisions were harmful and would not ensure a society's progress if some classes failed to advance in life. One editorial in 1850 summarized this perspective, stating, "Improvement in this respect, depends upon our system of Free Schools, which may open a strait to the threshold of every College, to all who may choose to enter—however humble they may be—they may enter into an equal competition for the high places of usefulness and honor."[159] If Oregon was to succeed, many settlers believed, then Oregon's youth must have the opportunity to succeed.

By the 1850s national papers had grown critical of Oregon's approach to education and the delayed development of its public institutions. One *New York Times* article suggested that "Education, carried on according to the prevalent idea here, would, after one or two generations, provide only the qualification of a nation of shop-keepers."[160] The editorial maintained that Oregonians did not desire a complete public education system, because they had not yet created one. Furthermore, by the end of the decade, national papers still discussed the continued need for eastern states to support private schools in Oregon. Organizations that had supported private institutions in Oregon for almost a decade, therefore, did not feel secure about the education of Oregon's youth.[161]

Regardless of national comments, Oregon delegates of the Constitutional Convention in 1857 also addressed whether all Oregon children required a college education. Again arguing that state universities had proved ineffective in other states, delegate Matthew Deady motioned to strike out in its entirety the section that would create a university and asserted that universities were better "left to private enterprise" then managed by a state government.[162] Oregon legislators such as Deady and William H. Farrar maintained that sending one's children to either the private institutions of Oregon or colleges in the East was a viable solution to the need to educate Oregon's youth at a collegiate level. David Logan echoed this sentiment and argued that many of the poor "would be remote from the state university and could not afford to send [students to] it." While Logan believed that many of the poor would be unable to benefit from a state university, he also felt that Oregon should not turn down the funds allotted to a university; rather, Logan suggested that the money should become part of the common school fund. Although distance was a factor in the cost of education, access to a state university located in their home state remained the easiest and most affordable opportunity for Oregon youth to receive a college education. Moreover, as mentioned earlier, the question posed to delegates was not whether Oregon should have a university but what immediate action should take place regarding funds that they were to receive from Congress for a university. The common (public) schools had allotted funds apart from those allocated for a state university, and therefore a state university would not be taking resources from the precollegiate public school system; Oregon legislators could not reappropriate that university money into the common school funds, either.[163] Nevertheless, debates continued as to whether Oregon delegates wanted a state university and, by extension, whether they wanted to create a more accessible form of college education for Oregon's youth.

Delegate Reuben Boise questioned his colleagues' understanding of the issue at hand and the ability of Oregon's private nonsecular institutions to "furnish means for a complete education" in the long term. Boise insisted that the question delegates needed to address was whether Oregon should immediately act to develop a state university, a college not focused on theology and creating future ministers, or watch "[Oregon's] children go uneducated in the higher branches." Recognizing that the debate over a state university had become an issue of whether everyone should have the right to an education, delegates such as John H. Reed further argued for children's complete access to education in Oregon and asserted that delegates had an obligation to "open every avenue to the acquisition of Knowledge."[164] If class divisions threatened the prosperity of Oregon, as they believed, and education could alleviate such a division, then the children of Oregon needed to have access to general and collegiate education. Without a state university this class division could exist, because, as Delazon Smith pointed out, "It was the poor who wanted the university, not the rich. The rich could send their children anywhere."[165] The lack of a state university would restrict poorer families' access to a college education and thus hinder them from the right to an education.

In the end, Section 5 of the education article in the Oregon Constitution specified that no action would take place with funds designated for a university until ten years after the adoption of the constitution. Oregon delegates, however, did include the loophole that funds would remain idle "unless the same shall be disposed of by the consent of Congress for Common school purposes."[166] But Congress, as some delegates had anticipated, did not reappropriate the university money for the common school fund—the money to develop a state university remained idle, and the Oregon Constitution enacted an education article that prevented the development of a state university. Granted, a state university would require substantial financial support from the state beyond that provided by Congress, but the delegates did not debate the issue of state funding or tax revenue; rather, they argued over whether a university education was necessary for all classes of Oregon's youth. Enough Oregon delegates did not believe a college education should be available to the poor or those otherwise restricted from private institutions, and therefore they made the right to an education an exclusive right.

Religion existed as its own contributing piece to Oregon's educational history, but it also allowed for a defense of class arguments within Oregon laws. Without the involvement of religious groups in Oregon's education, the region would have entered statehood with a dismal education system to show for itself. The very existence of these private institutions, however, became a means for Oregon legislators to suggest that public education was not necessary or at least did not warrant immediate attention. Objection to the role that religion could play in a state university by Oregon delegates in the Constitutional Convention had some legitimate footing, but this argument came from some of the same individuals who had objected to a state university altogether. Some Oregonians with fewer financial resources could have benefited from a public university in their state, but Oregon lawmakers denied them access to this education and left the right to an education at the college level reserved for those who could afford to attend a private or out-of-state institution.

The Legacy of Oregon's Education Laws

Unlike other laws that restricted specific groups from rights in the region, Oregon's education laws did not overtly exclude residents from rights as citizens. The issues involved in Oregon's education laws pertained almost entirely to matters in Oregon itself. And because these laws did not appear to contradict the U.S. Constitution or deny citizens of other states their rights, members of Congress did not object to the education article in the Oregon Constitution as they had done with Oregon's other articles. Education laws, nonetheless, held great significance in explaining the social and political dynamics of Oregon. These dynamics continued to evolve, and the elements of settler colonialism, arguments of morality, and the role of race in education laws ultimately merged.

Even after Oregon had become a state in 1859 the colonial settlement of the U.S. West was not complete, and American Indians remained the majority in several areas throughout the region. Issues between the settlers and Indigenous communities continued to arise as the settler population increased, and land claims infringed upon American Indians' homelands, if not completely removing Indigenous communities from an area. Throughout the nation, mission schools that had focused on American Indians' conversion to Christianity gave way to government-sponsored education systems for Indigenous children that were aimed at vocational, especially agricultural, training.[167] In the Pacific Northwest this also manifested with the "agricultural and industrial schools" promised to numerous American Indian groups through treaties between 1854 and 1855. The "free education" was to include a "suitable instructor or instructors" with the expenses "to be defrayed by the United States, and not deducted from the annuities."[168] Issues with annuities, among other problems, would plague the relationships between the U.S. and these treaty groups, but the focus on agricultural education remained consistent.[169] By the late 1870s the prevailing idea on how to address the "Indian problem" was to turn American Indians into farmers (eventually culminating with the Dawes Act of 1887) and to educate Indigenous children to become adults whose lifestyle and work were representative of American culture—although they were to be educated separately from U.S. children and with different curricula.[170]

Nearly half a century after morality arguments had been used by the U.S. to legitimize the settlement of Oregon, those who supported American Indian education adopted similar language to explain the U.S. government's involvement. One Boston newspaper praised efforts by the federal government and insisted that such education for Indigenous children would assist in "weaning them from their natural wildness" and bestow upon them "principles of the civilization that ameliorates and enlarges life."[171] Through the implementation of educational systems and arguments of morality, the colonization of the West continued, and Oregon served as one of the nation's leading examples.

In 1879 Congress approved the construction of the Hampton Normal and Agricultural Institute in Virginia and the Carlisle Indian Industrial School in Pennsylvania for American Indian children east of the Mississippi "to receive elementary English education and practical instruction in farming and other useful industries."[172] The following year the Indian Training School in Forest Grove, Oregon, was established, and it served as the only federally funded western school of its kind. The Department of the Interior designed all three of these schools with the intent of removing Indigenous children from their homes, parents, and communities for full immersion into the focus of the institute and their complete acculturation. These schools hoped that removing the children and disassociating them with their communities and homelands would transform the students into individuals who would no longer oppose the acquisition of lands not yet ceded by American Indian groups and would no longer identify with their native cultures.[173] Maintaining the position that the U.S. government had developed these schools to benefit Indigenous children, the empire further charged these schools with "commend[ing] themselves to the liberality of Congress and to the philanthropic munificence of the American people."[174] Moreover, appropriations by Congress supported these schools through "the permanent civilization fund," revealing both the government's goal to "civilize" American Indians as well as its current attitudes toward American Indians and their cultures.[175]

Oregon's Forest Grove Indian Training School was under the instruction of Superintendent M. C. Wilkinson, who reported in 1882 that this school served ninety-one students, with fifty-four boys and thirty-seven girls. Forest Grove claimed to include students from twelve tribes among the numerous American Indian groups in the West. Wilkinson added that instruction focused on vocational training "directed to the blacksmithing, shoemaking, and carpentering departments." Output production took center stage in Wilkinson's report to the commissioners of Indian Affairs, and he noted the several thousands of dollars' worth of products made by the students, including "the girl's department [where] 1,118 articles were manufactured."[176] Schools similar to this Oregon institution claimed they provided services to American Indians and resolved issues between this group and U.S. settlers. The controlled labor of students, however, reflected the perception of Indigenous bodies in the homes of missionaries fifty years earlier and appeared to benefit the goals of the instructors rather than the students. Furthermore, such labors were not reflective of the students' own cultures; rather, they reflected a pseudo-American lifestyle specifically tailored to create laborers suitable for U.S. society. Educational systems such as the one at Forest Grove, therefore, helped continue the process of settler colonization. These localized institutions removed Indigenous children from their homes and promoted the embodiment of a different culture that would not prevent further settlement.

Another element of Oregon's educational system and its policies that emerged again during the 1870s and 1880s was the issue of supporting public education and maintaining established institutions. It was not until 1872, thirteen years after it had become a state and ten years after the Morrill Act had helped establish land grant colleges throughout the nation, that Oregon established a state university. The state legislature transformed the private college of the Union University Association of Eugene into the State University, including the construction of new buildings. By 1876 the State University was fully functioning, and it became an accessible form of collegiate education for Oregon's youth.[177] Support for a state university, however, was still not universal. Some Oregon legislators immediately took positions against the establishment of a state-run college, citing its existence as overly expensive in a state with multiple private universities. Within a decade Oregon's governor Sylvester Pennoyer had begun recommending that the Oregon legislature reconsider its support of a state university, and even suggested withdrawing funds entirely.[178] The presence of numerous private institutions once again provided opponents of a state university with the argument that a state university was unnecessary, but this time the public opposition to nonsecular schools had gained political proponents for public education.

In one Oregon editorial, the author, R. H. Willis, discussed the fact that while Oregon possessed several institutions of higher education operated by "religious denominations" and that these schools would benefit economically from the absence of a state university, he believed it to be unwise for the state to dismantle the State University. Willis argued that because "the public sentiment so strongly opposed to sectarian influence in the schools," he doubted if "the state [could] afford to do this" and let nonsecular institutions control college-level education in Oregon. Furthermore, the author insisted that the state should consider how to increase access to public education rather than limiting such a right, and he criticized Oregon's decisions in comparison to those of other states. Willis maintained, "If the legislature would increase the appropriations and give free tuition to all collegiate students, as California does, thus making the university the great head of our public school system, it would be a great step in the march of progress. But if we are to have no head or a weak and disordered one, the body of our educational system must suffer correspondingly."[179]

Free college education would grant Oregon youth complete, unrestricted access to an education, but although the State University did not close and exists today as the University of Oregon, the state did not provide free tuition to its residents.[180] The right to an education, therefore, became a notion that was as malleable as Oregon settlers' perception of education. During the 1840s and 1850s Oregon settlers struggled to achieve a public educational system for Oregon children and viewed access to such an education as a right. By the end of the century, some Oregonians felt college education from a free public university embodied what it meant to be progressive about the right to an education, but the majority still felt that providing a state school sufficiently met this need. Nevertheless, Oregon lawmakers continued to debate the necessity of a state university even during the boom of state-sponsored universities.

Overall, Oregonians' perceptions and treatment of education perpetuated the process of settler colonialism in Oregon because they supported and helped legitimize the settlement of the region. Oregon's education laws also reflected its specific understandings of miscegenation and the role of gender and race in the right to an education. Finally, the discussion of private schools and religious instruction in Oregon's education laws redefined the role of education in Oregon and influenced which social classes had access to a public education.

CHAPTER 6

Implications of Citizenship in Suffrage and Naturalization Laws

The gentleman from New York stated, that while the [Oregon] constitution allowed aliens to vote, it excluded free negroes from the State. He stated that was inequality. While the constitution of his State allows negroes to vote, does it allow them to vote on equal footing with the white persons?

—**John Clark**, Missouri, "Admission of Oregon," *Congressional Globe*, 35th Cong., 2nd sess.

I do solemnly swear that I renounce all allegiances and fidelity to all and any foreigner prince, potentate, state and sovereigns of whatever, and particularly in Victoria, Queen of the United Kingdom of Great Britain and Ireland, and that I will support the Constitution of the United States, and the provisions of an act to establish the Territorial Government of Oregon, so help me God.

—**John McLoughlin**, "Communications," *Oregon Spectator* (Oregon City, Oregon Territory), March 27, 1849.

In the fall of 1856 the *Oregon Argus* newspaper published a story about a group of American actors touring Europe with a minstrel show who found themselves detained for lacking U.S. passports. European officials wrote to H. H. Rice, the clerk of the Superior Court in New York, on behalf of the actors and requested that passports be issued to these Americans now stranded abroad. Rice then sent applications for the actors' passports to the Department of State. The response to this application, by Assistant Secretary J. A. Thomas, found its way into many newspapers across the nation, because the Department of State had denied the applicants' request.[1]

Assuring Rice that the U.S. government "would regard it to be its duty to protect them [the actors] if wronged by a foreign government," the Department of State responded (not surprisingly) that it could not issue these men U.S. passports because the federal government did not presently acknowledge Black Americans as U.S. citizens. Thomas explained that former U.S. Attorney General William Wirt had ruled on a 1821 congressional act regarding "foreign and coasting trade" that Black Americans "were not [citizens], and moreover held that the words 'citizen of the United States,' were used in this act of Congress in the same sense as in the constitution."[2] Thomas continued that the present U.S. attorney general concurred with this opinion and that the state supreme courts of Connecticut and Tennessee had later upheld Judge Wirt's ruling. The letter concluded, "Such being the construction of the constitution in regard to free persons of color, it is conceived that they cannot be regarded, when beyond the jurisdiction of this Government, as entitled to the full rights of citizens."[3] According to U.S. newspapers, the group of Black Americans had stopped in Bremen, Germany, to await their passports, but what became of these men was unclear.[4] The race of the U.S. actors excluded them from full rights as U.S. citizens and thus U.S. citizenship.

It is likely, given what we have already learned about views in Oregon on the issue of immigration restriction, land ownership, and education, that those white Oregonians who had read this news item agreed with the State Department and the U.S. attorney general. A year after this incident Oregonians also learned of the controversial and highly influential Supreme Court decision in *Dred Scott v. Sanford*. The definitions of citizenship in the United States prior to the Civil War, thus, remained complicated, contradictory, and continuously evolving.[5] Oregonians not only read about changed interpretations in newspapers but also actively participated in the legal transformation of U.S. citizenship.

Not unlike other western places in the United States, Oregonians constructed suffrage and naturalization laws to capture the definitions of "citizen" that they intended and desired for their territory and then state. The issues of suffrage and naturalization were vitally interconnected in this discussion about citizenship, especially in regions that had large immigrant populations and provisions related to naturalization within their suffrage articles, such as Oregon. Although the access to and protection of personal and political rights contributed to the definition of U.S. citizenship, suffrage remained one of the most exclusive rights in the nation and carried more weight in debates about U.S. citizenship.[6]

In evaluating the construction of Oregon's suffrage and naturalization laws, this chapter explains the complicated process of naturalization in a region with shifting borders; it demonstrates how the treatment of Oregonians identified as "half breed" and of Chinese descent complicated national interpretations of citizenship. Oregon also presents an example of a colonial outpost whose laws had established an earlier legal precedent of including racial qualifications in the right of suffrage. Oregon lawmakers further protected Oregon's definition of a "voter" and a "citizen" by including and reinforcing the necessity of excluding specific racial and gender groups. Additionally, this chapter demonstrates Oregon's influence on the legal interpretations and perceptions of Black American citizenship in post-Reconstruction America.

Settler Colonialism through Citizenship

The settler colony known as Oregon harbored a diverse population. By 1840 various American Indian groups, French Canadian fur traders, British and Kanaka employees of the Hudson's Bay Company, as well as European, Chinese, and U.S. immigrants all called Oregon home. Although American Indians were the only group that could claim a long ancestral heritage to the region, Oregonian's interpretation of "native" came to encompass a wide range of those who had made Oregon their permanent residence.[7] With the lack of a nation-state claiming jurisdiction over the settler colony, the nationalities of white settlers initially held little social or political importance.[8] In 1843 a group of Willamette residents identified as the "Canadian Citizens of Oregon" drafted legislation to recognize their existence and that of others in the region with hopes of ensuring peaceful relations among all Oregonians. These residents stated that the country was "free, at present, to all nations, till [the] government shall have decided; open to every individual wishing to settle, without any distinction of origin, and without asking him anything, either to become an English, Spanish, or American citizen."[9] In acknowledging the differences between Oregon settlers, the group further stated, "So we, English subjects, proclaim to be free, as well as those who came from France, California, United States, or even native of this country; and we desire unison with all the respectable citizens who wish to settle in this country."[10]

According to colonizing empires, the settler colony whose boundaries ran west of the Rocky Mountains, north of the forty-second parallel, and south of Russian territories was unattached to a nation. The Canadians hoped their nationality would not prevent them from being recognized as members of the settler colony by other groups—namely the Willamette U.S. settlers, who were also constructing legislation for the region.[11] Acknowledging that Oregon would eventually fall under the jurisdiction of either Great Britain or the United States, these Canadian settlers further included in their decree, "we are willing to submit to any lawful government, when it comes."[12] Ultimately, early Oregon settlers constructed laws and government structures for more than one national group.[13]

While power structures existed among Oregon settlers, the lack of a nation-state's jurisdiction over the region made a specific naturalization process unnecessary. The first suffrage laws, therefore, did not address nationality as a qualification for the right to vote. In 1843 the "Legislative Committee" proposed a law to define eligible voters in Oregon. The committee determined, "Every free male descendent of a white man, an inhabitant of this territory, of the age of twenty-one years and upwards, who shall have been an inhabitant of this territory at the time of this organization, shall be entitled to vote at the election of officers, civil and military, and be eligible to any office in the territory."[14] The elements of race and gender within this law will be addressed in later sections. Oregonians then used this very same language in 1845 for the Organic

Laws; if a settler was not living in Oregon by the time this law came into effect, six months of residence were required before that qualified settler became "an inhabitant" and eligible to vote in Oregon elections. In just six months, a white male settler could become an Oregon voter and citizen of the settler colony. The right of suffrage, therefore, was technically accessible to multiple nationalities.

Meanwhile the U.S. Congress grappled with revisions to the nation's naturalization laws. Reflecting a growing resentment toward recent immigrant populations among the public, Congress debated if the time of residency before application for naturalization should be extended and whether immigrants with criminal records should be excluded from naturalization altogether.[15] Senator Henry Johnson of Louisiana expressed that "He was opposed to extending to these swarms of ignorant men the civil rights of citizens, until they had been in this country long enough to comprehend and understand our institutions, and acquire an attachment to them and to the country."[16] What time was necessary to become an "American" became a point of common debate in Congress, with some states such as Massachusetts pushing for a period of residence prior to naturalization exceptionally longer than the one-year requirement contained in the Constitution.[17]

The U.S. federal government was also in discussion with Great Britain about the matter of sovereignty over Oregon. The Oregon Territory would bring into the national fold several nationalities and racial groups that, in some cases, were functioning as Oregon citizens alongside of U.S. immigrants. Those whom the American public understood to be living in Oregon, however, were not reflective of the settler colony or the early territory's inhabitants. One Washington DC newspaper expressed the belief that Oregon was composed almost entirely of U.S. immigrants, with only a few Hudson's Bay Company employees from Great Britain. The journalist also praised U.S. settlers' apparent unchallenged occupation of the region.[18] This was an incorrect belief. Furthermore, Oregon's provisional laws, which extended rights to multiple nationalities, demonstrated both the diverse population as well as the fact that the Oregon leaders shared authority within the settler colony among multiple nationalities. Even though U.S. immigrants were the largest settler group in Oregon, especially after the wagon trains from the East had commenced in 1844, the suggestion that any one nationality controlled the region while Oregon was a settler colony would be difficult to prove; it varied from place to place. Very few settlers moved north of the Columbia River during those years, for example, with most heading south into the Willamette Valley. This changed once Oregon became a U.S. territory.[19]

While Congress debated the Oregon Bill—for the creation of the Oregon Territory—they also considered developments in the territorial governments of New Mexico and California. Giving a reason for why Oregon deserved different consideration than the other territories, Representative William J. Phelps of Illinois explained that the creation of an elective government in Oregon was "nothing more nor less than the exercise of the elective franchise by [Oregon's] own people." Providing a territorial delegate to the "mongrel population" of California or New Mexico, on the other hand, would be a terrible "farce."[20] The settler colony in the Pacific Northwest, Phelps believed, was worthy of elective franchise, and that by extending to it a territorial government the U.S. federal government was enfranchising the people of Oregon. Once Oregonians had become an enfranchised group, however, lawmakers would need to decide who held the right to this enfranchisement and, likewise, define those who did not qualify as citizens.

When Oregon came under U.S. jurisdiction in 1846, the borders of Oregon took shape to reflect U.S. jurisdiction, and the northern border was drawn at the forty-ninth parallel. Falling below that border were several Oregonians who were not from the United States. The settlers did not move, but the national borders created by the Oregon Treaty transformed non-U.S. settlers into foreign populations. Oregon's Territorial Constitution of 1848 made this distinction within its article on elections, citing that suffrage extended to foreigners so long as they were "white male inhabitants" of twenty-one years of age and had "declared, on oath, their intention to become such [U.S. citizens], and shall have taken an oath to support the constitution of the United States." Otherwise, suffrage was restricted to white males identified as "citizens of the United States."[21] As a settler colony, this declaration and taking of an oath had not been necessary for white males to vote in Oregon. With Oregon's new status as a U.S. territory, those not originally from the United States became required to prove both their worthiness to vote in Oregon and their loyalty to the nation now claiming ownership over the region.

Oddly, the Oregon territorial constitution did not require those of foreign birth to reside in Oregon for a specific period prior to taking an oath and then receiving the ability to vote. This was not in line with current U.S. policies toward naturalization or suffrage. As with other territories, Oregon's first election was controlled by Congress. The section containing the naturalization clause also included the statement that "the qualifications of voters and of holding office, at all subsequent elections, shall be such as shall be prescribed by the [Oregon] legislative assembly."[22] Congress may have determined the right of suffrage in Oregon's first election, but Oregonians brought legislation to the territorial government reflective of their settler-colonial policies.

In December 1850 Oregon's congressional delegate Samuel R. Thurston wrote to U.S. congressman William Strong from the Committee on Elections and requested his opinion on suffrage and naturalization in Oregon. Thurston explained a situation in which a white male foreigner had cast a vote the previous July; because this voter was not a naturalized resident, the election judge had rejected the vote. Thurston was seeking the opinion of someone with authority on suffrage, but he was also testing to see where congressional control ended in relation to Oregon laws. Oregon's territorial constitution did not require naturalization for white male foreigners to qualify for suffrage, but Thurston suggested the reason for disenfranchisement was that the voter was not naturalized. This Oregon law did not follow national policies; therefore, Thurston wanted to see (based on Strong's opinion) whether the federal government permitted Oregon's laws to stand in contrast to federal law. Thurston maintained that the territorial government could draw from its Organic Laws the basis of what defined a voter in Oregon, regardless of federal policy.[23]

Representative Strong confirmed Thurston's opinion, stating that Oregonians could exclude whomever they saw fit and that "the right to vote is a political and not a natural right, and belongs to none except those . . . [upon whom it is] conferred by law."[24] The Oregon Territory had the power to determine its own suffrage laws, and it could influence the national discussion on both suffrage and naturalization with this capability. So why did the federal government not regulate Oregon's suffrage law in relation to naturalization? Part of the reason, as discussed in previous chapters, was the perceived need by the U.S. government and some Oregon settlers for further white settlement to sufficiently control Pacific Northwest lands. The racial identification of "white" also applied to people outside of the United States, such as those from European nations. The other main reason rested in the demographics of Oregon and the fact that persons other than U.S. immigrants held political and social authority within the settler colony. Oregon lawmakers such as Thurston, therefore, argued that Oregon required more malleable definitions of suffrage, naturalization, and citizenship than the federal government provided.

In 1851 Oregon's Legislative Assembly debated a revision to the suffrage law that would drop the declaration and oath component of the current policy and only allow white foreign born men to vote if they were naturalized citizens. Although it did not pass, Oregon's evolving interpretation of who could become a voter (and thus who could become a naturalized citizen) reflected legal definitions of suffrage in numerous states at the time.[25] Oregon initially specified that "inhabitants" could vote but revised its constitution to indicate that only "citizens" held the right of suffrage—though becoming a "citizen" remained accessible to white foreigners. Not all U.S. states or territories, however, included a section about noncitizens' access to suffrage in their constitutions.[26]

In fact, as evidenced in table 6, only nine states had included a naturalization component in their suffrage laws prior to 1860, and many of these states were in western regions.[27] In the case of Oregon, requiring white foreign men to become naturalized before gaining the right to vote would have been a large departure from its laws a decade earlier.

Technically, if Oregon legislators had adopted such a revision, white males born in Oregon prior to 1846 (regardless of their parents' nationalities) would have been foreign born, because the region was not yet a U.S. territory at the time. Oregon's diverse population and the fact that it had existed as a multinational settler colony only a few years earlier resulted in a complex discussion about the issue of naturalization and U.S. citizenship.

A region with shifting boundaries, Oregon's construction and implementation of laws connected to naturalization had to consider the non-U.S. groups that had existed in Oregon prior to its becoming a U.S. territory. Those identified as British subjects—which encompassed a diverse population—comprised the largest foreign group and represented those with the greatest influence outside of U.S. immigrants before 1846. One of the most influential individuals in Oregon during the colonization of the region was the Hudson's Bay Company's chief factor Dr. John McLoughlin. Born in Canada, McLoughlin came to the Oregon Country with the fur-trade franchise in 1824 (twenty-two years before the region became the Oregon Territory). There, he constructed Fort Vancouver and, as mentioned in chapter 1, became a vital contributor to the development of missions and settlements in Oregon. McLoughlin had contributed to Oregon's earliest colonial governments, and his trade relations with American Indian groups were unmatched by leaders among U.S. immigrants.[28] In 1846, however, McLoughlin went from being one of the most influential nonnative men in the far West to being a foreigner. Once under U.S. jurisdiction, this influential white member of Oregon faced legal restrictions due to his origin of birth.

On May 30, 1849, Dr. McLoughlin met with George L. Curry, clerk of the County Court of Clackamas County, and formally declared his intention to become a naturalized U.S. citizen, thereby renouncing any allegiance to other governments. According to the Oregon Territory's constitution, ratified in the previous year, this action permitted him to vote and to enjoy other rights granted to U.S. citizens. The Donation Land Act, passed by the federal government one year later, acknowledged this naturalization option and should have retroactively awarded

Table 6. State constitution suffrage articles—"citizen" (prior 1860)

SPECIFICATION	STATE	SLAVE / FREE	YEAR	ORIGINAL / REVISION	NATURALIZATION SECTION (Y/N)
Allowed non-U.S. citizens possible access to suffrage	New Hampshire	Free	1784	Original	Y
	Vermont	Free	1793	Original	Y
	Georgia	Slave	1798	Original	N
	South Carolina	Slave	1810	Revision	N
	Mississippi	Slave	1817	Original	N
	Connecticut	Free	1818	Revision	N
	Alabama	Slave	1819	Original	N
	Maine	Free	1819	Original	N
	Missouri	Slave	1820	Original	N
	Massachusetts	Free	1822	Revision	N
	Delaware	Slave	1831	Revision	N
	Tennessee	Slave	1834	Original	N
	Michigan	Free	1835	Original	Y
	Arkansas	Slave	1836	Original	N
	Florida	Slave	1838	Original (approved 1845)	N
	Pennsylvania	Free	1838	Revision	N
	New Jersey	Free	1844	Revision	N
	Texas	Slave	1845	Original	N
	Iowa	Free	1846	Original	N

New York	Free	1846	Revision	N
Illinois	Free	1848	Revision	Y
Wisconsin	Free	1848	Original	Y
Oregon	**Free**	**1848**	**Territorial constitution**	**Y**
California	Free	1849	Original	N
Kentucky	Slave	1850	Revision	N
Maryland	Slave	1850	Revision	N
New Mexico	Slave	1850	Territorial constitution	N
Indiana	Free	1851	Revision	Y
Ohio	Free	1851	Revision	N
Virginia	Slave	1851	Revision	N
Louisiana	Slave	1852	Revision	N
Washington	Free	1853	Territorial constitution	Y
North Carolina	Slave	1854	Revision	Y
Minnesota	Free	1857	Original	Y
Oregon	Free	1858	Original (approved 1859)	Y
Kansas	Free	1859	Original (statehood 1861)	Y

Total (States) = 33
Total (Territories) = 3

Source: Created by author based on ratified constitutions; Swindler, *Sources and Documents*.

McLoughlin a grant for lands claimed—the oldest of which went back to 1829.[29] The former chief factor, however, faced an uphill battle to prove that he had legally declared his intentions to become a U.S. citizen and that he possessed the rights of suffrage and land ownership.

In December 1849 Oregon's territorial delegate Samuel R. Thurston and Supreme Judge of the Oregon Territory W. P. Bryant stated that they did not recognize McLoughlin's recorded declaration to become a citizen. Thurston went so far as to report to the U.S. Congress that although McLoughlin had chosen to vote in the August elections that year (which he did), the doctor had not demonstrated any desire to become a citizen. Thurston and Bryant further questioned the authority of Clerk Curry to record McLoughlin's declaration to become a U.S. citizen given the timing of the event, which had taken place between the operation of the provisional courts and the establishment of the territorial courts.[30] Responding to these accusations, McLoughlin asked Oregonians, in multiple newspaper editorials, why Thurston had solicited McLoughlin's vote during the time leading up to the election if the latter's declaration to become a citizen had not been legal and McLoughlin had not been an eligible voter. McLoughlin also pointed out to Oregon readers the role he had played in the colonial settlement of the region, noting, in one article, "if I had acted differently, the Government would have had difficulties, and this community would perhaps not have enjoyed the peace it has, nor be in so prosperous a condition as it is."[31]

Thurston and other authors of the Donation Land Act were primarily concerned about allowing Hudson's Bay Company employees (whether current or former), including influential individuals such as McLoughlin, the right to own land in Oregon.[32] As addressed in chapter 4, Oregonians were determined to restrict the ownership of land and access to the Donation Land Act. This exclusion applied to employees of the Hudson's Bay Company, who obtained limited rights to lands occupied by British subjects in the Oregon Treaty of 1846.[33] McLoughlin and several others, however, had left the company around the time of the Oregon Treaty, and McLoughlin had settled on and claimed land in Oregon City several years before the Donation Land Act. By denying

5. Dr. John McLoughlin, neg. no. 49848, Oregon Historical Society Research Library.

that McLoughlin had declared his intention to become a U.S. citizen in 1849, Thurston attempted to restrict McLoughlin from retaining his land claims through the federal land grant act.[34]

In May 1851 Judge O. C. Pratt weighed in on the matter of McLoughlin's naturalization. Pratt stated that Curry had been authorized to record McLoughlin's declaration to become a citizen, because the provisional government structure remained active until the territorial government had been appointed and was active.[35] Pratt also noted the unique position of Oregon, stating that it "was entirely unlike other Territorial districts . . . Left for years by the only right of power having authority to make needful rules for its government, and without protection." And yet, despite "all neglect by congress," Pratt asserted that Oregon had "accumulated within its limits large numbers of American citizens, and others who wished to become such, all loudly demanding aid and immediate extension of laws with means to enforce them."[36] Oregon lawmakers and the policies they created had to contend with Oregon's history as a colonial outpost, including the influence of the Hudson's Bay Company and leaders such as McLoughlin.[37]

The problem for some Oregon settlers seeking authority in the region was that even though Oregon was no longer identified as a colony, the process of settler colonialism continued. Those involved in the construction of Oregon's initial provisional laws, and who had commanded authority in the settler communities, still had power within the developing political and social systems of Oregon. There were, however, several U.S. settlers within the territorial government who believed that the treatment of McLoughlin's claim, regardless of his nationality, had been wrong. When the House of the Oregon territorial government discussed a memorial to construct a university in Oregon City on McLoughlin's disputed land claim, a majority of representatives voiced their opinion that McLoughlin's continuous legal fight for said lands would eventually side in his favor, and many expressed the opinion that they did not see it as appropriate to presume otherwise. McLoughlin's claims were eventually awarded to his estate, but only after his death in 1857.[38]

Disenfranchising a powerful member of the community could help political leaders consolidate their authority in Oregon. With the McLoughlin incident, for example, McLoughlin pointed out that Thurston had solicited his vote, leading McLoughlin to conclude, "I voted and voted against him, as he well knows, and as he seems well to remember."[39] Regardless of whether that had been Thurston's intention in challenging McLoughlin's declaration to become a U.S. citizen, McLoughlin's experience reflects how Oregonians negotiated power during their transition from a settler colony to a territory. Settler colonialism created power structures in Oregon that required U.S. politicians to consider the role of white foreign-born men within the region when developing legislation connected to naturalization. Thus, Oregon legislators continued to adapt naturalization policies as they deemed fit at that specific time. Additionally, the role of settler colonialism explains why these legislators continuously voted down the language that implied only citizens had access to the right of suffrage. The existence of multiple nationalities with authority and claims to the region became a uniquely Oregon feature in its suffrage and naturalization laws. Moreover, the federal government did not challenge Oregon's interpretation of naturalization; rather, it allowed Oregon's colonial structures to continue to dictate such policies as the territory developed.

Oregon's incoming immigrants also contributed to legislators' approach to naturalization laws. Although Oregon officials reported to Secretary of State John Clayton in April 1849 that the territory only counted 2,509 voters, Oregon Democrats had recognized the potential voting strength of the region's white immigrant population by the mid-1850s.[40] Regional Democrats focused on associating Whig and eventually Republican candidates with the (notoriously antiforeign) Know-Nothing ideology. Preceding the election of a councilman to Oregon's Legislative Assembly in 1854, Democrat Shubbicke Norris encouraged the *Oregon Statesman* editor Asahel Bush to "Give [Thomas] Dryer hell also the know nothings as they are getting quite numerous in this place and we are making a desperate effort to get all the foreigners which I think can be done by all the Democratic papers pitching in."[41] As editor, Bush had the ability to use his paper to not only promote Democrat candidates but also rouse fear among Oregonians that the opposing parties would strip white foreign men of their rights or make naturalization impossible. The *Oregon Statesman* ran numerous articles criticizing policies against white foreigners in Oregon and within the nation. Among other arguments made, the paper suggested that the Alien and Sedition Acts under the John Adams administration "stripped both native and alien of the liberty of speech and press."[42] Bush connected this perspective of federalism to Oregon's Anti-Democrat groups, suggesting that "we see here exhibited this same hostility to adopted citizens."[43] Since the days of the provisional government, politicians from multiple partisan groups had supported the assimilation and naturalization of European immigrants, but Democrats still successfully associated their opponents with carrying prejudices toward foreign residents.

In discussing the upcoming election of Oregon's territorial delegate to Congress and the reelection of General Joseph Lane, G. H. Ambrose wrote to Bush in 1855 that the newspapers' "remarks upon 'that expedition to fight the emigrants' will meet with appropriation of a majority of the people in this vally [*sic*]. It was believed at the time to have been gotten up for speculation by those very persons who advanced most liberally."[44] Ambrose believed that Oregonians were accepting statements from the *Oregon Statesman* about the strength and determination of Know-Nothings in Oregon. These articles promoted the idea that the region's foreigners were only truly safe with the leadership of the Democratic Party. The Know-Nothings had influence within Oregon, but the groups that supported such anti-immigrant ideology were quite small. The Democratic Party, on the other hand, was growing and had consistently held a majority of Oregon's public offices.[45]

The Democrats of Oregon were not without their prejudices against immigrants. In one *Oregon Statesman* article, the author explained the moral and economic benefit European immigrants received from coming to the United States, claiming that immigrants beheld "a mighty spectacle—a land teeming with the fruits of the earth—a commerce rapidly reaching towards the first among nations—a world of rivers ploughed by the steam vessel—near nine thousand miles of railway and numerous canals—and the electric telegraph threading its wires in every direction." The editorial continued that unlike the "idle, slovenly, and unthrifty habits, acquired in Europe," "the improvement of both the physical and mental condition of the new-comer" would be realized by moving to Oregon.[46] Although it may not have intended to be anti-immigrant, the article depicted European immigrants as being less advanced in the ways of technology and industry and insinuated that they could be "improved" through the process of coming to the United States and living with Americans.

Some Oregon settlers depicted Europeans as too inferior to criticize immigrants' influence on U.S. politics, contrasting European governance with what some viewed as a purely U.S. form of democracy. Reminiscent of the arguments used during the Revolutionary War era and again during the War of 1812, Anti-Democrats in Oregon associated the Democrats' platforms with European ideas and drew connections between them and the continuous resentment toward European influence within U.S. politics.[47] Democrats did not necessarily disagree with this aversion to European governments or their influence, but they recognized that Oregon's current and future demographics comprised a large white foreign-born group.

The growing national trend against foreign immigration and the negative perception of Europeans in the United States may have influenced some Oregonians' opposition to former Hudson's Bay Company employees such as McLoughlin. For example, the Anti-Democrat newspaper *Oregon Argus* appealed to its readers to "take the American side in politics, and advocate, as the last and best hope of our poor distracted country, an abandonment of old party platforms, a clear emancipation from the shackles that party demagogues have so long forged for the people."[48] But unlike anti-immigrant sentiments in the East, Oregon had to reconcile with its past as a settler colony with multiple nationalities and its contemporary existence as a region in need of white immigrant settlement to increase its population numbers. At the federal level, Oregon's approaching application for statehood meant that its position on naturalization and foreign suffrage would become a national concern, as many states continued to redefine citizenship and debate the meaning of U.S. citizenship.

From its colonial beginnings Oregon continued to be a land ruled by immigrants, and foreign-born white men continued to become public officeholders throughout the 1850s. This group of Oregonians was aided by suffrage laws that granted white foreign men intending to become U.S. citizens the right to vote. In fact, during an Oregon Council session, legislators questioned the nomination of Alexander Campbell for the prosecuting attorney because he was foreign-born and had not become a naturalized citizen as defined by the U.S. Constitution. Supporters of Campbell referenced the Oregon suffrage law that had just passed both the Council and House. This Oregon legislation granted Campbell, as a white male who had declared his intention to become a citizen, the right to vote and thus qualified him to hold the position of prosecuting attorney.[49] Oregon's suffrage law, therefore, informed naturalization policy within the region and determined who was eligible to hold public office, thus permitting unnaturalized residents of Oregon access to other rights as citizens.

States' naturalization processes varied across the country during the mid-nineteenth century, and during Oregon's Constitutional Convention disagreement over naturalization plagued the Committee on Suffrage and Elections. The states that were new to statehood in the West—today considered the Midwest—upon whose constitutional articles Oregonians molded many of their own, did not have the same (perceived) level of nonwhite immigrants that California and Oregon experienced.[50] Furthermore, the required time of residence for foreigners prior to receiving the right of suffrage held deep political implications. As discussed above, accusations that politicians who were associated with or held sympathies for the Know-Nothings closely followed delegates who pushed for longer periods of naturalization. Minimizing the requirements for naturalization, however, granted foreign-born residents greater access to rights as citizens, which made some delegates apprehensive about white U.S.-born males losing authority in Oregon. This latter fear was particularly true in sparsely populated regions, where immigrant numbers could easily surpass those of "native" residents in a matter of years.[51] Oregon legislators, therefore, had to reach a decision on the political standing of Oregon's white foreign population and include this group within its definition of citizenship.

Reflecting past Oregon laws on suffrage, the article on Suffrage and Elections permitted white males of foreign birth who declared their intention of becoming U.S. citizens the right to vote. Additionally, the law required potential voters to have lived in Oregon for at least six months prior to voting in an election. In comparison to other state constitutions, as well as the federal constitution, six months was a short period of residence for one to receive the right to vote. Delegates such as William H. Farrar disagreed with this timeline and drew direct connections between the right of suffrage and naturalization, arguing that Congress had established that a foreigner must reside in the United States for at least five years before being eligible for naturalization and gaining the right to vote.[52] Oregon legislators who shared this opposition to the short six-month requirement questioned whether Oregon should establish qualifications for naturalization that were different from federal policy. *Oregonian* editor and Portland delegate Thomas Dryer argued "that a foreigner was not as capable of administering the laws of the country as was a native-born citizen. He [explained that he] was in favor of foreigners voting when they had become qualified, but [that] they should never control him, or the rights and liberties of the people."[53] Dryer maintained that foreigners needed to live in the United States for a period longer than six months before they could politically act in the best interests of the nation.

Although this debate focused on naturalization, the law in question was about suffrage. If a white male foreigner received the right to vote and the other rights of a citizen in connection to suffrage, then Oregon's constitutional article on suffrage would establish a policy on naturalization within the future state. Even other states that included a naturalization component in their suffrage laws (to provide easier access to voting) matched the federal government's requirements for naturalization, whereas Oregon reduced the time requirement.[54]

Oregonians' departure from federal policy, however, bothered even delegates who supported easy access to naturalization. For example, delegate Matthew Deady argued that keeping Oregon's naturalization policy on par with the federal constitution would "strip those who oppose foreigners of their strongest argument against them," because opposition to the Oregon law would imply a disapproval of federal policy. Deady further stated that "he had no sympathy for those who opposed foreigners—his father was a foreigner, and every drop of blood in his veins was of foreign origin."[55] Although Deady was born in the United States, and was identified as a U.S. citizen despite his parent's nationality, many settlers of the American West were not that far removed from their European descendants. While having Oregon's laws reflect established national policies would have gone a long way toward garnering favor with Congress during the statehood application, Oregon instead forced Congress to debate and possibly reject such a liberal policy on naturalization.

Nevertheless, most delegates at Oregon's Constitutional Convention supported the six-month residency requirement for suffrage. Delazon Smith insisted that foreigners who came here faced a perilous journey knowing full well what awaited them in Oregon; therefore, he believed anyone willing to take the risk of immigrating here was worthy of the trust bestowed in the right to vote.[56] Smith's argument also spoke to the desire for further settlement of Oregon and the need for additional immigrants to obtain land for settlement. This factor should not be overlooked, he claimed, because one of the main reasons why Congress had pushed for Oregon to become a territory and to establish a territorial government—and would later refer to when Oregon applied for statehood—was that Oregon still contained "open" and unprotected, therefore vulnerable, lands. The region, this argument insisted, needed further settlement for the United States to control the lands and its assets from outside forces, which included American Indian groups native to the region.[57] Delegates such as Smith, therefore, reminded their colleagues of what exactly European immigrants had contributed to Oregon. Anti-Democrat David Logan added to this, stating, "We all know in a new state but sparsely populated the population will, in all probability, be made up of many foreigners. Shall we tie up their hands for five years?"[58] Moreover, Democrat A. L. Lovejoy urged his colleagues to recognize that "the property of foreigners was taxed to support the government . . . [therefore they] should be allowed to vote; that it would be unjust if otherwise."[59] Of course, Oregonians did not seem to have trouble taxing the property of other groups who were ultimately denied the right to vote, such as women and nonwhite foreigners; this is addressed in later sections of this chapter.

Oregon delegates adopted the six-month requirement, and the second section of the Suffrage and Election article provided an allowance for foreigners (who had declared their intention to naturalize) the right to vote as long as they were also male, white, and of twenty-one years of age. Oregon legislators determined that this specific group of foreigners was worthy of receiving both the right of suffrage and other rights accessed through suffrage, such as holding public office. Regardless of the minimal time they had spent in the country, let alone in Oregon, delegates saw this group of foreigners as white men with desires to "settle" the region. Perpetuating the process of colonization in Oregon was still deemed necessary; therefore, the structures employed by the provisional government that acknowledged white men as equal regardless of nationality extended to Oregon's state constitution.[60]

In 1858 Oregonians' approval of the state constitution moved their interpretations of suffrage and subsequent naturalization to Congress for consideration. The need to negotiate with Oregon's colonial structures, even if not described as such, became apparent. Among other objections to Oregon's proposed state constitution, Congress debated the constitutionality of Oregon's article on suffrage.[61] Specifically, Congress discussed how Oregon had extended to foreigners the right to vote. The author of the Minority Report for the House of Representatives, Congressman Felix Zollicoffer of Tennessee, argued that "the clause allowing unnaturalized aliens to vote for members of the Legislature . . . [was] as violative [*sic*] of a fundamental principle of the Constitution of the United States." Zollicoffer believed that by granting foreigners the right to vote in all future state elections, the Oregon constitution allowed foreigners to also vote on federal offices, thus giving them "direct or indirect power of control over every department of the Federal Government." The Minority Report maintained that because voting for federal offices was a right reserved for U.S. citizens, Oregon's suffrage law extending suffrage to unnaturalized foreigners was in violation of the federal constitution.[62] This opinion, however, also addressed the debated position of the federal government's relationship to state rights.

Supporting Oregon's admittance and its constitutional policy toward foreigner voters, Georgia Congressman Alexander Stephan insisted that while a state can define suffrage differently from the federal government, no state possessed the authority to grant the rights of U.S. citizenship to an unnaturalized person. An unnaturalized white foreign male, therefore, might have the right to vote in Oregon, but access to citizenship rights in Oregon did not then extend to them the rights of U.S. citizenship.[63] This specific interpretation allowed states to have laws separate from and beyond the control of the federal government while also acknowledging that state laws do not always transfer outside of the state.

Congressional representative John Clark of Missouri supported this states' rights argument and drew a connection between Oregon's right to construct its own suffrage laws and the need to protect states from a tyrannical federal government, stating, "Whenever we surrender the right to determine who shall vote in the States, we do not know how soon we will be deprived of suffrage ourselves."[64] Neither Missouri nor Georgia, however, had naturalization policies attached to their state suffrage laws, although both were slave states.[65] Oregon's liberal policy toward foreigners, therefore, was defended by state representatives who did not necessarily share Oregon's sentiments toward European immigrants; rather, these representatives wanted Congress to recognize a state's right to its own suffrage law regardless of that law's nature.

By 1859 political tension over the federal government's legal reach had already manifested as violence across the nation, evidenced by events such as "Bleeding Kansas." Although partisan groups disagreed on how the federal government should enact legislation in the territories,

Democrats saw value in federal laws protecting certain state rights (e.g., Fugitive Slave Act).[66] The timing of Oregon's statehood application, therefore, garnered it support among representatives wanting to legitimize the authority of the federal government to uphold state rights. Oregon's legislation on suffrage may have run contrary to federal policy, but it provided representatives an opportunity to control and clarify federal interference in state legislation.

Congress admitted Oregon to statehood in February 1859, but national objection to Oregon's extending the right to vote to foreigners continued. Reprinted from a Virginia paper, one opinion piece on Oregon's admission referred to the suffrage articles as "infamous" and their acceptance as "one of the greatest mistakes—to say the least of it—ever committed by [the] U.S. Congress."[67] One editorial in a Boston newspaper suggested that Oregon Democrats, as well as those with influence in the Democratic Party, had purposely colonized Oregon with foreigners so that the party could control the region. The author further asserted "that Oregon has been hitherto too freely colonized and ruled by Democratic office-seekers."[68] Oregon Democrats had more aggressively campaigned for immigrants' votes during the 1850s, and the *Oregon Statesman* editorials connecting Know-Nothings to the Anti-Democrats certainly aided that cause. Whether Democrats had brought immigrants into Oregon, however, was less clear. Immigration to Oregon was part of colonization in that region, and politicians from all partisan groups had supported the settlement of Oregon. Nevertheless, the Boston editorial was correct to associate Oregon's suffrage law with colonization. In the case of Oregon, the multiple nationalities created a unique political and social dynamic within the settler colony (once it had become a U.S. Territory) requiring American lawmakers to adopt policies that granted other white inhabitants access to rights as citizens regardless of their nationalities.

Overall, Oregon's specific allowances to the right of suffrage and its related naturalization policy revealed the impact of settler colonialism on Oregon power structures. It also demonstrated the influence such processes had on national discussions of naturalization, citizenship, and the legal interpretations of suffrage as a right defined by a territory or state. Congress's acceptance of Oregon's suffrage laws at the territorial and then state level were due in part to timing and national tensions but also to Oregon's vulnerable situation regarding sparse settlement and its proximity to other non-U.S. groups. Oregonians remained in control of their laws, even when their constitutional articles on suffrage and naturalization conflicted with federal policies. Ultimately, suffrage laws cultivated within the process of settler colonialism had to continue to ensure future control over the region.

Racial Definitions through Suffrage Laws

As one of the most protected rights in U.S. citizenship, the right of suffrage in the United States has had a long history of excluding groups. In the mid-nineteenth century the political and social structures that had existed before universal white male suffrage were not yet a distant memory. Those fortunate enough to gain U.S. citizenship, therefore, felt it necessary to continuously scrutinize which groups possessed the right to vote, because controlling access to citizenship limited competition over political authority. Oregon's diverse population and complex relationships between the region's inhabitants, as well as the timing of its transition from a settler colony to a territory and finally to statehood, created an environment that supported specific racial exclusions to the right of suffrage.

To justify a group's exclusion from the right of suffrage, Oregon and federal representatives attempted to demonstrate that these groups needed to be restricted from rights connected to U.S. citizenship. For example, excluding Black Americans from the right to vote would make them politically ineffective. Lawmakers could then argue that because this group was not able to practice political rights (the very rights legislators had stripped from them), the nation should restrict Black Americans from the West, because the West remained a space where persons endowed with the rights of citizenship were needed for successful settlement.[69] This justification for racial exclusions in the American West was partially rooted in the continued colonization process of the region. Settlement was not complete, meaning land remained unsecured by U.S. settlers—

specifically, lands from American Indians. As most nonwhite groups in the United States did not possess full citizenship, legislators argued for the need to exclude nonwhite groups and ensure only those with political authority would settle and maintain control of the region. But congressional representatives missed an important component of the settler colony's provisional laws: the fact that early Oregon laws permitted nonwhite men to vote so long as the voters had white fathers.

In 1843 the Oregon provisional government defined those qualified to vote: "Every white male descendant of a white man, inhabitant of this territory, of the age of twenty-one years and upwards, who shall have been an inhabitant of this territory at the time of its organization, shall be entitled to vote at the election of officers." Two years later when Oregon adopted its Organic Laws, this qualification for suffrage remained in place. As with a similar specification in Oregon's early land laws, legislators intended to address a population of Oregonians with American Indian mothers and white U.S. or European fathers. The suffrage law did not specify that the individual had to be half American Indian, rather, merely the son of a white man.[70] Suffrage, therefore, became a transferable right that a white father could pass down to his son, and this established a racial criterion to suffrage laws.

By 1845 seventeen state constitutions included suffrage laws with the racial specification of "white." This number, however, did not represent all incoming states or revisions by existing states to include this language. Rather, when Oregon drafted its suffrage laws with the racial exclusion, twelve of the seventeen states to include "white" in their suffrage laws were slave states. Additionally, as table 7 demonstrates, out of the free states with the specification of "white," only two were not western states or former slave states.[71] Some slave states added this racial specification to distinguish between white men and the growing number of free Black Americans. Western regions such as Oregon did not have large populations of free Black Americans, and Oregon's largest nonwhite group was American Indians. Many western states, however, wanted to restrict the presence of Black Americans, whether enslaved or free, from their regions.[72] Oregon's inclusion of "white" to identify eligible voters in its settler colony, therefore, joined a national movement toward explicitly classifying qualified voters as white citizens. Oregon also joined a western trend of adopting this racial specification even when populations did not support its necessity; rather, racial prejudice and support of local law carried the day.

As mentioned above, when Oregon became a U.S. territory in 1848 Oregonians altered their suffrage law to include a section on naturalization. Oregon legislators, however, also dropped the section that identified eligible voters as "descendants of white men," including instead "Every white male inhabitant only by citizens of the United States above the age of twenty-one years, and those above that age who shall have declared, on oath, their intention to become such, and shall have taken an oath to support the constitution of the United States, and the provision of this act."[73] Oregonians generated numerous pieces of legislation in the next decade that proposed extending the right to vote and citizenship to "Half Breed" men, specifically those with white fathers and Indigenous mothers, but none passed.[74] In part, the need to grant nonwhite men with white fathers the right to vote lost favor among Oregon lawmakers once Oregon had become a U.S. territory and more white women had moved to the region. By restricting those of Indigenous ancestry from the right of suffrage, Oregon lawmakers also removed American Indians' access to U.S. citizenship. Like the argument that only citizens should be able to live in Oregon, which lawmakers made to deny Black Americans the right to come and settle in the region, denying citizenship to American Indians supported settlers' reasoning for their removal.[75] Oregon's racial restrictions to suffrage, therefore, transitioned with the process of settler colonialism.

In 1854 the Oregon territorial government passed an act related to elections and "the mode of supplying vacancies in office" that reified the racial specification within its suffrage article.[76] Oregon's revised suffrage policy more closely resembled the language applied by states with racial specifications and indicated a trend unique to the West and South. Throughout the 1840s and 1850s, western states continued to adopt racial qualifications within their suffrage laws, and slave states

Table 7. State constitution suffrage articles—"white" (prior 1860)

SPECIFICATION	STATE	SLAVE/ FREE	YEAR	ORIGINAL / REVISION
Included the word "white" to identify voting population	South Carolina	Slave	1790	Revision
	Delaware	Slave	1792	Revision
	Ohio	Free	1802	Original
	Maryland	Slave	1810	Revision
	Louisiana	Slave	1812	Original
	Mississippi	Slave	1817	Original
	Indiana	Slave	1816	Original
	Connecticut	Free	1818	Revision
	Alabama	Slave	1819	Original
	Missouri	Slave	1820	Original
	Virginia	Slave	1829	Revision
	Tennessee	Slave	1834	Original
	Michigan	Free	1835	Original
	Arkansas	Slave	1836	Original
	Florida	Slave	1838	Original (approved 1845)
	Pennsylvania	Free	1838	Revision
	New Jersey	Free	1844	Revision
	Oregon	**Free**	**1845**	**Organic Law—Provisional**
	Iowa	Free	1846	Original
	Illinois	Free	1848	Revision
	Wisconsin	Free	1848	Original
	Oregon	**Free**	**1848**	**Territorial Constitution**
	California	Free	1849	Original
	Kentucky	Slave	1850	Revision
	New Mexico	Slave	1850	Territorial Constitution
	Washington	Free	1853	Territorial Constitution
	North Carolina	Slave	1854	Revision
	Oregon	**Free**	**1858**	**Original** (approved 1859)
	Kansas	Free	1859	Original
	Total (States) = 25; Free = 11, Slave = 14 Total (Territories) = 2; Free = 1, Slave = 1			

Source: Created by author based on ratified constitutions; Swindler, *Sources and Documents*.

such as Kentucky and North Carolina eventually followed, revising their voting legislation to include this specification in 1850 and 1854 respectively.[77] The West did not follow the South; rather, both enacted similar laws around the same time. Specific to the West, however, was the discussed inclusion of men with Indigenous mothers and white fathers.

Despite the passionate appeals by friends and family members of this excluded group, "Half Breed" men remained restricted from the right to vote in Oregon's constitution due to the racial specification of "white" and the lack of a paternal qualification.[78] Following the constitution's passage, representatives again brought several bills forward asking the legislative assembly to extend the right of suffrage to "Half Breed" men.[79] The suffrage article in the constitution did not include "half breed" males, but neither did it specifically exclude them as had been done to other groups (addressed later in this section). Thus, the Oregon constitution left the fate of males with white fathers and Indigenous mothers unclear. This was contrary to Oregon's provisional and territorial government policies and a move away from states such as Minnesota, California, and Wisconsin, which made allowance for this mixed-race group.[80] By not permitting "half breed" men the right of suffrage, Oregon codified voting as a white right, without exception.

By the 1850s the North and South had become more cautious of laws specifically pertaining to Black Americans, in hopes of avoiding the discussion of dissolution, but Oregon and western states created laws directed at this group as well as others.[81] Many western states carried Democratic majorities, but, believing that the national partisan groups did not or would not fully support their needs, westerners employed policies that best served their specific states or territories. Similarly, Oregonians passed legislation with racial exclusions to specific groups and refined the definition of citizenship in their settler colony, territory, and eventual state to suit their own purposes.[82]

After the Oregon Treaty of 1846 a significant number of Kanaka immigrants, many of whom were connected to the Hudson's Bay Company, wanted to remain in Oregon and become U.S. citizens. As mentioned above, the federal naturalization policy included a racial specification that limited naturalization to persons identified as both free and white. When a group of Kanaka settlers attempted to become naturalized citizens in 1848 the chief justice of the Oregon Territory Supreme Court, Justice William P. Bryant, ruled that extending citizenship to the Hawaiian subjects would be in violation of the U.S. Constitution due to the race of the applicants.[83] Federal legislation prevented Kanaka settlers from becoming naturalized citizens, and Oregonians even considered excluding them from specific political rights in the state constitution.[84] Ultimately, as with "half breed" men, the Oregon constitution did not list Kanaka as an excluded group. Oregon legislators, however, did specifically exclude two groups from the right of suffrage: Black Americans and persons of Chinese descent.

As early as 1844 Oregon legislators began adding racial specifications to various rights and referencing exclusions to suffrage as justification for other legal restrictions. Reflecting on meetings under Oregon's provisional government, Peter Burnett argued that if Black Americans were to be restricted from voting in Oregon elections because they were not white, then it would be in the settler colony's best interest to prohibit the presence of Black Americans in the region altogether. Burnett believed that such an exclusion would be an act of compassion, stating that "the principle is no doubt correct that when a State, for reasons satisfactory to itself, denies the right of suffrage and office to a certain class, it is sometimes the best humanity also to deny the privilege of resident."[85] Later, as Congress discussed the establishment of Oregon's territorial government, national debates surrounding Oregon's provisional laws continued to associate the settler colony's racial restrictions to suffrage with the restriction of Black Americans from coming to or settling in Oregon.

In 1848 representatives such as Senator John Dix of New York described Oregon's exclusion of Black Americans from rights as citizens (such as suffrage) as a necessary step to keep Black Americans from the "fertile spaces of the West." Dix argued, "A class thus degraded will not multiply. This is the first step in retrogradation," and further stated that he held "it to be our sacred duty to consecrate these [western] spaces to the multiplication of the white race." Citing the fact that northeastern states had revised laws to limit or eliminate free Black Americans' access to suffrage, Dix and other representatives viewed the exclusion of this group from suffrage as necessary to preserve Oregon for white settlement.[86] Additionally, Senator Hannibal Hamlin of Maine identified Oregon's steps to exclude Black Americans as an action that California should replicate, once Congress had constructed California a territorial government. "I know there is a mixed population in California," Hamlin once stated, "and so it is in Oregon; but the same limitations and restrictions which apply in one case can be applied in the other. The right of voting had been confined in Oregon to the 'free white inhabitants.' The same limitation may apply to California."[87] The ability to maintain control in the region, it was believed, rested with the settlement of white Americans (or white foreigners) endowed with rights as citizens.[88]

Free Black Americans had limited rights throughout the United States by the 1850s. Moreover, when national tension over slavery increased, so did exclusionary laws that targeted Black Americans in the West. Many western lawmakers went out of their way to argue that racially exclusive laws were necessary to secure white Americans' social and political authority and boisterously opposed "negro equality."[89] Access to the right of suffrage in states such as New York, which included a property requirement and at least three years of residence for "men of color," therefore, provided a small avenue of political rights for Black Americans.[90] In territories or states such as Oregon, disenfranchisement by racial specifications in suffrage laws denied this group access to other rights as citizens. Yet only Indiana and Oregon found it necessary to include a section in their suffrage policy that listed Black Americans as a group that did not have the right to vote.[91]

Oregon's transition from just using the specification of "white" in its suffrage policy to the specific exclusion of groups from the right of suffrage was significant, as it took additional steps to clarify the qualification of "white." To justify exclusions to suffrage, Oregon lawmakers attempted to prove that such groups were potentially problematic inhabitants and therefore not worthy of the right to vote. Even legislation such as the proposed amendment to the immigration restriction in 1851, which provided that Black Americans could come to Oregon if they paid a bond, were not "idle," or did not adopt a "vicious habit" and swore to conduct themselves as "good and law abiding citizen[s] of the Territory," promoted a negative image of Black Americans as nonproductive community members.[92] No such requirements were necessary for white foreign immigrants or white American migrants, only for Black Americans wishing to come to Oregon. This amendment did not pass, and Black Americans continued to be excluded from migrating to Oregon.[93] Discussions and ensuing debates surrounding this bill revealed the continued perception that those ineligible for suffrage in the territory (including women and nonwhite men) were presumed incapable of being contributing members of the community.

Attempting to challenge this perception of Black Americans in Oregon, an *Oregonian* editorial addressed the immigration restriction in the proposed state constitution and suggested that Black Americans "who by education, habits and qualifications, have become voters in other States," should be allowed to come to and reside in Oregon.[94] This article went on to list other revisions to Oregon laws that promoted the Anti-Democrats' arguments, but more important, it acknowledged that Black Americans identified as voters in other states qualified as contributing members of society and, therefore, that they should be able to reside in Oregon. The *Oregon Statesman* editor Asahel Bush recognized the repercussions of this language and idea; Bush responded with a scathing article about the Anti-Democrats' platform and the relationship the *Oregonian*'s editor, Thomas Dryer, held with Black Americans in Oregon. In addition to questioning the sanity and masculinity of Dryer, Bush accused his competitor and political adversary of only promoting the rights of Black Americans because "one of Dryer's regular advertisers is 'of the African race'."[95] The *Oregon Statesman* continued that the advertiser "thinks he ought to be invested with the rights of citizenship, in addition to being able to come and remain here, and of course Dryer's platform must contain an exception covering his case, or he might order out his advertisements, and Dryer would lose his patronage."[96]

The *Oregonian* editor may have considered the business of Black Americans when stating his opinion on their rights, but the fact remained that the right to vote made Black Americans active political members of the community. The right to suffrage, therefore, could open a group up to more rights connected to citizenship. Oregon delegates of the Constitutional Convention understood this potential connection, as evidenced in their decision on the immigration restriction of Black Americans, but the general racial specifications in the suffrage laws were deemed insufficient for keeping Black Americans from gaining access to the rights of citizens.[97] In 1857 Oregon delegates deemed it necessary to specifically exclude Black Americans from the right of suffrage.

Several debates during the Oregon Constitutional Convention addressed citizenship and referred to the definition of "citizen" ultimately established in the Article on Suffrage and Elections. Section 6 of that article states, "No negro, chinaman, or mulatto shall have the right of suffrage."[98] In creating these specific restrictions, Oregon politicians excluded entire populations within Oregon from the right to vote and left them without a formal political voice. According to Oregon delegates who supported this section, the specific exclusion was necessary to prevent said groups from attempting to exercise suffrage. Some Anti-Democrats, however, viewed the exclusion of Black Americans from suffrage and other rights as proslavery Democrats' attempt to prove that a "n—aint a white man."[99] According to this argument, if Black Americans could not be identified as white, they would not have access to the right of suffrage, then they would therefore become a pitied and destitute group. As such, proslavery men could then argue that slavery was really the only moral solution for Black Americans' existence. In response to this, Anti-Democrat delegates, including Thomas Dryer, associated the usage of this specific exclusion with proslavery leaders' need to make slavery seem a "moral, religious, natural, and probably in general a necessary institution."[100]

Alternatively, some supporters of Section 6 viewed the voting exclusion as a means of upholding one of the federal definitions of a citizen. La Fayette Grover argued that only a free white person could become a

U.S. citizen, stating, "No race of color—no negro, no mulatto, no kanaka, no Chinaman, can become a citizen of the free republic of the United States."[101] Black Americans were not unnaturalized foreigners and did possess some rights as citizens in select states. The *Dred Scott v. Sanford* court decision in 1857, however, became interpreted in a multitude of ways—one of these was that Black Americans, regardless of enslavement, were not U.S. citizens.[102] Grover's association with Black Americans and the federal naturalization policy, therefore, reflected the opinion that Black Americans were not U.S. citizens; by his understanding, they could not acquire citizenship and therefore should be specifically excluded from the right to vote. In identifying Black Americans as a group ineligible for suffrage, Oregon's constitution reified the perspective that Black Americans were not U.S. citizens.

For other Oregon delegates, the racial specification of "white" and the addition of Section 6 were still not sufficient measures to guarantee that suffrage would be exclusively a white male right. Aiming to address this issue, Matthew Deady proposed to strike out the specific list of those ineligible for suffrage, stating, "No person, other than those of the white race, shall have the right of suffrage."[103] Even "white race," however, became a debate, because some delegates believed that confusion remained over the meaning of "white." While most Oregon legislators supported exclusionary laws that prohibited Black Americans from gaining access to rights in their future state, some Anti-Democrats took advantage of these discussions about race to inject opinions against slavery. Thus, when David Logan proposed to insert the term "free" before "white" in Section 2 of the suffrage article, Anti-Democrat Thomas Dryer again took the opportunity to engage in a debate on what the term "free" meant.[104]

When discussing the article on Oregon's militia, John Kelsay argued that the racial specification of white was not sufficient to keep Black Americans (both free and enslaved) from joining the militia. Kelsay insisted that he had witnessed several "light-skinned" Black American slaves while he lived in Missouri and suggested such men could pass as being white.[105] Dryer capitalized on Kelsay's testimony of "white slaves" to question whether Kelsay himself was a fugitive light-skinned slave from Missouri. An intense argument followed this baseless accusation, but it permitted Anti-Democrats to debate the issue of slavery despite the delegates' decision to let the people vote on the matter. Thus, after Logan had introduced the term "free" for the suffrage article, Dryer resumed his questioning of Kelsay's race. Dryer maintained that because individuals of questionable races could vote, Oregon needed to define the term "white" rather than add the word "free."[106] Although Dryer had political motives behind these accusations, in making these statements he questioned both Kelsay's race and freedom, which also challenged Kelsay's claims to the right of suffrage. Kelsay attempted to combat these accusations by implying Dryer was the better candidate for being a fugitive slave, arguing "that was why [Dryer] carried a cane—to defend himself against United States [election] officers," and that Dryer opposed adding the term "free" because "he wanted to get to vote himself."[107]

The term "free," as table 8 demonstrates, would not have been a new addition to Oregon legislation, as both Oregon's provisional and territorial governments included this language in their suffrage laws. Having identified itself as a free settler colony and then a free territory, Oregon joined the state of Pennsylvania as the only other nonslave government to include the status of "free" as a qualification for voting.[108] The term "free" may have been necessary to distinguish between enslaved Black Americans and free Black or white Americans in slave states. Within a free territory or state, the term "free" still connected to the issue of slavery, because it suggested the government recognized some kind of nonfree status. In part, this was why Oregon delegates ultimately left the term "free" out of the suffrage article in their state constitution.

As discussed in chapter 3, the earlier presence of "free" in Oregon laws reflected the continuous debate over slavery's existence in Oregon and how support for slavery remained among Oregon leaders. Oregonians, however, chose to drop this politically charged language in 1857. Unlike the evolving issue of racial equality, debate over slavery presented itself clearly between slave and free states during congressional discussions of statehood applications. The absence of the "free" qualification, there-

Table 8. State constitution suffrage articles—"free" (prior 1860)

SPECIFICATION	STATE	SLAVE / FREE	YEAR	ORIGINAL / REVISION
"Free"	North Carolina	Slave	1776	Original ("Freemen")
	South Carolina	Slave	1790	Revision
	Delaware	Slave	1792	Revision
	Kentucky	Slave	1792	Original
	Maryland	Slave	1810	Revision
	Louisiana	Slave	1812	Original
	Mississippi	Slave	1817	Original
	Missouri	Slave	1820	Original
	Tennessee	Slave	1834	Original
	Arkansas	Slave	1836	Original
	Florida	Slave	1838	Original (approved 1845)
	Pennsylvania	Free	1838	Revision ("Freeman")
	Oregon	**Free**	**1845**	**Organic Law—Provisional**
	Texas	Slave	1845	Original
	Oregon	**Free**	**1848**	**Territorial Constitution**
	New Mexico	Slave	1850	Territorial Constitution
	Total (States) = 13; Free = 1, Slave = 12			
	Total (Territories) = 2; Free = 1 Slave = 1			

Source: Created by author based on ratified constitutions; Swindler, *Sources and Documents*.

fore, guaranteed favor with free states. But the removal of "free" was not without debate, and Oregon legislators would in fact discuss the existence of slavery again after statehood.[109]

Overall, debates among Oregon delegates over the suffrage article reflected a concern with free nonwhite men attempting to vote in Oregon and a general confusion over how to ensure only white men voted. For example, Dryer further argued, in a jab at his fellow delegates, that "it was hard to determine who was pure white. There was his friend Kelsay; he was not as white as his friend Burch, and Mr. Waymire's nose was not as sharp as his."[110] Those with constituents who possessed both "white" and American Indian heritage earnestly shared Dryer's opposition to the word "pure." If elected delegates struggled to identify the race of their colleagues, how were election officers going to be able to determine the race of potential voters? The classification of "pure white" might not only potentially exclude men that the delegates and other Oregonians had identified as "white" from voting but also allow nonwhite men to vote. Delegate William Watkins suggested as much when he noted that such a classification would still not "exclude two men of doubtful white color in his county who had voted for his opponent."[111] Ultimately, race as a category remained too malleable for Oregon delegates to feel confident in providing a definition of "white"; therefore, the Oregon constitution retained the terminology of "white male" for its article on suffrage.[112]

Additionally, because Oregon legislators wanted to exclude Black Americans and those of Chinese descent as specific groups, they created separate sections that listed those groups who, regardless of their skin color, were not eligible to vote in Oregon. Race was and continues to be a negotiable concept, and "white" therefore did not necessarily address all groups of European ancestry.[113] Once Oregon had included the term "white," it found itself having to define "white" as a group, and one way to clarify this language was to separately identify groups they deemed in contrast to their understanding of "white." But Oregon's specific exclusions to the right of suffrage were not in line with the rest of the nation. Oregonians had placed restrictions on residents identified as Chinese since their provisional government, but in 1859 they became the *only* state to specifically exclude persons of Chinese descent (regardless of their place of birth) from the right to vote.[114]

During the debate over Oregon's statehood other regions as well as congressional representatives took positions on this fact.[115] A Wisconsin newspaper broached the subject when questioning how the United States could have a treaty with China and then permit a state to exclude Chinese immigrants "from civil rights."[116] How could a future state deny persons of Chinese descent basic rights and tax "Chinese" miners, one Boston newspaper asked, after the federal government had sworn the United States and China "shall be forever at peace with each other."[117] The editorial continued that Oregon would not have offended other treaty-bearing nations, specifically Great Britain, in this manner.

Drawing a difference between Chinese and British subjects highlighted the racial element of Oregon's suffrage exclusions, because Oregon did not apply exclusions to any other specific nationality. Under Oregon law, a British immigrant (presumably white) not only was eligible to all the rights as a citizen but also held the possibility of becoming a U.S. citizen. Granted, Chinese immigrants could not become naturalized citizens due to the racial specification of "white" within the federal policy on naturalization, but persons of Chinese descent had lived in Oregon since the early 1840s. Technically, there were those with Chinese ancestry who had been born in the U.S. Territory and qualified as citizens under jus soli, or the "birthright citizenship orientation of English law."[118] Nevertheless, it would not be until the Fourteenth Amendment that natural-born Americans of Chinese ancestry could challenge this exclusion to U.S. citizenship. Prior to the Civil War, not being identified as "white" had been grounds for exclusion to rights in parts of the country, but Oregon legislators again did not deem this specification sufficient. Oregon singled out its residents of Chinese ancestry and excluded them from the right to vote. This exclusion, Oregon delegates believed, would remove the possibility of election officials incorrectly identifying someone as "white" and reiterate Oregon's objection to such nonwhite groups holding political authority in their future state.

Even California, whose congressional representative William Gwin had praised Oregon for its treatment of persons of Chinese descent in its proposed state constitution, did not pass such exclusionary laws against the Chinese.[119] As Gwin explained during the debate over Oregon's admission as a state, "In California [the Chinese are] not received in the courts of law. They are not citizens of the U.S. and Oregon has done right in rejecting both Chinese and negroes."[120] Yet, Oregon's laws took the exclusion of persons of Chinese descent to another level, according to Gwin, and in doing so narrowed the definition of U.S. citizenship by excluding those of Chinese descent.

Historians have argued that the Chinese Exclusion Act and subsequent immigration policies that specifically excluded Asian groups made those nationalities a racial classification.[121] These acts did define the point at which such legislation became federal policy. However, Oregon's territorial and state laws, which prohibited Chinese from the right to own property and the right to vote as well as levied a tax on Chinese miners, not only classified persons of Chinese descent as a race but also influenced national policy once Oregon had become a state.[122] That is, when Congress admitted Oregon to the union as a state, the federal government institutionalized Oregon's laws on persons of Chinese descent. The existence of such laws in Oregon's constitution did not make these laws federal policy, but it contributed to national debate about the rights of Asian immigrants and Asian Americans and established a legal precedent for later legislation that did become federal policy.

Although not as unique, Oregon's specific exclusion of Black Americans from voting also differed from national trends. Leading up to the Civil War, the state of Texas had listed "Indians not taxed, Africans and descendants of Africans" as "excepted" from its definition of "free male" voters, but prior to Oregon's statehood only the state of Indiana had specified, "No negro or mulatto shall have the right of suffrage."[123] In fact, the state of Kentucky had identified "negroes, mulattoes, and Indians [as] excepted" in 1799, but when it revised its constitution in 1850, it dropped this specific exclusion and defined a voter in Kentucky as a "free white male citizen."[124] In 1859, therefore, Oregon joined a slave state and a former slave territory in specifically excluding Black Americans from the right of suffrage—in addition to identifying a voter as "white." Oregon's constitution left little room for interpreting the right of suffrage, frustrating sections of the country and requiring Congress to decide if these exclusions were acceptable.

Examples of national interest in Oregon's treatment of Black Americans can be found in newspaper articles across the country focusing on how Oregon's legislation stood in contrast to other states' laws or the U.S.

Constitution. Discussions either centered on how Oregon and other western regions were within their rights to restrict Black Americans from political rights or how they violated the rights of Black Americans who originated from states such as Maine or New York (wherein this group possessed certain rights).[125]

With the distinctiveness of Oregon's exclusions to suffrage, discussion of citizenship in relation to race had reached the national stage by the time Oregon applied for statehood. Oregon's suffrage article, however, provided federal politicians another opportunity to debate issues of racial equality. One editorial from Vermont speculated on why Oregon had so many racial exclusions to suffrage and connected the reason to a partisan divide within Oregon. The article expressed the belief that Oregon's Democrats supported white foreigners' right to vote in order to gain the immigrant vote, whereas Oregon's Whigs and Republicans chastised the exclusionary legislation against the Chinese and Black Americans only to belittle Democrats' authority in the region. Ultimately, congressional representatives concerned about which party Oregon would vote with promoted the racial exclusion that suited their needs. This, the author believed, was why American Indians were effectively ignored as potential voters, stating, "There are some hundreds of thousands of Indians; but as Indian sympathy is not now in fashion, their rights are disregarded. There is no political capital to be made out of the real live Indians; and so Republican Senators have to fall back upon the imaginary African and prospective Chinese."[126]

Partisan politics certainly contributed to why congressional representatives ultimately accepted the exclusions to suffrage that Oregonians had adapted from their settler colony days, which they then proposed in a state constitution. Oregon lawmakers' choice to include racial specifications and exclude entire groups demonstrated their attempt to define suffrage, as well as citizenship, as a white right. Moreover, congressional representatives recognized this as Oregon's decision, with one noting the possible repercussions of such exclusions and raising the question, "Who are persons not qualified to become citizens of the United States?" He answered, "They are evidently negroes or mulattoes, or person[s] of color of foreign birth."[127] Oregon did not define U.S. citizenship, but it forced Congress to consider the constitutionality of such restrictive legislation. Thus, Oregon developed a narrow definition of "citizen" by including racial exclusions in its suffrage laws, and this definition (both unique and reflective of other states' policies) influenced national interpretations of suffrage and citizenship.

Constructing Gender in Suffrage Laws

Oregon's earliest laws on suffrage included a seemingly simple but revealing word: "male." In 1843, Oregon settlers constructed a voting law specifying that "Every free male descendent of a white man, and inhabitant of this territory," could enjoy the right of suffrage.[128] As discussed earlier in this chapter, this provisional law temporarily permitted men with white fathers to vote and ensured that voting remained a white right. The inclusion of the words "male" and "man," however, also safeguarded the right of suffrage as a male right.[129] Even within the settler colony's general political documents, Oregonians identified the parties involved as "gentlemen" and used male-gendered words, such as "he," "himself," and "his own," to reflect the possession of rights.[130] It was not just by default that male-gendered language found its way into suffrage laws. Oregon legislators intentionally included these terms and purposely used them to clarify that the right to vote was a male right.

By the 1840s national groups promoting the rights of women had gained widespread attention, particularly after the Seneca Falls Convention in 1848. These groups grounded their arguments about women's rights in legal interpretations of the U.S. Constitution, citing suffrage as an inalienable right protected by the constitution and applicable to all citizens—as larger political reform movements such as abolition had begun to argue.[131] Legislators and judges countered this growth of activism among disenfranchised groups by emphasizing the status of women as a "disabled caste" dependent on a patriarch. Such groups argued that when it came to a married couple, the husband had the responsibility to protect his wife, and the wife reciprocated this protection with allegiance to her husband. Instead of a state protecting the rights of its citizens, who then defended the state, this perception suggested a wife held allegiance to her husband first and the state second. Without full allegiance to the state, lawmakers reasoned, the wife could not receive full constitutional protection, which included the right to vote. This application of "paternal consideration," however, did not prevent the growth of women's rights groups, nor did it lay to rest the issue of women's citizenship. Rather, the reality remained that women across the country, and increasingly in the West, were taxpayers. A single woman without a father, brother, or son to claim authority over her taxable property became a unique problem, because she paid taxes but was denied the right to vote.[132]

To address this both potential and real matter, Oregon legislators constructed and revised laws to specify a gender qualification for the right to vote but also actively avoided discussing women's suffrage. It is important to note that the absence of debates on women's suffrage here (as in other parts of the nation) does not suggest that legislators simply used default language in suffrage laws.[133] Gendered language such as "he" or "his" did not inherently mean women were excluded from rights—as arguments made in the twentieth century against the Equal Rights Amendment and explanations for its ultimate failure later note—but neither did the inclusion of such language extend rights to women. The term "male" differentiated between men's and women's political authority. Oregon lawmakers found the word "male" necessary to prevent women from voting, and legislators' subsequent silence on women's suffrage reinforced this gendered exclusion.[134]

Oregon's Organic Laws in 1845 had echoed the settlers' initial law on suffrage, with the gender qualifications of being "male" and/or a descendant of a white "man" as a requirement.[135] Public discussion on the act of voting also revealed an association with the right of suffrage and the male sex. For example, leading up to a vote on amendments to the Organic Laws, an Oregon newspaper article stressed the importance of voting and insisted, "No man should hesitate to perform this important duty. His single vote may be of great consequence, and it is as much due to his fellow-citizens as it is to himself, that he should exercise his right of suffrage . . . Let no one, then, who has the right, neglect to vote—and, in doing so, each voter should feel the importance and responsibility of his act."[136] Although the author never referenced those who did not possess this right to vote, the language clearly indicates that the intended audience of this article was enfranchised males, with several references to the sex of the potential voter. Moreover, the article does not provide any information as to why this "important duty" was something only a man had to honor; rather, it noted how "his" vote impacted the community as well as "himself," portraying the act of voting as a "responsibility" of men.[137] This ingrained usage of male gendered terms, it goes without saying, was not unique to Oregon.

In 1848, as table 9 portrays, the Oregon Territorial Constitution joined most states to include the term "male" or "men" in its suffrage laws. States such as New York, Rhode Island, and New Jersey were slow to revise their constitutions to include the word male, but only the state of Georgia did not include a gender specification before 1860.[138] The fact remained, however, that several states revised their constitutions' suffrage laws after 1830 to include the gender qualification. This suggests that the inclusion of male language was not the default in voting laws; rather, state legislators came to see the inclusion of "male" or "men" as necessary to define the right of suffrage as a male right, and these revisions took place when the United States began to question such a restriction.[139] Although Oregon laws generally reflected the needs of Oregonians more than national trends, revisions to state suffrage laws had taken place prior to the development of provisional laws in Oregon; thus, in this case, Oregon settlers joined a movement to include male language and keep groups, including women, from voting.

Throughout the 1850s Oregon legislators went on to develop and revise acts that reinforced the exclusion of women from voting. In 1851 the territorial government considered an amendment to the suffrage law that would provide this additional section: "and when any person shall present himself to give his vote, and either of the judges shall suspect that such person does not pass the perquisite qualification of an elector," the election judge had authority to reject said person's vote.[140] Legislators' repetitive use of "male" terms in this section to identify who was an eligible voter helped reaffirm that one of the qualifications for suffrage was being identified as male. Even amendments focused on the naturalization section of suffrage laws reinforced the inclusion of a gender qualification, as policies on white foreigners' eligibility for suffrage—and thus their eligibility for becoming citizens of Oregon—contained the requirement that white foreigners also be "male."[141]

Regardless of this language and what it represented, Oregon women did not remain on the sidelines of Oregon politics, nor did they refrain from exercising the right to vote in avenues available to them. In 1853 the Oregon Territory granted women who paid taxes the right to vote in school elections. Two years later legislators extended this same right to property-owning widows.[142] It was not, however, until 1889 that legislators dropped the land requirement for widows, viewing such women as heads of households and thus eligible to vote in school elections.[143] Due to Oregon land laws' recognition of women holding land claims in their own names, the inclusion of property-owning women in school elections allowed for a significant number of Oregon women to participate in this limited, though significant, field of politics.[144]

School elections were an important step in the advancement of women's suffrage in Oregon as well as elsewhere in the nation, but it has been viewed as more of a "social" rather than a truly "political" realm of participation. Western women, viewed as moral leaders of their households, extended their socially acceptable talents in childrearing to the schools in which their children were educated. This logical step out of the house, however, reinforced women's connection to the home. Women could vote in school elections and in environments that did not challenge the gendered division between the home and the public, because these female voters remained connected to their domestic roles while voting. Furthermore, domesticity linked to social status; therefore, Oregon women could (conceivably) safely involve themselves in matters of children's education without breaching this gendered wall that defined their social worth.[145]

The social ramifications of a woman entering the public arena as a voter in general elections weighed heavily on Oregon women. The

Table 9. State constitution suffrage articles—"male identifier" (prior 1860)

SPECIFICATION	STATE	SLAVE / FREE	YEAR	ORIGINAL / REVISION
Includes male identifiers	North Carolina	Slave	1776	Original ("Freemen")
	New Hampshire	Free	1784	Original
	South Carolina	Slave	1790	Revision
	Delaware	Slave	1792	Revision
	Kentucky	Slave	1792	Original
	Vermont	Free	1793	Original
	Ohio	Free	1802	Original
	Maryland	Slave	1810	Revision
	Louisiana	Slave	1812	Original
	Indiana	Slave	1816	Original
	Mississippi	Slave	1817	Original
	Connecticut	Free	1818	Revision
	Illinois	Free	1818	Original
	Maine	Free	1819	Original
	Alabama	Slave	1819	Original
	Missouri	Slave	1820	Original
	Massachusetts	Free	1822	Revision
	Virginia	Slave	1829	Revision
	Tennessee	Slave	1834	Original
	Michigan	Free	1835	Original
	Arkansas	Slave	1836	Original
	Florida	Slave	1838	Original (approved 1845)
	Pennsylvania	Free	1838	Revision ("Freeman")
	New Jersey	Free	1844	Revision
	Oregon	**Free**	**1845**	**Organic Law—Provisional**
	Texas	Slave	1845	Original
	New York	Free	1846	Revision
	Rhode Island	Free	1846	Revision
	Wisconsin	Free	1848	Original
	Oregon	**Free**	**1848**	**Territorial Constitution**
	California	Free	1849	Original

New Mexico	Slave	1850	Territorial Constitution
Washington	Free	1853	Territorial Constitution
Minnesota	Free	1857	Original
Oregon	**Free**	**1858**	**Original** (approved 1859)
Kansas	Free	1859	Original
Total (States) = 32; Free = 17, Slave = 15			
Total (Territories) = 2; Free = 1, Slave = 1			

Source: Created by author based on ratified constitutions; Swindler, *Sources and Documents*.

opinion of one young Oregon woman, Maria Morfitt, in 1859 reflected this consideration. Born in 1840 in Yorkshire, England, Morfitt migrated with her family to Oregon seven years later. In the Pacific Northwest, she corresponded with her friend Sophie Cornelius about Oregon legislators' decision to exclude women from the right of suffrage in their state constitution. At the time, she expressed the opinion that women did not belong in politics. Morfitt instructed her friend, who evidentially did not share this opinion, "Perhaps you say 'Woman has ideas, refined and noble, capable of benefitting the human race, which never would be given to the world, if she remained in the privacy of her own home.' Then let her use the pen." According to Morfitt, although women were quite capable of forming valid political opinions, attending public elections would violate a woman's delicacy. This female quality, Morfitt asserted, allowed her to rule as "queen of the home" and serve as the moral compass within the family. It was within the home, she maintained, where a woman could "shine as a star, gladdening the hearts she loved and [was] loved by," whereas women's political opinions should be voiced through the medium of newspaper editorials or through a wife's support of her husband—allowing him to enter the public realm of suffrage in her place. If a woman did enter the "public lecture rooms," Morfitt insisted, she would be "divested of this delicacy"; she stated further that in her opinion, such a female would become "a mere machine no[t] deserving the name" of woman.[146]

Disagreeing with Cornelius's opinion that the Oregon legislators should extend the right of suffrage to women, Morfitt continued that women's restrictions from the public arena, "preventing us from acting, and speaking as we would wish, and sometimes as we ought," was a result of gender roles society had constructed and women had enforced. Morfitt further stated, "Woman is wronged by the overstrained customs of society, but these are in a great measure of her own making, and woman is ever ready to 'haul' her poor sisters over the coals, for the slightest infringement upon them."[147] Although Morfitt sidestepped the role of legislation in defining the right of suffrage, her observation on the social enforcement of this legal exclusion is important to note. Women in Oregon would not gain the right to vote for many years after this letter had been written, but it only took another decade before women such as Abigail Scott Duniway took up the pen and challenged Oregonians to reconsider the social and political role of women, thus challenging dominant gender roles.[148] Possessing the right to vote required both political and social acceptance, and early Oregon women such as Morfitt did not see the advantage of challenging political structures when society was positioned to question her social authority as a woman for doing so.

From the political side of how Oregonians excluded women from rights such as suffrage, the Oregon Constitutional Convention of 1857 appears anticlimactic at first glance. As with earlier laws in Oregon, the article on suffrage contains male pronouns and identifies eligible voters as male. Throughout the debate, delegates primarily compared the groups restricted from the right to vote against the specification of "white male" in Section 1.[149] During a debate on the naturalization of white foreign men and their access to the right of suffrage, however, David Logan moved to strike out the term "male" before "citizen," which would leave that specific section of the suffrage article reading "every white citizen of the United States."[150] The *Oregonian*, one of the two newspapers reporting on the Constitutional Convention, did not document this motion, but the *Oregon Statesman* did. Yet, in doing so it only briefly mentioned that the motion had been lost. Neither the newspaper reporters nor the House recorded any discussion after Logan had made this motion.[151] It is possible that no discussion had occurred and another delegate had simply called for an immediate vote on the motion, but the fact that Logan had suggested removing the word "male" was itself significant. Any question, or departure from a consensus, as to why "male" was necessary suggests that "male" was not the default language. Oregon delegates used "male" to identify that women were not eligible voters. Even the relative inaction of debate on women's suffrage, in this case, still demonstrated action.

During Oregon's application for statehood Congress did not question the male qualifications within its suffrage article, but the growing political activism of women's groups made it unlikely that Oregon delegates or members of Congress had not considered women's suffrage at the time.[152] The Washington Territory, only a year after separating from Oregon, came just one vote shy of extending suffrage to white women in 1854. Scholars suggest that Washington's lawmakers ultimately voted the inclusion down, interestingly enough, due to a race issue rather than opposition to women's right to vote.[153] Moreover, Oregon delegates, aware of political discussions in the Washington Territory and elsewhere, included the gendered qualification and identified the right to vote as male. With suffrage restricted to men, access to full citizenship was also limited to men. In terms of gendered definitions, Oregon delegates further debated the appropriate type of men eligible to vote while constructing Section 10 in the suffrage article.

Initially listed as Section 9 in Oregon's suffrage article, the Committee on Suffrage and Elections included a provision on dueling to serve as an indication of what criminal actions would lead to disenfranchisement. The section stated, "Every person who shall give or accept a challenge to fight a duel, or shall knowingly carry to another person such challenge, or who shall agree to go out of the state the fight a duel, shall be ineligible to any office of trust or profit."[154] According to the Oregon constitution, only eligible voters qualified to hold a public office, and this section would therefore also prevent a white male who met the other qualifications for suffrage from becoming an elected official. Although the provision did not state that the person who had participated in dueling was not eligible to vote, the section still restricted his right of suffrage, because access to public office was connected to the right to vote. Debates between delegates ensued, however, as to whether dueling should qualify as an infamous crime. The split that emerged among Oregon legislators rested on gendered assumptions.

During the early American Republic, particularly in the South but elsewhere as well, dueling had been associated with honor and reputation. While in the North this gave way to interpretations that dueling was irrational and unmanly, scholars such as Joanne Freeman demonstrate that the practice of dueling continued to resonate with southern and western politicians up to the Civil War.[155] In the case of Oregon, however, lawmakers felt that participation in dueling warranted exclusion from the right to hold a public office. Trust, some Oregon delegates argued, could not be extended to men unable to control their emotions. In addition to viewing dueling as "barbarous," Oregonians such as Delazon Smith voiced the general sentiment against dueling in society, noting "that nearly every southern state in the Union has a clause in their constitution against the practice of dueling. The moral and civilized world has set their face against dueling," and therefore Oregon should as well.[156] Not all states, southern or otherwise, restricted those convicted or accused of dueling from rights as citizens. Rather, many states recognized dueling as a crime worthy of a nonfelony conviction.[157] Oregon's constitutional provision, however, took the offense as cause for disenfranchisement. This position on dueling, therefore, further identified males eligible for suffrage as those who demonstrated appropriate manliness and civility.

During Oregon's Constitutional Conventions some Oregon delegates still defended the act of dueling. For example, Perry Maple explained to his colleagues that dueling only affected those immediately involved and argued that it was "an honorable and gentlemanly mode of settling difficulties," further noting that to "adopt this section was to protect the cowardly and low-minded."[158] Maple, along with a minority of delegates, saw dignity and manliness in dueling. This division of interpretations between Oregon legislators reflected the complex understanding of manhood and manliness during the mid-nineteenth century. The confused application of these gender roles within legislation was apparently evident to lawmakers such as Thomas Dryer, who spoke out against dueling but also argued that disenfranchisement seemed an extreme prosecutorial measure for dueling.[159] The delegates ultimately sided with the interpretation that dueling was not honorable or manly, and the dueling provision became the tenth section of the suffrage article.[160]

Although the section on dueling may seem removed from the inclusion of male language in Oregon's suffrage laws, the provision on dueling further gendered the right to vote. White males unable to embody the traits of the franchised (men), such as controlling one's emotions, were prohibited from rights connected to suffrage. The provision on dueling, therefore, also reinforced the gendered perceptions that females (with their femininity) were the opposite of the enfranchised group. Overall, Oregon's suffrage laws took two distinct steps to identify the acceptable gender of those who could vote, and this ultimately came down to males with the appropriate masculine traits.

The Legacy of Oregon Suffrage Laws

Celebrating the fortieth anniversary of Oregon's statehood, Judge L. B. Cox of Portland addressed the state legislature in 1899 with a speech on law and governance. "In every age of the world," Cox explained to the assembly, "its population has been divided into two classes—those who possessed power and those who demanded it. The latter class has never been numerous, and when contest have come, although often baffled and often defeated, it has pertinacious and defiantly kept up the struggle, and in the end it has ever proved victorious."[161] Although optimistic about the future of those without power, Cox did not address the fact that under current legislation (such as that governing the right to vote) political power in Oregon remained exclusive. In fact, whether through calculated decisions or conditioned forgetfulness, the state of Oregon did not ratify the fourteenth amendment until it celebrated its centennial anniversary as a state in 1959.[162] Overall, Oregon's past as a settler colony and then territory with exclusionary laws on suffrage held repercussions for Oregonians and the nation.

As part of Reconstruction, the Fifteenth Amendment in 1870 forced states to revise its suffrage laws to include Black men as a group entitled to vote. In Oregon, this meant removing the racial qualification in Section 1 and striking out the section that specifically excluded Black American men from the right of suffrage.[163] Oregon legislators, however, did not change other state laws with racial specifications that excluded Black Americans from certain rights.[164] One of the racialized laws that remained was the legislation prohibiting Black Americans from coming to or settling in Oregon. This constitutional provision stood in conflict with the Fourteenth Amendment but remained an Oregon law. Southern states creating new constitutions as part of their readmission to the Union and those that did not want Black Americans to receive full rights as citizens cited Oregon's constitution as justification for excluding Black Americans from political and natural rights.[165]

In 1891 Mississippi senator James George defended his state's choice to exclude Black Americans from suffrage and referenced Oregon's current constitution as an example for why Mississippi should have such an option. George further chastised northwestern and western representatives for objecting to such a racial exclusion, as their states had held or did hold similar policies. Responding to his Mississippi colleague, Senator Joseph Dolph of Oregon argued that "the Constitution in question had been framed when Oregon was hopelessly under the control of General Jo Lane" but that "the Constitution had not since been amended." George then replied, "I understand that those provisions were physically in the Constitution of Oregon. They may have fallen into innocuous desuetude and may not now be enforced, but they stand today as the expression of the judgment of the people of Oregon on this subject . . . and the people of Oregon have not seen proper to recall them in the same solemn formal manner."[166] Neither Senator Dolph nor other representatives wanting to prevent Mississippi from excluding Black American men from the right of suffrage could explain away Oregon's active law contradicting the federal constitution, but he argued that Mississippi's law stood in violation of the Fifteenth Amendment. Representative George maintained that an inconsistency of reasoning had taken place on the floors of Congress toward the rights of Black Americans, which did not prevent Mississippi from restricting a specific group from the right to vote. Oregon laws originally established under the settler colony government, therefore, continued to haunt the halls of Congress.

While Oregon's federal representatives argued that laws such as those proposed by Mississippi were illegal, Oregon's constitution continued to provide ammunition for states that wanted to deny Black Americans certain rights. Senator James Eustis of Louisiana, for example, referenced the Oregon constitution in a discussion about laborers on public work projects. Eustis argued that labor was more hospitable to Black Americans in the South than in Oregon, stating that "although black men are in various ways discriminated against in the South, yet they are allowed to work and toil in common with other men in every avenue of industry and labor." A California newspaper, commenting on the usage of Oregon's racially exclusive laws by southern politicians, informed readers, "The moral which it points out is worthy of the consideration of Northern Republicans. We know full well that while the Southern Democrat bulldozer has succeeded in nullifying, practically, the Negro vote, he has been almost entirely dependent on upon Negro labor, and although no Northern State has ever been represented in Congress by a Negro, or have had a Negro to govern them, many instances of the kind have been recorded in favor of the South."[167] The editor drew attention to the contradictory actions of the Republican Party, which had attempted to prevent the South from passing laws to disenfranchise Black American men but did not recognize its own prejudices toward Black Americans. Overall, southern representatives may have found that the federal government would not permit racial exclusions, but they also learned that states could add other specific qualifications to suffrage laws. Thus, southern states continued to use Oregon's constitution and its incorporation of racially exclusive provisions to support their own legal restrictions to the right of suffrage.[168]

As with other states, by 1870 Oregon had removed the racial qualifications in its suffrage law after the passage of the Fifteenth Amendment. At that time, Oregon also struck out many of the male-related terms within the article on suffrage. Oregon did not grant women the right to vote until 1912, but with the absence of a gender qualification, Oregon women made the argument that they were not legally excluded from the right to vote and, therefore, were eligible for suffrage. One such example of Oregon women attempting to exercise their right to vote captured national attention and solidified Oregon suffragists within the historical narrative of the women's rights movement.[169]

On January 11, 1872, a group of Oregon women—Abigail Scott Duniway, E. F. Hendee, M. A. Lambert, and Mary Beatty—entered the Morrison precinct polls in Portland to register their ballots. Upon being stopped by Judge Mayer from the Election Office, Duniway responded, "I am a peaceable law-abiding citizen of this Republic. I pay taxes, own lands, and possess other immunities and responsibilities of citizenship, and I am here to deposit my ballot as a duty I owe to the commonwealth." Replicating the reasons for why men were obligated to vote, which Oregon lawmakers had voiced since the 1850s, Duniway covered herself and her fellow would-be voters in language that embodied the rights and duties of a U.S. citizen. The second election officer then interjected, "I see no law requiring me to receive your vote, madam," to which Duniway replied, "There is no law prohibiting you from doing so. I have read the Constitution of the United States and of the State of Oregon and come here under those instruments to claim the equal protection of the laws."[170] As past Oregon suffrage laws had specifically listed groups restricted from the right of suffrage, Duniway suggested that no law specifically restricted women from voting. The law still included some male pronouns but did not explicitly list women as a group prohibited from voting. Legislators and election officers, however, did not interpret suffrage as a right accessible to both men and women, nor did they feel socially obligated to do so.

Insinuating that these Oregon women attempting to vote had misunderstood the situation for their right to vote in school elections instead, the election officer informed Duniway, "The statute says that women, if heads of families, may vote at school meetings." As mentioned earlier in this chapter, women had received the right to vote in school elections in the 1850s; Duniway was aware of such legislation and responded,

"This is not a school meeting, and if it were I shouldn't want to kill my husband to get a vote."[171] The women's knowledge of the suffrage laws and their persistence, however, did not get them access to the ballot box, and they left the precinct unable to register an official vote.[172] Nevertheless, arguments as to why women should be eligible for suffrage reached the public, and their actions reflected a change in how Oregon women approached the issue of voting and interpreted U.S. citizenship. In fact, Maria (Morfitt) Locey, addressed earlier, returned to her 1859 letter, which explained why women should not vote or get involved in politics; she wrote along the letter's margins, "This was written by an enthusiastic girl of eighteen. The same woman at the age of 32 adds 'Fiddle-sticks.'"[173] The unmarried Morfitt had recognized the social restrictions to women entering the public arena of suffrage, but as a wife and mother during a time when more women were speaking out for equal rights, Locey changed her opinion and joined the groups of women who sought the right to vote.

Moreover, public discussion about women's suffrage in Oregon had not really appeared until the 1870s, when women began using their association with morality and purity as reasons for why they should have the right to vote. Duniway became the most notable figure employing this tactic in Oregon, which combined arguments on middle-class gender roles focused on domesticity with the experience of living in a region that was sparsely populated, was slowly developing, and contained isolated farms. Through a series of newspaper editorials, Duniway addressed the need for direct moral guidance in Oregon and insisted that this could be obtained through women's participation in politics. She further argued that women's involvement and sacrifices in the settlement of the region granted them the right to political participation through suffrage. Western men had been using this argument for years, and Duniway extended the principal idea of settler colonialism to include the role of female Oregonians in settlement, therefore making them deserving of the right to vote.[174]

Another step in the evolution of Oregon's suffrage laws, however, was the fact that one of the women who had attempted to vote that day in 1872 was Mary Beatty, a Black American woman. Beatty was a member of the National Women's Suffrage Association, and in 1873 she both attended and was a speaker at the Oregon State Woman's Suffrage Association's first annual convention. Although she was not the only Black American female suffragist in the West, Beatty was one of few mentioned in reports and records as early as the 1870s.[175] Beatty represented two groups excluded from the right of suffrage when Oregon had become a state, and even though state laws still restricted her from several rights due to her race, she had become a part of the movement to promote female suffrage. Without the specific racial and gender exclusions from the right to vote, disenfranchised individuals such as Beatty took advantage of the revised laws and worked to establish a legal claim to suffrage. Many Black and white women throughout the United States had joined this effort by the end of the nineteenth century, but Oregon's laws provided opponents of women's and Black Americans' suffrage legal examples of how a state could exclude groups presumably protected by the U.S. Constitution.

Overall, Oregon's suffrage and naturalization laws demonstrated how politicians intentionally constructed legislation to exclude specific groups from the right to vote and revealed how a colony and then territory's laws could both reflect and impact national interpretations of citizenship. Moreover, Oregon's suffrage and naturalization laws provide earlier foundations to the national development of exclusionary policies based on race. Finally, Oregon's laws demonstrated how the use of racial specifications to restrict groups from rights within a state constitution, regardless of whether those laws were enforced, allowed other states to legally justify racially exclusive legislation.

Conclusion

Defiant Subjects and Their Legacies

> There is fire in the mountain. It is struggling to burst forth. You cannot smother it. It will come out. Lay the axe to the foot of the mountain. Let the fires come from the mountain. There is not need of fear.—As Jefferson said, let the truth and error grapple together. Who ever knew truth to be worsted in a struggle with error? No one need fear the result. Who fears the fire? Let it come! We are all Union loving men. The people of Oregon—young, vigorous Oregon—are patriotic, Union-loving people. They love their country. They love the name of Washington, and the republican institutions he labored to establish.
>
> —Delazon Smith, "House," *Oregon Statesman*, January 20, 1857

There once was a man named Louis. According to one source (who listed him as a friend), Louis was born somewhere near the Columbia River to a French father and a Klickitat mother. He was raised among the Nez Perce Indians, where he served as an interpreter for U.S. missionaries Henry and Eliza Spalding. Although living in the area when a group of American Indians attacked the Waiilatpu mission, Louis did not partake in the killings. In fact, Louis "gave Mr. Spalding timely warning of his danger," aiding in the Spaldings' ultimate safety.[1] He later served in the Umpqua Valley militia during the Rogue River War. Louis, the source continued, lived on his own farm and "considers himself an American citisen [*sic*]." Despite his past actions and markers of white manhood, however, Louis was arrested in 1855 along with a group of Indigenous people for "intended" violence to white settlers of Oregon.[2]

White U.S. settler Jesse Applegate was the source of this information, and he wrote to *Oregon Statesman* editor Asahel Bush seeking assistance in clearing Louis of these charges. Applegate believed that publishing "a true version of things" in the newspaper would lead Oregonians to see that Louis was not a threat to their settlement.[3] The *Oregon Statesman*, however, ran a story contrary to Applegate's account that depicted Louis as a "hostile" American Indian and "infamous wretch" likely to be hanged for his actions.[4] The series of events that befell Louis was not out of the ordinary for the mid-nineteenth-century American West. Nevertheless, Louis's story is reflective of Oregon's developing definitions of rights and citizenship on the eve of the Civil War.

Louis's experience also demonstrates how perceptions of race had changed over the years to accommodate the overall needs of Oregon settlers, dictating when a mixed-race individual was viewed as a contributing member of society (such as when one served in the militia) and when an individual was not. Moreover, it portrays how the diverse group of settlers and existing groups of fur traders and Indigenous communities continuously negotiated social and political authority in Oregon. The unfortunate circumstances of one individual can demonstrate a plethora of information when evaluated within the historical context of that individual's place of residence. For those persons who were not male, white, American or European born, or appropriately masculine, Oregon did not provide them with a socially or politically accepting environment. And even those who represented these modifiers were confined to the narrow legal definitions constructed to exclude others.

Oregon was not alone in the creation and enforcement of exclusionary legislation. Laws throughout the nation in the early to mid-nineteenth century made the lives of specific groups difficult or even unbearably cruel, as was the case where slavery existed. But Oregon's existence as a settler colony and the timing of its transition into a U.S. territory and then state provided the region a unique vantage point from which to evaluate both the construction of exclusionary laws and the impact of Oregon legislation on national discussions of race, gender, and citizenship.

Settler Colonialism

The romantic notions of western expansion that emerged prior to foreign settlement in Oregon, and that continues even today, interlocked with the national perspective of Manifest Destiny and overshadowed the narrative of colonization and dispossession. In arguing for the admittance of Oregon as a state in February 1859, Massachusetts congressman Eli Thayer recounted the visions of his youth and the "wonderment" of adventures to be found "upon the western shore of the American continent," as described by the likes of Lewis and Clark. Thayer referred to Oregon settlers as "pilgrims of the Pacific coast" and noted the towns, schools, and churches they had developed since the 1840s as proof of their groundbreaking industriousness. Thayer further asserted that Oregon settlers had "laid the foundations of a free State, and they come here, like the wise men of the East, not asking gifts, but bringing gifts . . . They bring all, all the products of their labor, and place them upon the altar of the Union, a pledge for the common welfare and the common defense."[5] For these reasons, he believed Congress should admit Oregon as a state and finalize this story of discovery and the "salvation" of western lands.

If the land that became Oregon was, in fact, vacant of any other group of people and not a disputed region between empires, then perhaps this portrayal of pioneers simply extending the United States to the Pacific would have some foundational truths. But this was not the case. The lands were forcibly taken from Indigenous communities whose connections to the region predated colonization by thousands of years. Oregon was a settlement at the edge of empires, and its population reflected diverse ancestries, nationalities, races, and citizenships. Oregon settlers acted on their own behalf, extending their own legislation throughout the region of settlement, and only eventually (well after settlement had begun to take place) did Oregon become a U.S. territory. The idea of natural expansion, therefore, provides an inaccurate portrayal of the event. To perpetuate the idea of organic expansion is also to ignore the role of Oregon settlers and the multileveled process of colonization that occurred. Settler colonialism shaped the overall construction of Oregon and fundamentally impacted the ways in which the United States received the region and its laws.

Land ownership and education laws demonstrated the Oregon settlers' ability to establish and continue permanent settlement within the region. Although laws pertaining to land and education varied from national practices—and the former shaped the first federal land act on territorial lands, U.S. representatives viewed them as necessary elements for a civilized and established society. The permanent presence of Oregon settlers was also essential for U.S. claims to the sparsely populated region. The desire and need for permanent settlement, therefore, assisted in the acceptance of Oregon's laws on education and property ownership, regardless of what restrictions or allowances the laws possessed.

Related to permanent settlement, the need to control the region was vital to the success of the settlement and U.S. claims to Oregon. The settler colony drafted its own policies on the seizure of American Indians' property and informed the direction and urgency of treaty making by U.S. officials. The dispossession of Indigenous communities had begun prior to U.S. treaties with American Indian groups, but the removal treaties supported actions taken by Oregon settlers and increased the settlers' control over the region. To protect this exclusive authority, Oregon's suffrage laws established definitions of citizenship by specifying who had access to political authority. Oregon's suffrage and naturalization laws both promoted the presence of settlers who possessed political authority and suppressed the involvement of those ineligible for the rights of suffrage. Although Oregon's liberal allowances for the naturalization of white foreigners stood in contrast to both national standards and the U.S. Constitution, legislation established by the settler colony and carried into governments under U.S. jurisdiction compelled national discussion on the rights of suffrage and naturalization, ultimately informing the definition of U.S. citizenship.

Oregon laws restricting the immigration and settlement of Black Americans demonstrated not only how exclusionary laws impacted national debates on controversial issues but also how those national tensions opened the door to such legislation. Oregon's immigration restrictions connected to issues of slavery and partisan representation within the federal government, but the settler colony also reflected both sides of the argument: nonslavery with a Democratic majority. As a result, settler laws, such as the immigration restriction, which stood in contrast to the U.S. Constitution and other states' laws, were transferred into the territorial government and finally into the Oregon state constitution.

The United States was dependent on these settlers. It was dependent on settlers' permanent settlement of the region and on settlers' enforcement of laws (even when the United States had no jurisdiction over the region). Overall, Oregon's position as a settler colony and the timing of its transition to a territory and then to statehood prevented the federal government from changing or denying Oregon's exclusionary laws. Oregon settlers and U.S. officials' effective erasure of American Indians from the narrative and dissociation of Indigenous peoples from regional lands was a critical part of settler colonialism in the Pacific Northwest. The ongoing legacy of this process is evidenced by a long history of violence against Indigenous women going overlooked and underreported.

In May 2019 a young woman from Muckleshoot Tribal School competed at the Washington State 1B Track Meet with a red handprint painted across her face and the letters "MMIW" on her leg. Like other competitors at the meet, Rosalie Fish wanted to win her events, but unlike the other high school students, she ran for thousands of missing and murdered Indigenous women. The issue of missing and murdered Indigenous women (MMIW) reached the national stage in October 2017 when Congress first considered the Savanna's Act (Stat. 227). The bill proposes "to review, revise, and develop law enforcement and justice protocols to address missing and murdered Indians" in memory of Savanna LaFontaine-Greywind, a twenty-two-year-old pregnant member of the Spirit Lake Nation who was murdered in 2017. As of spring 2020 the U.S. Senate has passed the Savanna's Act, and it is currently held at the desk in the House of Representatives.[6] The Pacific Northwest has some of the highest number of crimes against American Indian women in the country, though many go unreported, with the state of Washington holding the second highest number of crimes in 2016.[7] According to findings from S.227 sponsors, "on some reservations, Indian women are murdered at more than 10 times the national average," and 84.3 percent of American Indian and Alaska Native women have experienced violence.[8] Fish, a member of the Cowlitz Indian Tribe, faced questions from fellow student competitors about the red handprint, with some assuming it was related to "war paint." But despite feelings of vulnerability created by the visibility of the red handprint and peoples' misunderstandings, she medaled in multiple events and continues to exist for those women who have been denied that right.[9]

Race

In 1850 a trunk containing coins, silver, and gold dust was stolen from an Oregon City family while they attended church. The family lived in a neighborhood with adjacent homes. Upon discovery of the theft, "A colored family, residing opposite, [was] arrested on suspicion," resulting in an immediate trial before Justice S. W. Moss. The Oregon newspaper that reported this event did not cite any other theories for this crime, only that the court eventually released the Black American family due to insufficient evidence, and the money remained missing.[10] The Black American family did live across the street from the burglarized home, but what the newspaper article did not address was whether their neighbors had been supportive of them living there.

Over the next ten years, Oregonians continued to develop laws that illegalized Black Americans' presence, culminating in a constitutional provision to restrict Black Americans from coming to or residing in the future state of Oregon. One delegate, concerned about what such a law would mean for Black Americans already living in Oregon, asked his colleagues, "Is it a sin to be black?"[11] Although legislators did not state that being Black was a sin, being a Black American or otherwise nonwhite resident did mean that the person was prohibited from several political rights within Oregon. Legislators made numerous arguments to justify the exclusion of nonwhite groups. With each exclusion came further racialization of citizenship in Oregon.

Of course, the right to exist had to first be secured before groups in Oregon could fight for access to citizenship. Oregon newspapers as well as Oregon officials racialized warfare in the Pacific Northwest to justify violence against Indigenous communities and the removal of American Indians from the region. Consistent depictions in editorials of American Indians being the "hostile" aggressors stood in contrast to U.S. reports about atrocities committed by Oregon militias against Indigenous men, women, and children. Nevertheless, Oregon settlers' racial depiction of American Indians garnered them support from the U.S. military to both engage in warfare against Indigenous peoples and hasten the application of removal treaties. American Indians who survived the warfare then found themselves members of marginalized groups, if recognized at all, in a settlement that increasingly restricted the rights of nonwhite residents.

Laws pertaining to land ownership and slave labor in Oregon demonstrated the ability of legislators to justify the restricted presence and excluded political role of nonwhite settlers in Oregon. By associating Black American labor with slave labor and racializing the efficiency of labor, Oregonians used labor arguments to portray Black Americans as noncontributing members of society that threatened Oregon's development as a settlement. This association racialized the perception of civic contributions in Oregon. Legislators and community leaders gave similar justifications for the restriction of Black Americans and other nonwhite Oregonians (apart from "half breed" males with white fathers) from land ownership.

Laws that specifically prohibited Black Americans and those of Chinese descent from the right of suffrage and naturalization served as a reifying force for other exclusionary legislation throughout Oregon's transition from a settler colony to a territory and then a state. Those classified as having limited political participation rights (due to restrictions from specific rights or the ability to become naturalized citizens), legislators argued, did not help secure the land for Oregon settlers, because race prevented them from becoming citizens. The exclusionary suffrage and naturalization laws therefore solidified a racialized citizenship in Oregon.

In contrast to those of land, labor, or suffrage laws, the process by which Oregon legislators constructed education legislation reveals how race, as it pertains to the act of miscegenation, forced legislators to avoid racial specifications to protect white (American or European) men's rights in Oregon. These laws demonstrated how a lack of racial specification did not necessarily mean a piece of legislation did not contribute to racial definitions of citizenship. Protecting the rights of white men's children, regardless of the children's race, became a way to avoid challenging white men's rights. Thus, the lack of racial specification, in this instance, allowed Oregon legislators to maintain their overall racial specification of citizenship as something only accessible to white men.

Racial specifications in the Pacific Northwest stood in contrast to other state laws and the U.S. Constitution. These differences resulted in heated national debates over the issue of race and citizenship that ultimately influenced the interpretation of both at the national level. The more drastic exclusions, such as in the immigration restriction and naturalization laws, also impacted future legislation in relation to nonwhite groups and their access to U.S. citizenship. Moreover, the ongoing legacy of these racial restrictions is reflected in the demographics of the region.

Racially exclusionary legislation remained on the books and continued to be created in the Pacific Northwest throughout the nineteenth century. By the early twentieth century the Ku Klux Klan had held a significant presence in cities such as Tacoma, Washington, and Portland, Oregon.[12] Despite the mass population growth in the Pacific Northwest and the related diversification of the region's demographics during World War II, the city of Portland continues to be in the running for "whitest city in America" in the twenty-first century.[13] In May 2017 a white Oregon man shouted racist slurs, which included anti-Muslim remarks, at two Black teenage girls on a Portland MAX train. When fellow passengers Taliesin Myrddin Namkai-Meche, Micah Fletcher, and Rick Best intervened, they were stabbed by the shouting man. Namkai-Meche and Best died as a result of the attack.[14] A good deal of national attention on Portland followed the event, not only because it connected to the rise of anti-Muslim rhetoric and violence throughout the United States but also because Oregon and the city of Portland had taken on a more inclusive appearance in recent decades.[15] During the trial in February 2020, one of the young women who had been accosted on the train testified about her confusion and pain from the attacker's remarks, explaining to the courtroom, "I was born and raised in Portland, Oregon"; she continued, "I don't feel like I should go somewhere else, I don't feel like I have to go back to where I came from because I'm born here."[16] But as with other states in the United States, a reckoning with Oregon's racially restrictive legal foundations is required to move forward in a more effective and genuine manner.

Gender

In 1851 an Ohio newspaper article noted how the unmarried female teachers sent to Oregon by Governor William Slade of Vermont would likely find themselves married within a year of their arrival. The newspaper article continued that "as the land bill makes every lady worth 320 acres, if taken [married] before December next, you will be quite safe in believing that Oregon will soon be without teachers, unless another supply is dispatched immediately."[17] The need for teachers competed with the need for marriageable women in Oregon. Although such discussion about the need for women reduced them to desired property assets, it also reflected the important social and political roles of women in Oregon and the complicated nature of gendered exclusionary laws from 1841 to 1859.

As a group restricted from political participation because of their sex and gender, Oregon women were settlers not only influenced by the process of colonialism but who also reinforced it. Both the region's land and education laws demonstrate how women became key components of permanent settlement and necessary for the greatest accessibility to land claims as well as to education for settlers' children. Men could also serve as teachers, but the combination of marriage being necessary to claim the largest land donation possible for white men and the disproportionate ratio of settler men to settler women in the region made white female teachers more desirable settlers. The need for women as wives and mothers in connection to education and land ownership laws, however, reinforced gender roles that restricted women's social and political authority within Oregon. Although necessary for permanent settlement to take place, Oregon legislators continuously developed laws that prevented women from achieving complete control over themselves, their children, and their property.

Gendered exclusionary laws pertained to all groups within mid-nineteenth-century Oregon, as everyone possessed some sort of connection to gender roles and the restrictions of such roles were imposed on both men and women. By maintaining that femininity was the opposite of those characteristics that defined political participation and citizenship, Oregon legislators crafted laws pertaining to slavery and suffrage that eliminated women from specific rights and challenged the access certain male groups had to those rights. These same arguments about gender, however, were also used to draw distinctions between groups of women, namely between Indigenous and white women. In portraying Indigenous women as less feminine than their white counterparts or excluding them from narratives on warfare and treaty making entirely, Oregon newspapers and officials diminished the perception of Indigenous women's roles and authority in their communities. Oregon lawmakers then reinforced perceptions about gender in relation to social status and rights as a citizen.

Oregon's exclusionary laws also reveal how a region can construct legislation that is seemingly common or even progressive (as was the case for land and property ownership) but ultimately define rights as gender specific. In considering the process of settler colonialism, women's roles greatly broadened to include their participation in and their necessity to the permanent settlement of Oregon. Oregon legislation, however, perpetuated the perception of women and femininity as being contrary to political participation, which influenced the rights granted to women as well as the general understanding of women's roles in the West.

Although the Pacific Northwest would go on to join many of the western states by granting women the right to vote prior to the Nineteenth Amendment, this path was never an easy one. In Oregon, despite the presence of long-standing and influential leaders such as Abigail Scott Duniway, the state legislature voted women's suffrage down five times before its final passage in 1912.[18] Oregon was also home to one of the first female governors in the nation, with the interim appointment of Carrie Bertha Shelton for a little over two days in 1909. Shelton held the position between the departure of George Chamberlain and the arrival of F. W. Benson, securing these men's rights to hold a public office while Shelton herself was still denied the right to cast a ballot for the position of state governor.[19] Lawmakers in the region continued to restrict gains in women's individual rights and political participation, through both legislation and rhetoric.

Although Oregon's state government now includes a large number of female officeholders, including the governor, using gendered language to disparage male politicians remains an effective tactic in the United States.[20] A recent example, vaguely similar to rhetoric used by mid-nineteenth-century politicians, occurred in March 2014 when Republican news syndicates depicted the U.S. president and Democrat Barack Obama as wearing "mom jeans."[21] These reporters directly contrasted images of President Obama in high-waisted jeans with pictures of a shirtless Russian president Vladimir Putin, whom they described as displaying proper masculinity. These media outlets insinuated, without further explanation, that President Obama's choice in clothing reflected his timidity toward issues with Russia.[22] Criticism of dress and associations between displays of masculinity and leadership qualities persist in American politics.[23] As of summer 2020, while the nation celebrates the centennial of women's suffrage, the United States has yet to have a female president. Although Senator Kamala Harris is the third woman to be nominated by a major party as a vice-presidential candidate, objections to having women serve in the nation's top political leadership positions continue to find an audience. Sometimes the past provides us a map for the continuation of exclusionary practices, but in learning from those practices, we can also see how they work and how they can be undone.

Oregon's Legacy

The present is always a product of the past. Although Oregon legislators eventually changed or repealed mid-nineteenth-century exclusionary laws, the presence of these laws influenced perceptions of race, gender, and citizenship that continue in some form today. Some laws impacted the sectional tensions leading up to the Civil War, and some had clear effects on the Reconstruction era and late nineteenth-century state and federal policies. Gender and race-based ideas are powerful, and laws institutionalize those ideas. Oregon's development of exclusionary laws, such as those addressed here, reveals how a region can construct laws to legitimize certain definitions of rights specific to itself. The process of settler colonialism and the timing in which Oregon transitioned from a settler colony to a territory and then a state, however, ensured that these laws did not remain regional. Even a small population of people can affect the majority, for better or for worse, especially when that small group develops laws contrary to other states' laws and the U.S. Constitution.

I hope this book encourages more questions, because Oregon was not the only place settler colonialism had occurred during the nineteenth century. As with other western territories on the North American continent, such as the colony of British Colombia, Oregon experienced similar developments to regions across the globe.[24] During the same time that Great Britain held a joint occupation of Oregon with the United States, the British were in negotiations with the Dutch over regions in the Malay Peninsula.[25] While labor issues and laws pertaining to slavery, education, and immigration took place within the settler colony of Oregon, Hawaii experienced numerous challenges with labor laws and a growing foreign population—including missionaries and European merchants—which influenced its economies and education.[26] Toward the end of the nineteenth century, the colonies of New Zealand, Australia, and South Africa also revealed processes of settler colonialism, and these colonies could be evaluated in a similar fashion as this project has examined Oregon.[27]

The gendered and racial implications of Oregon laws in the late nineteenth century and the twentieth century can also be further examined.

Similarities between state constitutions in the West and those in the South during the mid-nineteenth century suggest that such connections continued. Jim Crow legislation did not emerge out of thin air. As Oregon developed unprecedented laws on immigration and naturalization, connections can also be found between the region and national laws pertaining to those issues throughout the twentieth century. Finally, U.S. citizenship is gendered as well as racialized. I hope that this project contributes to the continued need to illuminate this fact.

Notes

Preface

1. Jefferson-Brown, *Daffodil*, 26, 49, 171.

2. Jefferson-Brown, *Daffodil*, 26–27. For a discussion of foreign plants and their adoption by immigrants throughout North America, see DeJohn Anderson, *Creatures of Empire*; Prescott, *Gender and Generation*; Boag, *Environment and Experience*; Scharff, *Seeing Nature through Gender*.

3. Jefferson-Brown, *Daffodil*, 39.

Introduction

1. W. W. Bristow to Asahel Bush, April 11, 1859, MS 581, Asahel Bush Letters.

2. Bristow to Bush, April 11, 1859.

3. Bristow to Bush, April 11, 1859.

4. Bowen, *Willamette Valley*; Duncan, *Minority without a Champion*; Johansen, "Working Hypothesis"; this list included Mexican-American settlers and Mexican immigrant labor by 1855.

5. Much of this book derived from my dissertation, "The Power of Political Chatter: Settler Colonialism and the Construction of Race, Gender, and Citizenship in Oregon" (PhD diss., Washington State University, 2015).

6. For a more in-depth discussion of this process, see chapter 1. Whaley, *Oregon and the Collapse*; Johansen, *Empire of the Columbia*, 43–47; Cebula, *Plateau Indians*.

7. Cong. Globe, 17th Cong., 1st Sess., 2345–46 (1822).

8. Boag, *Environment and Experience*; Whaley, *Oregon and the Collapse*, 19–20; Johansen, *Empire of the Columbia*, 26–27.

9. Specific descriptions of Oregon as a place will be addressed in chapter 1.

10. Histories that address early to mid-nineteenth-century Oregon as well as, in some cases, immigration restriction and legal exclusion include Johansen, *Empire of the Columbia*; Dion Ashton, *Moulders of Public Opinion*; Berwagner, *Frontier against Slavery*; Bowen, *Willamette Valley*; Johannsen, *Frontier Politics and the Sectional*; Johnson, *Founding the Far West*; Mahoney, "Oregon Democracy," 202–27; Simms, "Controversy over the Admission," 355–74; Taylor, *In Search*.

11. See Richter, *Facing East*.

12. One example of this diverse historiography is Linda Gordon's work on orphan trains in Arizona and the influence of "internal colonialism" in the American Southwest; see *Great Arizona Orphan Abduction.*

13. Hietala, *Manifest Dream*, 271. For more recent support of Hietala's claims, see Aron, "Returning the West," 53–60. For a specific evaluation of Oregon and empire, see Whaley, *Oregon and the Collapse.*

14. Cebula, *Plateau Indians*; Whaley, *Oregon and the Collapse*; Ostler, *Plains Sioux.*

15. Schafer, "Notes on the Colonization," 379–90.

16. Veracini, "Introducing Settler Colonial Studies," 1–12.

17. Price, "Experiments in Colonization."

18. Wolfe, *Settler Colonialism and the Transformation.*

19. Wolfe, "Settler Colonialism and the Elimination," 393.

20. Jacobs, *White Mother.*

21. For examples of settler colonialism in nineteenth-century North America, see Jacobs, *White Mother*; Faragher, "Settler Colonial Studies," 181–91; Hoxie, "Retrieving the Red Continent," 1153–67; Russell, *Colonial Frontiers*; Rifkin, *Settler Common Sense*; Asaka, *Tropical Freedom*; Copland, *Burden of Empire*; Haycox, *Alaska*; Perry, *On the Edge*; Simpson, *Mohawk Interruptus*; Bruyneel, "Exiled, Executed, Exalted," 711–32; Edmonds, "Unpacking Settler Colonialism's Urban Strategies" 4–20; Goldstein and Lubin, "Settler Colonialism," 611–866; Kauanui, "Colonialism in Equality," 636–50; Blackhawk, *Violence over the Land.*

22. Sinha, "Gender and Nation," 229–74.

23. Morrison, *Slavery and the American West*; Potter, *Impending Crisis*, 51–225. For a discussion of Western influence during the mid-nineteenth century, see, among others, Forbes, *Missouri Compromise*; Smith, *Freedom's Frontier*; Berwagner, *Frontier against Slavery*; Johannsen, *Frontier Politics and the Sectional*; Johnson, *Founding the Far West*; Aarim-Heriot, *Chinese Immigrants, African Americans*; Foner, *Free Soil, Free Labor*; Freeman, *Field of Blood*; Holt, *Fate of Their Country.*

24. For examples of legal histories with a focus on the American West, see Farrington and Bakken, *Racial Encounters*, 200; Grossberg and Tomlins, *Cambridge History of Law*; Jacobs, *White Mother*; Kwong, *Forbidden Workers*; Pascoe, *What Comes Naturally*; Shah, *Stranger Intimacy*; Jagodinsky, *Legal Codes and Talking Trees*; Lew-Williams, *Chinese Must Go.*

25. Scott, *Gender and the Politics*, 178–98; Smith, *Women's History in Global Perspective*, 229–74.

26. For example, see Bederman, *Manliness & Civilization*; Block, *Rape and Sexual Power*; Brown, *Good Wives, Nasty Wenches*; Hoganson, *Fighting for American Manhood*; Gilmore, *Gender and Jim Crow*; Isenberg, *Sex and Citizenship*; Johnson, *Roaring Camp*; Lott, *Love and Theft*; Pascoe, *What Comes Naturally*; Stoler, *Carnal Knowledge and Imperial Power*; Hyde, *Empires, Nations, and Families.*

27. Kendi, *Stamped from the Beginning*; Dain, *Hideous Monster*; Horsman, *Race and Manifest Destiny*; Pierce, *Making the White Man's West*; Tomlins, *Freedom Bound.*

28. The dichotomy of white and Black was entrenched in American perceptions of race during the nineteenth century; therefore, this book uses these terms to represent white Americans (those of European ancestry and identified as white or Anglo) and Black Americans (those of African ancestry and identified as negro or mulatto). The capitalization of "Black" and not "white" in reference to these groups is in keeping with University of Nebraska Press policies. Immigrant groups are identified by their nations of origin rather than this racial classification attributed to white and Black Americans. Groups such as "half breed" individuals from white and American Indian parents are acknowledged either as being from this mixed ancestry or as nonwhite.

29. Wolfe, *Settler Colonialism and the Transformation*; Getz and Streets-Salter, *Modern Imperialism and Colonialism*, 11; Osterhammel, *Colonialism*, 20.

30. See chapter 1 for a discussion on both the development of a settler colony and usage of colonial language in Oregon.

31. Mahoney, "Oregon Democracy," 202–27.

32. Himes, "History of the Press," 327–70; Johansen, *Empire of Columbia*, 259–62; Johnson, *Founding the Far West*, 50–70.

33. For histories that have focused on how the nation impacted policies in the Pacific Northwest, see Woodward, *Rise and Early History*; Johannsen, *Frontier Politics and the Sectional*; Pomeroy, *Pacific Slope*; Johansen, *Empire of the Columbia*; Bowen, *Willamette Valley*; Lamar and Thompson, *Frontier in History*; Johnson, *Founding the Far West*; Whaley, *Oregon and the Collapse*; Etulain, *Lincoln and Oregon Country*.

1. Making of a Settler Colony

1. See "Journal of Mary Richardson Walker, March 5, 1838–October 1848," January 25, 1839, Elkanah and Mary Richardson Walker Papers, Cage 57, Manuscripts, Archives, and Special Collections, Washington State University Libraries, Pullman WA. Mary Walker recorded this diary entry while still en route to Tshimakain.

2. Speer, *Oldest and the Newest*; Cook, *Flood Tide of Empire*; Hyde, *Empires, Nations, and Families*, 91–95, 375.

3. For a discussion of how language such as "colony" was used to describe settlements in the Pacific Northwest, see Faragher, "Settler Colonial Studies," 181–91; Hyde, *Empires, Nations, and Families*; Johansen, *Empire of the Columbia*; Galbraith, *Hudson's Bay Company*; Perry, *On the Edge*; Beckham, *Requiem for a People*; Edmonds, "Unpacking Settler Colonialism's Urban Strategies," 4–20.

4. Grover, *Oregon Archives*, 8.

5. Grover, *Oregon Archives*, 8–13, 37–38, 56–59, 84.

6. Oregon Emigration Society, *Articles of Agreement*, 15.

7. "Journal of Mary Richardson Walker," April 23, 1838, and July 7, 1838.

8. West, *Last Indian War*, 29–34.

9. Gray, *History of Oregon*, 245, 219–327.

10. Drawn from definitions in Osterhammel, *Colonialism*; Getz and Streets-Salter, *Modern Imperialism and Colonialism*; see also Simpson, *Mohawk Interruptus*; Asaka, *Tropical*

Freedom; Blackhawk, *Violence over the Land*; Copland, *Burden of Empire*; Goldstein and Lubin, "Settler Colonialism," 611–866.

11. Cong. Globe, 56th Cong., 1st Sess., S. Doc. No. 194, 50–52 (1900); Pierce, *Making the White Man's West*, 130.

12. Boag, *Environment and Experience*, 41–42.

13. Augustus, *General View*, 96.

14. Cong. Globe, 31st Cong., 1st Sess., Senate 2 (1850); West, *Last Indian War*, 59–60; Cong. Globe, 56th Cong., 1st Sess., S. Doc. No. 194, 39–49 (1900).

15. Cong. Globe, 31st Cong., 1st Sess., Senate, 2 (1850); West, *Last Indian War*, 59–60.

16. For discussion of the colonization of Oregon by the United States, see Whaley, *Oregon and the Collapse*; Ostler, *Plains Sioux*; Hyde, *Empires, Nations, and Families*; Ronda, *Astoria and Empire*; Cebula, *Plateau Indians*; Addis, "Whitman Massacre," 221–58; Thrush, *Native Seattle*; Miller, *Native America*.

17. Boag, *Environment and Experience*, 40–43.

18. Cebula, *Plateau Indians*, 9; Hyde, *Empires, Nations, and Families*, 35. That said, accounts such as the following placed the entire population of Pacific Northwest American Indians in 1846 (half a century after contact) at fifty thousand individuals; Mitchell, *General View*, 16.

19. For lists of Indigenous nations and tribes in the Pacific Northwest, see Fixico, *Treaties with American Indians*; Boag, *Environment and Experience*; Hyde, *Empires, Nations, and Families*; Cebula, *Plateau Indians*; Whaley, *Oregon and the Collapse*; Miller, *Native America*; see also "Tribes Map," Washington Tribes (website), accessed July 2019, https://www.washingtontribes.org/; "Washington State Tribal Map," Washington State Department of Social and Health Services, accessed July 2019, https://www.dshs.wa.gov/office-of-the-secretary/washington-tribes; "Honor Native Land: A Guide and Call to Acknowledgement," U.S. Department of Arts and Culture (website), accessed July 2019, https://usdac.us/nativeland; "Native Land—Map," Native Land Digital (website), accessed July 2019, https://native-land.ca/; "The Peoples of Idaho: Native Settlers," Digital Atlas of Idaho (website), accessed July 2019, Idaho State University, https://digitalatlas.cose.isu.edu/geog/native/natvfr.htm; "Tribal Directory," (website), accessed July 2019, National Congress of American Indians, http://www.ncai.org/tribal-directory.

20. For discussion of the economic motivations for colonization, as well as trade connections between the Pacific Northwest furs and Chinese markets, see Hyde, *Empires, Nations, and Families*, 91–95, 375; Blackhawk, *Violence over the Land*, 151; Ronda, *Astoria and Empire*, 31, Whaley, *Oregon and the Collapse*, 20–31; Perry, *Colonial Relations*, 115; Tomlins, *Freedom Bound*, 21–66; Asaka, *Tropical Freedom*, 5–6; Speer, *Oldest and the Newest*; Cook, *Flood Tide of Empire*.

21. For discussion of U.S. concerns with its western borders during the beginning of the nineteenth century, see Bender, *Rethinking American History*; Bemis, *John Quincy Adams*; Muldoon, "Discovery, Grant, Charter," 25–46.

22. Black, *Fighting for America*; Hyde, *Empires, Nations, and Families*; Hafen, *Mountain Men*; Hayes and Morris, *Manifest Destiny and Empire*; Johansen, *Empire of the Columbia*, 34–62, 67–72.

23. Whaley, *Oregon and the Collapse*, 22–30; Blackhawk, *Violence over the Land*, 148; Johansen, *Empire of the Columbia*, 72–81; Tomlins, *Freedom Bound*, 89, 105; Miller, *Native America*, 100–107; Asaka, *Tropical Freedom*, 40–42; Ronda, *Astoria and Empire*, 31.

24. Although major overland emigration to Oregon did not begin until the 1840s, newspapers across the United States had posted articles about "occupying" and "colonizing" the region as early as 1824. See also Cong. Globe, 18th Cong. 1st Sess., Rep. 110, 2345–46 (1824).

25. Cong. Globe, 17th Cong., 1st Sess., 2345–46 (1822).

26. Cook, *Flood Tide of Empire*, 435–37.

27. Cong. Globe, 17th Cong., 1st Sess., 2345–46 (1822); see also Muldoon, "Discovery, Grant, Charter," 29, 30, 32, 41, 46.

28. Tomlin, *Freedom Bound*, 67, 142; Whaley, *Oregon and the Collapse*, 21–23; Cook, *Flood Tide of Empire*, 250–70; Miller, *Native America*, 48.

29. Cook, *Flood Tide of Empire*, 250–70.

30. Hyde, *Empires, Nations, and Families*, 14, 94; Perry, *On the Edge*, 111–16; Johansen, *Empire of the Columbia*, 39–43.

31. Tomlin, *Freedom Bound*, 105; Johansen, *Empire of the Columbia*, 42; Miller, *Native America*, 17–22, 48.

32. Tomlin, *Freedom Bound*, 160, 185; Muldoon, "Discovery, Grant, Charter," 30; Elliot, *Empires of the Atlantic*; see also Cong. Globe, 17th Cong., 1st Sess., 2345–46 (1822).

33. Among the many histories that address this treaty, see McDougall, *Tragedy of U.S.*; Nagel, *John Quincy Adams*; Fehrenbacher, *Slaveholding Republic*.

34. Cong. Globe, 17th Cong., 1st Sess., 2345–46 (1822). American maps that represent the land acquired from Spain in the Transcontinental Treaty do not include this northwest region, but the treaty technically granted the United States all of Spain's previous claims above the new boundary line. Of course, this transference of claims was not recognized by all parties involved, as Great Britain did not acknowledge Spain's claims to the region and, therefore, did not accept that the United States had gained that land in the treaty.

35. Cong. Globe, 17th Cong., 1st Sess., 2345–46 (1822).

36. Cong. Globe, 17th Cong., 1st Sess., 2345–46 (1822); Hyde, *Empires, Nations, and Families*, 92–97, 126; Johnson, *Roaring Camp*.

37. Cong. Globe, 17th Cong., 1st Sess., 2345–46 (1822); Cook, *Flood Tide of Empire*, 435–37.

38. Cong. Globe, 19th Cong., 1st Sess., 30–37 (1826); Miller, *Native America*, 4, 135, 136.

39 . Cong. Globe, 19th Cong., 1st Sess.,790–97 (1826); Cong. Globe, 19th Cong., 1st Sess., 30–37 (1826).

40. Cong. Globe, 19th Cong., 1st Sess., 8 (1826).

41. Cong. Globe, 19th Cong., 1st Sess., 8 (1826); McDougall, *Tragedy of U.S.*, 60–79; Johansen, *Empire of the Columbia*, 113–19. For further discussion of Russian settlements in the Northwest and claims to the Pacific coastline, see Haycox, *Alaska*.

42. Tomlin, *Freedom Bound*, 95–96; Cong. Globe, 19th Cong., 1st Sess., 790–97 (1826).

43. Cong. Globe, 19th Cong., 1st Sess., 790–97 (1826); Cong. Globe, 19th Cong., 1st Sess., 30–37 (1826).

44. Cong. Globe, 19th Cong., 1st Sess., 30–37 (1826).

45. Tomlin, *Freedom Bound*, 160–83; Cong. Globe, 19th Cong., 1st Sess., 30–37 (1826).

46. Whaley, *Oregon and the Collapse*, 23; Cong. Globe, 19th Cong., 1st Sess. (1826).

47. Cong. Globe, 19th Cong., 1st Sess., 30–37 (1826).

48. Ostler, *Plains Sioux*, 28–31; Nagel, *John Quincy Adams*, 241–60; Cong. Globe, 19th Cong., 1st Sess., 790–97 (1826); Hyde, *Empires, Nations, and Families*, 105.

49. Galbraith, *Hudson's Bay Company*, 178, 177–80.

50. Cong. Globe, 19th Cong., 1st Sess., 8 (1826). Americans later applied the interpretation of natural dominion to their construction of Manifest Destiny.

51. Isenberg and Burstein, *Problem of Democracy*, 285–320; Johansen, *Empire of the Columbia*, 110–11; Hyde, *Empires, Nations, and Families*, 95–105; Perry, *Colonial Relations*, 114–20.

52. Cong. Globe, 19th Cong., 1st Sess., 8 (1826).

53. Cong. Globe, 19th Cong., 1st Sess., 8 (1826); see also Bemis, *John Quincy Adams*.

54. For some examples of congressional and public discussion of the occupation of Oregon, see "Congressional," *Supporters and Scioto Gazette* (Chilicothe OH), March 17, 1825; "Proceedings of Congress," *Daily National Intelligencer* (Washington DC), March 25, 1825; "By Authority," *Providence Patriot and Columbian Phenix* (Providence RI), June 7, 1825; "Washington," *Daily National Journal* (Washington DC), December 30, 1828; "Settlement of West America," *Louisiana Advertiser* (New Orleans LA), February 22, 1828; "From the Nashville Republican," *New York Spectator* (New York NY), August 12, 1828; "A Subscriber," *Missouri Republican* (St. Louis MO), June 27, 1825; as well as more than twenty-five other newspaper articles in 1829 from across the United States.

55. Cong. Globe, 18th Cong., 1st Sess., 2345–46 (1824).

56. Cong. Globe, 18th Cong., 1st Sess. (1824).

57. Hyde, *Empires, Nations, and Families*, 91–99; Cong. Globe, 19th Cong., 1st Sess., 8 (1824).

58. Bemis, *John Quincy Adams*; Isenberg and Burstein, *Problem of Democracy*, 293–315; Cong. Globe, 19th Cong., 1st Sess., 8 (1824).

59. Cong. Globe, 19th Cong., 1st Sess., 8 (1824).

60. Howe, *What Hath God*.

61. Cong. Globe, 19th Cong., 1st Sess., 8 (1824). See also discussion of trade interests east of the Cascade Mountains in Cebula, *Plateau Indians*.

62. Johansen, *Empire of the Columbia*, 119–21; Isenberg and Burstein, *Problem of Democracy*, 293–315; Miller, *Native America*, 125–36; Whaley, *Oregon and the Collapse*, 71, 228. Maps of the Pacific Northwest prior to the Oregon Treaty were full of curiosities,

such as the Oregon map from 1843, which incorrectly identified the region as a territory of the United States, but also focused on Great Britain's presence and its claims to the Oregon. The inscription on the map states, "Exhibiting the various Trading Depots or Forts occupied by the British Hudson Bay Company, connected with the Western and northwest Fur Trade"; Map of Oregon Territory of the United States, 1843, G4240.1843.H87/MAP-086, Oregon Historical Society Research Library.

63. The presence of settlers from other European nations was likely, as Mary Richardson Walker reported seeing a "company of Portuguese across the river" in the spring of 1838; "Journal of Mary Richardson Walker," March 5, 1838–October 1848.

64. For an example of western settlement being an effective tool in acquiring the West, see Hayes and Morris, *Manifest Destiny and Empire.*

65. Mitchell, *General View*, 96; Cebula, *Plateau Indians*, 54; Hyde, *Empires, Nations, and Families*, 91–114.

66. Cebula, *Plateau Indians*, 57, map 2.

67. Blackhawk, *Violence over the Land*, 158–61.

68. For examples of scouting groups and military reports on Oregon during the joint-occupation tenure, see Cong. Globe, 18th Cong., 1st Sess., 2345–46 (1824); Cong. Globe, H.R. 19th Cong., 1st Sess., 213 (1826); Cong. Globe, 19th Cong., 1st Sess., H.R. 35, 156, (1826); both refer to reports of groups sent out earlier in the decade.

69. Cong. Globe, 20th Cong., 2nd Sess., H.R. Doc. No. 13, 126–29 (1829).

70. Cong. Globe, 20th Cong., 2nd Sess., H.R. Doc. No. 13 (1828).

71. Cong. Globe, 20th Cong., 2nd Sess., H.R. Doc. No. 13 (1828).

72. See Ostler, *Plains Sioux*; Blackhawk, *Violence over the Land*, 168; Cong. Globe, 20th Cong., 2nd Sess., H.R. Doc. No. 13, 126–92 (1829); Cong. Globe, 19th Cong., 1st Sess., H.R. Rep. 213, 566 (1826); Cong. Globe, 20th Cong., 1st Sess., 280 (1828).

73. Blackhawk, *Violence over the Land*, 160–66.

74. Hyde, *Empires, Nations, and Families*, 71.

75. Whaley, *Oregon and the Collapse*, 32, 68.

76. Hyde, *Empires, Nations, and Families*, 71, 114; Whaley, *Oregon and the Collapse*, 95.

77. Blackhawk, *Violence over the Land*, 168–69; Ronda, *Astoria and Empire*, 40, 314–15; see also Galbraith, *Hudson's Bay Company*.

78. Mudge, *Sketches of the Mission*; Lee and Frost, *Ten Years in Oregon*; see also Whaley, *Oregon and the Collapse*, 99–123; Cebula, *Plateau Indians*, 68–78.

79. Jessett, *Reports and Letters*, 22.

80. Jessett, *Reports and Letters*, 31.

81. Jessett, *Reports and Letters*, 79, 78–79.

82. Johansen, *Empire of the Columbia*, 178–82; Jessett, *Reports and Letters*, 22–23.

83. Cebula, *Plateau Indians*, 90–110; Jessett, *Reports and Letters*, 77–80.

84. Mudge, *Sketches of the Mission*, 15.

85. West, *Last Indian War*, 46.

86. Mudge, *Sketches of the Mission*, 38.

87. Whaley, *Oregon and the Collapse*, 133; Hyde, *Empires, Nations, and Families*, 141.

88. Cong. Globe, H.R., 20th Cong., 1st Sess., 280 (1828).

89 . Cong. Globe, H.R., 20th Cong., 1st Sess. (1828).

90. Mitchell, *General View*, 96.

91. See Whaley, *Oregon and the Collapse*; Hyde, *Empires, Nations, and Families*; Cebula, *Plateau Indians*; Johnson, *Founding the Far West.*

92. The provisional government of Oregon and its documents are recognized as beginning in 1843, although the earliest meeting minutes go back to 1841, as documented by the territorial government and its commissioner La Fayette Grover. See Grover, *Oregon Archives*. Henceforth, the laws established by emigration societies in Oregon will be considered as legislation during the provisional government period.

93. Tomlin, *Freedom Bound*, 67–92.

94. Oregon Emigration Society, *Articles of Agreement*, 4.

95. Tomlin, *Freedom Bound*, 180–85.

96. Johansen, *Empire of the Columbia*, 184–86; Whaley, *Oregon and the Collapse*, 110.

97. In a meeting referenced as "Of the Canadian Citizens of Oregon, to the meeting at Champoeg, March 4th, 1843," the writers asserted that they considered the land "free, at present, to all nations, till government shall have decided; open to every individual wishing to settle, without any districting of origin, and without asking him anything, either to become an English, Spanish, or American citizen. . . . So we, English subjects, proclaim to be free, as well as those who came from France, California, United States, or even native of this country." Grover, *Oregon Archives*, 12.

98. Senator Linn, as well as other Midwestern representatives, were very supportive of granting land to settlers in the Far West, as chapter 3 addresses; "Debate in the Senate," *Daily National Intelligencer* (Washington DC), September 19, 1850.

99. Grover, *Oregon Archives*, 8.

100. See Burnett, *Recollections and Opinions.*

101. See Grover, *Oregon Archive.*

102. Conlin, *Constitutional Origins*, 134–67; Freeman, *Field of Blood*; Johnson, *Founding the Far West*; Fehrenbacher, *Slaveholding Republic*; Etulain, *Lincoln and Oregon Country*, 15. For one example—though chapter 3 includes several—of the national discussion about the occupation of Oregon and whether it should be open to slavery, see "Oregon—Western Convention: Oregon, Address to the South," *The Globe* (Washington DC), June 20, 1843.

2. American Indians and the Right to Exist

1. Burnett, *Recollections and Opinions*, 219.

2. Burnett, *Recollections and Opinions*, 220.

3. Ned Blackhawk, *Violence over the Land*, 147; Cebula, *Plateau Indians*; Hyde, *Empires, Nations, and Families*, 94, 289; Spores, "Too Small a Place," 172.

4. Cebula, *Plateau Indians*, 27.

5. Boag, *Environment and Experience*, 10–11, 21; Cebula, *Plateau Indians*, 37, 73–74; Boyd, *Coming of the Spirit.*

6. Whaley, *Oregon and the Collapse*; see also West, *Last Indian War*; Ostler, *Plains Sioux*; Perry, *Colonial*; Prucha, *American Indian Treaties*; Simpson, *Mohawk Interruptus*; Hyde, *Empires, Nations, and Families*; Blackhawk, *Violence over the Land*; Cebula, *Plateau Indians*; Hoxie, *Final Promise.*

7. Unlike other chapters in this book that focus on laws connected to the region identified as Oregon (from Oregon Country to the State of Oregon), this chapter addresses treaties pertaining to lands in Oregon and what became the Washington Territory, because American Indians existed beyond these borders made by the United States. For example, joint treaties were negotiated by officials from the Oregon Territory and Washington Territory with Indigenous peoples in southwestern Washington, in the central region of the Columbia River basin, and in eastern Washington, as well as with groups with connections to the Snake River.

8. See chapter 1 for a more detailed discussion of these groups and the impact of their presence in the Pacific Northwest.

9. Among the many scholars who address the histories of the fur trade and missionaries in Oregon, see Blackhawk, *Violence over the Land*, 145–75; Cebula, *Plateau Indians*, 57–78; Hyde, *Empires, Nations, and Families*, 89–136; Whaley, *Oregon and the Collapse*, 71–160; West, *Last Indian War*, 35–51; Pierce, *Making the White Man's West.*

10. For examples of these sentiments, see "Journal of Mary Richardson Walker, March 5, 1838–October 1848"; Mudge, *Sketches of the Mission*; Elliot, *Coming of the White Women*; "Papers of Jason Lee."

11. Tomlins, *Freedom Bound*, 22, 67, 142, 155, 176.

12. Tomlins, *Freedom Bound*, 67–92, 144, 148, 155, 335–570; Muldoon, "Discovery, Grant, Charter," 25–46; Kauanui, "Colonialism in Equality," 636–50; Miller, *Native America.*

13. U.S. Const. art. I, § 8, cl. 2.

14. Fletcher v. Peck, 10 U.S. 6 Cranch 87 (1810); Worcester v. the State of Georgia, 31 U.S. 6 Pet. 515 (1832); Tomlins, *Freedom Bound*, 151–52, 163; Miller, *Native America*, 49–50.

15. Johnson v. McIntosh, 21 U.S. 8 Wheat. 543 (1823); Goldstein, "Where the Nation Takes Place," 833–62; Tomlins, *Freedom Bound*, 120–310; Miller, *Native America*, 53; West, *Last Indian War*, 60.

16. *Journal of Council of Oregon*, 28.

17. *Journal of Council of Oregon*, 32; repeated verbatim in Article 1, Section 3 of the Organic Laws in 1845; Semple, *Organic and Other General Laws*, 47.

18. Cong. Globe, 19th Cong. 1st Sess., H.R. Ex. Doc. No. 65, at 30–37 (1826); Fletcher v. Peck, 10 U.S. 6 Cranch 87 (1810); Worcester v. the State of Georgia, 31 U.S. 6 Pet. 515 (1832); Johnson v. McIntosh, 21 U.S. 8 Wheat. 543 (1823); "President Polk's Message," *Oregon Spectator* (Oregon City OT), June 11, 1846; Cong. Globe, 30th Cong., 1st Sess., Ex. Doc. No. 47, Senate, at 3–14 (1848).

19. White, *Concise View*, 3–4.

20. Tomlins, *Freedom Bound*, 144–48.

21. Boag, *Environment and Experience*; Cebula, *Plateau Indians*, 22; Kozloff, *Plants of Western Oregon.*

22. Swindler, *Sources and Documents*, 7:407.

23. United States v. Rogers, 45 U.S. 4 How. 567 (1846)

24. Semple, *Organic and Other General Laws*, 48. The *Oregon Spectator* (Oregon City OT) ran a copy of the Organic Laws in every publication of the newspaper between February 5, 1846, and July 8, 1846, as a public notice to Oregon settlers.

25. "President Polk's Message," *Oregon Spectator* (Oregon City OT), June 11, 1846.

26. McCarver, M. M., "For the Spectator," *Oregon Spectator* (Oregon City OT), August 6, 1846.

27. The first provisional government meetings to leave official records and recognize their settlements as part of a colony began in 1841.

28. For example, "Public Meeting," *Oregon Spectator* (Oregon City OT), October 1, 1846.

29. For discussion of the "Whitman Massacre" and the Cayuse War, see, among the many publications on this subject, Cebula, *Plateau Indians*, 124–26, 130; Hyde, *Empires, Nations, and Families*, 144; Blackhawk, *Violence over the Land*, 252; Whaley, *Oregon and the Collapse*, 94, 117–20, 178; West, *Last Indian War*, 49–58; Johnson, *Founding the Far West*; O'Donnell, *Arrow in the Earth*; Johansen, *Empire of the Columbia*; Addis, "Whitman Massacre," 221–58.

30. Cong. Globe, 30th Cong., 1st Sess., Ex. Doc. No. 47 (1848); Whaley, *Oregon and the Collapse*, 177; Hyde, *Empires, Nations, and Families*, 424.

31 . Grover, *Oregon Archives*, 207.

32. Grover, *Oregon Archives*, 210.

33. Grover, *Oregon Archives*, 322.

34. Grover, *Oregon Archives*, 323–24.

35. Cong. Globe, 30th Cong., 1st Sess., Ex. Doc. No. 47, at 7–8 (1848).

36 . Cong. Globe, 30th Cong., 1st Sess., Ex. Doc. No. 47, at 3 (1848).

37. Cong. Globe, 30th Cong., 1st Sess., Ex. Doc. No. 47 (1848).

38. Brown, *Brown's Political History of Oregon*, 333; Grover, *Oregon Archives*, 325.

39. *Oregon Archives*, 325–26; *Brown's Political History of Oregon*, 330–434; It should also be noted that Oregon's Organic Acts extended the power to "relate the intercourse of the people with the Indian tribes" to their House of Representatives; see Semple, *Organic and Other General Laws*, 48.

40. "Mr. Curry," *Oregon Free Press* (Oregon City OT), July 15, 1848.

41. Grover, *Oregon Archives*, 326–30.

42. Semple, *Organic and Other General Laws*, 52.

43. Semple, *Organic and Other General Laws*, 62.

44. Coan, "First Stage of the Federal," 49–51.

45. "Oregon," *Oregon Spectator* (Oregon City OT), August 22, 1850; Coan, "First Stage of the Federal," 49.

46. "An act providing for the extinguishment of the Indian title to the lands in the settled portion of the country in Oregon," December 20 and 21, 1849, *Oregon Provisional and Territorial Government Records*, index 3803.

47. Coan, "First Stage of the Federal," 51–52.

48. "Congressional," *Oregon Spectator* (Oregon City OT), July 1850.

49. Minto, *Statutes at Large*, chap. 16.

50. Semple, *Organic and Other General Laws*, 63–75. For a more in-depth and specific discussion of the Oregon Donation Act, see chapter 4.

51. Vine and De Mallie, *Documents of American Indians*, 205; Coan, "First Stage of the Federal," 54–55, 88.

52. "Indian Treaties," *Vermont Watchman and State Journal* (Montpelier VT), July 31, 1851.

53. Coan, "First Stage of the Federal," 66.

54. Vine, *Documents of American Indians*, 221–27.

55. Scholars argue that this inclusion of traditional lands was due in part to the successful negotiations made by the American Indians involved in the treaties. For additional discussion on the role of American Indians in the negotiations of these unratified treaties, see Vine, *Documents of American Indians*, 206; Whaley, *Oregon and the Collapse*, 185–86.

56. Washington Hall to Joseph Lane, September 1, 1851, MS 1146, Joseph Lane Papers, Oregon Historical Society Research Library, Portland OR.

57. Prucha, *American Indian Treaties*, 246–50; Coan, "First Stage of the Federal," 55, 62, 76, 88.

58. Coan, "First Stage of the Federal," 1; Whaley, *Oregon and the Collapse*, 196–200; West, *Last Indian War*, 60–71; Cebula, *Plateau Indians*, 158.

59. Whaley, *Oregon and the Collapse*, 201.

60. Kappler, *Indian Affairs*, 1049.

61. Fixico, *Treaties with American Indians*, 229.

62. Kappler, *Indian Affairs*, 603–5.

63. Kappler, *Indian Affairs*, 606–7.

64. Kappler, *Indian Affairs*, 603–7, 1049; Coan, "Adoption of the Reservation," 8; Whaley, *Oregon and the Collapse*, 196.

65. "Annual Report of Joel Palmer."

66. Prucha, *American Indian Treaties*, 248.

67. For a discussion of these early temporary reservations and forts, see Beckham, *Requiem for a People*; Whaley, *Oregon and the Collapse*, 196–98, 214–16; Fixico, *Treaties with American Indians*, 226.

68. Beckham, *Oregon Indians*, 220–21; Cow Creek Band of Umpqua Tribe of Indians, "Tribal Story," Cow Creek Band of Umpqua Tribe of Indians (website), accessed July 2019, https://www.cowcreek.com/tribal-story/. According to the Oregon Secretary of State website, the Cow Creek Band of Umpqua's treaty remained unfulfilled until 1982; https://sos.oregon.gov/blue-book/Pages/national-tribes-cow-creek.aspx.

69. Kappler, *Indian Affairs*, 654–64.

70. Fixico, *Treaties with American Indians*, 229.

71. Kappler, *Indian Affairs*, 657–60; Beckham, *Oregon Indians*, 220–21.

72. Kappler, *Indian Affairs*, 665–68, 669–84, 694–725, 740–41; Beck, "'Standing Out Here,'" 6–37.

73. Cong. Globe, 34th Cong. 1st Sess., Ex. Doc. No. 93, at 1–144 (1856); source referenced hereafter as "Indian Hostilities in the Territories," with specific letters when relevant.

74. Beckham, *Oregon Indians*, 144.

75. For discussion of positions American Indians faced when negotiating treaties with the U.S. government, see Blackhawk, *Violence over the Land*; Fixico, *Treaties with American Indians*; Beckham, *Oregon Indians*.

76. For example, "Notice," *Oregon Argus* (Oregon City OT), July 7, 1855; "Notice," *Oregon Argus* (Oregon City OT), July 14, 1855; "Notices," *Oregon Argus* (Oregon City OT), January 19, 1856.

77. "Notice," *Oregon Argus* (Oregon City OT), July 7, 1855; "Notice," *Oregon Argus* (Oregon City OT), July 14, 1855; "Notices," *Oregon Argus* (Oregon City OT), January 19, 1856; West, *Last Indian War*, 70.

78. The reservations created in 1855: Umatilla Reservation, Warm Springs Reservation, Nez Perce Reservation, Coast Reservation; Beckham, *Oregon Indians*, 219–22.

79. Blackhawk, *Violence over the Land*, 10.

80. Kappler, *Indian Affairs*, 665–68, 669–84, 694–725, 740–41.

81. Beckham, *Oregon Indians*, 119–22, 156–71; Beck, "'Standing Out Here'"; Whaley, *Oregon and the Collapse*, 191–226.

82. Beckham, *Oregon Indians*, 154.

83. For example, in reference to the Umpqua Reservation, an Indian Agent wrote, "The ration of decrease vastly exceeds that of the increase"; G. H. Ambrose, Indian Agent to General Palmer, superintendent of Indian Affairs, November 30, 1855, from "Indian Hostilities in the Territories."

84. Whaley, *Oregon and the Collapse*, 233.

85. Numerous reports by Oregon Indian Agents noted the desperate conditions of Indigenous peoples at the Oregon reservations; see "Indian Hostilities in the Territories."

86. Whaley, *Oregon and the Collapse*, 196.

87. For a few examples of the racialization of American Indians by European nations and the United States, see Lepore, *Name of War*; Elliot, *Empires of the Atlantic*; Brown, *Good Wives, Nasty Wenches*; Morgan, *American Slavery, American Freedom*; Taylor, *American Colonies*; Ballantyne and Burton, *Bodies in Contact*; Plane, *Colonial Intimacies*.

88. For example, see Kendi, *Stamped from the Beginning*; Pierce, *Making the White Man's West*; Dain, *Hideous Monster*; Buss, *Winning the West*; Asaka, *Tropical Freedom*; Benton, *Law and Colonial Cultures*; Black, *Fighting for America*; Horsman, *Race and Manifest Destiny*; Painter, *History of White People*.

89. "For the Spectator," *Oregon Spectator* (Oregon City OT), August 6, 1846.

90. "Indian Treaties in Oregon," *Vermont Watchman and State Journal* (Montpelier VT), July 31, 1851.

91. For some examples on the political discussion of racialized ideas of civility, see Russell, *Colonial Frontiers*; Kendi, *Stamped from the Beginning*; Pierce, *Making the White Man's West*; Dain, *Hideous Monster*; Whaley, *Oregon and the Collapse*; Ostler, *Plains Sioux*; Tomlins, *Freedom Bound*; Shah, *Stranger Intimacy*.

92. West, *Last Indian War*, 3–120; Hyde, *Empires, Nations, and Families*, 122; presumed at least in comparison to American Indian groups with lands on the Waiilatpu and Whitman missions. Cebula, *Plateau Indians*, 101–7, 151; "Oregon Indians," *Ohio Observer*

(Hudson OH), November 19, 1840; "The Oregon Territory," *Daily National Intelligencer* (Washington DC), February 15, 1844.

93. "Oregon Indians," *Daily Atlas* (Boston MA), August 7, 1846.

94. "Indian Hostilities in the Territories"; for an example of this sentiment, see "Latest from the Army," *Oregon Free Press* (Oregon City OT), June 10, 1848.

95. West, *Last Indian War*, 123–243; Cebula, *Plateau Indians*, 163–72; Kappler, *Indian Affairs*, 702–5, 843–47, 1024–25; Ostler, *Plains Sioux*, 298.

96. Whaley, *Oregon and the Collapse*, 56–59, 80. Several examples of Oregonians using these terms appear in the discussion of war reports, but for a later reference of these terms in even a casual discussion, see "Asahel Bush Letters," October 30, 1855, MS 581, Oregon Historical Society, Portland OR.

97. Blackhawk, *Violence over the Land*, 172–75; Perry, *Colonial Relations*, 118–19.

98. Cong. Globe, 25th Cong. 2nd Sess., Senate, 445 (1838); see also Cong. Globe, 18th Cong., 1st Sess., Rep. 110 (1824).

99. See further discussion of this perspective of American Indians asking for and taking compensation for their lands from settlers in the following: Whaley, *Oregon and the Collapse*; Cebula, *Plateau Indians*; Blackhawk, *Violence over the Land*; Hyde, *Empires, Nations, and Families*.

100. Grover, *Oregon Archives*, 9–11.

101. Grover, *Oregon Archives*, 11.

102. Grover, *Oregon Archives*, 33–34.

103. Jesse Applegate to Asahel Bush, November 18, 1855, MS 581, Asahel Bush Letters, Oregon Historical Society, Portland OR. See also chapters 4 and 6 of this volume for a discussion of rights held by men with white fathers and Indigenous mothers.

104. Swindler, *Sources and Documents*, 7:241, 372. Indiana removed this exclusion in its 1851 revision (7:390), but Kentucky added the exclusion of American Indians from the militia in its 1850 revision (4:177).

105. Grover, *Oregon Archives*, 33–34.

106. Grover, *Oregon Archives*, 34.

107. Grover, *Oregon Archives*, 36–37. For additional discussion of how violence skewed the specific histories of American Indian groups, which in cases such as the Pacific Northwest made precise names difficult to record, see Blackhawk, *Violence over the Land*, 8–10.

108. Boag, *Environment and Experience*, 64, 82.

109. For example: "Indian Difficulty," *Oregon Spectator* (Oregon City OT), July 9, 1846; "More Indian Difficulties," *Oregon Spectator* (Oregon City OT), August 6, 1846; "For the Spectator," *Oregon Spectator* (Oregon City OT), October 14, 1847; "Indian Depredations, Etc.," *Oregon Free Press* (Oregon City OT), June 24, 1848. The research focus in the selection of newspapers was placed on Oregon City newspapers for the first half of this section, because the Willamette Valley was the most populous settlement at this time; in addition, many of the events involving the Cayuse War, including the final execution of "murderers," took place in or near Oregon City.

110. "For the Spectator," *Oregon Spectator* (Oregon City OT), September 3, 1846.

111. Grover, *Oregon Archives*, 84.

112. "Mr. Editor," *Oregon Spectator* (Oregon City OT), June 11, 1846.

113. For discussions of Oregon immigration and conflicts in the 1840s, see Hyde, *Empires, Nations, and Families*, 400–407, 421–34; Cebula, *Plateau Indians*, 125–26; Coan, "Adoption of Reservation," 23, 29, 37.

114. Grover, *Oregon Archives*, 163.

115. Grover, *Oregon Archives*, 208–9.

116. Grover, *Oregon Archives*, 209.

117. Grover, *Oregon Archives*, 210.

118. "Indian Difficulty," *Oregon Spectator* (Oregon City OT), July 9, 1846.

119. Douglas, "Letter to George Abernethy, December 7, 1847," *Oregon Spectator* (Oregon City OT), December 19, 1847.

120. McBean, "Letter to Board of Management, Nov. 30, 1847," *Oregon Spectator* (Oregon City OT), December 19, 1847.

121. McBean, "Letter to Board of Management, Nov. 30, 1847," *Oregon Spectator* (Oregon City OT), December 19, 1847.

122. "Oregon City, Dec. 8, 1847," *Oregon Spectator* (Oregon City OT), December 9, 1847.

123. Cong. Globe, 30th Cong., 1st Sess., Ex. Doc. No. 47, at 4 (1848).

124. Grover, *Oregon Archives*, 225.

125. For a military history of the Cayuse War, see Victor, *Early Indian Wars of Oregon*.

126. "No Title," *Oregon Spectator* (Oregon City OT), December 23, 1847.

127. *Oregon Archives*, 324.

128. *Oregon Archives*, 322.

129. For further discussion of the HBC during the Cayuse War, see Hyde, *Empires, Nations, and Families*, Perry, *Colonial Relations*, Beckham, *Oregon Indians*.

130. Several articles on the second page of the *Oregon Spectator* between December 19 and 23 carried reprints of letters from Oregon lawmakers to fort officials as well as speculation on how the conflict would progress; for an example, see "No Title," *Oregon Spectator* (Oregon City OT), December 23, 1847.

131. Cong. Globe, 30th Cong., 1st Sess., Ex. Doc. No. 47, at 7 (1848).

132. "Incidents of the War," *Oregon Free Press* (Oregon City OT), April 29, 1848.

133. "Alarm!," *Oregon Spectator* (Oregon City OT), April 30, 1848.

134. "Indian Depredations, Etc.," *Oregon Free Press* (Oregon City OT), June 24, 1848; for other examples of this type of report, see "Intelligence from the Interior," *Oregon Spectator* (Oregon City OT), July 27, 1848; "Volunteers," *Oregon Free Press* (Oregon City OT), July 7, 1848.

135. "Army Matters," *Oregon Free Press* (Oregon City OT), June 17, 1848.

136. "Free Press Correspondence," *Oregon Free Press* (Oregon City OT), May 13, 1848.

137. Cong. Globe, 30th Cong., 1st Sess., Ex. Doc. No. 47, at 1 (1848).

138. Cong. Globe, 30th Cong., 1st Sess., Ex. Doc. No. 47, at 1–2 (1848).

139. Cong. Globe, 30th Cong., 1st Sess., Ex. Doc. No. 47, at 2 (1848).

140. Cong. Globe, 30th Cong., 1st Sess., Senate, 1147 (1848).

141. Marschner, *Oregon 1859*, 70.

142. Cong. Globe, 31st Congress, 1st Sess., Senate, 2–3 (1850).

143. Cong. Globe, 31st Congress, 1st Sess., Senate, 2 (1850).

144. Beckham, *Oregon Indians*, 110–15; Cebula, *Plateau Indians*, 1–2.

145. See previous section on the acquisition of lands from the Cayuse War, as well as government documents on the Oregon Donation Act that include claims from Cayuse lands prior to a treaty with the Cayuse Indians.

146. For examples of these actions during the Cayuse War, see "Intelligence from the Interior," *Oregon Spectator* (Oregon City OT), July 27, 1848; "Volunteers," *Oregon Free Press* (Oregon City OT), July 7, 1848; "Indian Depredations, Etc.," *Oregon Free Press* (Oregon City OT), June 24, 1848.

147. Jesse Applegate to Joseph Lane, October 5, 1851, MS 1146, Joseph Lane Papers.

148. *Oregon Archives*, 248,

149. Cong. Globe, 31st Cong., 1st Sess., Senate, 11–12 (1850); *Oregon Archives*, 248, 320.

150. This is addressed in greater detail in chapter 3. For an example, see *Oregon Provisional and Territorial Government Records*, HB 37, index 3515.

151. Cpt. J. W. T. Gardiner of the First Dragoons to Maj. E. D. Townsend, assistant adjutant general, Fort Tejon CA, July 28, 1855, from "Indian Hostilities in the Territories."

152. For histories on these specific wars, see Schwartz, *Rogue River Indian War*; Whaley, *Oregon and the Collapse*; Blackhawk, *Violence over the Land*; Holbrook and Nikol, "Navy in the Puget Sound," 10–20; Burns, "Bancroft Library Manuscript," 54–57; Glassley, *Pacific Northwest Indian Wars*; Beckham, *Oregon Indians*, 131–224; Jacob, *Yakama Rising*.

153. "Another Indian Outbreak," *Oregon Argus* (Oregon City OT), August 18, 1855.

154. "Indian Outbreak on Rogue River," *Oregon Argus* (Oregon City OT), June 15, 1855.

155. "Indian Difficulties in the South," *Oregon Argus* (Oregon City OT), August 25, 1855; "Signs of the End," *Oregon Argus* (Oregon City OT), October 6, 1855; "Startling News!," *Oregon Argus* (Oregon City OT), October 13, 1855; "More Indian Murderers!," *Oregon Argus* (Oregon City OT), October 20, 1855; "Our Confederated Indian War," *Oregon Argus* (Oregon City OT), October 27, 1855; "Further Massacres!," *Oregon Argus* (Oregon City OT), November 3, 1855; "Stirring News from Puget Sound," *Oregon Argus* (Oregon City OT), November 19, 1855.

156. G. H. Ambrose, Indian Agent, to General Palmer, sup. of Indian Affairs, September 30, 1855, from "Indian Hostilities in the Territories."

157. A. Miner to Editor, October 11, 1855, MS 581, Asahel Bush Letters.

158. Cebula, *Plateau Indians*; Whaley, *Oregon and the Collapse*.

159. B. F. Harding, "By the Governor of the Territory of Oregon," *Oregon Argus* (Oregon City OT), October 13, 1855; B. F. Harding, "By the Governor of the Territory of Oregon," *Oregon Argus* (Oregon City OT), October 20, 1855.

160. B. F. Harding, "By the Governor of the Territory of Oregon," *Oregon Argus* (Oregon City OT), October 13, 1855.

161. "General Order," E. M. Barnum, adjutant general of Oregon, October 16, 1855, from "Indian Hostilities in the Territories."

162. John Withers, 1st Lt., Fourth Infantry, to Col. S. Cooper, adjutant general U.S., November 12, 1855, from "Indian Hostilities in the Territories."

163. John E. Wool, Maj. Gen., to Lt. Col. L. Thomas, assistant adjutant general, December 13, 1855, from "Indian Hostilities in the Territories."

164. "General Order," E. M. Barnum, adjutant general of Oregon, October 20, 1855, from "Indian Hostilities in the Territories."

165. "General Order," E. M. Barnum, adjutant general of Oregon, October 16, 1855, from "Indian Hostilities in the Territories."

166. "General Order," E. M. Barnum, adjutant general of Oregon, October 17, 1855, from "Indian Hostilities in the Territories."

167. Isaac Stevens, governor and sup. of Indian Affairs (WA), to Hon. Gen. George W. Manypenny, commissioner of Indian Affairs, Washington DC, January 29, 1856, from "Indian Hostilities in the Territories."

168. For examples of numbers reported from both the volunteer side and from U.S. officials, see "Stirring News from Puget Sound!," *Oregon Argus* (Oregon City OT), November 19, 1855; Beeson, *Plea for the Indians*; Edward R. Geary, agent, to General Palmer, sup. of Indian Affairs, October 21, 1855; E. M. Barnum, adjutant general of Oregon, to Col. S. Cooper, adjutant general U.S., October 24, 1855, from "Indian Hostilities in the Territories"; "Maj. Haller Driven In to The Dalles," *Oregon Argus* (Oregon City OT), October 20, 1855; John Withers, 1st Lt., Fourth Infantry, to Col. S. Cooper, adjutant general U.S., November 12, 1855, from "Indian Hostilities in the Territories"; G. H. Ambrose, Indian Agent, to General Palmer, sup. of Indian Affairs, November 30, 1855, from "Indian Hostilities in the Territories."

169. G. H. Ambrose, Indian Agent, to General Palmer, sup. of Indian Affairs, October 28, 1855, from "Indian Hostilities in the Territories."

170. R. R. Thompson, Indian Agent, to Gen. Joel Palmer, sup. Indian Affairs, November 19, 1855, from "Indian Hostilities in the Territories."

171. Nathan Olney, "From the Seat of War," *Oregon Argus* (Oregon City OT), October 27, 1855.

172. Nathan Olney, Indian Agent, to Gen. Joel Palmer, sup. Indian Affairs, December 5, 1855, from "Indian Hostilities in the Territories."

173. Nathan Olney, Indian Agent, to Gen. Joel Palmer, sup. Indian Affairs, December 5, 1855, from "Indian Hostilities in the Territories"; Nathan Olney, "From the Seat of War," *Oregon Argus* (Oregon City OT), October 27, 1855.

174. John E. Wool, Maj. Gen., to Lt. Col. L. Thomas, assistant adjutant general, January 19, 1856, from "Indian Hostilities in the Territories"; John E. Wool, Maj. Gen., to Isaac I. Stevens, governor of Washington Territory, February 12, 1856, from "Indian Hostilities in the Territories."

175. Joel Palmer, superintendent of Indian Affairs OT, to Office of Superintendent of Indian Affairs, November 21, 1855, from "Indian Hostilities in the Territories"; John E. Wool, Maj. Gen., to Lt. Col. L. Thomas, assistant adjutant general, January 19, 1856, from "Indian Hostilities in the Territories"; Joel Palmer, superintendent of Indian Affairs OT, to Maj. Gen. John E. Wool, commanding Pacific Division, U.S. Army, December 1, 1855, from "Indian Hostilities in the Territories."

176. John E. Wool, Maj. Gen., to Lt. Col. L. Thomas, assistant adjutant general, January 19, 1856, from "Indian Hostilities in the Territories."

177. For example, "The Volunteers were generally in good health and spirits; they stood in need of clothing and flour; they had plenty of beef, straight. Dr. Shaw brought down, as a trophy, old Pu-pu-max's [*sic*] ear, and Mr. Story brought down a portion of his scalp to Thomas Stevens which was sent him by his son John, who cut it off." "From the War," *Weekly Times* (Portland OT), January 1856.

178. Edward R. Geary, agent, to General Palmer, sup. Indian Affairs, October 21, 1855, from "Indian Hostilities in the Territories"; see also Joel Palmer, superintendent of Indian Affairs, to Hon. G. W. Manypenny, October 16, 1855, from "Indian Hostilities in the Territories."

179. "To his Excellency Franklin Pierce, President of the United States," January 8, 1856, from "Indian Hostilities in the Territories."

180. John E. Wool, Maj. Gen., to J. N. Johnson, governor of California, January 21, 1856, from "Indian Hostilities in the Territories."

181. Joel Palmer, sup. of Indian Affairs, to Hon. G. W. Manypenny, November 12, 1855, from "Indian Hostilities in the Territories."

182. Franklin Pierce, U.S. president, to Senate and House of Representatives of the U.S., March 5, 1856, from "Indian Hostilities in the Territories."

183. For an example of national discussion on the cost of the Oregon wars, see "Indian War in Oregon," *Nebraskian* (Omaha NT), November 12, 1856; "The Oregon War," *North American and United States Gazette* (Philadelphia PA), May 20, 1856; "The Indian War," *Fayetteville Observer* (Fayetteville NC), September 20, 1858; "Indian War in Oregon," *Daily National Intelligencer* (Washington DC), October 18, 1858.

184. For examples see G. H. Ambrose, Indian Agent, to General Palmer, sup. of Indian Affairs, November 30, 1855, from "Indian Hostilities in the Territories"; Joel Palmer, sup. of Indian Affairs, to Hon. G. W. Manypenny, January 9, 1856, "Indian Hostilities in the Territories"; Joel Palmer, sup. of Indian Affairs, to Maj. Gen. John E. Wool, commanding Pacific Division, December 1, 1855, from "Indian Hostilities in the Territories."

185. John E. Wool, Maj. Gen., to Isaac Stevens, governor of Washington Territory, February 12, 1856, from "Indian Hostilities in the Territories."

186. Joel Palmer, sup. of Indian Affairs, to Maj. Gen. John E. Wool, commanding Pacific Division, December 1, 1855, from "Indian Hostilities in the Territories."

187. Joel Palmer, sup. of Indian Affairs, to Maj. Gen. John E. Wool, commanding Pacific Division, U.S. Army, November 1, 1855, from "Indian Hostilities in the Territories"; Joel Palmer, superintendent of Indian Affairs OT, to Maj. Gen. John E. Wool, commanding Pacific Division, U.S. Army, November 1, 1855, from "Indian Hostilities in the Territories"; Geo. (Gen.) W. Manypenny, commissioner, to Joel Palmer, superintendent of Indian Affairs OT, December 4, 1855, from "Indian Hostilities in the Territories"; Manypenny, commissioner, to Joel Palmer, superintendent of Indian Affairs OT, November 1, 1855, from "Indian Hostilities in the Territories."

188. See chapters 4 and 5 for a more detailed account of unions between American Indians and white men, land laws, and other specific rights available to men with American Indian mothers. Other examples include newspaper articles, such as the following, that depicted Oregon thus: "There are about seventy-five to eighty French-Canadians settled in this country, principally discharged from the service of the Hudson's Bay Company; there are also about fifty Americans settled in and about this country, making, perhaps, one hundred and twenty-five to one hundred and thirty male inhabitants, who are married to Indian women." "From Oregon: Extract of a Letter Dated Willamette, February 19, 1842," *New York Tribune* (New York NY), January 18, 1843; Beckham, *Oregon Indians*, 87; see also Jagodinsky, *Legal Codes and Talking Trees*, 60–70.

189. In addressing the impact of gender on arguments for the dispossession of American Indians, I was informed by many works on gender history but especially influenced by Audra Simpson, who demonstrates in *Mohawk Interruptus* that American Indian women's "bodies have historically been rendered less valuable because of what they are taken to represent: land, reproduction, Indigenous kinship and governance"; Simpson, *Mohawk Interruptus*, 156. See also Jagodinsky, *Legal Codes and Talking Trees*, 80–81.

190. For discussion on perceived gender roles for women and ideas of womanhood in the Antebellum era, see, among many others, Prescott, *Gender and Generation*; Kerber, *No Constitutional Right*; Isenberg, *Sex and Citizenship*; Stansell, *City of Women*; Norton, *Liberty's Daughters*; Clinton, *Plantation Mistress*.

191. For a more detailed discussion of race in relation to the portrayal of American Indian women, see chapter 5.

192. G. H. Ambrose, Indian Agent, to Gen. Palmer, October 11, 1855, from "Indian Hostilities in the Territories."

193. A. Miner to Editor, October 11, 1855, MS 581, Asahel Bush Letters.

194. Edward R. Geary, agent, to General Palmer, sup. of Indian Affairs, October 21, 1855, from "Indian Hostilities in the Territories." Even when reporting on a missing white female settler whose first name he did not know, an Indian Agent still identified the women as the "wife" of Mr. Hains and noted that she had a daughter.

195. For discussion of the settlers' and the United States' reaction to the death of Narcissa Whitman, see Addis, "Whitman Massacre," 221–58; Cebula, *Plateau Indians*, 1–5.

196. "James Douglas to George Abernethy," *Oregon Spectator* (Oregon City OT), December 19, 1847.

197. For example, see Robert Newell, speaker of Oregon Assembly, to the U.S. Senate and House, December 29, 1848, from "Indian Hostilities in the Territories"; "Late Massacre in Oregon," *Daily Cleveland Herald* (Cleveland OH), July 17, 1848.

198. Although the "Whitman Massacre" has been credited with being the moment the nation was alarmed by the situation in Oregon, several newspapers east of the Mississippi did not even have the correct surname connected to the killings. Papers at the time of killings did not include the phrase "Whitman Massacre," and, evidentially, the *Pittsburg Gazette* reported that a Dr. "White" and his wife had been killed, with numerous papers repeating the mistake. See "Indian War in Oregon," *Daily National Intelligencer* (Wash-

ington DC), May 25, 1848; "Reported Massacre of Missionaries in Oregon," *Vermont Chronicle* (Bellow Falls VT), May 31, 1848; "Indian War in Oregon," *Mountaineer* (Waynesville NC), June 2, 1848.

199. As noted in chapter 5, even when Indigenous women were married to white men, settlers did not always identity the woman as a "Mrs." or with a proper title of any kind.

200. G. H. Ambrose, Indian Agent, to General Palmer, October 11, 1855, from "Indian Hostilities in the Territories."

201. Bancroft, *Works of Hubert Howe*, 216.

202. For further discussion of the importance placed on the female population and the need for more female settlers, see the gender sections of chapter 4 and chapter 5.

203. "Response of the Volunteers," *Oregon Free Press* (Oregon City OT), June 17, 1848.

204. For examples, see "More Indian Difficulties," *Oregon Spectator* (Oregon City OT), July 9, 1846; "A Villain Caught," *Oregon Statesman* (Salem OT), January 20, 1852; "From the Seat of War," *Oregon Argus* (Oregon City OT), October 27, 1855; Joel Palmer, sup. of Indian Affairs, to Hon. G. W. Manypenny, November 12, 1855, from "Indian Hostilities in the Territories"; Cpt. H. M. Judah, Fourth Infantry, to Maj. E. D. Townsend, assistant adjutant general, November 2, 1855, from "Indian Hostilities in the Territories"; and even as late as "Dreadful Massacred of Emigrants—The Oregon Senatorial Election," *Weekly Raleigh Register and North-Carolina Gazette* (Raleigh NC), October 31, 1860.

205. For examples of U.S. groups connecting the protection of white women to the security of their territories, states, or regions, see Greenberg, *Manifest Manhood*; Block, *Rape and Sexual Power*; Freemen, *Field of Blood*; Black, *Fighting for America*; Hayes and Morris, *Manifest Destiny and Empire.*

206. "Indian Massacre in Oregon," *Daily Atlas* (Boston MA), October 30, 1854; based on the article "Indian Massacre in Oregon," *San Francisco Herald* (San Francisco CA), September 30, 1854.

207. "Indian Massacre in Oregon," *San Francisco Herald* (San Francisco CA), September 30, 1854.

208. One of the few examples of motherhood or another feminine trait being attributed to an Indigenous woman was a report that noted a pregnant American Indian woman had been shot in the stomach by an Oregon settler. See Whaley, *Oregon and the Collapse*, 203.

209. Hill, *Everyday Language of Racism*, 58–59; see also McWilliams, *Brothers under the Skin*.

210. Beeson, *Plea for the Indians*, 17.

211. For example: "Journal of Mary Richardson Walker, March 5, 1838–October 1848," June 2, 1838, August 26, 1838, September 22, 1838.

212. "From Oregon Territory," *Daily Scioto Gazette* (Chillicothe OH), April 14, 1854.

213. Maj. Gen. John H. Wool to Lt. Col. L. Thomas, assistant adjutant general, March 5, 1856, from "Indian Hostilities in the Territories."

214. Maj. Gen. John H. Wool to Lt. Col. L. Thomas, assistant adjutant general, March 5, 1856, from "Indian Hostilities in the Territories."

215. Whaley, *Oregon and the Collapse*, 203.

216. For an example of abuse of American Indian women by American missionary Henry Spalding, see Cebula, *Plateau Indians*, 121.

217. For example, see General Order—E. M. Barnum, adjutant general of Oregon, October 20, 1855, from "Indian Hostilities in the Territories"; Joel Palmer, sup. of Indian Affairs in Oregon Territory, to Maj. Gen. John E. Wool, December 1, 1855, from "Indian Hostilities in the Territories."

218. A. Miner to Editor, October 11, 1855, MS 581, Asahel Bush Letters.

219. For example, see reports from Joel Palmer, John Wool, Edward Geary, and G. H. Ambrose, from "Indian Hostilities in the Territories"; Whaley, *Oregon and the Collapse*, 181, 202.

220. Joel Palmer, sup. of Indian Affairs, to Hon. G. W. Manypenny, September 28, 1855, from "Indian Hostilities in the Territories"; R. R. Thompson, Indian Agent, to Gen. Joel Palmer, sup. Indian Affairs, November 19, 1855, from "Indian Hostilities in the Territories."

221. G. H. Ambrose, Indian Agent, to Gen. Palmer, sup. of Indian Affairs, October 9, 1855, from "Indian Hostilities in the Territories."

222. G. H. Ambrose, Indian Agent, to Gen. Palmer, sup. of Indian Affairs, October 9, 1855, from "Indian Hostilities in the Territories."

223. A. Miner to Editor, October 11, 1855, MS 581, Asahel Bush Letters.

224. G. H. Ambrose, Indian Agent, to General Palmer, superintendent of Indian Affairs, October 20, 1855, from "Indian Hostilities in the Territories."

225. John Withers, 1st Lt., Fourth Infantry, to Col. S. Cooper, adjutant general U.S., November 12, 1855, from "Indian Hostilities in the Territories."

226. For other examples of women not listed when they may have been present, see General Order, E. M. Barnum, adjutant general of Oregon, October 17, 1855, from "Indian Hostilities in the Territories"; R. R. Thompson, Indian Agent, to Gen. Joel Palmer, superintendent of Indian Affairs, November 19, 1855, from "Indian Hostilities in the Territories."

227. General Order, E. M. Barnum, adjutant general of Oregon, October 17, 1855, from "Indian Hostilities in the Territories."

228. G. H. Ambrose, Indian Agent, to General Palmer, sup. of Indian Affairs, October 28, 1855, from "Indian Hostilities in the Territories."

229. "News from the Army," *Oregon Free Press* (Oregon City OT), June 10, 1848; "Latest from the Army," *Oregon Free Press* (Oregon City OT), June 10, 1848.

230. Joel Palmer, sup. of Indian Affairs, to Hon. G. W. Manypenny, November 12, 1855, from "Indian Hostilities in the Territories."

231. For an example of this understanding by Palmer, see Joel Palmer, sup. of Indian Affairs, to Hon. G. W. Manypenny, October 19, 1855, from "Indian Hostilities in the Territories."

232. 1st Lt. John Withers, Fourth Infantry, to Col. S. Cooper, adjutant general U.S., November 12, 1855, from "Indian Hostilities in the Territories."

233. Whaley, *Oregon and the Collapse*, 185.

234. Coan, "First Stage of the Federal," 70.

235. For further discussion of "head-of-household" interpretations in Oregon, see chapter 4.

236. For examples of these exclusions and specific language, see the following treaties of Pacific Northwest American Indian groups from Kappler, *Indian Affairs*: "Agreement with the Rogue River, 1853," September 8, 1853, 1049; "Treaty with the Rogue River, 1853," September 10, 1853, 603–5; "Treaty with the Umpqua—Cow Creek Band, 1853," September 19, 1856, 606–7; "Treaty with the Rogue River, 1854," November 15, 1854, 654–55; "Treaty with the Chasta, Etc., 1854," November 15, 1854, 655–57, "Treaty with the Umpqua and Kalapuya, 1854," November 29, 1854, 657–60; "Treaty with the Nisqually, Puyallup, Etc., 1854," December 26, 1854, 661–64; "Treaty with the Kalapuya, etc., 1855," January 22, 1855, 665–68; "Treaty with the Dwamish, Squamish, Etc., 1855," January 22, 1855, 669–73; "Treaty with the Makah, 1855," January 31, 1855, 682–84; "Treaty with the Wallawalla, Cayuse, Etc., 1855," June 9, 1855, 694–97; "Treaty with the Yakima, 1855," June 9, 1855, 698–701; "Treaty with the Nez Perces, 1855," June 11, 1855, 702–5; "Treaty with the Tribes of Middle Oregon, 1855," June 25, 1855, 714–19; "Treaty with the Quinaielt, Etc.," July 1, 1855 and January 25, 1856, 719–21; "Treaty with the Molala, 1855," December 21, 1855, 740–42; "Treaty with the Flatheads, Etc., 1855," July 16, 1856, 722–25.

237. For post-1859 treaties, including changed treaties, see the following in Kappler, *Indian Affairs*: "Treaty with the Nez Perces, 1863," June 9, 1863, 843–47; "Treaty with the Klamath, Etc., 1864," October 14, 1864, 865–68; "Treaty with the Snake, 1865," August 12, 1865, 876–78; "Treaty with the Osage, 1865," September 29, 1865, 878–80; "Treaty with the Middle Oregon Tribes, 1865," November 15, 1865, 908–10; "Treaty with the Nez Perces, 1868," August 13, 1868, 1024–25; "Treaty with the Eastern Band Shoshoni and Bannock, 1868," July 3, 1868, 1020–22.

238. Whaley, *Oregon and the Collapse*, 219, 238.

239. Simpson, *Mohawk Interruptus*, 10.

240. "Treaty with the Yakima, 1855," June 9, 1855, in Kappler, *Indian Affairs*, 698–701; Washington State Department of Licensing v. Cougar Den, Inc., 586 U.S. 16–1498 (2019).

241. United States Supreme Court, *Tulee v. State of Washington*, 315 U.S. 681 (March 30, 1942); Washington State Department of Licensing v. Cougar Den, Inc., 586 U.S. 16–1498 (2019); "Treaty with the Yakima, 1855," June 9, 1855, in Kappler, *Indian Affairs*, 698–701.

242. For examples of modern histories of Indigenous Women in the Pacific Northwest, see Jagodinsky, *Legal Codes and Talking Trees*; Baldy, *We Are Dancing*; Thrush, *Native Seattle*; Youst, *She's Tricky Like Coyote*.

243. See Simpson, *Mohawk Interruptus*, 147–76; and the conclusion of this volume for a discussion of the continued legacy of these laws.

3. Understanding Immigration Restrictions

1. "Oregon Constitutional Convention," *Daily Citizen and News* (Lowell MA), October 8, 1857. This is a reprint of an article originally printed by the *New York Tribune*, which claimed to have been at the Oregon Constitutional Convention.

2. "Oregon Constitutional Convention," *Daily Citizen and News* (Lowell MA), October 8, 1857.

3. "Oregon Constitutional Convention," *Daily Citizen and News* (Lowell MA), October 8, 1857.

4. Freeman, *Field of Blood*, 249, 248–64.

5. Conlin, *Constitutional Origins*, 153–68; Johnson, *Founding the Far West*, 48–70.

6. Burnett, *Recollections and Opinions*, 215; Though Black Americans would become migrants like other U.S. newcomers to the Oregon by 1849 (when the territory was formally organized by Congress), lawmakers first prevented Black Americans from coming to and residing in Oregon under the provisional government; therefore, all non-Indigenous occupants were immigrants. I have chosen to keep the term "immigration restriction" to highlight this earlier period and to more efficiently reference laws with this specific exclusion.

7. This does not suggest that American Indian groups' practices ceased to exist but that the colonial communications between settlers and the empires that wanted to claim the region began cutting other parties involved in Oregon out and, as chapter 2 demonstrates, forcibly removing Indigenous communities. See, among others, Wolfe, "Settler Colonialism and the Elimination," 387–409; Faragher, "Settler Colonial Studies," 181–91; Hoxie, "Retrieving the Red Continent," 1153–67; Horsman, *Race and Manifest Destiny*.

8. See, for example, "Oregon—Slavery," *Vermont Watchman and State Journal* (Montpelier VT), March 1, 1844.

9. Hyde, *Empires, Nations, and Families*, 375.

10. Hyde, *Empires, Nations, and Families*, 401; Pierce, *Making the White Man's West*, 132–33.

11. For example: "Great Britain—Her Hypocrisy—The Slave Trade," *Pittsfield Sun* (Pittsfield MA), May 1845.

12. During the Treaty of Ghent the British continually brought up the need for the United States to aid the policing of the African slave trade, and during such discussions U.S. diplomats accused the British of wanting such participation solely because it would grant the British the authority to board U.S. vessels. The long-standing disagreement over how to enforce the prohibition of the slave trade continued up to the American Civil War; see Fehrenbacher, *Slaveholding Republic*; Conlin, *Constitutional Origins*, 41–58; Bolster, *Black Jacks*.

13. For a more detailed discussion of how anti-British arguments aided western expansion, see chapter 1.

14. Belohlavek, "Race, Progress, and Destiny," 29.

15. "Editorial," *Oregon Spectator* (Oregon City OT), July 9, 1846. This article was in response to an article from the Polynesian newspaper, which stated that Oregon's business connections with the Sandwich Islands were exaggerated. The article states, "Perhaps friend Jarvis is not thoroughly acquainted with the American character, and may not be aware that, while the American[s] speak of things in language that may seem to other nations highly extravagant, they are really capable to effecting measures and accomplishing ends, which are marvelous indeed in the eyes of the world, especially in matters of

trade and traffic—settling new countries, &c., &c., and we hope they will soon give our island friends and all the world, a practical demonstration of their wonder-working powers, by taking hold of Oregon and making it all they have ever represented it as capable of being made."

16. "Oregon-Slavery," *Vermont Watchman and State Journal* (Montpelier VT), March 1, 1844; "Great Britain—Her Hypocrisy—The Slave Trade," *Pittsfield Sun* (Pittsfield MA), May 1845.

17. Goldstein and Lubin, "Settler Colonialism," 611–866.

18. Grover, *Oregon Archives*, 32.

19. For a discussion of the application of the Northwest Ordinance in the Far West, see Smith, *Freedom's Frontier*; Taylor, *In Search*; Morrison, *Slavery and the American West*.

20. Tomlins, *Freedom* Bound, 133–90, 409–508; Davis, *Inhuman Bondage*.

21. "The Organic Laws," *Oregon Spectator* (Oregon City OT), March 19, 1846.

22. Burnett, *Recollections and Opinions*, 213–14. The enslaved individual had to leave within two years if male or three years if female.

23. For a discussion of how removal projects of Black Americans were used by both the United States and Great Britain, see Asaka, *Tropical Freedom*, 5–6.

24. Burnett, *Recollections and Opinions*, 215. This revision made it more reflective of an Illinois state statute from 1819; see Pierce, *Making the White Man's West*, 131.

25. Burnett, *Recollections and Opinions*, 215.

26. Article 1, Section 4 of the Oregon Organic Laws uses the same language as the Northwest Ordinance in the first half of the first sentence, but the Oregon law ends there, whereas Article 6 of the Ordinance continues. Furthermore, unlike in the Oregon Territorial Constitution of 1848, nowhere in the Oregon Organic Laws does it state that the region was extending the Northwest Ordinance over itself. Congressional representatives implied this during the debate over the Oregon Bill, but the Oregon Organic Laws did not specify any such connection. Semple, *Organic and Other General Laws*, 47, 59–60. See also Johansen, *Empire of the Columbia*.

27. For examples of U.S. officials' criticizing British legal protections in Oregon, see Cong. Globe, 30th Cong., 1st Sess., Ex. Doc. No. 47, at 3–14 (1848); also, for examples of U.S. citizens' knowledge of the U.S. Constitution, see Conlin, *Constitutional Origins*, xxvi–xxx, 1–38.

28. See, among others, Rayback, *Free Soil*; Fehrenbacher, *Slaveholding Republic*; Johnson, *Founding of the New West*; Johannsen, *Frontier Politics and the Sectional*.

29. See Cong. Globe, 30th Cong., 1st and 2nd Sess.; Forbes, *Missouri Compromise*; Woodworth, *Manifest Destinies*.

30. Cong. Globe, 30th Cong., 1st Sess., 34 (1848); Morrison, *Slavery and the American West*; Holt, *Fate of Their Country*.

31. The exact use of this constitutional amendment appeared again during Oregon's statehood debates. Representatives who opposed Oregon's immigration restriction of Black Americans cited this amendment and argued that the law denied Black Americans who were viewed as citizens in their states of origin their federal right. During the Oregon

Bill debates, however, the focus remained on Oregon's ability to exclude slavery from its territory. Cong. Globe, 30th Cong., 1st Sess., 34–36 (1848).

32. Cong. Globe, 30th Cong., 1st Sess., 44 (1848); "Editorial," *Oregon Argus* (Oregon City OT), March 28, 1857. National newspapers ran with news of this proposed amendment, speculating as to whether this meant a government bodied by Southern politicians would make up the Oregon territorial government. One New Hampshire paper reported the rumor that former South Carolina senator Bedford Brown had been on his way to Oregon with eighty slaves and was awaiting his appointment as Oregon territorial governor by President Polk. See "Oregon—Slavery—An Intrigue," *New Hampshire Statesman and State Journal* (Concord NH), February 26, 1847.

33. "Speech of John C. Calhoun: The Oregon Bill—Extension of Slavery," *North Star* (Rochester NY), July 7, 1848.

34. "Letter from Senator Benton, to the People of Oregon," *Oregon Spectator* (Oregon City OT), September 17, 1848; Morrison, *Slavery and the American West*; Freeman, *Field of Blood*, 154–72.

35. "Letter from Senator Benton, to the People of Oregon," *Oregon Spectator* (Oregon City OT), September 17, 1848.

36. Miller, *Native America*, 115–16.

37. *Mr. Webster's Speech*. Iowa was in the process of applying for statehood during this time.

38. Cong. Globe, 30th Cong., 1st Sess., 1148–49 (1848).

39. Johnson, *Founding the Far West*; *Mr. Webster's Speech*; Foner, *Free Soil, Free Labor*.

40. "Polk's Last," *Liberator* (Boston MA), August 25, 1848; "Mr. Polk on Slavery, Oregon, and the New Territories," *Liberator* (Boston MA), August 25, 1848.

41. "Polk's Last," *Liberator* (Boston MA), August 25, 1848.

42. "Slavery in Oregon," *Weekly Raleigh Register and North-Carolina Gazette* (Raleigh NC), October 21, 1857.

43. Cong. Globe, 30th Cong., 1st Sess., 944–1045 (1848); Johannsen, *Frontier Politics on the Eve*.

44. Kappler, *Indian Affairs*, 2:658, 664, 670, 675, 683.

45. For discussion of the Kansas-Nebraska Act, see Potter, *Impending Crisis*; Foner, *Free Soil, Free Labor*; Johannsen, *Frontier Politics and the Sectional*; Pierce, *Making the White Man's West*, 130–36.

46. Cong. Globe, 30th Cong., 1st Sess., 962 (1848); Johnson, *Founding the New West*, 23–40.

47. Technically, Florida could also fall under the category of states predating Oregon's exclusion of Black Americans, as the document that eventually became the Florida state constitution was drafted in 1838. Whether Oregonians were aware of these documents prior to their acceptance into Florida's state constitution is unknown. See Swindler, *Sources and Documents*, 5:481, 2:329.

48. Swindler, *Sources and Documents*, 2:329.

49. Swindler, *Sources and Documents*, 3:268–69, 272.

50. Swindler, *Sources and Documents*, 10:79.

51. *Journal of the House of Representatives of the Territory of Oregon Being the Third Regular Session*.

52. Smith, *Freedom's Frontier*; Pierce, *Making the White Man's West*, 128–30.

53. See Johannsen, "Political Picture," 38–48; Hubbart, "'Pro-Southern' Influences," 45–62; Himes, "History of the Press," 327–70.

54. For examples, see "Slavery in Oregon," *Milwaukee Daily Sentinel* (Milwaukee WI), October 20, 1857; "Democracy Going for Slavery in Oregon," *Bangor Daily Whig & Courier* (Bangor ME), September 5, 1857; "Our San Francisco Correspondence," *New York Herald* (New York NY), August 9, 1857; "The Prospect in Oregon," *Liberator* (Boston MA), July 10, 1857; "Later from Oregon," *Daily Evening Bulletin* (San Francisco CA), August 25, 1857; "Oregon As a State," *North American and United States Gazette* (Philadelphia PA), December 16, 1857.

55. "Oregon," *North American and United States Gazette* (Philadelphia PA), November 6, 1857.

56. Judgment in the U.S. Supreme Court Case *Dred Scott v. John F.A. Sanford*, March 6, 1857, Case Files 1792–1995, Record Group 267, Records of the Supreme Court of the United States, National Archives.

57. Potter, *Impending Crisis*; Johnson, *Founding the Far West*; Holt. *Fate of Their Country*.

58. Cong. Globe, 35th Cong., 1st Sess., 987–88 (1858).

59. "Oregon," *Mississippian and State Gazette* (Jackson MS), May 26, 1858.

60. Tomlins, *Freedom Bound*, 534. For a discussion of arguments for preventing Black Americans entry to states and territory during the mid-nineteenth century, see Tyler, "Unwanted Sailor," 506–35.

61. "A Handsome Rebuke—The Admission of Oregon," *Newark Advocate* (Newark OH), May 19, 1858; "Debate on the Oregon Bill," *Boston Daily Advertiser* (Boston MA), February 15, 1859; "Last Night's Report—Congressional," *Daily Cleveland Herald* (Cleveland OH), May 19, 1858.

62. Asaka, *Tropical Freedom*, 3; Dain, *Hideous Monster*, 121.

63. Tomlins, *Freedom Bound*, 73.

64. See Richardson, "Unwelcomed Settlers," 193–95.

65. Taylor, *In Search of a Racial Frontier*, 77.

66. Swindler, *Sources and Documents*, 5:481.

67. Hammer, "Great Britain," 3–28; Langley, "Negro in the Navy," 273–86; January, "South Carolina Association," 191–201.

68. "Missouri," *Oregon Spectator* (Oregon City OT), July 23, 1846; Swindler, *Sources and Documents*, 5:481. Wisconsin's revised constitution of 1846 once again "made it the duty of [the] general assembly to pass laws to prevent free negroes from coming into the state."

69. Kendi, *Stamped from the Beginning*, 174, 1–3.

70. Cong. Globe, 30th Cong., 1st Sess., 1140 (1848).

71. Slavery had also existed prior to white settlement in Oregon, as several coastal American Indian groups practiced slavery. In fact, American Indian slaves were reported to have existed in Fort Vancouver with the Hudson Bay Company at least five years before

the first overland wagon train had come to Oregon Country. See Whaley, *Oregon and the Collapse*; Jessett, *Reports and Letters*; Nokes, *Breaking Chains*.

72. For examples of U.S. politicians using these arguments, see "Speech of John C. Calhoun: The Oregon Bill—Extension of Slavery," *North Star* (Rochester NY), July 7, 1848; "Letter from Senator Benton, to the People of Oregon," *Oregon Spectator* (Oregon City OT), September 17, 1848; "Speech of the Hon. R. B. Rhett."

73. Many histories and much racial theory scholarship address these perceptions of race as well as the transformation of racial beliefs during the nineteenth century. For a discussion of racial theory in the United States and its application to the American West, see Pierce, *Making the White Man's West*, 15–18; Dain, *Hideous Monster*, 69–72, 227–63; Roediger, *Wages of Whiteness*; Kendi, *Stamped from the Beginning*; Horsman, *Race and Manifest Destiny*, 92–157; Hietala, *Manifest Design*; Asaka, *Tropical Freedom*; Painter, *History of White People*.

74. "Slavery," *Oregon Statesman* (Salem OR), July 1, 1857.

75. "Slavery," *Oregon Statesman* (Salem OR), July 1, 1857.

76. "Slavery," *Oregon Statesman* (Salem OR), July 1, 1857.

77. "What the Present Legislature Finds to Do," *Oregonian* (Portland OT), January 6, 1855.

78. See Taylor, *In Search*, 82; Richardson, "Unwelcomed Settlers."

79. Semple, *Organic and Other General Laws*, 52–62; *See Journal of Council of Oregon*; *Journal of the Council of the Legislative Assembly*; *Journal of the House of Representatives of the Territorial of Oregon During the Sixth Regular Session*; *Journal of the House of Representatives of the Territory of Oregon: During the Seventh Regular Session*; *Journal of the House of Representatives of the Territory of Oregon (Salem, Oregon: Asahel Bush, Territorial Printer, 1852–56).*

80. "Editorial," *Oregon Spectator* (Oregon City OT), August 22, 1850.

81. *Oregon Provisional and Territorial Government Records*, index 612.

82. *Oregon Provisional and Territorial Government Records*, index 612.

83. Johnson, *Founding the Far West*; Mahoney, "Oregon Democracy," 202–27.

84. Taylor, *In Search*, 82–91.

85. "Case Files for *Vanderpool vs. Magruder*, 1851," MS 996, Philip Foster Collection.

86. "Case Files for *Vanderpool vs. Magruder*, 1851," MS 996, Philip Foster Collection.

87. For discussion of the Vanderpool case, see Taylor, "Slaves and Free Men," 153–70; McLagan, *Peculiar Paradise*.

88. "What the Present Legislature Finds to Do," *Oregonian* (Portland OT), January 6, 1855.

89. "What the Present Legislature Finds to Do," *Oregonian* (Portland OT), January 6, 1855.

90. "What the Present Legislature Finds to Do," *Oregonian* (Portland OT), January 6, 1855.

91. For discussion of laborers of Chinese descent in the Pacific Northwest during the mid-nineteenth century, see Lew-Williams, *Chinese Must Go*; Aarim-Heriot, *Chinese Immigrants, African Americans, and Racial Anxiety in the United States*; Zhu, *Chinaman's Chance*.

92. "What the Present Legislature Finds to Do," *Oregonian* (Portland OT), January 6, 1855.

93. "What the Present Legislature Finds to Do," *Oregonian* (Portland OT), January 6, 1855.

94. See Carey, *Oregon Constitution and Proceedings*; Morrison, *Slavery and the American West*; Litwack, *North of Slavery*; Woodward, *Rise and Early History*.

95. Semple, *Organic and Other General Laws*, 78.

96. "Oregon Legislator," *Oregon Argus* (Oregon City OT), January 31, 1857.

97. "Oregon Legislator," *Oregon Argus* (Oregon City OT), January 31, 1857. The article identifies this speaker as Smith of Jackson, but the only Smith at the convention was Delazon Smith of Linn, who also happened to have been open about his proslavery position.

98. "Editorial," *Oregonian* (Portland OT), August 8, 1857. Arguments about miscegenation, morality, and naturalization within debates about excluding Black Americans from coming into or settling in Oregon appear in chapter 5 of this volume.

99. "Oregon Legislator," *Oregon Argus* (Oregon City OT), January 31, 1857.

100. "House," *Oregon Statesman* (Salem OR), January 20, 1857.

101. For a discussion on definitions of labor and class leading to the Civil War, see, among others, Foner, *Free Soil, Free Labor*; Wilentz, *Chants Democratic*; Blumin, *Emergence of the Middle Class*.

102. Lott, *Love and Theft*.

103. Cong. Globe, H.R., 30th Cong., 2nd Sess., 47 (1848).

104. *Mr. Webster's Speech*.

105. For discussions of arguments about slavery in comparison to northern laborers, see Walters, *Anti-Slavery Appeal*; Fox-Genovese, *Within the Plantation Household*; Potter, *Impending Crisis*.

106. "House," *Oregon Statesman* (Salem OR), January 20, 1857. An exception to this perspective was the argument some proslavery individuals made that suggested northern laborers degraded white labor because they allowed white and Black labor to exist within the same professions, whereas plantation labor always elevated the work done by white men over that performed by enslaved Black Americans. See "Slavery in Oregon," *Occidental Messenger* (Corvallis OT), October 17, 1857.

107. "Young Men of Oregon—Slavery," *Oregon Argus* (Oregon City OT), January 31, 1857.

108. Kendi, *Stamped from the Beginning*, 1–3.

109. "Young Men of Oregon—Slavery," *Oregon Argus* (Oregon City OT), January 31, 1857.

110. "Slavery and Freedom," *Oregon Argus* (Oregon City OT), January 3, 1857.

111. "Constitution," *Oregon Argus* (Oregon City OT), October 17, 1857.

112. "Bush and Slavery," *Oregonian* (Portland OT), March 7, 1857.

113. Marschner, *Oregon 1859*, 51–52. According to Marschner, the *Occidental Messenger* was created in 1857 as a proslavery newspaper.

114. "Astonishing Absurdity," *Occidental Messenger* (Corvallis OT), September 26, 1857.

115. *Journal of the Ninth Regular Session*.

116. See Stacey Smith, *Freedom's Frontier*.

117. *Oregon Provisional and Territorial Government Records*, indexes 8661, 9671, 10974; "House," *Oregonian* (Portland OT), December 26, 1857; "Bill to Protect Slave Property," *Oregon Sentinel* (Jacksonville OT), February 6, 1858; "Report of the Judiciary Committee from Slave Petitions," *Oregon Sentinel* (Jacksonville OT), February 10, 1859; copy of a letter

from Owen Wade from the Oregon Territory pertaining to a bill to protect slave property, dated November 18, 1858, see "Slavery in Oregon," *North American and United States Gazette* (Philadelphia PA), February 22, 1859.

118. "All Hail! The State of Oregon," *Oregon Statesman* (Salem OR), November 14, 1857.

119. See Litwack, *North of Slavery*; Hahn, *Nation under Our Feet.*

120. As addressed above, Missouri included a provision that instructed its legislators to create a law to prohibit free Black Americans from coming to or settling in the state, but its constitution did not possess a law that enforced this exclusion. Furthermore, other states' similar restrictions to the presence of free Black Americans came during revisions to their state constitutions or were later enacted as state statutes. See Swindler, *Sources and Documents.*

121. Cong. Globe, H.R., 35th Cong., 1st Sess., 987 (1859).

122. He was possibly referring to the Fugitive Slave Act as well, which is why he repeatedly used the language "hunted down."

123. Cong. Globe, H.R., 35th Cong., 1st Sess., 987 (1859).

124. Cong. Globe, H.R., 35th Cong., 1st Sess., 987 (1859). Hoard finished his argument with the statement, "Sir, in conclusion, I protest, in the name of justice, against this inhumanity; and, in the name of humanity, against this injustice."

125. See Johannsen, *Frontier Politics and the Sectional*; Hill, "Negro as a Political," 130–45.

126. "The Constitution of Oregon," *Boston Daily Advertiser* (Boston MA), January 24, 1859.

127. "Why the Oregon Bill Is Opposed by Republican Members of Congress," *Milwaukee Daily Sentinel* (Milwaukee WI), January 15, 1859.

128. See Zaeske, *Signatures of Citizenship*; Walters, *Anti-Slavery Appeal*; McPherson, *Battle Cry of Freedom*; Potter, *Impending Crisis*; Foner, *Free Soil, Free Labor.*

129. Minto, "Antecedents of the Oregon," 38–63.

130. Cong. Globe, 30th Cong., 2nd Sess., 1142 (1848). This section of the *Congressional Globe* focused on the "Review of the Select Committee to establish a Territorial Government in Oregon."

131. Welke, "Law, Personhood, and Citizenship," 353; Kerber, *No Constitutional Right*; Kerber, "Paradox of Women's Citizenship," 349–78; Boag, *Re-dressing America's Frontier Past*; Greenberg, *Manifest Manhood*; Varon, *We Mean to Be Counted*; Edwards, *Angels in the Machinery*; Kerber, "Separate Spheres, Female Worlds."

132. Wallach, *Obedient Sons*, 86–88.

133. Zboray and Zboray, "Gender Slurs," 431–46.

134. See Varon, *We Mean to Be Counted*; Edward, *Angels in the Machinery*; Blumin, *Emergence of the Middle Class.*

135. Roth, *Gender and Race*; Varon, "Gender History," 19–23; Varon, *We Mean to Be Counted*; Edward, *Angels in the Machinery*; Kerber, *No Constitutional Right*; Blumin, *Emergence of the Middle Class*; Sklar and Steward, *Women's Rights and Transatlantic.*

136. Cong. Globe, 30th Cong., 1st Sess., 37 (1848).

137. See Zaeske, *Signatures of Citizenship*; Greenberg, *Manifest Manhood*; Boag, *Re-dressing America's Frontier Past*; Zboray and Zboray, "Gender Slurs"; Kendi, *Stamped from the Beginning*, 187; Kolp and Snyder, "Women and the Political," 272–92.

138. Cong. Globe, 30th Cong., 1st Sess., 30 (1848).

139. Deady to Bush, MS 581, Asahel Bush Letters, Oregon Historical Society.

140. Articles from the *Oregonian* between 1855 and 1857 that insinuated or completely identified Bush as supporting slavery are a good example of this. Although *Oregonian* editor Thomas Dryer took the most shots at Bush over this issue, the *Oregon Argus* also publicized Bush's position on slavery.

141. "What the Present Legislature Finds to Do," *Oregonian* (Portland OT), January 6, 1855.

142. "Slavery in Oregon," *Oregon Statesman* (Salem OR), June 9, 1857.

143. See the reprint of the *New York Tribune* article reporting on a riot in Oregon, "Oregon Constitutional Convention," *Daily Citizen and News* (Lowell MA), October 8, 1857.

144. "Our Admission," *Oregon Statesman* (Salem OR), August 3, 1858.

145. See Kendi, *Stamped from the Beginning*; Dain, *Hideous Monster*, 121.

146. See *Oregon Argus* (Oregon City OT), articles from 1855 to 1860.

147. "Important," *Oregon Statesman* (Salem OT), November 14, 1854.

148. "Notes to Old Granny Gray," *Maryland Gazette and Political Intelligencer* (Annapolis MD), June 29, 1820.

149. "Editorial," *Vermont Patriot and State Gazette* (Montpelier VT), September 26, 1832.

150. "Granny Harrison, the Red Petticoat Candidate for the President of the United States," *Weekly Raleigh Register and North-Carolina Gazette* (Raleigh NC), January 31, 1840.

151. Zboray and Zboray, "Gender Slurs" 421–23.

152. "Editorial," *North American and Daily Advertiser*, April 2, 1840.

153. "Granny Harrison," *Weekly Raleigh Register and North-Carolina Gazette* (Raleigh NC), March 20, 1840; "Some Incidents in the Life of an Old Granny," *New Hampshire Statesman and State Journal* (Concord NH), February 1, 1840, originally printed in the *Providence Journal* but reprinted by several papers; "Granny Harrison," *Boston Courier*, April 16, 1840.

154. "Vote for Old Granny," *Ohio Statesman* (Columbus OH), March 20, 1840; "No Title," *Ohio Statesman* (Columbus OH), February 14, 1840.

155. Eyal, *Young American Movement*.

156. Wallach, *Obedient Sons*, 72–81.

157. See Eyal, *Young American Movement*; Freeman, *Field of Blood*, 57.

158. See Varon, *We Mean to Be Counted*; Edwards, *Angels in the Machinery*.

159. Zboray and Zboray, "Gender Slurs," 432–39.

160. For a discussion of Oregon's partisan groups during the 1850s, see Johnson, *Founding the Far West*; Berwagner, *Frontier against Slavery*.

161. For a discussion of the generational argument in the late nineteenth century, see Hoganson, *Fighting for American Manhood*.

162. See *Oregon Statesman* (Salem OR), January 1850–December 1857.

163. "Cool!," *Oregon Statesman* (Salem OR), July 14, 1855.

164. See Klepp, "Revolutionary Bodies," 910–45; Stansell, *City of Women*; Varon, *We Mean to Be Counted*; Blumin, *Emergence of the Middle Class*; Zboray and Zboray, "Gender Slurs"; Edwards, *Angels in the Machinery*; Isenberg, *Sex and Citizenship*.

165. Kolp and Snyder, "Women and the Political," 277–80.

166. "Political Party," *Oregon Statesman* (Salem OR), September 25, 1852.

167. "Abolitionism," *Oregon Statesman* (Salem OR), July 21, 1855.

168. "The Old and the New," *Oregon Statesman* (Salem OR), November 11, 1856.

169. "Granny Alta Rubbing Her Eyes," *Daily Evening Bulletin* (San Francisco CA), June 1, 1858; "The Impotent Spite of Granny Alta," *Daily Evening Bulletin* (San Francisco CA), August 30, 1858; "The Foolish Granny Alta," *Daily Evening Bulletin* (San Francisco CA), August 31, 1858; "Granny Indecent," *Daily Evening Bulletin* (San Francisco CA), January 26, 1860.

170. "The Vote in Oregon—Slavery Restricted," *Daily Evening Bulletin* (San Francisco CA), November 16, 1857.

171. "Oregon and Eli Thayer," *Kansas Herald of Freedom* (Wakarusa KS), September 30, 1859.

172. See Johnson, *Founding the Far West*; Taylor, *In Search*; Brooks, "Race, Politics, and Denial," 731–62.

173. "Blacks in Oregon," Oregon Encyclopedia (website), Oregon Historical Society, accessed July 20, 2018, https://oregonencyclopedia.org/articles/blacks_in_oregon/; Pierce, *Making the White Man's West*; Limerick, *Legacy of Conquest*; see the conclusion of this volume for a discussion on the continued legacy of these laws.

174. Chapter 5 specifically references the influence of the immigration restriction on voting rights.

175. Gray, *History of Oregon*, 378–79.

176. Gray, *History of Oregon*, 379.

177. Pierce, *Making the White Man's West*, 144.

178. See Burnett, *Recollections and Opinions*; Whaley, *Oregon and the Collapse*, 201.

179. Johansen, "Political Picture," 38.

180. Semple, *Organic and Other General Laws*, 95.

181. "House," *Oregon Sentinel* (Jacksonville OT), February 6, 1858; "Taxing Chinamen," *Oregon Sentinel* (Jacksonville OT), April 3, 1858.

182. For example, see "John Chinaman," *Table Rock Sentinel* (Jacksonville OT), December 6, 1859; "The Chinese in Oregon—A Howl at John," *Milwaukee Daily Sentinel* (Milwaukee WI), August 29, 1866.

183. Aarim-Heriot, *Chinese Immigrants, African Americans*; Kwong, *Forbidden Workers*; Lew-Williams, *Chinese Must Go*; Zhu, *Chinaman's Chance*; Kanazawa, "Immigration, Exclusion, and Taxation," 779–805.

184. "Popular Sovereignty in Ohio: Speaking Up So Granny Can Hear," *Vermont Patriot and State Gazette* (Montpelier VT), January 28, 1860.

185. "A Political Convention of Granny-Dears, Calling Itself the 'Constitutional Union Party,' Was Held on Boston Thursday Last," *Bangor Daily Whig & Courier* (Bangor ME), April 3, 1860.

186. See the conclusion of this volume for a discussion on the continued legacy of this political practice.

187. See Parker, "Citizenship and Immigration Law," 168–203.

4. Definitions of Land Ownership

1. "Atrocious Murder," *Western Star* (Oregon City OR), January 16, 1851; "Coroner's Inquest," *Western Star* (Oregon City OR), January 30, 1851.

2. The person leasing a land claim, however, typically did not possess his own separate claim, as did Hamilton. Bergquist, "Oregon Donation Act," 29–31; for a discussion of violence among federal politicians during this same time, see Freeman, *Field of Blood*.

3. "He was laying [*sic*] rather on his back, with his head down the hill toward the house—Blood was running from him freely, apparently very near the collar bone and breast. I came up and spoke to him but received no answer from him. He never moved hand or foot. I discovered a little quiver in his face. I then screamed out for the neighbors to come." In "Trial of William Kendal for the Murder of William Hamilton, in Marion County Circuit, at March Special Term, 1851," *Oregon Statesman* (Salem OR), April 18, 1851.

4. "Trial of William Kendal for the Murder of William Hamilton, in Marion County Circuit, at March Special Term, 1851," *Oregon Statesman* (Salem OR), April 18, 1851.

5. Grover, *Oregon Archives*, 28.

6. West, *Last Indian War*, 47.

7. Hyde, *Empires, Nations, and Families*, 425.

8. Burnett, *Recollections and Opinions*, 200.

9. Burnett, *Recollections and Opinions*, 201.

10. Taylor, *In Search of a Racial Frontier*, 75–77.

11. Swindler, *Sources and Documents*; see also chapter 6 for further discussion of the term "free" in Oregon legislation.

12. *Oregon Provisional and Territorial Government Records*, index 1317.

13. Tomlins, *Freedom Bound*, 21–78.

14. See, among others, Johnson, *Founding the Far West*; Kenner, *Comanchero*.

15. Cong. Globe, 30th Cong., 2nd Sess., 1139 (1848).

16. Pierce, *Making the White Man's West*, 30–39.

17. Miller, *Native America*, 115–16.

18. Technically, federally appointed positions were not filled until 1851; therefore, Oregon settlers continued to operate under their own government until that time.

19. Grover, *Oregon Archives*, 291.

20. Whaley, *Oregon and the Collapse*, 161.

21. See Burnett, *Recollections and Opinions*, Semple, *Organic and Other General Laws*.

22. "Hudson's Bay Company—The Oregon Land Law," *Oregon Statesman* (Salem OR), July 18, 1854; see also Semple, *Organic and Other General Laws*, 44.

23. *Oregon Provisional and Territorial Government Records*, index 3803.

24. Whaley, "Oregon, Illahee," 166–70.

25. "Congressional," *Oregon Spectator* (Oregon City OT), July 1850.

26. For further discussion of how Oregon land acquisitions were retroactively legalized by the federal government, see Whaley, *Oregon and the Collapse*, 161–89.

27. "Debate in the Senate," *Daily National Intelligencer* (Washington DC), September 19, 1850. An Ohio newspaper echoed this sentiment, asking why the unsettled nature of

other regions in the country would not benefit from such land donations. Focusing more on European immigration, the editorial argued that German and Irish immigrants should set their sights on Arkansas, Mississippi, or Florida, suggesting that the availability of Oregon lands would remain an option for the foreseeable future. "Oregon Land Law," *Daily Scioto Gazette* (Chillicothe OH), November 15, 1851.

28. Johansen, *Empire of the Columbia*, 234–37.

29. Johnson, *Founding the Far West*, 6–61.

30. Ostler, *Plains Sioux*, 18.

31. "Debate in the Senate," *Daily National Intelligencer* (Washington DC), September 19, 1850.

32. "Debate in the Senate," *Daily National Intelligencer* (Washington DC), September 19, 1850.

33. Johnson, *Founding the Far West*, 41–60.

34. Whaley, *Oregon and the Collapse*, 171.

35. "Oregon Correspondence," *Daily Cleveland Herald* (Cleveland OH), November 29, 1850.

36. "Indian Treaties," *Vermont (Montpelier) Watchman & State Journal*, July 31, 1851.

37. Tomlins, *Freedom Bound*, 335–59.

38. Boag, *Environment and Experience*, 99–102.

39. Burnett, *Recollections and Opinions*, 201.

40. "Murder—Two Men Killed," *Oregon Spectator* (Oregon City OT), April 18, 1850.

41. Whaley, *Oregon and the Collapse*, 235.

42. "Homicide at Fort Vancouver," *Oregon Spectator* (Oregon City OT), September 12, 1850. One of the more well-known accounts of violence in the name of land ownership in Oregon was the murder of Jeremiah Mahoney by Nimrod O'Kelly. For a detailed account of the Mahoney murder, see Lansing, *Nimrod*.

43. "Question Settled," *Western Star* (Oregon City OR), February 13, 1851.

44. For a discussion of land ownership's connection to citizenship and rights, see Brown, *Good Wives, Nasty Wenches*; Isenberg, *Sex and Citizenship*; McCurry, *Masters of Small Worlds*; Morgan, *American Slavery, American Freedom*.

45. "Colored Voters," *Oregon Spectator* (Oregon City OT), October 18, 1849.

46. *Oregon Provisional and Territorial Government Records*, index 1317.

47. Whaley, *Oregon and the Collapse*, 176.

48. Three years before the Oregon Treaty, the U.S. Senate had attempted to enforce Iowa land laws on Oregon, but that bill died in the House of Representatives.

49. "Corresponder of the Spectator," *Oregon Spectator* (Oregon City OT), October 12, 1846.

50. Hyde, *Empires, Nations, and Families*, 55, 144.

51. The usage of "negro equality" as an argumentative tactic was apparent in the debates for both the Donation Land Act and the Oregon Bill for Oregon's statehood. Politicians accused of being in support of "negro suffrage" would at the very least be taken off their lines of argument to defend themselves and/or berate their accusers, and at best

the accusation would end the accused's speech. See Cong. Globe, 31st Cong., 2nd Sess. (1850) and 35th Cong., 2nd sess. (1859) as well as Walters, *Antislavery Appeal*; Pierce, *Making the White Man's West*, 134; Freeman, *Field of Blood*, 132–33.

52. "Right of Colored Men in Oregon, &c.," *North Star* (Rochester NY), June 30, 1850.

53. "Right of Colored Men in Oregon, &c.," *North Star* (Rochester NY), June 30, 1850. Bayly's objection to the exclusion of Black Americans from land donations stemmed from the fact that he wanted to encourage the migration of free Black Americans to the West and out of the slave states. See chapter 3 of this volume and Asaka, *Tropical Freedom*.

54. See Richardson, *West from Appomattox*; Potter, *Impending Crisis*; Smith, *Freedom's Frontier*.

55. Semple, *Organic and Other General Laws*, 63–64.

56. Oregon politicians were also concerned that the father of a "half breed" could be British (or rather, a Hudson's Bay employee) without this clarification as well.

57. Whaley, *Oregon and the Collapse*, 176.

58. Pascoe, *What Comes Naturally*, 96.

59. Semple, *Organic and Other General Laws*, 66.

60. "Land in Oregon," *Mississippian* (Oxford MS), October 11, 1850.

61. "Right of Colored Men in Oregon, &c.," *North Star* (Rochester NY), June 30, 1850.

62. For a discussion of race as an element and product of power relations in the West, including Oregon, see Aarim-Heriot, *Chinese Immigrants, African Americans*.

63. *Journal of the House of Representatives of the Territory of Oregon Being the Third Regular Session*, 36.

64. "Afternoon Session," *Oregon Statesman* (Salem OR), December 16, 1851.

65. Semple, *Organic and Other General Laws*, 77.

66. "State Legislature," *Oregonian* (Portland OT), October 3, 1857.

67. "House," *Oregon Statesman* (Salem OR), September 15, 1857. See also Potter, *Impending Crisis*; Foner, *Free Soil, Free Labor*.

68. "House," *Oregon Statesman* (Salem OR), September 15, 1857. See also Baum, "Know-Nothing and the Republican," 959–86.

69. "House," *Oregon Statesman* (Salem OR), September 15, 1857.

70. "State Legislature," *Oregonian* (Portland OT), October 3, 1857.

71. Semple, *Organic and Other General Laws*, 77–78.

72. Semple, *Organic and Other General Laws*, 77–78; Johnson, *Founding the Far West*, 139–45.

73. Taylor, *In Search of a Racial Frontier*, 82.

74. For discussion of how resistance demonstrated political activism, see Hahn, *Nation under Our Feet*.

75. Ripley, *Black Abolitionist Papers*, 102–4. Further discussion of this letter can be found in chapter 6 of this volume.

76. Shah, *Stranger Intimacy*, 10.

77. Semple, *Organic and Other General Laws*, 95. The section pertaining to those of Chinese descent stated, "No chinaman, not resident of the state at the adoption of this

constitution, shall ever hold any real estate or mining claim, or work any mining claim therein." For discussion of this restriction, see chapter 3 of this volume.

78. Semple, *Organic and Other General Laws*, 78.

79. Cong. Globe, 35th Cong., 2nd Sess., 110 (1859).

80. For constitutions from southern states that address the rights of slaves, see Swindler, *Sources and Documents*.

81. Cong. Globe, 35th Cong., 2nd Sess., 110 (1859).

82. Piece, *Making the White Man's West*, 133–45.

83. Cong. Globe, 35th Cong., 2nd Sess., 984 (1859).

84. Potter, *Impending Crisis*; Johnson, *Founding the Far West*; Holt, *Fate of Their Country*.

85. For a discussion on how the definition of independence transformed in the Antebellum era to accommodate all white male landowners, thereby turning wives and children into dependents, see McCurry, *Masters of Small Worlds*.

86. For a discussion of the complex structures of masculinity, particularly those associated with the settlement of the American West, see Greenberg, *Manifest Manhood*; Rotundo, *American Manhood*; Shah, *Stranger Intimacy*; Compton, "Proper Women/Propertied Women"; Kolp and Snyder, "Women and the Political," 272–92.

87. Kendi, *Stamped from the Beginning*, 171–73; Johnson, *Founding the Far West*; Pierce, *Making the West White*, 234; Hyde, *Empires, Nations, and Families*, 406–8; Johnson, *Roaring Camp*.

88. Brown, *Good Wives, Nasty Wenches*; Block, *Rape and Sexual Power*; Kolp, "Women and the Political," 283.

89. Welke, "Law, Personhood, and Citizenship," 353; see also Kerber, *No Constitutional Right*.

90. Chused, "Oregon Donation Act," 44–78; see also Salmon, *Women and the Law*; Jones-Rogers, *They Were Her Property*, 29.

91. Oregon Emigration Society, *Articles of Agreement*, 3.

92. Rotundo, *American Manhood*, 2.

93. Boag, "Thinking Like Mount Rushmore," 44–46.

94. Oregon Emigration Society, *Articles of Agreement*, 5.

95. Mrinalini Sinha addresses the complex position of women's rights within the larger context of social rules and perceptions, with the explanation that "the anomalous status of women as citizens is reflected in the dual construction of women both as individuals in their own right subject to the general laws of the state, and as men's legal appendages, subject to the provision of special laws." See "Gender and Nation," 260.

96. *Oregon Provisional and Territorial Government Records*, index 1317.

97. Swindler, *Sources and Documents*, 1:457, 4:95, 5:237, 9:271.

98. Semple, *Organic and Other General Laws*, 63, 65.

99. Chused, "Oregon Donation Act," 44–54.

100. An example of Thurston's letters to newspapers can be seen in "Squatters Rights in Oregon," *Ohio Statesman* (Columbus OH), October 10, 1850.

101. "Editorial Correspondence," *Oregon Spectator* (Oregon City OT), July 10, 1851.

102. Ostler, *Plains Sioux*; Whaley, *Oregon and the Collapses*, 171.

103. Asahel Bush, "Women and Taxes in Oregon," *Milwaukee Daily Sentinel* (Milwaukee WI), March 28, 1851.

104. Whaley, *Oregon and the Collapse*, 188.

105. "Editorial," *Oregon Spectator* (Oregon City OT), November 11, 1851.

106. "Tired of Oregon," *Daily Scioto Gazette* (Chillicothe OH), May 19, 1853.

107. "For the Statesman," *Oregon Statesman* (Salem OR), July 15, 1851.

108. "Divorce in Oregon," *Vermont Patriot and State Gazette* (Montpelier VT), April 21, 1853.

109. Semple, *Organic and Other General Laws*, 63, 65, 71.

110. Boag, *Environmental and Experience*, 28.

111. For examples of these proposals and laws pertaining to widows' rights, see "Oregon Laws: Article II," *Oregon Spectator* (Oregon City OT), September 12, 1850; "Squatters Rights in Oregon," *Ohio Statesman* (Columbus OH), October 10, 1850 "Oregon Legislature," *Western Star* (Oregon City OR), December 23, 1850.

112. Perry, *Colonial Relations*; Sinha "Gender and Nation," 260; Welke, "Law, Personhood, and Citizenship."

113. Kerber, *No Constitutional Right*, 81–123.

114. *Journal of Council of Oregon*, 27–29; William Allphin to Joseph Lane, November 22, 1852, MS 1146, Joseph Lane Papers.

115. Semple, *Organic and Other General Laws*, 63, 65, 71; "Oregon," *Ohio Statesman* (Columbus OH), October 29, 1851; the Oregon Supreme Court set a legal precedent that land claims taken by a married couple favored the husband's authority in *Vandolf v. Otis* (1854), in which the court ruled that claims made by white husbands and Indigenous wives were still legal because the claim rested on the white husbands' right to land ownership. See Whaley, *Oregon and the Collapse*, 170–71; chapter 5 of this volume.

116. Welke, "Law, Personhood, and Citizenship," 352–54; Greenberg, *Manifest Manhood*, 7. See also Blumin, *Emergence of the Middle Class.*

117. See note 108 as well as Pascoe, *What Comes Naturally*, 95–97; Jones-Rogers, *They Were Her Property*, 28–30.

118. Chused, "Oregon Donation Act," 55–56. Chused suggests that Congress had omitted the section only because they had thought the Oregon territory already had such a law in their statutes that protected "agricultural families," which they did not until 1851.

119. *Oregon Provisional and Territorial Government Records*, indexes 3974, 3954, 3955; *Journal of the House of Representatives of the Territory of Oregon* (1852), 80, 94; "In the Council," *Oregon Statesman* (Salem OR), January 20, 1852.

120. "Laws of Oregon," *Oregon Statesman* (Salem OR), January 27, 1852.

121. Chused, "Oregon Donation Act," 75.

122. The rights of a widow's heirs, however, remained complicated if not entirely unclear. One Oregon settler was denied the claim under his children, who were heirs of his deceased wife. The settler was informed that because his wife had died before the

Land Donation Act was enacted, his children would not receive the claim as heirs. The entire act, however, retroactively recognized claims that settlers had made prior to this federal law. Granted, women did not have separate property rights prior to the act (although widows could claim land); thus when enforced in Oregon, the federal law did not always override existing provisional government laws. For sources on the fact that laws were retroactively applied, see "Amendments to the Land Law—Misapprehension Misrepresentation" *Oregon Statesman* (Salem OR), May 21, 1853; Whaley, "Oregon, Illahee."

123. "State Legislature," *Oregonian* (Portland OT), September 22, 1857.

124. "House," *Oregon Statesman* (Salem OR), September 22, 1857.

125. Whaley, *Oregon and the Collapse*, 189.

126. Boag, *Environmental Experiences*; Johansen, *Empire of the Columbia*; Whaley, *Oregon and the Collapse*, 188.

127. "House," *Oregon Statesman* (Salem OR), September 22, 1857.

128. Kerber, *No Constitutional Right*, 11–15.

129. See Greenberg, *Manifest Manhood*; Kolp, "Women and the Political," 273.

130. "House," *Oregon Statesman* (Salem OR), September 22, 1857.

131. "State Legislature," *Oregonian* (Portland OT), October 10, 1857.

132. "House," *Oregon Statesman* (Salem OR), September 22, 1857.

133. Jones-Rogers, *They Were Her Property*, 35–36.

134. "State Legislature," *Oregonian* (Portland OT), October 10, 1857.

135. Welke, "Law, Personhood, and Citizenship," 352–54; Kerber, *No Constitutional Right*, 16–28.

136. Cong. Globe, 35th Cong., 2nd Sess., 110 (1859).

137. "Another Pioneer Gone," *Umpqua Weekly Gazette* (Scottsburg OT), August 23, 1855.

138. Limerick, *Legacy of Conquest*, 35–54.

139. Cong. Globe, 35th Cong., 2nd Sess., 124 (1859).

140. "Editorial," *Daily Picayune* (New Orleans LA), October 12, 1887.

141. "The Constitution of Oregon," *Atchison Daily Globe* (Atchison KS), June 19, 1882.

142. The Chinese Exclusion Act influenced the racial specifications for the Johnson-Reed Act of 1924, McCarran-Walter Act 1952, and the Hart-Cellar Act of 1965, which led to the repealing the racialized portions of immigration law. See Ngai, *Impossible Subjects*; Aarim-Heriot, *Chinese Immigrants, African Americans.*

143. Swindler, *Sources and Documents*, 4:95.

144. For discussion of women's suffrage in Oregon, see, among many others, Blackwell and Oertel, *Frontier Feminist.*

5. Privileged Right to an Education

1. Mudge, *Sketches of Mission Life*, 143–49.

2. Mudge, *Sketches of Mission Life*, 148.

3. Mudge, *Sketches of Mission Life*, 159–60.

4. Mudge, *Sketches of Mission Life*, 148.

5. Although the term "half breed" should be hyphenated, the Oregon documents from this period did not hyphenate the term when using it, thus it appears unhyphenated hereafter. Russell, *Colonial Frontiers: Indigenous-European Encounters in Settler Societies.*

6. For discussions on missions and missionary-based education in the American West, see, among others, Schreibeis, *Pioneer Education*; Whaley, *Oregon and the Collapse*; David Alan Johnson, *Founding the Far West.*

7. "Society in Oregon," *Oregon Spectator* (Oregon City OT), September 3, 1846.

8. See Ostler, *Plains Sioux*; Findlay, "SPCTEW and Western Colleges," 62; Horsman, *Race and Manifest Destiny*; Whaley, *Oregon and the Collapse*; Limerick, *Legacy of Conquest*; Perry, *On the Edge.*

9. See Kendi, *Stamped from the Beginning*, 81–97; Dain, *Hideous Monster*; Pierce, *Making the White Man's West.*

10. Shah, *Stranger Intimacy*, 9. As did colonizing groups before them, U.S. settlers also identified American Indians' rejection of or perceived incompatibly with Christianity as further validation for the removal of Indigenous communities; Tomlins, *Freedom Bound*, 99–113.

11. Gray, *History of Oregon*, 247.

12. Boag, *Environment and Experience*; Whaley, *Oregon and the Collapse*, 94–150; Cebula, *Plateau Indians*, 83–96.

13. "Methodist Mission at the Oregon," *New York Spectator* (New York NY), March 26, 1838.

14. "Belgian Missionaries for the Oregon," *Ohio Statesman* (Columbus OH), February 9, 1844.

15. J. Quinn Thornton, "Historical Notice of the Colonization of Oregon," *Oregon Spectator* (Oregon City OT), November 1, 1849.

16. Goldstein and Lubin, "Settler Colonialism."

17. Tomlin, *Freedom Bound*, 93–131.

18. "Education," *Oregon Spectator* (Oregon City OT), April 29, 1847.

19. Tomlin, *Freedom Bound*, 359–400.

20. Oregon Emigration Society, *Articles of Agreement*, 1–2.

21. Miller, *Native America*, 115–16; Horsman, *Race and Manifest Destiny*, 86–88.

22. See "The Oregon Territory," *Daily National Intelligencer* (Washington DC), February 15, 1844; "For Oregon," *Oregon Spectator* (Oregon City OT), November 7, 1850, reprinted from the *Cincinnati Gazette*; "Oregon," *Barre Gazette* (Barre MA), November 21, 1845; see also chapter 1.

23. "Mr. Adam's Speech on Oregon," *Oregon Spectator* (Oregon City OT), August 6, 1848.

24. Hyde, *Empires, Nations, and Families*; Johansen, *Empire of the Columbia.*

25. Horsman, *Race and Manifest Destiny*, 89–90.

26. Benton, *Selections of Editorial Articles*, 5–6.

27. Grover, *Oregon Archives*, 163.

28. Grover, *Oregon Archives*, 210.

29. "School Law," *Oregon Spectator* (Oregon City OT); October 18, 1849.

30. "Public Acts—Passed During the Second Session of the Thirty-First Congress," *Daily Cleveland Herald* (Cleveland OH), March 1, 1851.

31. For discussion of national concerns with the behavior of the federal government, see Freeman, *Affairs of Honor*; Prescott, *Gender and Generation*; Greenberg, *Manifest Manhood*.

32. "Slander," *Oregon Spectator* (Oregon City OT), August 19, 1847.

33. "For the Spectator," *Oregon Spectator* (Oregon City OT), May 14, 1846.

34. Johnson, *Founding of the Far West*, 140–85.

35. "Letter to the President," *Western Star* (Oregon City OR), December 12, 1850.

36. "Slander," *Oregon Spectator* (Oregon City OT), August 19, 1847; Johnson, *Founding of the Far West*, 140–85.

37. "Proceedings of the Oregon Legislature," *Oregonian* (Portland OT), January 24, 1857.

38. "State Legislature," *Oregonian* (Portland OT), October 10, 1857.

39. For additional examples of Oregon legislators making this argument and defending the moral image of Oregon, see "House," *Oregon Statesman* (Salem OR), January 13, 1857.

40. Cong. Globe, 35th Cong., 2nd Sess., 980 (1859).

41. Cong. Globe, 35th Cong., 2nd Sess., 110 (1859).

42. Cong. Globe, 35th Cong., 2nd Sess., 169 (1859).

43. Cong. Globe, 35th Cong., 2nd Sess., 988.

44. For discussion of mixed-race marriages between male fur traders and American Indian women in the American West, see Wellman, *Peace*; Whaley, *Oregon and the Collapse*; Van Kirk, *Many Tender Ties*; Brown, J. S. H., *Strangers in Blood*; Within Oregon, "half breed" could also refer to child of a Kanaka or Sandwich Island mother, as these women were sometimes viewed as racially comparable to American Indians.

45. See Hafen, *Mountain Men*; Hine and Faragher, *American West*.

46. The vast number of "half breed" children and American Indian mothers unceremoniously abandoned by white European and American fathers prove that this was not the case; see Van Kirk, *Many Tender Ties*; Brown, *Stranger in Blood*; Whaley, *Oregon and the Collapse*; Perry, *On the Edge*. Fort Vancouver chaplain Herbert Beaver noted in one report to London that "one problem facing the Company was the disposal of the part Indian 'orphans' so often abandoned at the posts"; Jesset, *Reports and Letters*, xxi.

47. Cebula, *Plateau Indians*, 79–32; Hyde, *Empires, Nations, and Families*, 404.

48. See Jesset, *Reports and Letters*, 1–11; these include a letter to McLoughlin that ridiculed American missionaries Narcissa Whitman and Eliza Spalding for attempting to administer education to the children of the fort. Beaver believed that he was the only person capable of giving such instruction to the children.

49. Jesset, *Reports and Letters*, 1–11.

50. McLoughlin's first marriage had also been to an Indigenous woman, an Ojibwe woman and mother of McLoughlin's son Joseph. This first wife had died in childbirth. See Hyde, *Empires, Nations, and Families*, 10–11.

51. Jesset, *Reports and Letters*, 29–31; According to a follow-up report, John McLoughlin assaulted Beaver for insulting Marguerite McLoughlin; see 93–97.

52. Jesset, *Reports and Letters*, 67–89. Oddly, many of the biographies on Dr. John McLoughlin as well as histories of the Pacific Northwest do not address the race of his wife, Marguerite Wadin McKay McLoughlin.

53. "Journal of Mary Richardson Walker, March 5, 1838—October 1848," cage 57, Elkanah and Mary Richardson Walker Papers, Manuscripts, Archives, and Special Collections, Washington State University Libraries, Pullman WA, April 20, 1838.

54. "Journal of Mary Richardson Walker," August 29, 1838. Even when chastising them within the pages of her journal for their actions or behavior, Walker still addressed white women with the title of "Mrs." or "Miss."

55. "Journal of Mary Richardson Walker," August 25, 1838; August 26, 1838.

56. See "Journal of Mary Richardson Walker, March 5, 1838—October 1848."

57. Cebula, *Plateau Indians*, 90–106.

58. For a discussion on a similar type of relationship between missionary women and Indigenous women during the mid-nineteenth century in Hawaii, see Thigpen, *Island Queens and Mission Wives.*

59. Although predominately addressing these relationships in the late nineteenth and early twentieth century, see Stoler, *Carnal Knowledge and Imperial Power*; Jacobs, *White Mother*; Pascoe, *Relations of Rescue*; Deutsch, *No Separate Refuge.*

60. Gray, *History of Oregon*, 243.

61. See Pascoe, *Relations of Rescue*; Jacobs, *White Mother*; Thigpen, *Island Queens and Mission Wives.*

62. Deutsch, *No Separate Refuge*; Cebula, *Plateau Indians*, 110–27.

63. "Journal of Mary Richardson Walker," February 3, 1839.

64. "Journal of Mary Richardson Walker," February 3, 1839; see also Stoler, *Carnal Knowledge and Imperial Power*; Addis, Cameron, "Whitman Massacre," 221–58.

65. "Journal of Mary Richardson Walker," February 3, 1839 and January 6, 1839. Although Narcissa Whitman notes on at least one occasion that a Black American had been associated with the Whitman mission; it is unlikely that the "black breast" belonged to a Black American woman, as records note the presence of American Indian women. See T. C. Elliot, *Coming of the White Women.*

66. Jones-Rogers. *They Were Her Property*, 103, 101–5.

67. Cebula, *Plateau Indians*, 123.

68. Oregon Emigration Society, *Articles of Agreement*, 4.

69. Whaley, *Oregon and the Collapse*, 110.

70. Oregon Emigration Society, *Articles of Agreement*, 15.

71. "From Oregon: Extract of a Letter Dated Wilhamet," *New York Tribune* (New York NY), January 18, 1842.

72. See Mitchell, *General View*; Bowen, *Willamette Valley.*

73. Whaley, *Oregon and the Collapse*, 170.

74. Perry, *Colonial Relations*, 4.

75. Jagodinsky, *Legal Codes and Talking Trees*, 19–92.

76. Grover, *Oregon Archives*, 28.

77. Grover, *Oregon Archives*, 59.

78. Grover, *Oregon Archives*, 163, 210.

79. "Education Law," *Oregon Spectator* (Oregon City OT), January 10, 1850.

80. "Education Law," *Oregon Spectator* (Oregon City OT), January 10, 1850.

81. "Oregon Laws," *Oregon Statesman* (Salem OR), March 14, 1854.

82. "House," *Oregon Statesman* (Salem OR), September 15, 1857.

83. "State Legislature," *Oregonian* (Portland OT), October 3, 1857.

84. "State Legislature," *Oregonian* (Portland OT), October 3, 1857.

85. "House," *Oregon Statesman* (Salem OR), September 15, 1857; Keith, "Unwelcome Settlers," 29–55.

86. "State Legislature," *Oregonian* (Portland OT), October 3, 1857.

87. Asaka, *Tropical Freedom*.

88. Eugene Semple, *Organic and Other General Laws*, 90–91.

89. Swindler, *Sources and Documents*, 4:210.

90. Swindler, *Sources and Documents*, 4:90.

91. "Slavery in Oregon," *Oregon Statesman* (Salem OR), June 9, 1857; reprinted from the *New York Tribune*.

92. Although this generally only applied to children with American Indian mothers, some "half breed" children had mothers with Hawaiian ancestry. See Whaley, *Oregon and the Collapse*.

93. Jun, "Black Orientalism," 1047–66; Hill, "Negro as a Political," 130–45; Pierce, *Making the White Man's West*.

94. For discussion of how marriages between white American men and American Indian women helped Americans gain land in Oregon prior to the cession of said lands by American Indian groups, see Pascoe, *What Comes Naturally*.

95. "An Act to Prohibit the Amalgamation and the Intermarriage of Races," *Oregonian* (Portland OT), November 2, 1866.

96. Whaley, *Oregon and the Collapse*, 168–75; Hyde, *Empires, Nations, and Families*, 55; Simpson, "From White into Red: Captivity Narratives as Alchemies of Race and Citizenship," 251–57.

97. Vandolf v. Otis, 1 Ore. 153, 151–55 (1854).

98. Ostler, *Plains Sioux*.

99. "In the House," *Oregon Statesman* (Salem OR), December 27, 1853.

100. See Tomlin, *Freedom Bound*, 411–31; Wanhalle, "Indigenous Women," 209–32; Simpson, *Mohawk Interruptus*.

101. "In the House," *Oregon Statesman* (Salem OR), December 27, 1853.

102. Jagodinsky, *Legal Codes and Talking Trees*, 31–32.

103. "In the House," *Oregon Statesman* (Salem OR), December 27, 1853.

104. Jagodinsky, "'In Family Way,'" 160–77; Prescott, *Gender and Generation*.

105. Kelley, *Learning to Stand and Speak*.

106. "Oregon Indians," *Ohio Observer* (Hudson OH), November 19, 1840; Cebula, *Plateau Indians*, 96–118. The Spaldings also had a mission school at Lapwai where both Eliza and Henry Spalding taught. West. *Last Indian War*, 44–48.

107. "For the Spectator," *Oregon Spectator* (Oregon City OT), March 19, 1846.

108. Prescott, *Gender and Generation*; Edwards, *Angels in the Machinery*.

109. "Education of Women," *Oregon Spectator* (Oregon City OT), July 10, 1851.

110. Norton, *Liberty's Daughters*; Troen, "Popular Education," 23–40.

111. "Education of Women," *Oregon Spectator* (Oregon City OT), July 10, 1851.

112. "Female School," *Oregon Spectator* (Oregon City OT), January 7, 1847; "Female School," *Oregon Spectator* (Oregon City OT), May 13, 1847.

113. "Education Correspondence," *Daily Cleveland Herald* (Cleveland OH), July 26, 1850.

114. Boag, *Environment and Experience*; Taylor, *In Search*.

115. "Education Correspondence," *Daily Cleveland Herald* (Cleveland OH), July 26, 1850.

116. "Female Teachers in Oregon," *Western Star* (Oregon City OR), February 27, 1851; "Education in California and Oregon," *Vermont Chronicle* (Bellow Falls VT), January 11, 1853.

117. "Female Teachers in Oregon," *Western Star* (Oregon City OR), February 27, 1851.

118. "Female Teachers for Oregon," *Daily Cleveland Herald* (Cleveland OH), March 22, 1851; reprinted from the *New York Commercial*.

119. Whaley, *Oregon and the Collapse*, 182.

120. "From Oregon," *Weekly Herald* (New York NY), December 17, 1853.

121. "From Oregon," *Weekly Herald* (New York NY), December 17, 1853, based on letters the newspaper received from Oregon subscribers.

122. Roth, *Gender and Race*; Compton, "Proper Women/Propertied Women."

123. For discussion of secular education systems in mid-nineteenth-century Oregon and the United States, see Kelley, *Learning to Stand and Speak*; Lange, "Oregon City Public School," 92–108; Lange, "Oregon City Private Schools," 308–28; Troen, "Popular Education," 23–40; Wren, "American Business Philanthropy," 321–46.

124. Lange, "Oregon City Private Schools," 308–28.

125. "Journal of Mary Richardson Walker," July 7, 1838.

126. Jesset, *Reports and Letters*, xiv. McKay's grandmother was half Cree, but he had been raised in the socially elevated position of a white family under the legal coverage of white fathers. Hyde, *Empires, Nations, and Families*, 509.

127. *Oregon Provisional and Territorial Government Records*, index 1500.

128. *Oregon Provisional and Territorial Government Records*, indexes 2892, 3654, 3682.

129. "Education Law," *Oregon Spectator* (Oregon City OT), January 10, 1850.

130. Subscription schools were a type of private education during the mid-nineteenth century, predominately in the Midwest, but the term "subscription school" became more commonly used to describe such institutions in Oregon until after the Civil War. The term was thus retroactively applied to certain religion-based private schools in Oregon. For example, see Eells, *Biography of Rev. G. H. Atkinson*.

131. Lange, "Oregon City Private Schools," 308–28.

132. Gray, *History of Oregon*, 246–47.

133. Hines, *Oregon and Its Institutions*, 160.

134. Hines, *Oregon and Its Institutions*, 160–75.

135. Lange, "Oregon City Public School," 92–95.

136. "For the Spectator," *Oregon Spectator* (Oregon City OT), December 13, 1849. See also, among others, "Editorial," *Western Star* (Oregon City OR), December 19, 1850; "Popular Education," *Umpqua Weekly Gazette* (Scottsburg OT), February 10, 1855.

137. "Education in Oregon," *Oregon Argus* (Oregon City OT), April 22, 1855.

138. Schreibeis, *Pioneer Education*; "Education in Oregon," *Oregon Argus* (Oregon City OT), April 22, 1855; "Popular Education," *Umpqua Weekly Gazette* (Scottsburg OT), February 10, 1855.

139. Findlay, "SPCTEW and Western Colleges," 31–50.

140. "A New England College in Oregon," *Vermont Chronicle* (Bellow Falls VT), July 26, 1859.

141. Byrne, *Co-ordinated Control of Higher Education*, 26–28.

142. "Oregon Legislature," *Oregon Statesman* (Salem OR), September 15, 1857.

143. Swindler, *Sources and Documents*, 7:566, 10:433.

144. See Swindler, *Sources and Documents*.

145. "Oregon Legislature," *Oregon Statesman* (Salem OR), September 15, 1857.

146. "Constitutional Convention," *Oregonian* (Portland OT), October 3, 1857.

147. "Oregon Legislature," *Oregon Statesman* (Salem OR), September 15, 1857.

148. Ashton, *Moulders of Public Opinion*; Schreibeis, *Pioneer Education*.

149. "Constitutional Convention" *Oregonian* (Portland OT), October 3, 1857.

150. *Journal of the House of Representatives of the Territory of Oregon Being the Third Regular Session*, 22.

151. Hyde, *Empires, Nations, Families*; Whaley, *Oregon and the Collapse*; Marschner, *Oregon 1859*.

152. "Correspondence," *Umpqua Weekly Gazette* (Scottsburg OT), February 24, 1855.

153. "Correspondence," *Umpqua Weekly Gazette* (Scottsburg OT), February 24, 1855. In 1856 Oregon legislators also debated whether to divert any funds received from Congress for a public university to the common school funds, but the bill was lost; see *Journal of the House of Representatives of the Territory of Oregon Being the Eighth Regular Session*, 38.

154. Swindler, *Sources and Documents*, 7:407, 1:456.

155. The exception, of course, being slave states with restrictions on the education of slaves, but this was included in state statutes or under an article that addressed the laws of slavery within that specific state.

156. Swindler, *Sources and Documents*, 5:485.

157. Swindler, *Sources and Documents*, 8:395.

158. "Education," *Oregon Spectator* (Oregon City OT), April 29, 1847.

159. "Editorial," *Western Star* (Oregon City OR), December 19, 1850. Other Oregon articles with this perception include, "Education, No. 3," *Oregon Spectator* (Oregon City OT), July 8, 1847; "Education, No. 5," *Oregon Spectator* (Oregon City OT), August 19, 1847; "For the Spectator," *Oregon Spectator* (Oregon City OT), December 13, 1849; "Popular Education," *Umpqua Weekly Gazette* (Scottsburg OT), February 10, 1855; "Correspondence," *Umpqua Weekly Gazette* (Scottsburg OT), February 24, 1855.

160. "Oregon—Her Education Prospects," *Ohio Observer* (Hudson OH), June 21, 1854; reprint of *New York Times* article.

161. See, among others, "Affairs in Oregon," *North American and United States Gazette* (Philadelphia PA), November 4, 1857; "Slavery in Oregon," *North American and United*

States Gazette (Philadelphia PA), February 6, 1857; "A New England College in Oregon," *Vermont Chronicle* (Bellow Falls VT), July 26, 1859; "Collegiate Education in Oregon," *Vermont Chronicle* (Bellow Falls VT), September 6, 1859; "The Pacific University of Oregon," *Boston Daily Advertiser* (Boston MA), May 25, 1859.

162. "Constitutional Convention" *Oregonian* (Portland OT), October 3, 1857.

163. "Oregon Legislature," *Oregon Statesman* (Salem OR), September 15, 1857.

164. "Constitutional Convention," *Oregonian* (Portland OT), October 3, 1857.

165. "Oregon Legislature," *Oregon Statesman* (Salem OR), September 15, 1857.

166. "Oregon Legislature," *Oregon Statesman* (Salem OR), September 15, 1857.

167. Blackhawk, *Violence over the Land.*

168. Kappler, *Indian Affairs*, 2:664, 668, 673, 676, 684.

169. Beckham, *Oregon Indians*, 293–99.

170. See among others, Hoxie, *Final Promise*; Jacobs, *White Mother*; Sarah Deutsch, *No Separate Refuge*; Whaley, *Oregon and the Collapse*; Ostler, *Plains Sioux.*

171. "Educating the Indian," *Boston Daily Advertiser* (Boston MA), May 17, 1882.

172. "Presidential Message," *Daily Inter Ocean* (Chicago IL), December 1, 1879.

173. See Stout, *Native American Boarding Schools*; Hoxie, *Final Promise*; Jacobs, *White Mother*; Adam, *Education for Extinction.*

174. Stout, *Native American Boarding Schools*; see also "The Indian Question," *Daily Cleveland Herald* (Cleveland OH), August 30, 1881; "The President's Message," *Georgia Weekly Telegraph Journal and Messenger* (Macon GA), December 10, 1880. "Educating the Indian," *Boston Daily Advertiser* (Boston MA), May 17, 1882.

175. "The President's Message," *Georgia Weekly Telegraph Journal and Messenger* (Macon GA), December 10, 1880.

176. "Indian Education," *Rocky Mountain News* (Denver CO), November 11, 1882.

177. See Byrne, *Co-ordinated Control of Higher Education.*

178. "A Word for Higher Education in Oregon," *Oregonian* (Portland OT), January 22, 1889.

179. "A Word for Higher Education in Oregon," *Oregonian* (Portland OT), January 22, 1889.

180. See Byrne, *Co-ordinated Control of Higher Education.*

6. Implications of Citizenship

1. "Colored Persons Not Citizens of the United States," *Oregon Argus* (Oregon City OT), January 3, 1857. Likely taken from "Claims of Free Negroes to the Rights of Citizenship," *New York Herald* (New York NY), November 8, 1856.

2. "Colored Persons Not Citizens of the United States," *Oregon Argus* (Oregon City OT), January 3, 1857.

3. "Colored Persons Not Citizens of the United States," *Oregon Argus* (Oregon City OT), January 3, 1857. No follow-up article addressing what had happened to these U.S. actors appeared in the *New York Herald* either; what happened to these stranded Americans remains unclear.

4. See "Claims of Free Negroes to the Rights of Citizenship," *New York Herald* (New York NY), November 8, 1856.

5. Potter, *Impending Crisis*; Isenberg, *Sex and Citizenship*; Holt, *Fate of Their Country*.

6. Grossberg and Tomlins, *Cambridge History of Law*.

7. Whaley, *Oregon and the Collapse*; Ostler, *Plains Sioux*; Hyde, *Empires, Nations, and Families*; Ronda, *Astoria and Empire*; Cebula, *Plateau Indians*.

8. In this instance, as with much of western expansion in North America, the title of "nation-state" applied only to those nations recognized by colonizing powers.

9. Grover, *Oregon Archives*, 12.

10. Grover, *Oregon Archives*, 13.

11. Grover, *Oregon Archives*, 28–32.

12. Grover, *Oregon Archives*, 13.

13. That said, a growing faction of anti-British (more specifically, anti–Hudson's Bay Company) Oregon lawmakers did emerge—they are addressed later in this section.

14. Grover, *Oregon Archives*, 28. The law continues, "Provided, that all persons of the description entitled to vote by the provision of this section, who shall have emigrated to this territory after organization, shall be entitled to the rights of citizens after having resided six months in the territory."

15. Tomlins, *Law, Labor, and Ideology*; Ngai, *Impossible Subjects*.

16. "Congress—Finances—Naturalization Laws—Oregon," *Vermont Watchman and State Journal* (Montpelier VT), December 27, 1844.

17. See Cong. Globe, 35th 1st and 2nd Sess. (1858–59) and 36th Cong., 1st Sess. (1859).

18. S. C. Damon, "A Visit to Oregon," *Daily National Intelligencer* (Washington DC), August 30, 1849; reprinted from the *New York Observer*.

19. Johansen, "Working Hypothesis," 1–12; Boag, *Environment and Experience*.

20. Cong. Globe, 30th Cong., 2nd Sess. 1148 (1848).

21. Semple, *Organic and Other General Laws*, 54.

22. Semple, *Organic and Other General Laws*, 54.

23. "Legal Opinions," *Oregon Spectator* (Oregon City OT), December 4, 1850.

24. "Legal Opinions," *Oregon Spectator* (Oregon City OT), December 4, 1850.

25. Semple, *Organic and Other General Laws*, 64.

26. Hatter, *Citizens of Convenience*.

27. Swindler, *Sources and Documents*.

28. Hyde, *Empires, Nations, and Families*; "For the Oregon Statesman," *Oregon Statesman* (Salem OR), June 8, 1852; Johansen, *Empire of the Columbia*, 127–35.

29. "Editorial," *Oregon Spectator* (Oregon City OT), September 12, 1850; "Editorial," *Oregon Spectator* (Oregon City OT), May 1, 1851. See also Whaley, *Oregon and the Collapse*, 125.

30. "Communications," *Oregon Spectator* (Oregon City OT), March 27, 1851.

31. "Editorial," *Oregon Spectator* (Oregon City OT), September 12, 1850; "Editorial," *Oregon Spectator* (Oregon City OT), May 1, 1851; "For the Oregon Statesman," *Oregon Statesman* (Salem OR), June 8, 1852

32. "Editorial," *Oregon Spectator* (Oregon City OT), September 12, 1850.

33. As McLoughlin had not been seen as eligible for a land claim prior to the Donation Land Act, his claim could not be retroactively granted through the federal act, and white male citizens could claim the land he had previously recorded with provisional officers as his own. "Hudson's Bay Company—The Oregon Land Law," *Oregon Statesman* (Salem OR), July 18, 1854.

34. See "Editorial," *Oregon Spectator* (Oregon City OT), September 12, 1850; Johnson, *John McLoughlin*.

35. According to the inscription on the back of the photograph of McLoughlin, this is a photograph of a painting done by William Cogswell, but the painting was destroyed in 1937 during the "Capital fire."

36. "Legal Opinion," *Oregon Spectator* (Oregon City OT), May 22, 1851.

37. Hyde, *Empires, Nations, and Families*, 406, 508.

38. "Oregon Legislature," *Oregon Statesman* (Salem OR), January 22, 1853; Johannsen. *John McLoughlin*.

39. "Editorial," *Oregon Spectator* (Oregon City OT), September 12, 1850.

40. Cong. Globe, 31st Cong., 1st Sess., Senate (1850).

41. Shubbike Norris to Asahel Bush, MS 581, Asahel Bush Letters.

42. "Native Americanism," *Oregon Statesman* (Salem OR), March 30, 1852.

43. "Native Americanism," *Oregon Statesman* (Salem OR), March 30, 1852. See also "America," *Oregon Statesman* (Salem OR), September 18, 1852. For an explanation of who "Anti-Democrat" groups were, see the introduction of this volume.

44. "G. H. Ambrose to Asahel Bush," MS 581, Asahel Bush Letters.

45. See, for example, "The Knownothings of Oregon," *Umpqua Weekly Gazette* (Scottsburg OT), May 19, 1855; see also Johnson, *Founding the Far West*; Johannsen, *Frontier Politics and the Sectional*.

46. "European Immigration," *Oregon Statesman* (Salem OR), August 26, 1851.

47. For a discussion of anti-British and anti-European sentiments in the American West in conjunction with national perceptions of British and European people during the Antebellum era see, among others, Hayes and Morris, *Manifest Destiny and Empire*.

48. "Our Excuse for Entering the Field," *Oregon Argus* (Oregon City OT), April 21, 1855. Some articles directly attacked Oregon's European immigrants; see, for example, "To the 'Foreigners' of Oregon," *Oregon Argus* (Oregon City OT), May 26, 1855; "Was Jefferson a Know Nothing," *Oregon Argus* (Oregon City OT), May 26, 1855.

49. "Resolved by the Council," *Oregon Statesman* (Salem OR), February 12, 1853.

50. Aarim-Heriot, *Chinese Immigration, African Americans*, 54–62; Carey, *Oregon Constitution and Proceedings*, 468–82.

51. Johannsen, *Frontier Politics and the Sectional*, 51–88.

52. "State Legislature," *Oregonian* (Portland OT), October 3, 1857.

53. "State Legislature," *Oregonian* (Portland OT), October 3, 1857. Delegates also debated whether this different requirement for naturalization would allow an immigrant naturalized by Oregon's suffrage law to receive citizenship in another state.

54. See Swindler, *Sources and Documents*; table 6 of this chapter.

55. "House," *Oregon Statesman* (Salem OR), September 15, 1857.

56. "House," *Oregon Statesman* (Salem OR), September 15, 1857.

57. See chapter 4 of this volume on property ownership.

58. "State Legislature," *Oregonian* (Portland OT), October 3, 1857.

59. "House," *Oregon Statesman* (Salem OR), September 15, 1857.

60. Semple, *Organic and Other General Laws*, 78.

61. Woodward. *Rise and Early History, 1843–68*; Johnson, *Founding of the Far West*; Woodworth, *Manifest Destinies*.

62. Cong. Globe, 35th Cong., 2nd Sess., 973 (1859).

63. Cong. Globe, 35th Cong., 2nd Sess., 123 (1859).

64. Cong. Globe, 35th Cong., 2nd Sess., 969 (1859).

65. Swindler, *Sources and Documents*.

66. See Conlin, *Constitutional Origins*; Freeman, *Field of Blood*.

67. "Oregon," *Weekly Raleigh Register and North-Carolina Gazette* (Raleigh NC), September 14, 1859; a reprint of an article from the *Lynchburg Virginian*.

68. "Oregon—Its Constitution—Its Admission," *Liberator* (Boston MA), March 4, 1859.

69. Not all representatives felt this way, evidenced by those who opposed the immigration restriction of Black Americans, as discussed in chapter 3 of this volume; see also Finkelman, *Slavery and the Founders*; Forbes, *Missouri Compromise*; Litwack, *North of Slavery*.

70. Grover, *Oregon Archives*, 28.

71. Swindler, *Sources and Documents*.

72. See, among others: Berwagner, *Frontier against Slavery*; Taylor, *In Search of a Racial Frontier*.

73. Semple, *Organic and Other General Laws*, 54.

74. *Journal of the House of Representatives of the Territory of Oregon Being the Eighth Regular Session*, 41, 49, 74. See also *Oregon Provisional and Territorial Government Records*.

75. Simpson, *Mohawk Interruptus*, 23. See also chapter 3 of this volume for a discussion of the immigration restriction of Black Americans and chapter 5 of this volume for a detailed discussion of the transition of rights for American Indian women married to white settlers and men identified as "half breed."

76. "Laws of Oregon," *Oregon Statesman*, March 14, 1854.

77. Swindler, *Sources and Documents of United States Constitutions*, 4:168, 7:411.

78. Semple, *Organic and Other General Laws*, 78.

79. *Journal of the House of Representatives of the Territory of Oregon Being the Tenth Regular Session*, 172, 183, 310.

80. Swindler, *Sources and Documents*, 5:310, 1:448–49, 10:421.

81. See Litwack, *North of Slavery*; Morrison, *Slavery and the American West*; Johannsen, "Political Picture," 38–48.

82. For scholarship that addresses the influence of southern politics in the American West, see Smith, *Freedom's Frontier*; Berwagner, *Frontier against Slavery*; Johannsen,

Frontier Politics on the Eve; Hubbart, "'Pro-Southern' Influences," 45–62; Johnson, *Founding the Far West*; Taylor, *In Search of a Racial Frontier*; Hill, "Negro as a Political," 130–45; Pierce, *Making the White Man's West.*

83. Duncan, *Minority without a Champion*, 17; Perry, *On the Edge.*

84. Tomlins, *Law, Labor, and Ideology*; Waldstreicher, *In the Midst.*

85. Burnett, *Recollections and Opinions*, 219.

86. Cong. Globe, 30th Cong., 2nd Sess., 46 (1848).

87. Cong. Globe, 30th Cong., 1st Sess., 1147 (1848).

88. Refer to chapters 2, 3, and 4 of this volume for discussions on Congress's wanting to secure Oregon.

89. Freeman, *Field of Blood*; Forbes, *Missouri Compromise*; Finkelman, *Slavery and the Founders*; Berwagner, *Frontier against Slavery*, 123–37.

90. Swindler, *Sources and Documents*, 7:194. In 1834 the state of Tennessee included the racial specification of "free white male citizen" but also stated, "Provided that no person shall be disqualified from voting in any election on account of color, who is now, by the laws of this State, a competent witness in a court of justice against a white man." See also Litwack, *North of Slavery*; Dain, *Hideous Monster*, 120.

91. Indiana revised its constitutional article on suffrage in 1851 to include a section that cited, "No negro or mulatto shall have the right of suffrage." See Swindler, *Sources and Documents*, 3:380.

92. *Oregon Provisional and Territorial Government Records*, index 3864.

93. See chapter 3 of this volume.

94. "Reader! Let Us Stop and Think," *Oregonian* (Portland OT), April 26, 1856.

95. "Another Platform—The Oregonian in Favor of N— Suffrage," *Oregon Statesman* (Salem OR), May 6, 1856. Although Bush never revealed his name, the advertiser was likely Abner Hunt Francis (a Black American business owner in Portland). For a discussion of Democrats' intentional association of antislavery politicians with Black Americans, see Kendi, *Stamped from the Beginning*, 124–25, 205.

96. "Another Platform—The Oregonian in Favor of N— Suffrage," *Oregon Statesman* (Salem OR), May 6, 1856; For discussion of Abner Hunt Francis, see also Taylor, *In Search of a Racial Frontier*, 88–102.

97. Hill, "Negro as a Political," 130–45.

98. Semple, *Organic and Other General Laws*, 79.

99. "What Black Democracy is," *Oregon Argus* (Oregon City OT), October 11, 1856.

100. "What Black Democracy is," *Oregon Argus* (Oregon City OT), October 11, 1856. See also "January & Council," *Oregon Argus* (Oregon City OT), January 17, 1857; "House," *Oregon Statesman* (Salem OR), January 13, 1857.

101. "House," *Oregon Statesman* (Salem OR), January 13, 1857.

102. For examples of how this court decision was interpreted differently, see Kendi, *Stamped from the Beginning*, 203–5; Conlin, *Constitutional Origins*, 168–74; Taylor, *In Search of a Racial Frontier*; Litwack, *North of Slavery*; Hahn, *Nation under Our Feet.*

103. "House," *Oregon Statesman* (Salem OR), September 15, 1857.

104. Logan believed that the inclusion was necessary to prevent "quarter-blood negroes" (who possessed white blood) from being "entitled to vote," if the qualification only specified "white race." "House," *Oregon Statesman* (Salem OR), September 15, 1857.

105. "State Legislature," *Oregonian* (Portland OT), September 12, 1857.

106. "House," *Oregon Statesman* (Salem OR), September 15, 1857.

107. "House," *Oregon Statesman* (Salem OR), September 15, 1857.

108. Swindler, *Sources and Documents*.

109. For a detailed discussion of slavery debates in Oregon, please see chapter 3 of this volume.

110. "House," *Oregon Statesman* (Salem OR), September 15, 1857. Contributing to the questionable nature of who was "free," Mr. Farrar argued, "It was uncertain who were free. That requirement might exclude the countrymen of Mr. Deady and Mr. McCormick. Irishmen were not free at home. They lived under the worst slavery in the world."

111. "House," *Oregon Statesman* (Salem OR), September 15, 1857.

112. Semple, *Organic and Other General Laws*, 79.

113. See among others, Dain, *Hideous Monster*; Horsman, *Race and Manifest Destiny*; Pierce, *Making the White Man's West*; Taylor, *In Search of a Racial Frontier*; Limerick, *Legacy of Conquest*; Farrington and Bakken, *Racial Encounters*.

114. Swindler, *Sources and Documents*.

115. California did have laws restricting the rights of those with Chinese ancestry, but they did not list this group as excluded from the right of suffrage. See Kwong, *Forbidden Workers*.

116. "Latest News!," *Milwaukee Daily Sentinel* (Milwaukee WI), May 6, 1858.

117. "Debate on the Oregon Bill," *Boston Daily Advertiser*, February 15, 1859.

118. Parker, "Citizenship and Immigration Law," 171.

119. Smith, *Freedom's Frontier*; Lew-Williams, *Chinese Must Go*.

120. "Last Night's Report—Congressional," *Daily Cleveland Herald* (Cleveland OH), May 19, 1858. For additional discussion of Oregon's laws against persons of Chinese descent, see "Chinamen in California," *Ripley Bee* (Ripley OH), May 15, 1858; "Minnesota and Oregon and the Black Republicans," *New York Herald* (New York NY), May 11, 1858; "The Opposition of the Oregon Bill," *Bangor Daily Whig & Courier* (Bangor ME), May 27, 1858; "Debate on the Oregon Bill," *Boston Daily Advertiser* (Boston MA), February 15, 1859; "The Debate on the Oregon Bill," *Daily Citizen and News* (Lowell MA), February 16, 1859.

121. For example, see Ngai, *Impossible Subjects*.

122. For Oregon laws pertaining to a tax on Chinese miners, see *Oregon Provisional and Territorial Government Records*; *Journal of the House of Representatives of the Territory of Oregon Being the Eighth Regular Session*.

123. Swindler, *Sources and Documents*, 9:262, 3:380.

124. Swindler, *Sources and Documents*, 4:154, 168.

125. For example, see, "The Bangor Union Argues for the Rightfulness and Constitutionality of That Provision of the Oregon Constitution which Excludes All Persons of the Colored Race," *Bangor Daily Whig & Courier* (Bangor ME), May 29, 1858; "Minnesota and Oregon and the Black Republicans," *New York Herald* (New York NY), May 11, 1858;

"Why the Oregon Bill is Opposed by Republican Members of Congress," *Milwaukee Daily Sentinel* (Milwaukee WI), January 15, 1859.

126. "Admission of Oregon and Minnesota," *Vermont Patriot and State Gazette* (Montpelier VT), May 21, 1858.

127. Cong. Globe, 35th Cong., 2nd Sess., 169 (1859).

128. Grover, *Oregon Archives*, 28.

129. Isenberg, *Sex and Citizenship*; Kerber, *No Constitutional Right.*

130. Grover, *Oregon Archives*, 12–13.

131. See Varon, *We Mean to Be Counted*; Sklar and Steward *Women's Rights and Transatlantic*; Stansell, *City of Women*; Edwards, *Angels in the Machinery.*

132. Isenberg, *Sex and Citizenship*, 28–38; Prescott, *Gender and Generation.*

133. For discussion about the use of silence, see Boag, *Same-Sex Affairs*; Waldstreicher, *In the Midst.*

134. For discussion on the Equal Rights Amendment, see Kyvig, "Historical Misunderstandings," 45–63; Evans, *Tidal Wave*; Rosen, *World Split Open.*

135. Semple, *Organic and Other General Laws*, 50.

136. "The Election," *Oregon Free Press* (Oregon City OT), June 3, 1848. This had passed only a few months before Oregon's Territorial Government was established, and the amendments in question therefore became part of the Territorial Constitution.

137. "The Election," *Oregon Free Press* (Oregon City OT), June 3, 1848

138. Swindler, *Sources and Documents*, 2:464, 8:388, 7:194, 6:450.

139. Roth. *Gender and Race*; Lasser and Robertson, *Antebellum Women*; Zaeske. *Signatures of Citizenship.*

140. *Oregon Provisional and Territorial Government Records*, index 2759.

141. For example, see "Laws of Oregon," *Oregon Statesman* (Salem OR), March 14, 1854.

142. Semple, *Organic and Other General Laws*, 55.

143. Semple, *Organic and Other General Laws*, 565–68.

144. For further discussion of women in relation to Oregon land laws, see chapter 4 of this volume.

145. See chapter 5 of this volume for further discussion of Oregon women in education. See also Kelley, *Learning to Stand and Speak*; Prescott, *Gender and Generation*; Greenberg, *Manifest Manhood*; Varon, *We Mean to Be Counted*; Edwards, *Angels in the Machinery*; Roth, *Gender and Race.*

146. Letter from Maria Morfitt to Sophie Cornelius, 1859, MS 2968, Locey Family.

147. Letter from Maria Morfitt to Sophie Cornelius, 1859, MS 2968, Locey Family.

148. See Duniway, *Pathbreaking*. See also the "Legacy" section of this chapter.

149. See "State Legislature," *Oregonian* (Portland OT), September 12, 1857; "House," *Oregon Statesman* (Salem OR), September 15, 1857; "State Legislature," *Oregonian* (Portland OT), October 3, 1857.

150. "House," *Oregon Statesman* (Salem OR), September 15, 1857.

151. "House," *Oregon Statesman* (Salem OR), September 15, 1857; "State Legislature," *Oregonian* (Portland OT), October 3, 1857; Carey, *Oregon Constitution and Proceedings*, 318–24.

152. See Cong. Globe, 35th Cong., 1st & 2nd Sess. (1858–59); Zboray and Zboray, *Voices without Votes.*

153. Larson, "Woman Suffrage Movement," 45–50; Christen, "Winning, Losing and Regaining," 45–47; see also *Washington Territory Records*, University of Washington Libraries, Special Collections, Seattle WA.

154. "State Legislature" *Oregonian* (Portland OT), September 12, 1857

155. For this specific reference to the West, see Freeman, *Field of Blood*, 71. See also Freeman, *Affairs of Honor*; Isenberg, *Sex and Citizenship*; Greenberg, *Manifest Manhood*; Rotundo, *American Manhood*; Boag, *Re-dressing America's Frontier*. For a discussion of how politicians argued that "rational thought and self-control" was also out of reach for nonwhite men, see Pierce, *Making the White Man's West*, 40.

156. "State Legislature" *Oregonian* (Portland OT), October 3, 1857.

157. See Swindler, *Sources and Documents.*

158. "House," *Oregon Statesman* (Salem OR), September 15, 1857.

159. "State Legislature," *Oregonian* (Portland OT), October 3, 1857.

160. Carey, *Oregon Constitution and Proceedings*, 404.

161. "Address of L. B. Cox—His Tribute Paid to the Constitution of Oregon," *Oregonian* (Portland OT), February 15, 1899.

162. For a discussion of why this had occurred, see Brooks, "Race, Politics, and Denial."

163. Semple, *Organic and Other General Laws*, 565–70.

164. Additionally, Oregon repealed its ratification of the Fourteenth Amendment, which is why the state had to reratify the amendment in 1959.

165. Foner, *Second Founding*; Smith, *Freedom's Frontier*; Richardson, *West from Appomattox*.

166. "That Constitution—The Anti-Black Law Constitution of Oregon—It Gets Another Ventilation," *Atchison Daily Globe* (Atchison KS), January 20, 1891.

167. "A Black Law in Oregon," *New York Age* (New York NY), January 24, 1891; reprinted from the *San Francisco Sentinel.*

168. Oregonians attempted to combat the usage of their constitution by southern politicians. For example, an editorial argued, "The negro is excluded from the franchise by the constitution of Oregon, but he enjoys that and all political rights here, under the constitution of the United States. In Mississippi, the negro is entitled to the franchise under the federal constitution, but it is denied him by the white minority, who deliberately annul that provision of the organic law. This is the difference between the two states." "No Title," *Oregonian* (Portland OT), January 20, 1891.

169. Smith, *Presumptuous Dreamers.*

170. "Women Voting in Oregon," *North American and United States Gazette* (Philadelphia PA), January 12, 1872.

171. "Women Voting in Oregon," *North American and United States Gazette* (Philadelphia PA), January 12, 1872.

172. The article suggests that the women's ballots had been collected and placed in a "separate" register.

173. "Letter from Maria Morfitt to Sophie Cornelius," 1859, in the Locey family's possession.

174. Prescott, *Gender and Generation*; Greenberg, *Manifest Manhood*; Smith, *Presumptuous Dreamers*; Duniway, *Pathbreaking*.

175. Terborg-Penn, *African American Women*; Smith, *Presumptuous Dreamers*; Duniway, *Pathbreaking*; Materson, *For the Freedom*.

Conclusion

Epigraph: "House," *Oregon Statesman* (Salem OR), January 20, 1857. Smith was discussing the presence of free or enslaved Black Americans in Oregon and what the future state proposed to do about the slavery issue.

1. Jesse Applegate to Asahel Bush, November 18, 1855, MS 581, Asahel Bush Letters. Applegate never noted a last name for Louis, only referring to him as "Louis" throughout the letter to Bush.

2. Letter from Jesse Applegate to Asahel Bush, November 18, 1855, MS 581, Asahel Bush Letters.

3. Letter from Jesse Applegate to Asahel Bush, November 18, 1855, MS 581, Asahel Bush Letters.

4. See "Umpqua Correspondent," *Oregon Statesman* (Salem OR), October 31, 1855. Due to the fact that subsequent articles pertaining to the prosecution of American Indians did not provide individuals' names, especially when the trial included a group, it is unclear what exactly came of Louis.

5. Cong. Globe, H.R., 35th Cong., 1st Sess., 976 (1859).

6. "Savanna's Act," 116th Cong., 1st Sess., Senate, Stat. 227 (2019).

7. Rosay, "Violence against American Indian," 38–45.

8. "Savanna's Act," 116th Cong., 1st Sess., Senate, Stat. 227 (2019).

9. Rowe, "Leaving Her Mark: Native High Schooler Uses State Track Meet to Raise Awareness for Missing and Murdered Women," *Spokesman-Review* (Spokane WA), May 30, 2019.

10. "Robbery," *Oregon Spectator* (Oregon City OT), September 12, 1850.

11. "What the Present Legislature Finds to Do," *Oregonian* (Portland OT), January 6, 1855.

12. For a select example of this scholarship, see Toll, "Progress and Piety," 75–85; Pearson, "'Menace to the Neighborhood,'" 158–79; Trevor Griffey, "History of the KKK in Washington State," Seattle Civil Rights and Labor History Project, accessed May 16, 2020, https://depts.washington.edu/civilr/kkk_history.htm; Kristin Dimick, "The Klu Klux Klan and the Anti-Catholic School Bills of Washington and Oregon," Seattle Civil Rights and Labor History Project, accessed May 16, 2020, https://depts.washington.edu/civilr/kkk_i49.htm; Horowitz, "'Cross of Culture'"; Jason Morgan Ward, "Civil Rights and Anti-Black Violence in America and Oregon," presentation with Darrell Millner, April 13, 2018, Oregon Historical Society Public Lecture Series, https://www.ohs.org/events/civil-rights-and-anti-black-violence.cfm; Gill, "Idaho's 'Aryan' Education,"159–77; "30 Years

after Skinheads Beat to Death Immigrant on Portland Street, City Reflects," *Oregonian* (Portland OT), January 29, 2019, https://www.oregonlive.com/portland/2018/11/30_years_after_skinheads_beat.html.

13. For examples of Oregon's racial legacy and its title as the "whitest city in America," see Keegan Stephan, "Portland Isn't Portlandia. It's a Capital of White Supremacy," *Washington Post*, June 1, 2017; Tai Harden-Moore, "The Tale of Two Portlands: The Whitest and Arguably Most Racist City in America," *Huffington Post*, May 30, 2017.

14. Jim Ryan, "2 Killed in Stabbing on MAX Train in Northeast Portland as Man Directs Slurs at Muslim women, Police Say," *Oregonian* (Portland OT), May 26, 2017, https://www.oregonlive.com/portland/2017/05/police_responding_to_ne_portla.html; Matthew Haag and Jacey Fortin, "Two Killed in Portland While Trying to Stop Anti-Muslim Rant, Police Say," *New York Times*, May 27, 2017, https://www.nytimes.com/2017/05/27/us/portland-train-attack-muslim-rant.html; Laurel Wamsley, "White Supremacist Charged with Killing 2 in Portland, Ore., Knife Attack," *The Two Way*, NPR, May 27, 2017, https://www.npr.org/sections/thetwo-way/2017/05/27/530351468/2-dead-1-injured-after-stabbing-in-portland-ore; Maxine Bernstein, "Man Accused in MAX Attack Confessed to Stabbing, Said, 'I'm Happy Now. I'm Happy Now,'" *Oregonian* (Portland OT), January 9, 2019, https://www.oregonlive.com/portland/2017/05/man_accused_in_max_attack_cont.html.

15. Examples of national coverage: Madison Park and Stephanie Becker, "Portland Train Suspect: 'I Hope Everyone I Stabbed Died,'" CNN, May 31, 2017, https://www.cnn.com/2017/05/31/us/portland-train-stabbing-what-happened/index.html; Nate Hanson, "Portland Suspect in Courtroom Rant: 'You Call It Terrorism. I Call It Patriotism!,'" *USA Today*, May 31, 2017, https://www.usatoday.com/story/news/nation-now/2017/05/30/portland-train-stabbing-suspect/353963001/; "Portland: Race Against the Past," CBSN Originals, aired October 30, 2017, https://www.cbsnews.com/video/portlands-racist-past-explains-its-violent-present/; "Portland Train Murders Highlight Oregon's History of White Supremacy," *All Things Considered*, NPR, https://www.npr.org/2017/05/30/530769807/portland-train-murders-highlight-oregons-history-of-white-supremacy; Paul Vercammen and Holly Yan, "Portland's Liberal Image Tempered by History as 'Skinhead City,'" CNN, https://www.cnn.com/2017/05/31/us/portland-white-supremacy-history/index.html.

16. "Jerry Christian Convicted of Killing Men Who Intervened in his Hate Tirade on Portland Train," CBS News, February 21, 2020, https://www.cbsnews.com/news/jeremy-christian-convicted-of-killing-men-who-intervened-in-his-hate-tirade-on-portland-train-2020-02-21/.

17. "Ladies in Oregon," *Daily Cleveland Herald* (Cleveland OH), July 12, 1851.

18. Duniway, *Pathbreaking*; Jensen, "'Neither Head nor Tail,'" 350–83; "Oregon and the 19th Amendment," National Park Service (website), https://www.nps.gov/articles/oregon-and-the-19th-amendment.htm.

19. Bryan M. Vance, "The Governor Who Couldn't Vote: Why History Forgot Oregon's 1st Female Head of State," *Oregon Public Broadcasting*, February 28, 2019, https://www.opb.org/article/2019/02/27/carrie-b-shelton-chamberlain-oregon-governor-history/.

20. Noting this current situation in Oregon politics, see Rachel Monahan, "Oregon State Government Already Led by Women Adds One More Woman," *Willamette Week*, March 29, 2019, https://www.wweek.com/news/state/2019/03/29/oregon-state-government-already-led-by-women-adds-one-more-woman/.

21. Although "Mom jeans" have been associated with Obama since 2008, in March 2014 *Fox News Channel* correspondent Sarah Palin (2008 Republican vice-presidential nominee) discussed Obama's "Mom jeans" with colleague Sean Hannity on air. Eric Brown, "Sarah Palin: Putin Is Out 'Wrestling Bears' while Obama is Wearing 'Mom Jeans,'" March 4, 2014, *International Business Times*, https://www.ibtimes.com/sarah-palin-putin-out-wrestling-bears-while-obama-wearing-mom-jeans-1559337.

22. Brown, "Sarah Palin." See also CNN Political Unit, "Obama Wants People to Quit Bashing His Jeans," accessed February 9, 2015, http://politicalticker.blogs.cnn.com/2014/03/14/; Connor Simpson, "Obama's Mom Jeans: A Wire Investigation," *Wire*, March 14, 2014, https://www.theatlantic.com/politics/archive/2014/03/obamas-mom-jeans-wire-investigation/359189/; Ben Wolfgang, "Obama: Michelle Got Rid of My 'Mom Jeans,'" *Washington Times*, May 22, 2014, https://www.washingtontimes.com/news/2014/may/22/obama-michelle-got-rid-of-my-mom-jeans/.

23. For examples of a discussion of gendered rhetoric and dress in contemporary U.S. politics, see Anderson, "From Spouses to Candidates"; Juliana Menasce Horowitz, and Ruth Igielnik, and Kim Parker, "Women in Leadership 2018: Wide Gender and Party Gaps in Views about the State of Female Leadership and the Obstacles Women Face," Social and Demographic Trends, Pew Research Center, September 20, 2018, https://www.pewsocialtrends.org/2018/09/20/women-and-leadership-2018/; Rohina Katoch Sehra, "For Women in Politics, Personal Style Is a Game of Chess with the Patriarchy," *Huffington Post*, last updated December 9, 2019, https://www.huffpost.com/entry/women-politics-dress-code-patriarchy_l_5d8ba3d6e4b01c02ca627f9c; Parry-Giles and Parry-Giles, "Gendered Politics and Presidential Image."

24. Faragher, "Settler Colonial Studies," 181–91. For an example of this research in British Colombia history, see Edmonds, "Unpacking Settler Colonialism's Urban Strategies," 4–20; Egan, "Toward Shared Ownership," 33–50.

25. See Copland, *Burden of Empire*; Getz and Streets-Salter, *Modern Imperialism and Colonialism*; Harris, "How Did Colonialism Dispossess?," 165–82.

26. For examples of scholarship that has started this process, see Thigpen, *Island Queens and Mission Wives*; Lyndon, *Anti-Chinese Movement*; Kauanui, "Colonialism in Equality," 636–50.

27. For examples of scholarship that has engaged in this process, see Jacobs, *White Mother*; Asaka, *Tropical Freedom*; Good, "Settler Colonialism," 597–620; Lester, "Reformulating Identities," 515–31.

Bibliography

Archival Materials

Oregon Historical Society Research Library, Portland OR.

Applegate Family Papers, MS 233.

Asahel Bush Letters, 1850–1908, MS 581.

Barker-Adair Family Papers, 1762–1967, MS 1131.

"Case Files for *Vanderpool vs. Magruder*, 1851," Philip Foster Collection, MS 996.

Delazon Smith Family Papers, coll. 26.

Ellendale Woolen Mills Records, MS 1169.

George Law Curry, 1848–77, MS 700.

Grover, La Fayette, *The Oregon Archives: Including Journals, Governors' Messages, and Public Papers of Oregon*. Salem OR: Asahel Bush, Public Papers of Oregon, 1853.

Hugh O'Bryant Papers, MS 1856.

John McCraken Papers, MS 2540.

John McLoughlin to Alex H. H. Stewart, 1851 July 15, MS 15000.

Joseph Lane Papers, MS 1146.

Journal of the House of Representatives of the Territory of Oregon Being the Third Regular Session of the Legislative Assembly, Begun and Held at Salem, December 1st, 1851. Salem OR: Asahel Bush, Territorial Printer, 1852.

Journal of Council of Oregon of the Territory of Oregon, during the Session of the Legislative Assembly, Begun and Held at Salem, December 6, 1852. Salem OR: Asahel Bush, Public Printer, 1853.

Journal of the Council of the Legislative Assembly of the Territory of Oregon, during the Fifth Annual Session, Begun and Held at Salem, 5th of December, 1853. Salem OR: Asahel Bush, Territorial Printers, 1854.

Journal of the House of Representatives of the Territorial of Oregon during the Sixth Regular Session of the Legislative Assembly, Begun and Held at Salem, December 4, 1854. Corvallis OR: Asahel Bush, Territorial Printer, 1855.

Journal of the House of Representatives of the Territory of Oregon: During the Seventh Regular Session, from Dec. 3, 1855, to Jan. 31, 1856. Salem OR: Asahel Bush, Territorial Printer, 1856.

Journal of the House of Representatives of the Territory of Oregon Being the Eighth Regular Session 1856–7. Salem OR: Asahel Bush, Territorial Printer, 1857.
Journal of the Ninth Regular Session of the House of Representatives of the Territory of the Legislative Assembly of Oregon Territory, Commencing December 7th, 1857. Salem OR: Asahel Bush, Territorial Printer, 1857.
Journal of the House of Representatives of the Territory of Oregon Being the Tenth Regular Session, 1858–9. Salem OR: Asahel Bush, Territorial Printer: 1859.
Journal of the House of Representatives of the Territory of Oregon. Salem OR: Asahel Bush, Territorial Printer, 1852–56.
La Fayette Grover Papers, MS 1069.
Locey Family Papers, 1858–1924, MS 2968.
Matthew P. Deady Papers, MS 48.
McLoughlin-Fraser Family Papers, 1796–1964, MS 927.
Oregon Provisional and Territorial Government Records Access Project, 1990, microfilm 020257, Oregon State Archives.
Orville C. Pratt, 1839–88, MS 426.
The Papers of Jason Lee, MS 1212.
Shubrick Norris Papers, 1849–66, MS 917.
Thurston Family Papers, 1838–87, MS 379.
Wall, Florence. "The Letters of Asahel Bush to Matthew Deady, 1851–1863," vault 979.105 B978w (1941).
Washington Hall Papers, 1848–51, MS 944.
Washington State University Libraries Manuscripts, Archives, and Special Collections, Pullman WA.
Cushing and Myra Fairbanks Eells Papers, cage 148.
Elkanah and Mary Richardson Walker Papers, cage 57.
Marcus and Narcissa Whitman Papers, cage 142.

Newspapers

Newspapers were extensively used in this book to understand how people throughout the nation discussed laws, politics, and social issues in Oregon. Additionally, many of the Oregon newspapers used were accessed through microfilm at the Oregon Historical Society Research Library. Town names and state or territorial abbreviations were also included to help identify specific newspapers, as many publications had short-lived runs, changed names, or moved to different locations during the mid-nineteenth century.

Atchison Daily Globe (Atchison KS)
Bangor Daily Whig & Courier (Bangor ME)
Barre Gazette (Barre MA)
Boston Daily Advertiser (Boston MA)
Boston Investigator (Boston MA)
Daily Atlas (Boston MA)
Daily Citizen and News (Lowell MA)
Daily Cleveland Herald (Cleveland OH)
Daily Evening Bulletin (San Francisco CA)
Daily Inter Ocean (Chicago IL)
Daily National Intelligencer (Washington DC)
Daily National Journal (Washington DC)

Daily Picayune (New Orleans LA)
Daily Scioto Gazette (Chillicothe OH)
Fayetteville Observer (Fayetteville NC)
Georgia Weekly Telegraph Journal and Messenger (Macon GA)
The Globe (Washington DC)
Kansas Herald of Freedom (Wakarusa KS)
The Liberator (Boston MA)
Louisiana Advertiser (New Orleans LA)
Maryland Gazette and Political Intelligencer (Annapolis MD)
Milwaukee Daily Sentinel (Milwaukee WI)
Mississippian (Oxford MS)
Mississippian and State Gazette (Jackson MS)
Missouri Republican (St. Louis MO)
Mountaineer (Waynesville NC)
Nebraskian (Omaha NT)
Newark Advocate (Newark OH)
New Hampshire Statesman and State Journal (Concord NH)
The New York Age (New York NY)
New York Herald (New York NY)
New York Spectator (New York NY)
New York Tribune (New York NY)
North American and United States Gazette (Philadelphia PA)
The North Star (Rochester NY)
Occidental Messenger (Corvallis OT)
Ohio Observer (Hudson OH)
Ohio Statesman (Columbus OH)
Oregon Argus (Oregon City OT)
Oregon Free Press (Oregon City OT)
Oregonian (Portland OT)
Oregon Sentinel (Jacksonville OT)
Oregon Spectator (Oregon City OT)
Oregon Statesman (Salem OR)
Pittsfield Sun (Pittsfield MA)
Providence Patriot and Columbian Phenix (Providence RI)
The Ripley Bee (Ripley OH)
Rocky Mountain News (Denver CO)
San Francisco Herald (San Francisco CA)
Supporters and Scioto Gazette (Chillicothe OH)
Table Rock Sentinel (Jacksonville OT)
Umpqua Weekly Gazette (Scottsburg OT)
Vermont Chronicle (Bellow Falls VT)
Vermont Patriot and State Gazette (Montpelier VT)
Vermont Watchman and State Journal (Montpelier VT)
The Weekly Herald (New York NY)
Weekly Raleigh Register and North-Carolina Gazette (Raleigh NC)
Weekly Times (Portland OT)
Western Star (Oregon City OR)

Published Works

Aarim-Heriot, Najia. *Chinese Immigrants, African Americans, and Racial Anxiety in the United States, 1848–1882*. Urbana: University of Illinois Press, 2003.

Adam, David Wallace. *Education for Extinction: American Indians and the Boarding School Experience, 1875–1928*. Lawrence: University of Kansas Press, 1995.

Addis, Cameron. "The Whitman Massacre: Religion and Manifest Destiny on the Columbia Plateau, 1809–1858." *Journal of the Early Republic* 25, no. 2 (Summer 2005): 221–58.

Anderson, Karrin Vasby. "From Spouses to Candidates: Hillary Rodham Clinton, Elizabeth Dole, and the Gendered Office of the U.S. President." *Rhetoric & Public Affairs* 5, no. 1 (Spring 2002): 105–32.

"Annual Report of Joel Palmer, Superintendent of Indian Affairs for Oregon Territory for 1853, Proposing the Reservation System." Office of the Secretary of Interior. Washington DC: U.S. Government Printing Office, 1853.

Aron, Stephen. "Returning the West to the World." *OHA Magazine of History* 20, no. 2 (March 2006): 53–60.

Asaka, Ikuko. *Tropical Freedom: Climate, Settler Colonialism, and Black Exclusion in the Age of Emancipation*. Durham NC: Duke University Press, 2017.

Ashton, Dion. *Moulders of Public Opinion: Oregon Newspapers and the Question of Statehood, 1850–1857*. Surrey UK: Ashton Dion, 1992.

Atcheson, Nathaniel. *American Encroachments on British rights: Or, Observations on the Importance of the British North American Colonies and on the Late Treaties with the United States: With Remarks on Mr. Baring's Examination and a Defense of the Shipping Interest from the Charge of Having Attempted to Impose on Parliament*. London: A. J. Valpy, 1815.

Baldy, Cutcha Risling. *We Are Dancing for You: Native Feminisms and the Revitalization of Women's Coming-of-Age Ceremonies*. Seattle: University of Washington Press, 2018.

Ballantyne, Tony, and Antoinette Burton, eds. *Bodies in Contact: Rethinking Colonial Encounters in World History*. Durham NC: Duke University Press, 2005.

Bancroft, Hubert Howe. *The Works of Hubert Howe Bancroft, Volume XXX, History of Oregon, 1848–1888*. Vol. 2. San Francisco: History Company, 1888.

Barkan, Elliot Robert. *From All Points: America's Immigrant West, 1870–1952*. Bloomington: Indiana University Press, 2007.

Basso, Matthew, Laura McCall, and Dee Garceau, eds. *Across the Great Divide: Cultures of Manhood in the American West*. New York: Routledge, 2001.

Baum, Dale. "Know-Nothingism and the Republican Majority in Massachusetts: The Political Realignment of the 1850s." *Journal of American History* 64, no. 4 (March 1978): 959–86.

Beck, David R. "'Standing Out Here in the Surf': The Termination and Restoration of the Coos, Lower Umpqua and Siuslaw of Western Oregon in Historical Perspective." *Oregon Historical Quarterly* 110, no. 1 (Spring 2009): 6–37.

Beckham, Stephen Dow, ed. *Oregon Indians: Voices from Two Centuries*. Corvallis: Oregon State University, 2006.

———. *Requiem for a People: The Rogue River Indians and the Frontiersmen*. Norman: University of Oklahoma Press, 1971.

Bederman, Gail. *Manliness & Civilization: A Cultural History of Gender and Race in the United States, 1880–1917*. Chicago: University of Chicago Press, 1995.

Beeson, John. *A Plea for the Indians: With Facts and Features of the Late War in Oregon*. New York: John Beeson, 1858.

Belich, James. *Replenishing the Earth: The Settler Revolution and the Rise of the Anglo-World*. Oxford: Oxford University Press, 2009.

Bemis, Samuel Flagg. *John Quincy Adams and the Foundations of American Foreign Policy*. New York: Alfred A. Knopf, 1949.

Bender, Thomas. *Rethinking American History in a Global Age*. Berkeley: University of California Press, 2002.

Benton, Lauren. *Law and Colonial Cultures: Legal Regimes in World History, 1400–1900*. Cambridge UK: Cambridge University Press, 2002.

Benton, Thomas Hart. *Selections of Editorial Articles from the St. Louis Enquirer on the Subject of Oregon and Texas: As Originally Published in That Paper in the Years 1818–19, and Written by Hon. Thomas H. Benton, To Which Is Annexed, His Speech in the Senate of the United States in March, 1825, on the Bill for the Occupation of the Columbia River*. St. Louis MO: Missourian Office, 1844.

Bergquist, James M. "The Oregon Donation Act and the National Land Policy." *Oregon Historical Quarterly* 58, no. 1 (March 1957): 17–35.

Berwagner, Eugene H. *The Frontier against Slavery: Western Anti-Negro Prejudice and the Slavery Extension Controversy*. Chicago: University of Illinois Press, 1967.

Bingham, John Armor. *Admission of Oregon: Speech of Hon. John A. Bingham, of Ohio, Delivered in the House of Representatives, February 11, 1859*. Washington DC: Buell and Blanchard, 1859.

Blackhawk, Ned. *Violence over the Land: Indians and Empires in the Early American West*. Cambridge MA: Harvard University Press, 2006.

Black, Jeremy. *Fighting for America: The Struggle for Mastery in North America, 1519–1871*. Bloomington: Indiana University Press, 2011.

Blackwell, Marilyn S., and Kristen T. Oertel. *Frontier Feminist: Clarina Howard Nichols and the Politics of Motherhood*. Lawrence: University Press of Kansas, 2010.

Block, Sharon. *Rape and Sexual Power in Early America*. Chapel Hill: University of North Carolina Press, 2006.

Boag, Peter. *Environment and Experience: Settlement Culture in Nineteenth-Century Oregon*. Berkeley: University of California Press, 1992.

———. *Re-Dressing America's Frontier Past*. Berkeley: University of California Press, 2011.

———. *Same-Sex Affairs: Constructing and Controlling Homosexuality in the Pacific Northwest*. Berkeley: University of California Press, 2003.

Bolster, Jeffrey W. *Black Jacks: African American Seamen in the Age of Sail*. Cambridge MA: Harvard University Press, 1997.

Bowen, William A. *The Willamette Valley: Migration and Settlement on the Oregon Frontier*. Seattle: University of Washington Press, 1978.

Boyd, Robert. *The Coming of the Spirit of Pestilence: Introduced Infectious Diseases and Population Decline among Northwest Coast Indians, 1774–1874*. Seattle: University of Washington, 1999.

Brooks, Cheryl A. "Race, Politics, and Denial: Why Oregon Forgot to Ratify the Fourteenth Amendment." *Oregon Law Review* 83 (February 2004): 731–62.

Brown, J. Henry. *Brown's Political History of Oregon*. Portland OR: Wiley B. Allen, 1892.

Brown, Jennifer S. H. *Strangers in Blood: Fur Trade Company Families in Indian Country*. Norman: University of Oklahoma, 1996.

Brown, Kathleen M. *Good Wives, Nasty Wenches, and Anxious Patriarchs: Gender, Race, and Power in Colonial Virginia*. Chapel Hill: University of North Carolina Press, 1996.

Bruyneel, Kevin. "Exiled, Executed, Exalted: Louis Riel, 'Homo Sacer' and the Production of Canadian Sovereignty." *Canadian Journal of Political Science* 43, no. 3 (September 2010): 711–32.

Burnett, Peter H. *Recollections and Opinions of an Old Pioneer*. New York: D. Appleton, 1880.

Burns, R. Ignatius. "A Bancroft Library Manuscript on the 1858 Indian War." *Oregon Historical Quarterly* 52, no. 1 (1951): 54–57.

Buss, James Joseph. *Winning the West with Words: Language and Conquest in the Lower Great Lakes*. Norman: University of Oklahoma Press, 2011.

Byrne, Charles David. *Co-ordinated Control of Higher Education in Oregon*. Redwood City CA: Stanford University Press, 1968.

Carbado, Devon W. "Racial Naturalization." *American Quarterly* 57, no. 3 (September 2005): 633–58.

Carey, Charles. *The Oregon Constitution and Proceedings and Debates of the Constitutional Convention of 1857*. Salem OR: State Printing Department, 1926.

Cebula, Larry. *Plateau Indians and the Quest for Spiritual Power, 1700–1850*. Lincoln: University of Nebraska Press, 2003.

Chused, Richard H. "The Oregon Donation Act of 1850 and Nineteenth Century Federal Married Women's Property Law." *Law and History Review* 2, no. 1 (Spring 1984): 44–78.

Clinton, Catherine. *The Plantation Mistress: Woman's World in the Old South*. New York: Pantheon Books, 1982.

Coan, C. F. "The Adoption of the Reservation Policy in the Pacific Northwest, 1853–1855." *Oregon Historical Quarterly* 23, no. 1 (March 1922): 1–38.

———. "The First Stage of the Federal Indian Policy in the Pacific Northwest, 1849–1852." *Oregon Historical Quarterly* 23, no. 1 (March 1922): 46–89.

Colonial Office, Great Britain. *Account Showing the Grants, Endowments and Appropriations Made for the Purpose of Religious Instruction or of Education in the Colonies: Stating the Particular Objects of Each of Such Grants, Endowments or Appropriations, for the Years 1840, 1841, and 1842, Including All Grants, Appropriations, or Endowments, Whether Made under the Authority of the Crown, of Parliament, or the Colonial Governments (So Far As the Returns Can Be Made Up in This Country)*. London: Colonial Office, 1845.

Congressional Globe, 14th–36th Cong. 1st–2nd Sess.

"Boundary on the Pacific Ocean. Message from the President of the United States, Transmitting the Correspondence with the British Government, in Relation to the Boundary of the United States on the Pacific Ocean." *Congressional Globe*. 19th Cong., 1st Sess. Doc. No. 65, HR Executive. 30–37, January 31, 1826.

"Correspondence with the British Government Relative to the Boundary of the United States on the Pacific Coast," *Congressional Globe*. 19th Cong., 1st Sess., No. 417, 790–97, January 31, 1826.

"The Committee to Who 'So Much of the Message of the President of the United States as Respects the Establishment of a Military Post at the Mouth of the Columbia River, and the Expediency of Providing for the More Perfect Exploring of the Northwest Coast of America' Was Referred, Report." *Congressional Globe*. 19th Cong., 1st Sess., Report 35, at 156, January 16, 1826.

"Department of State on Oregon." *Congressional Globe*. 31st Cong., 1st Sess., Senate., 2, May 13, 1850.

"Doc. No. 65." *Congressional Globe*. 19th Cong., 1st Sess., 8, January 31, 1826.

"Hunters of Oregon. Memorial of James M. Bradford and Others." *Congressional Globe*. 20th Cong., 2nd Sess., Doc. No. 13, HR, 126–92, 1829.

"Message from the President of the United States, Communicating Information Relative to Indian Hostilities in the Territories of Oregon and Washington." *Congressional Globe*. 34th Cong., 1st Sess., Ex. Doc. No. 93., at 1–144, April 17, 1856.

"Message from the President of the United States, in Answer to a Resolution of the Senate, Calling for Further Information in Relation to the Formation of a State Government in California; and Also, in Relation to the Condition of Civil Affairs in Oregon." *Congressional Globe*. 31st Cong. 1st Sess., Ex. Doc. 52, at 349–50, May 22, 1850.

"Message of the President of the United States, in Relation to the Indian Difficulties in Oregon." *Congressional Globe*. 30th Cong., 1st Sess., Ex. No. 47., at 3–14, March 29, 1848.

"Mr. Lane Submitted for Consideration in the Following Resolutions." *Congressional Globe*. 36th Cong., 2nd Sess., Mis. Doc. No. 4., 1861.

"Norwest Coast of America. The Committee to Who 'So Much of the Message of the President of the United States As Respects the Establishment of a Military Post at the Mouth of the Columbia River, and the Expediency of Providing for the More Perfect Exploring of the Northwest Coast of America' Was Referred, Report Further." *Congressional Globe*. 19th Cong. 1st Sess., Report 213, 156, May 15, 1826.

"Of the Select Committee, Appointed on the 10th Ultimo, to Inquire Into the Expediency of Occupying the Colombia River, and to Regulate the Intercourse with the Indian Tribes; Accompanied with a Bill to Authorize the Occupation of the Columbia River." *Congressional Globe*. 17th Cong. 1st Sess., Report 18, 161, January 18, 1822.

"Of the Select Committee, Appointed on the 29th of December Last, with Instruction to Inquire into the Expediency of Occupying the Mouth of the Columbia River." *Congressional Globe*. 18th Cong., 1st Sess., Report 110, 2345–46, April 15, 1824.

"Review of the Select Committee to Establish a Territorial Government in Oregon." *Congressional Globe*. 30th Cong., 1st Sess., Senate, 323–31, July 18, 1848.

"The Select Committee, To Which Was Referred a Bill to Authorize the President of the United States to Occupy the Oregon Territory, Submit to the Consideration of the Senate the Following Report." *Congressional Globe*. 25th Cong., 2nd Sess., Senate., 445, June 6, 1838.

"Settlement on the Oregon River. Memorial of Citizens of the United States, Praying for a Grant of Land, and the Aid of the Government in Forming a Colony on the Northwest Coast of the United States." *Congressional Globe*. 20th Cong., 1st Sess., Doc. No. 139, HR, 280, February 11, 1828.

The Colonizationist and the Journal of Freedom. Boston: Geo. W. Light, 1834.

Conlin, Michael F. *The Constitutional Origins of the American Civil War*. Cambridge UK: Cambridge University Press, 2019.

Cook, Warren L. *Flood Tide of Empire: Spain and the Pacific Northwest, 1543–1819*. New Haven CT: Yale University Press, 1973.

Compton, Tonia. "Proper Women/Propertied Women: Federal Land Laws and Gender Order(s) in the Nineteenth Century Imperial American West." PhD diss., University of Nebraska–Lincoln, 2009.

Copland, Ian. *The Burden of Empire: Perspectives on Imperialism and Colonialism*. Melbourne: Oxford University Press, 1990.

Cushing, Caleb. *Beyond the Rocky Mountains: Report on the Territory of Oregon*. Fairfield WA: Ye Galleon Press, 1999.

Dain, Bruce. *A Hideous Monster of the Mind: American Race Theory in the Early Republic*. Cambridge MA: Harvard University Press, 2002.

Daniel, Roger. "Westerners from the East: Oriental Immigrants Reappraised." *Pacific Historical Review* 35, no. 4 (November 1996): 373–83.

David, James Corbett. "The Politics of Emasculation: The Caning of Charles Sumner and Elite Ideologies of Manhood in Mid-Nineteenth-Century United States." *Gender and History* 19, no. 2 (August 2007): 324–45.

Davis, David Brian. *Inhuman Bondage: The Rise and Fall of Slavery in the New World*. New York: Oxford University Press, 2006.

DeJohn Anderson, Virginia. *Creatures of Empire: How Domestic Animals Transformed Early America*. New York: Oxford University Press, 2006.

Deutsch, Sarah. *No Separate Refuge: Culture, Class, and Gender on an Anglo-Hispanic Frontier in the American Southwest, 1880–1940*. Oxford: Oxford University Press, 1989.

Dudziak, Mary, and Leit Volpp. "Introduction Legal Borderlands: Law and the Construction of American Borders." *American Quarterly* 57, no. 3 (September 2005): 593–610.

Duncan, Janice K. *Minority without a Champion: Kanakas on the Pacific Coast, 1788–1850*. Portland: Oregon Historical Society, 1972.

Duniway, Abigail Scott. *Pathbreaking: An Autobiographical History of the Equal Suffrage Movement in the Pacific Coast States*. New York: Schocken Books, 1971.

Edmonds, Penelope. "Unpacking Settler Colonialism's Urban Strategies: Indigenous Peoples in Victoria, British Columbia, and the Transition to a Settler-Colonial City." *Urban History Review* 38, no. 2 (Spring 2010): 4–20.

Edwards, Rebecca. *Angels in the Machinery: Gender in American Party Politics from the Civil War to the Progressive Era*. Oxford: Oxford University Press, 1997.

Eells, Myron, ed. *Biography of Rev. G. H. Atkinson: Journal of Sea Voyage to Oregon in 1848, and Selected Addresses and Printed Articles, and a Particular Account of His Church Work in the Pacific Northwest*. Portland OR: F. W. Bates, 1893.

Egan, Brian. "Towards Shared Ownership: Property, Geography, and the Treaty Making in British Columbia." *Geografiska Annaler, Series B, Human Geography* 95, no. 1 (March 2013): 33–50.

Elliot, J. H. *Empires of the Atlantic World: Britain and Spain in America, 1492–1830*. New Haven CT: Yale University Press, 2006.

Elliot, T. C., ed. *The Coming of the White Women, 1836: As Told in Letters and Journals of Narcissa Whitman*. Whitefish MT: Literary Licensing, 2011.

Etcheson, Nicole. "Manliness and the Political Culture of the Old Northwest, 1790–1860," *Journal of the Early American Republic* 15, no. 1 (Spring 1995): 59–77.

Etulain, Richard W. *Lincoln and Oregon Country Politics in the Civil War Era*. Corvallis: Oregon State University Press, 2013.

Evans, Sara M. *Tidal Wave: How Women Changed America at Century's End*. New York: Free Press, 2003.

Eyal, Yonatan. *The Young American Movement and the Transformation of the Democratic Party, 1828–1861*. Cambridge UK: Cambridge University Press, 2007.

Faragher, John Mack. "Settler Colonial Studies and the North American Frontier." *Settler Colonial Studies* 4, no. 2 (December 2013): 181–91.

Farrington, Brenda, and Gordon Morris Bakken, eds. *Racial Encounters in the Multi-Cultural West*. New York: Garland, 2000.

Fehrenbacher, Don E. *The Slaveholding Republic: An Account of the United States Government's Relations to Slavery*. Edited by Ward M. McAfee. Oxford: Oxford University Press, 2001.

Findlay, James. "The SPCTEW and Western Colleges: Religious and High Education in Mid-Nineteenth Century America." *History of Education Quarterly* 17, no. 1 (Spring 1977): 31–62.

Finkelman, Paul. *Slavery and the Founders: Race and Liberty in the Age of Jefferson*. New York: M. E. Sharp, 2001.

Fixico, Donald L., ed. *Indian Treaties in the United States: An Encyclopedia and Documents Collection*. Santa Barbara CA: ABC-CLIO, 2018.

———, ed. *Treaties with American Indians: An Encyclopedia of Rights, Conflicts, and Sovereignty*. Vol. 1. Santa Barbara CA: ABC-CLIO, 2008.

Foner, Eric. *Free Soil, Free Labor, Free Men: The Ideology of the Republican Party before the Civil War*. Oxford: Oxford University Press, 1995.

———. *The Second Founding: How the Civil War and Reconstruction Remade the Constitution*. W. W. Norton, 2019.

Forbes, Robert Pierce. *The Missouri Compromise and Its Aftermath: Slavery and the Meaning of America*. Chapel Hill: University of North Carolina Press, 2007.

Fox-Genovese, Elizabeth. *Within the Plantation Household: Black and White Women of the Old South*. Chapel Hill: University of North Carolina, 1988.

Fraga, Sean. "Native Americans, Military Science, and Ambivalence on the Pacific Railroad Surveys, 1853–1855." *Princeton University Library Chronicle* 75, no. 3 (Spring 2014): 317–49.

Fraser, Alexander C., ed. *The Works of George Berkeley*. 3 vols. Oxford: Oxford University Press, 1871.

Freeman, Joanne B. *Affairs of Honor: National Politics in the New Republic*. New Haven CT: Yale University Press, 2002.

———. *The Field of Blood: Violence in Congress and the Road to Civil War*. New York: Farrar, Straus and Giroux, 2018.

Galbraith, John S. *The Hudson's Bay Company as an Imperial Factor, 1821–1869*. Berkeley: University of California Press, 1957.

Getz, Trevor, and Heather Streets-Salter. *Modern Imperialism and Colonialism: A Global Perspective*. Boston: Prentice Hall, 2011.

Ghosh, Durba. "Gender and Colonialism: Expansion or Marginalization." *Historical Journal* 47, no. 3 (September 2004): 737–55.

Gill, Jill K. "Idaho's 'Aryan' Education: Martin Luther King, Jr., Day and Racial Politics." *Pacific Northwest Quarterly* 102, no. 4 (2011): 159–77.

Gilmore, Glenda. *Gender and Jim Crow: Women and the Politics of White Supremacy in North Carolina, 1896–1920*. Chapel Hill: University of North Carolina Press, 1996.

Glassley, Ray Howard. *Pacific Northwest Indian Wars*. Portland OR: Binford and Mort, 1972.

Goldstein, Alyosha, and Alex Lubin, eds. "Settler Colonialism." Special issue, *South Atlantic Quarterly* 107, no. 4 (Fall 2008): 611–866.

Good, Kenneth. "Settler Colonialism: Economic Development and Class Formation." *Journal of Modern African Studies* 14, no. 4 (December 1976): 597–620

Gordon, Linda. *The Great Arizona Orphan Abduction*. Cambridge MA: Harvard University Press, 2001.

Gray, W. H. *A History of Oregon, 1792–1849: Drawn from Personal Observations and Authentic Information*. Portland OR: Harris & Holman, 1870.

Greenberg, Amy S. *Manifest Manhood and the Antebellum Empire*. Cambridge UK: Cambridge University Press, 2005.

Grossberg, Michael, and Christopher Tomlins, eds. *The Cambridge History of Law in America*. Vol. 2, *The Long Nineteenth Century (1789–1920)*, edited by Michael Grossberg and Christopher Tomlins. Cambridge UK: Cambridge University Press, 2008.

Hafen, LeRoy Reuben. *Mountain Men and Fur Traders of the Far West: Eighteen Biographical Sketches*. Lincoln: University of Nebraska Press, 1982.

Hahn, Steven. *A Nation under Our Feet: Black Political Struggles in the Rural South from Slavery to the Great Migration*. Cambridge MA: Belknap Press of Harvard University Press, 2005.

Hammer, Philip. "Great Britain, the United States, and the Negro Seaman Acts, 1822–1848." *Journal of Southern History* 1, no. 2 (May 1935): 3–28.

Hansen, Klaus J. "The Millennium, the West, and Race in the Antebellum American Mind." *Western Historical Quarterly* 3, no. 4 (October 1972): 373–90.

Harris, Cole. "How did Colonialism Dispossess? Comments from an Edge of Empire." *Annals of the Association of American Geographers* 94, no. 1 (March 2004): 165–82.

Hatter, Lawrence. *Citizens of Convenience: The Imperial Origins of American Nationhood on the U.S.-Canadian Border*. Charlottesville: University of Virginia Press, 2016.

Haycox, Stephen W. *Alaska: An American Colony*. Seattle: University of Washington Press, 2002.

Hayes, Sam W., and Christopher Morris, eds. *Manifest Destiny and Empire: American Antebellum Expansionism*. College Station: Texas A&M University Press, 1997.

Hietala, Thomas R. *Manifest Dream: Anxious Aggrandizement in Late Jacksonian America*. Ithaca NY: Cornell University Press, 1985.

Hill, D. G. "The Negro as a Political and Social Issue in the Oregon Country." *Journal of Negro History* 33, no. 2 (April 1948): 130–45.

Hill, Jane H. *The Everyday Language of White Racism*. West Sussex UK: Wiley-Blackwell, 2008.

Himes, George H. "History of the Press of Oregon, 1839–1850." *Quarterly of the Oregon Historical Society* 3, no. 4 (December 1902): 327–70.

Hine, Robert V., and John Mack Faragher. *The American West: A New Interpretive History*. New Haven CT: Yale University Press, 2000.

Hines, Gustavus. *Oregon and Its Institutions: Comprising a Full History of the Willamette University, the First Established on the Pacific Coast*. New York: Carlton and Porter, 1868.

Hoganson, Kristin L. *Fighting for American Manhood: How Gender Provoked the Spanish-American and Philippine-American Wars*. New Haven CT: Yale University Press, 1998.

Hogg, Thomas C. "Negroes and Their Institutions in Oregon." *Phylon* 30, no. 3 (3rd Qtr. 1969): 272–85.

Holbrook, Francis X., and John Nikol. "The Navy in the Puget Sound War, 1855–1857: A Documentary Study." *Pacific Northwest Quarterly*, 64, no. 1 (1976): 10–20.

Holt, Michael F. *The Fate of Their Country: Politicians, Slavery Extension, and the Coming of the Civil War*. New York: Hill and Wang, 2004.

Horsman, Reginald. *Race and Manifest Destiny: The Origins of American Racial-Anglo-Saxonism*. Cambridge MA: Harvard University Press, 1981.

Horowitz, David. "The 'Cross of Culture': La Grande, Oregon, in the 1920s." *Oregon Historical Quarterly* 93, no. 2 (1992): 147–67.

Howe, Daniel Walker. *What Hath God Wrought: The Transformation of America, 1815–1848*. Oxford: Oxford University Press, 2009.

Hoxie, Fredrick. *A Final Promise: The Campaign to Assimilate the Indians, 1880–1920*. Lincoln: University of Nebraska Press, 2001.

———. "Retrieving the Red Continent: Settler Colonialism and the History of American Indians in the U.S." *Ethnic and Racial Studies* 31, no. 6 (September 2008): 1153–67.

Hubbart, Henry Clyde. "'Pro-Southern' Influences in the Free West, 1840–1865." *Mississippi Valley Historical Review* 20, no. 1 (June 1933): 45–62.

Hyde, Anne E. *Empires, Nations, and Families: A New History of the North American West, 1800–1860*. Lincoln: University of Nebraska Press, 2011.

Isenberg, Nancy. *Sex and Citizenship in Antebellum America*. Chapel Hill: University of North Carolina Press, 1998.

Isenberg, Nancy, and Andrew Burstein. *The Problem of Democracy: The Presidents Adams Confront the Cult of Personality*. New York: Viking, 2019.

Jacob, Michelle M. *Yakama Rising: Indigenous Cultural Revitalization, Activism, and Healing*. Tucson: University of Arizona Press, 2013.

Jacobs, Margaret. "Getting Out of a Rut: Decolonizing Western Women's History." *Pacific Historical Review* 79, no. 4 (November 2010): 585–604.

———. *White Mother to a Dark Race: Settler Colonialism, Materialism, and the Removal of Indigenous Children in the American West and Australia, 1880–1940*. Lincoln: University of Nebraska Press, 2009.

Jacobson, Matthew Frye. *Whiteness of a Different Color: European Immigrants and the Alchemy of Race*. Cambridge MA: Harvard University Press, 1998.

Jagodinsky, Katrina. "'In Family Way': Guarding Indigenous Women's Children in Washington Territory." Native Adoption in Canada, the United States, New Zealand, and Australia, special issue, *American Indian Quarterly* 37, no. 1–2, (Winter 2013): 160–77.

———. *Legal Codes and Talking Trees: Indigenous Women's Sovereignty in the Sonoran and Puget Sound Borderlands, 1854–1946*. New Haven CT: Yale University, 2016.

January, Alan. "The South Carolina Association: An Agency for Race Control in Antebellum Charleston." *South Carolina Historical Magazine* 78, no. 3 (July 1977): 191–201.

Jefferson-Brown, M. J. *The Daffodil: Its History, Varieties and Cultivation*. London: Faber and Faber, 1951.

Jensen, Kimberly. "'Neither Head nor Tail to the Campaign': Esther Pohl Lovejoy and the Oregon Suffrage Victory of 1912." *Oregon Historical Quarterly* 108, no. 3 (2007): 350–83.

Jessett, Thomas E., ed. *Reports and Letters of Herbert Beaver, 1836–1838, Chaplain to the Hudson's Bay Company and Missionary to the Indians at Fort Vancouver*. Portland OR: Reed College Champoeg Press, 1959.

Johannsen, Robert W. *Frontier Politics and the Sectional Conflict: The Pacific Norwest on the Eve of the Civil War*. Seattle: University of Washington Press, 1955.

———. *John McLoughlin: Father of Oregon*. Hillsboro OR: Binford & Morit, 1958.

———. "A Political Picture of the Pacific Northwest in the Civil War: Spectators of Disunion." *Montana Magazine of Western History* 12, no. 2 (Spring 1962): 38–48.
Johansen, Dorothy O. *Empire of the Columbia: A History of the Pacific Northwest.* New York: Harper & Row, 1957.
———. "A Working Hypothesis for the Study of Migrations." *Pacific Historical Review* 36, no. 1 (February 1967): 1–12.
Johnson, David Alan. *Founding the Far West: California, Oregon, and Nevada, 1840–1890.* Berkley: University of California Press, 1992.
Johnson, Susan Lee. *Roaring Camp: The Social World of the California Gold Rush.* New York: W. W. Norton, 2000.
Jones-Rogers, Stephanie E. *They Were Her Property: White Women as Slave Owners in the American South.* New Haven CT: Yale University Press, 2019.
Jun, Helen H. "Black Orientalism: Nineteenth Century Narratives of Race and Citizenship." *American Quarterly* 58, no. 4 (2006): 1047–66.
Kauanui, J. Kēhaulani. "Colonialism in Equality: Hawaiian Sovereignty and the Question of U.S. Civil Rights." Settler Colonialism, special issue, *South Atlantic Quarterly* 107, no. 4 (Fall 2008): 636–50.
Kanazawa, Mark. "Immigration, Exclusion, and Taxation: Anti-Chinese Legislation in Gold Rush California." *Journal of Economic History* 68, no. 3 (September 2005): 779–805.
Kaplan, Sidney. "The Miscegenation Issue in the Election of 1864." *Journal of Negro History* 34, no. 3 (July 1949): 274–343.
Kappler, Charles J., ed. *Indian Affairs: Laws and Treaties.* In *Treaties*, edited by Charles J. Kappler, vol. 2. Washington DC: U.S. Government Printing Office, 1904.
Kelley, Mary. *Learning to Stand and Speak: Women, Education, and Public Life in America's Republic.* Chapel Hill: University of North Carolina, 2006.
Kendi, Ibram X. *Stamped from the Beginning: The Definitive History of Racist Ideas in America.* New York: Nation Books, 2016.
Kenner, Charles L. *The Comanchero Frontier: A History of New Mexican-Plains Indian Relations.* Norman: University of Oklahoma Press, 1969.
Kerber, Linda K. *No Constitutional Right to Be Ladies: Women and the Obligation of Citizenship.* New York: Hill & Wang, 1998.
———. "The Paradox of Women's Citizenship in the Early Republic: The Case of *Martin v. Massachusetts*, 1805." *American Historical Review* 97, no. 2 (April 1992): 349–78.
———. "Separate Spheres, Female Worlds, Woman's Place: The Rhetoric of Women's History." *Journal of American History* 75, no. 1 (1988): 9–39.
Klepp, Susan E. "Revolutionary Bodies: Women and Fertility Transition in the Mid-Atlantic Region, 1760–1820." *Journal of American History* 85, no. 3 (December 1998): 910–45.
Kökény, Andrea. "British and/or American: Colonization of the Oregon Country." PhD diss., University of Szeged (HU), 2008.

Kolp, John G., and Terri L. Snyder. "Women and the Political Culture of Eighteenth-Century Virginia: Gender, Property Law, and Voting Rights." In *The Many Legalities of Early America*, edited by Christopher L. Tomlins and Bruce H. Mann, 272–92. Chapel Hill: Published for the Omohundro Institute of Early American History and Culture, by the University of North Carolina Press, 2001.

Kozloff, E. *Plants of Western Oregon, Washington, and British Columbia*. Portland OR: Timber Press, 2005.

Kwong, Peter. *Forbidden Workers: Illegal Chinese Immigrants and American Labor*. New York: New Press, 1997.

Kyvig, David E. "Historical Misunderstandings and the Defeat of the Equal Rights Amendment." *Public Historian* 18, no. 1 (Winter 1996): 45–63.

Lamar, Howard, and Leonard Thompson. *The Frontier in History: North America and Southern Africa Compared*. New Haven CT: Yale University Press, 1981.

Lange, Erwin F. "Oregon City Private Schools, 1843–59." *Oregon Historical Quarterly* 37, no. 4 (December 1936): 308–28.

———. "The Oregon City Public School." *Oregon Historical Quarterly* 38, no. 1 (March 1937): 92–108.

Langley, Harold D. "The Negro in the Navy and Merchant Service, 1789–1860." *Journal of Negro History* 52, no. 4 (October 1967): 273–86.

Lansing, Ronald B. *Nimrod: Courts, Claims, and Killing on the Oregon Frontier*. Pullman: Washington State University Press, 2005.

Lasser, Carol, and Stacey Robertson. *Antebellum Women: Private, Public, Partisan*. Lanham MD: Rowman & Littlefield, 2010.

Lee, Daniel, and Joseph Frost. *Ten Years in Oregon*. New York: J. Collard, 1844.

Lee, Erika. "Immigrants and Immigrant Law: A State of the Field Assessment." *Journal of American Ethnic History* 18, no. 4 (Summer 1999): 85–114.

Lepore, Jill. *The Name of War: King Philip's War and the Origin of American Identity*. New York: Penguin Random House, 1998.

Lester, Alan. "Reformulating Identities: British Settlers in Early Nineteenth-Century South Africa." *Transactions of the Institute of British Geographers* 23, no. 4 (1998): 515–31.

Levine, Philippa, ed. *Gender and Empire*. Oxford: Oxford University Press, 2004.

Lew-Williams, Beth. *The Chinese Must Go: Violence, Exclusion, and the Making of the Alien in America*. Cambridge MA: Harvard University Press, 2018.

Lewis, David G. "Coast Indian Reservation." *The Oregon Encyclopedia*. Oregon Historical Society (website). Accessed June 2019. http://oregonencyclopedia.org/articles/coast_indian_reservation/.

———. "The 1851 Treaty Commission: Coquille, Euchre, and Totoan at Port Orford." Quartux Journal (website). Accessed June 2019. https://ndnhistoryresearch.com/2017/11/16/the-1851-treaty-commission-coquille-euchre-and-tototan-at-port-orford/.

Liestman, Daniel. "Horizontal Inter-Ethnic Relations: Chinese and American Indians in the Nineteenth-Century American West." *Western Historical Quarterly* 30, no. 3 (Autumn 1999): 327–49.

Limerick, Patricia Nelson. "Going West and Ending Up Global." *Western Historical Quarterly* 32, no. 1 (Spring 2001): 4–23.

———. *The Legacy of Conquest: The Unbroken Past of the American West.* New York: W. W. Norton, 1987.

Litwack, Leon F. *North of Slavery: The Negro in the Free States, 1790–1860.* Chicago: University of Chicago Press, 1961.

Lott, Eric. *Love and Theft: Blackface Minstrelsy and the American Working Class.* New York: Oxford University Press, 1993.

Lydon, Edward C. *The Anti-Chinese Movement in the Hawaiian Kingdom, 1852–1886.* San Francisco: R & E Research Associates, 1975.

Mahoney, Barbara. "Oregon Voices, Oregon Democracy: Asahel Bush, Slavery, and the Statehood Debate." *Oregon Historical Quarterly* 110, no. 2 (Summer 2009): 202–27.

Marschner, Janice. *Oregon 1859: A Snapshot in Time.* Portland OR: Timber Press, 2008.

Materson, Lisa G. *For the Freedom of Her Race: Black Women and Electoral Politics in Illinois, 1877–1932.* Chapel Hill: University of North Carolina Press, 2009.

McCoy, Kate, Eve Tuck, and Marcia McKenzie. *Land Education: Rethinking Pedagogies of Place from Indigenous, Postcolonial, and Decolonizing Perspectives.* London: Routledge, 2016.

McCurry, Stephanie. *Masters of Small Worlds: Yeoman Households, Gender Relations, and the Political Culture of the Antebellum South Carolina Low Country.* Oxford: Oxford University Press, 1997.

McDougall, Walter A. *The Tragedy of U.S. Foreign Policy: How America's Civil Religion Betrayed the National Interest.* New Haven CT: Yale University Press, 2016.

McHoul, Alec, and Wendy Grace, *A Foucault Primer: Discourse, Power, and the Subject.* New York: New York University Press, 1993.

McLagan, Elizabeth. *A Peculiar Paradise: A History of Blacks in Oregon, 1788–1940.* Portland OR: Georgian Press, 1980.

McWilliams, Carey. *Brothers under the Skin.* Boston: Little Brown, 1943.

Merk, Frederick. "The Genesis of the Oregon Question." *Mississippian Valley Historical Quarterly* 36, no. 4 (March 1950): 583–612.

Miller, Robert J. *Native America, Discovered and Conquered: Thomas Jefferson, Lewis & Clark, and Manifest Destiny.* Westport CT: Praeger, 2006.

Minto, George. *The Statutes at Large and Treaties of the United State of America, from December 1, 1845, to March 3, 1851, Arranged to the Matter of Each Act and to the Subsequent Acts on the Same Subject.* Vol. 9. Boston: Charles C. Little and James Brown, 1851.

Minto, John. "Antecedents of the Oregon Pioneers and the Light These Throw on Their Motives." *Oregon Historical Quarterly* 5, no. 1 (March 1904): 38–63.

Mitchell, S. Augustus. *A General View of the United States; Comprising, Also, a Description of Each Individual State and Territory in the Union; To Which Are Added, Various Tabular Statements, Comprehending Aggregates of the Population of the United States, at Different Periods, As Well As in the Year 1840*. Philadelphia PA: S. Augustus Mitchell, 1846.

Morgan, Edmund. *American Slavery, American Freedom*. New York: W. W. Norton, 1975.

Morrison, Michael A. *Slavery and the American West: The Eclipse of Manifest Destiny and the Coming of the Civil War*. Chapel Hill: University of North Carolina, 1997.

Mr. Webster's Speech at Marshfield, Mass.: Delivered September 1, 1848, and His Speech on the Oregon Bill, Delivered in the United States Senate, August 12, 1848. Boston: Press of T. R. Marvin, 1848.

Mudge, Zachariah Atwell. *Sketches of the Mission Life among the Indians of Oregon*. New York: Carlton & Porter, 1854.

Muldoon, James. "Discovery, Grant, Charter, Conquest, or Purchase: John Adams on the Legal Basis for English Possession of North America." In *The Many Legalities of Early America*, edited by Christopher L. Tomlins and Bruce H. Mann, 25–46. Chapel Hill: Published for the Omohundro Institute of Early American History and Culture, by the University of North Carolina Press, 2001.

Nagel, Paul C. *John Quincy Adams: A Public Life, a Private Life*. New York: Alfred A. Knopf, 1997.

Ngai, Mae M. *Impossible Subjects: Illegal Aliens and the Making of Modern America*. Princeton NJ: Princeton University Press, 2004.

Nokes, R. Gregory. *Breaking Chains: Slavery on Trial in the Oregon Territory*. Corvallis: Oregon State University Press, 2014.

Nordhoff, Charles. *Northern California, Oregon, and the Sandwich Islands*. New York: Harper and Brothers, 1874.

Norton, Mary Beth. *Liberty's Daughters: The Revolutionary Experience of American Women, 1750–1800*. New York: Cornell University Press, 1980.

O'Donnell, Terence. *An Arrow in the Earth: General Joel Palmer and the Indians of Oregon*. Portland: Oregon Historical Society Press, 1991.

Oliver, Egbert S. "Obed Dickinson and the 'Negro Question' in Salem." *Oregon Historical Quarterly* 92, no. 2 (Spring 1991): 4–40.

Osterhammel, Jürgen. *Colonialism: A Theoretical Overview*. Princeton NJ: Markus Wiener, 1997.

Ostler, Jeffrey. *The Plains Sioux and U.S. Colonialism from Lewis and Clark to Wounded Knee*. Cambridge UK: Cambridge University Press, 2004.

Painter, Nell Irvin. *The History of White People*. New York: W. W. Norton, 2010.

Parker, Kunal M. "Citizenship and Immigration Law, 1800–1924: Resolutions of Membership and Territory." In *The Long Nineteenth Century, 1789–1920*, edited by Michael Grossberg and Christopher Tomlins, 168–203. Vol. 2 of *The Cambridge History of Law in America*. Cambridge UK: Cambridge University Press, 2008.

Parker, Rev. Samuel. *Journal of an Exploring Tour beyond the Rocky Mountains: Under the Direction of the A.B.C.F.M.: With a Map of Oregon Territory*. New York: M. H. Newman, 1846.

Parry-Giles, Shawn J., and Trevor Parry-Giles. "Gendered Politics and Presidential Image Construction: A Reassessment of the 'Feminine Style.'" *Communication Monograph* 63, no. 4 (June 1996): 337–53.

Pascoe, Peggy. *Relations of Rescue: The Search for Female Moral Authority in the American West, 1874–1939*. New York: Oxford University Press, 1993.

———. *What Comes Naturally: Miscegenation Law and the Making of Race in America*. New York: Oxford University Press, 2009.

Paxon, Fredric L. "A Constitution of Democracy—Wisconsin, 1847." *Mississippian Valley Historical Review* 2, no. 1 (June 1915): 3–24.

Pearson, Rudy. "'A Menace to the Neighborhood': Housing and African Americans in Portland, 1941–1945." *Oregon Historical Quarterly* 102, no. 2 (2001): 158–79.

Perry, Adele. *Colonial Relations: The Douglas-Connolly Family and the Nineteenth-Century Imperial World*. Cambridge UK: Cambridge University Press, 2015.

———. *On the Edge of Empire: Gender, Race, and the Making of British Columbia, 1849–1871*. Toronto: University of Toronto Press, 2001.

Pierce, Jason E. *Making the White Man's West: Whiteness and the Creation of the American West*. Boulder: University of Colorado Press, 2016.

Plane, Ann Marie. *Colonial Intimacies: Indian Marriage in Early New England*. Ithaca NY: Cornell University Press, 2000.

Pomeroy, Earl. *The Pacific Slope: A History of California, Oregon, Washington, Idaho, Utah, and Nevada*. Reno: University of Nevada Press, 1965.

Potter, David. *The Impending Crisis, 1848–1861*. New York: Harper & Row, 1976.

Powell, J. W. *Eightieth Annual Report of the Bureau of American Ethnology by the Secretary of the Smithsonian Institution, 1896–97, Part 2*. Washington DC: U.S. Government Printing Office, 1899.

Prescott, Cynthia Culver. *Gender and Generation on the Far Western Frontier*. Tucson: University of Arizona Press, 2007.

Price, A. Grenfell. "Experiments in Colonization." In *Cambridge History of the British Empire*, edited by John Holland Rose, 207–42. Cambridge UK: Cambridge University Press, 1929.

Prucha, Francis Paul. *American Indian Treaties: The History of a Political Anomaly*. Berkeley: University of California Press, 1994.

Rayback, Joseph G. *Free Soil: The Election of 1848*. Lexington: University Press of Kentucky, 1970.

Richardson, Heather Cox. *West from Appomattox: The Reconstruction of America after the Civil War*. New Haven CT: Yale University Press, 2008.

Richardson, K. Keith. "Unwelcomed Settlers: Black and Mulatto Oregon Settlers." *Oregon Historical Quarterly* 84, no. 2 (Spring 1983): 29–55.

Richter, Daniel K. *Facing East from Indian Country: A Native History of Early America*. Cambridge UK: Harvard University Press, 2003.

Rifkin, Mark. *Settler Common Sense: Queerness and Everyday Colonialism in the American Renaissance*. Minneapolis: University of Minnesota Press, 2014.

Ripley, Peter C., ed. *United States, 1847–1858*. Vol. 4 of *The Black Abolitionist Papers*, edited by C. Peter Ripley. Chapel Hill: University of North Carolina Press, 1991.

Roediger, David R. *The Wages of Whiteness: Race and the Making of the American Working Class*. London: Verso, 2007

Ronda, James. *Astoria and Empire*. Lincoln: University of Nebraska Press, 1990.

Rosay, André B. "Violence against American Indian and Alaska Native Women and Men." *National Institute of Justice Journal* 277 (2016): 38–45.

Rosen, Ruth. *The World Split Open: How the Modern Women's Movement Changed America*. New York: Penguin, 2006.

Roth, Sarah N. *Gender and Race in Antebellum Popular Culture*. Cambridge UK: Cambridge University Press, 2014.

Rotundo, E. Anthony. *American Manhood: Transformations in Masculinity from the Revolution to the Modern Era*. New York: Basic Books, 1993.

Roy, Patricia E. *A White Man's Province: British Columbia and Chinese and Japanese Immigrants, 1858–1914*. Vancouver: University of British Columbia Press, 1989.

Russell, Lynette, ed. *Colonial Frontiers: Indigenous-European Encounters in Settler Societies*. Manchester UK: Manchester University Press, 2001.

Salmon, Marylynn. *Women and the Law of Property in Early America*. Chapel Hill: University of North Carolina, 1986.

Schafer, Joseph. "Notes on the Colonization of Oregon." *Quarterly of the Oregon Historical Society* 6, no. 4 (December 1905): 379–90.

Scharff, Virginia J., ed. *Seeing Nature through Gender*. Lawrence: University of Kansas Press, 2003.

Schreibeis, Charles D. *Pioneer Education in the Pacific Northwest, 1789–1847*. Portland OR: Metropolitan Press, 1937.

Schwartz, E. A. *The Rogue River Indian War and Its Aftermath, 1850–1980*. Norman: University of Oklahoma Press, 1997.

Scott, Joan. *Gender and the Politics of History*. New York: Columbia University Press, 1999.

Sears, Clare. "All That Glitters: Trans-ing California's Gold Rush Migrations." *GLQ: A Journal of Lesbian and Gay Studies* 14, no. 2–3 (June 2008): 383–402.

Semple, Eugene. *The Organic and Other General Laws of Oregon: Together with the National Constitution, and Other Public Acts and Statutes of the United States, 1843–1872*. San Francisco: A. L. Bancroft, 1874.

Shah, Nayan. *Stranger Intimacy: Contesting Race, Sexuality, and Law in the North American West*. Berkeley: University of California Press, 2011.

Simms, Henry H. "The Controversy over the Admission of the State of Oregon." *Mississippi Valley Historical Review* 32, no. 3 (December 1945): 355–74.

Simpson, Audra. "From White into Red: Captivity Narratives as Alchemies of Race and Citizenship." *American Quarterly* 60, no. 2 (June 2008): 251–57.

———. *Mohawk Interruptus: Political Life across the Borders of Settler States*. Durham NC: Duke University Press, 2014.

Sinha, Mrinalini. "Gender and Nation." In *Women's History in a Global Perspective*, edited by Bonnie Smith, 1–33. Chicago: University of Illinois Press, 2004.

Sklar, Kathryn Kish, and James Brewer Steward, eds. *Women's Rights and Transatlantic Antislavery in the Era of Emancipation*. New Haven CT: Yale University, 2007.

Smith, Bonnie, ed. *Women's History in Global Perspective*. Vol. 1. Urbana: University of Illinois Press, 2004.

Smith, Helen Krebs. *The Presumptuous Dreamers: A Sociological History of the Life and Times of Abigail Scott Duniway, 1834–1871*. Vol. 1. Lake Oswego OR: Smith and Smith, 1974.

Smith, Stacey L. *Freedom's Frontier: California and the Struggle over Unfree Labor, Emancipation, and Reconstruction*. Chapel Hill: University of North Carolina, 2013.

Sohoni, Deenesh. "Unsuitable Suitors: Anti-Miscegenation Laws, Naturalization Laws, and the Construction of Asian Identities." *Law and Society Review* 41, no. 3 (September 2007): 587–618.

"Speech of the Hon. R. B. Rhett of South Carolina on the Oregon Territory Bill: Excluding Slavery from that Territory—The Missouri Compromise Being Proposed and Rejected Delivered in the House of Representatives of the U.S., January 14, 1847." Washington DC: J. & G. S. Girdeon, 1847.

Speer, William. *The Oldest and the Newest Empire: China and the United States*. Hartford CT: S. S. Scranton, 1870.

Spence, Mark. "'Soyaapo' and the Remaking of Lewis and Clark." *Oregon Historical Quarterly* 105, no. 3 (Fall 2004): 482–99.

Spores, Ronald. "Too Small a Place: The Removal of the Willamette Valley Indians, 1850–1856." *American Indian Quarterly* 17, no. 2 (Spring 1993): 171–91.

Stansell, Christine. *City of Women: Sex and Class in New York, 1789–1860*. Urbana: University of Illinois Press, 1987.

Stoler, Ann Laura. *Carnal Knowledge and Imperial Power: Race and the Intimate in Colonial Rule*. Berkeley: University of California Press, 2010.

Stout, Mary. *Native American Boarding Schools*. Santa Barbara CA: Greenwood Press, 2012.

Swindler, William Finely, comp. *Sources and Documents of United States Constitutions, Vol. 1–11*. New York: Oceana Publications, 1973–79.

Taylor, Alan. *American Colonies: The Settling of North America*. London: Penguin Books, 2002.

Taylor, Quintard. *In Search of the Racial Frontier*. New York: W. W. Norton, 1998.

———. "Slaves and Free Men: Blacks in the Oregon Country, 1840–1860." *Oregon Historical Quarterly* 83, no. 2 (Summer 1982): 153–70.

Terborg-Penn, R. *African American Women in the Struggle for the Vote, 1850–1920*. Bloomington: Indiana University Press, 1998.

The Oregon Emigration Society. *Articles of Agreement of the Oregon Emigration Society*. Boston: D. H. Ela, 1839.

Thigpen, Jennifer. *Island Queens and Mission Wives: How Gender and Empire Remade Hawai'i's Pacific World*. Chapel Hill: University of North Carolina Press, 2014.

Thrush, Coll. *Native Seattle: Histories from the Crossing-Over Place*. Seattle: University of Washington, 2007.

Toll, William. "Progress and Piety: The Ku Klux and Social Changes in Tillamook, Oregon." *Pacific Northwest Quarterly* 69, no. 2 (1978): 75–85.

Tomlins, Christopher. *Freedom Bound: Law, Labor, and Civic Identity in Colonizing English America, 1580–1860*. Cambridge UK: Cambridge University Press, 2010.

———. *Law, Labor, and Ideology in the Early American Republic*. Cambridge UK: Cambridge University Press, 1993.

Traill, Catherine Parr Strickland. *The Backwoods of Canada: Being Letters from the Wife of an Emigrant Officer, Illustrative of the Domestic Economy of British America. To Which is Appended an Account of the Country of the Oregon*. London: M. A. Nattali, 1846.

Troen, Selwyn. "Popular Education in Nineteenth Century St. Louis." *History of Education Quarterly* 12, no. 1 (Spring 1973): 23–40.

Van Kirk, Sylvia. *Many Tender Ties: Women in Fur-Trade Society, 1670–1870*. Norman: University of Oklahoma Press, 1983.

Varon, Elizabeth. "Gender History and the Origins of the Civil War." *OAH Magazine of History* 25, no. 2 (April 2011): 19–23.

———. *We Mean to Be Counted: White Women and Politics in Antebellum Virginia*. Chapel Hill: North Carolina Press, 1998.

Veracini, Lorenzo. "Introducing: Settler Colonial Studies." *Settler Colonial Studies* 1, no. 1 (2011): 1–12.

Victor, Frances Fuller, ed. *The Early Indian Wars of Oregon*. Salem OR: Frank C. Baker, 1894.

Vine, Deloria J., and Raymond J. De Mallie. *Documents of American Indian Diplomacy: Treaties, Agreements, and Conventions, 1775–1979*. Vol. 1. University of Oklahoma Press, 1999.

Waldstreicher, David. *In the Midst of Perpetual Fetes: The Making of American Nationalism, 1776–1820*. Chapel Hill: University of North Carolina Press, 1997.

Wallach, Glenn. *Obedient Sons: The Discourse of Youth and Generations in American Culture, 1630–1860*. Amherst: University of Massachusetts Press, 1997.

Walters, Ronald G. *The Anti-Slavery Appeal: American Abolitionism after 1830*. Baltimore MD: Johns Hopkins University Press, 1976.

Wanhalle, Angela. "Indigenous Women, Marriage and Colonial Mobility." In *Indigenous Mobilities: Across and Beyond the Antipodes*, edited by Rachel Standfield, 209–32. Acton: Australian National University Press, 2018.

Webster, Daniel. *Mr. Webster's Speech at Marshfield, Mass., Delivered September 1, 1848: and His Speech on the Oregon Bill, Delivered in the United States Senate, August 12, 1848*. Boston: Press of T. R. Marvin, 1848.

Welke, Barbara Young. "Law, Personhood, and Citizenship in the Long Nineteenth Century." In *The Long Nineteenth Century, 1789–1920*. Edited by Michael Grossberg and Christopher Tomlins, 345–86. Vol. 2 of *The Cambridge History of Law in America*. Cambridge UK: Cambridge University Press, 2008.

Weller, Candace. *Peace Weavers: Uniting the Salish Coast through Cross-Cultural Marriages*. Pullman: Washington State University Press, 2017.

West, Elliott. *The Last Indian War: The Nez Perce Story*. Oxford: Oxford University Press, 2009.

———. "Reconstructing Race." *Western Historical Quarterly* 34, no. 1 (Spring 2003): 6–26.

Whaley, Gray H. *Oregon and the Collapse of Illahee: U.S. Empire and the Transformation of an Indigenous World, 1792–1859*. Chapel Hill: University of North Carolina Press, 2010.

———. "Oregon, Illahee, and the Empire Republic: A Case Study of American Colonialism, 1843–1858." *Western Historical Quarterly* 36, no. 2 (Summer 2005): 157–78.

White, Elijah. *Concise View of Oregon Territory, Its Colonial and Indian Relations: Compiled from Official Letters and Reports, Together with the Organic Laws of the Colony*. Washington DC: T. Barnard, 1846.

Wilentz, Sean. *Chants Democratic: New York and the Rise of the American Working Class, 1788–1850*. Oxford: Oxford University Press, 1984.

Wolfe, Patrick. "Settler Colonialism and the Elimination of the Native." *Journal of Genocide Research* 8, no. 4 (December 2006): 387–409.

———. *Settler Colonialism and the Transformation of Anthropology: The Politics and Poetics of Ethnographic Events*. London: Cassell, 1999.

Woodward, Walter Carleton. *The Rise and Early History of Political Parties in Oregon, 1843–1868*. Portland OR: J. K. Gill, 1913.

Woodworth, Stevens. *Manifest Destinies: Western Expansion and the Civil War*. New York: Knopf, 2010.

Worster, Donald. *Under Western Skies: Nature and History in the American West*. New York: Oxford University Press, 1992.

Wren, Daniel A. "American Business Philanthropy and Higher Education in the Nineteenth Century." *Business History Review* 57, no. 3 (Autumn 1983): 321–46.

Wright, Carroll D., and Chamberlin Hunt. "The History and Growth of the United States Census, prepared for the Census Committee on the Census." *Congressional Globe*, 56th Cong., 1st Sess., Senate. Doc. No. 194. February 24, 1900.

Wright, Mary C. "Economic Development and Native American Women in the Early Nineteenth Century." *American Quarterly* 33, no. 5 (Winter 1981): 525–36.

Youst, Lionel. *She's Tricky Like Coyote: Annie Miner Peterson, an Oregon Coast Indian Woman*. Norman: Oklahoma University Press, 1997.

Zaeske, Susan. *Signatures of Citizenship: Petitioning, Antislavery, and Women's Political Identity*. Chapel Hill: University of North Carolina Press, 2003.

Zboray, Ronald J., and Mary Saracino Zboray. "Gender Slurs in Boston's Partisan Press during the 1840s." *Journal of American Studies* 34, no. 3 (December 2000): 413–46.

———. *Voices without Votes: Women and Politics in Antebellum New England*. Durham: University of New Hampshire Press, 2010.

Zhu, Liping. *A Chinaman's Chance: The Chinese on the Rocky Mountain Mining Frontier*. Niwot: University Press of Colorado, 1997.

Index

Page numbers in italics indicate illustrations; page numbers with t indicate tables

www.ingramcontent.com/pod-product-compliance
Lightning Source LLC
Chambersburg PA
CBHW022253030426
42428CB00002B/86
* 9 7 8 1 4 9 6 2 1 9 0 4 6 *